1918　1919　1920　1921　1922　1923　1924

PAUL HINDEMITH (1895-1963)

Mörder, Hoffnung der Frauen
Op. 12 (1919)
Sonata for Cello
Op. 11/3 (1919-1922)
Eight Songs
Op. 18 (1920)
Sancta Susanna
Op. 21 (1921)
Kammermusik no. 1
Op. 24/1 (1922)
Die junge Magd
Op. 23/2 (1922)
Der Dämon
Op. 28 (1922)

KURT WEILL (1900-1950)

1st Symphony (1921)

Der Protagonist
Op. 14 (1924-1925)

ERNST KRENEK (1900-1991)

String Quartet I
Op. 6 (1921)
2nd Symphony
Op. 12 (1922)
Der Zwingburg
Op. 14 (1922)
Orpheus und Eurydike
Op. 21 (1923)

CARL RUGGLES (1876-1971)

Men and Mountains (1924)

Portals (1925)

Sun Treader
(1926-1931)

(Berg)

Lyric Suite (1925-1926)

(Bartók)

Miraculous Mandarin
Op. 19 (1918-1919)

Sonata No. 1 for Violin and Piano (1921)

Sonata No. 2 for Violin and Piano (1922)

(Ives)

Psalm 90 (1894, 1923-1924)

Expressionism in Twentieth-Century Music

Franz Marc, *Animal Destinies: (The Trees Showed Their Rings, the Animals Their Arteries)*, 1913. Oil on canvas, 195 x 263.5 cm. Kunstmuseum, Basel.

Expressionism in Twentieth-Century Music

John C. Crawford and
Dorothy L. Crawford

Indiana University Press | BLOOMINGTON & INDIANAPOLIS

Library of Congress Cataloging-in-Publication Data
Crawford, John C. (John Charlton), date.
   Expressionism in twentieth-century music / John C. Crawford and
Dorothy L. Crawford.
       p.   cm.
   Includes bibliographical references and index.
   ISBN 0-253-31473-9
   1. Expressionism (Music)   I. Crawford, Dorothy L.   II. Title.
ML197.C8   1993
780'.9'04—dc20   92-35291

1 2 3 4 5 97 96 95 94 93

Contents

Color Plates

Illustrations

Preface

Understanding of expressionism in music has lagged far behind what has been achieved with regard to literature and the visual arts.[1] Although the term *expressionism*[2] (which was only gradually accepted by composers late in the expressionist era) has come to be used frequently in writings about music, its connotations have remained vague and unexamined. The present study is an effort to provide a clearer understanding of the chronological limits and musical characteristics of musical expressionism, and to identify and examine a body of expressionist compositions crucially important to the subsequent development of twentieth-century music. We hope that enlightenment about this aspect of some of the great revolutionary works of the early twentieth century will make a fascinating and difficult musical repertoire more meaningful.

This book presents a new view of the music of the first quarter of the twentieth century. We have found that musical expressionism is not limited to Schoenberg, Berg, and Webern but is a potent force affecting the music of a larger group of important composers in this period. Our broader view of expressionism evolved gradually. For John Crawford's dissertation on the vocal works of Schoenberg, 1908–24,[3] it was necessary to know not only the expressionist works of Schoenberg, Berg, and Webern but also the works of their immediate predecessors Strauss and Mahler. The subject also demanded broadly based cultural research in expressionism. A year's residence in Vienna and subsequent research trips to Europe brought both authors into greater contact with original sources and with the cultural milieu of expressionism. Our experience in performing expressionist works as soprano and pianist was also of great value. We began searching for a cogent definition of musical expressionism. Close study suggested to us that certain works of Stravinsky, Bartók, and Ives, written during the first quarter of the century, also showed characteristics of expressionism. Further investigation of the creative attitudes as well as the societal and biographical situations of these composers revealed deeper parallels than we had expected.

Examination of previous attempts to arrive at a clear and inclusive definition of musical expressionism demonstrated that there was little scholarly agreement on the matter.[4] It was of great interest to us that two of the most substantive discussions (Arnold Schering's essay "Die expressionistiche Bewegung in der Musik" and the article on expressionism by Karl Wörner, Walter Maunzen, and Will Hofmann in *Die Musik in Geschichte und Gegenwart*) took the view that expressionism was not limited to Schoenberg and his disciples but was also present in the work of other composers during the first quarter of the century. An article by Elliott Carter supported the idea that such composers as Ives and Ruggles were indeed American expressionists.[5] Scholarship in the other arts gave further evidence of expressionism's importance beyond Central Europe.[6]

The description of the characteristics of expressionism in music which appears toward the end of chapter 1 (pp. 16-21) was arrived at from several different directions. The comparatively small number of previous efforts at such a description were carefully considered and evaluated. The far more numerous discussions of expressionism in literature and the visual arts were useful for the light they threw on expressionist music. Finally, we let the music itself be our guide, as we further developed and refined our description during our research and the writing of this book.

Expressionist music is best understood in its psychological, biographical, and cultural context. Some European writers, such as Theodor Adorno and Wörner, take this view, but most American writing about expressionist music has been purely analytical, contradicting the documented desire of the composers to rebel against "technique as the only means of salvation."[7] What has caused this contradiction? Joseph Kerman, in his valuable study *Contemplating Music,* suggests that musicologists have become too exclusively concerned with "the factual, the documentary, the verifiable, the analyzable, the positivistic." He questions why analysts should "concentrate solely on the internal structure of a work of art as an autonomous entity, and take no account of such considerable matters as history, communications, affect, texts and programs, the existence of other works of art, and so much else?"[8] In a similar vein, cultural historian Jost Hermand faults scholarship in twentieth-century music for its absorption in formal and structural problems unrelated to societal questions and its lack of interest in historical investigations of periods.[9] Surely this narrow point of view on the part of both musicologists and music theorists can be traced to the positivistic, technological nature of our present civilization, and to the desire of academics in the arts and humanities to be as "rigorous" as their colleagues in the sciences.

Another factor militating against a broadly humanistic view of expressionist music has been the continued influence in Western Europe and the United States of the "art-for-art's-sake" aesthetic characteristic of French-derived modernism. This influence has predominated to such an extent that the important role of expressionism as another aspect of modernism has been largely ignored. It is significant, however, that this aesthetic is beginning to be challenged in art museum circles and elsewhere.[10]

In order to truly understand expressionist music, it is necessary for us to think ourselves back to Europe before World War I, to an era and a culture very different from our own. Without this effort, our ignorance of the milieu of expressionism will prevent us from achieving a fully rounded view of the music. Problems of understanding are further intensified by language barriers. It is the aim of this book to overcome these difficulties in order to place the music in its proper context.

Since the book is necessarily an exploratory rather than a definitive treatment of its subject, we have not attempted to discuss all the twentieth-century works that could be considered expressionist. Rather, we hope that our attempt to clarify the concept will bring musical expressionism into the arena of intelligent discussion and ultimately render it more useful to future scholars and writers.

It is our conviction, arrived at after long years of study, that expressionist music, in spite of its tendency toward abstraction, is fundamentally content-oriented. The presence of a subtext or a hidden psychological program is confirmed in many expressionist works, even those that are exclusively instrumental. The writings of expressionist composers, along with biographical information and cultural history, provide important clues to this crucial inner content. There may be further evidence we have not uncovered in this region; there may be secrets which will not yield to investigation. In any case, we believe it is no accident that we are dealing, in the study of expressionism in music, with masterworks that revolutionized musical language. The deeply subjective phase in the work of the composers considered here has produced enigmatic but universal expression that is enduring precisely because it is so thought provoking.

We would like to acknowledge the help of Allen Sapp and the late Jack Stein for their mentorship in the initial stages of this investigation. The late Friedrich Wildgans gave us invaluable assistance in Vienna; Maria Halbich-Webern, the late Ernst Krenek, the late Felix Greissle, Lawrence Schoenberg, Nuria Schoenberg Nono, Ronald Schoenberg, the late Hans Moldenhauer, László Somfai, János Kárpáti, Jelena Hahl, Jane Kallir, Olda Kokoschka, Peter Bartók, Karl Kohn, Lewis Wickes, Regina Busch, and Jorun Johns have all been graciously helpful; Heidi Lesemann and Joseph Rovan assisted us in innumerable ways.

We are grateful to the following for reading all or parts of the manuscript, and offering beneficial advice and encouragement: Laurence Berman, Mark DeVoto, Douglass Green, Leonard Stein, the late John Kirkpatrick, Françoise Forster-Hahn, Robert Wohl, Peter Jelavich, Leon Kirchner, Elliot Forbes, Frans Boerlage, and Kenneth Barkin.

We pursued research in many libraries and archives, and are particularly indebted to the following: Research staff of the Getty Center for the History of Art and the Humanities; staff of the Paul Sacher Stiftung; Wayne Shoaf, Jerry McBride, and the late Clara Steuermann of the Arnold Schoenberg Institute; Timothy Benson, Associate Curator, Robert Gore Rifkind Center for German Expressionist Studies; Harold Samuel and Victor Cardell, Yale Music Library, Ives Collection; Wayne Shirley, Music Division, Library of Congress; Michael Ochs and David Schwarzkopf, Music Library, Harvard University; J. Rigbie Turner, Pierpont Morgan Library; and Benjamin Suchoff, New York Bartók Archives.

Important financial and material support came from the American Council of Learned Societies, the Humanities Institute of the University of California, a Visiting Fellowship at Harvard University, and a publication grant from Dean Brian Copenhaver, the University of California, Riverside.

Finally, we graciously thank our friends and family for their impatience over the decades it took to see this work in print.

Acknowledgments for Musical Examples

The authors are grateful to the publishers listed below for permission to reprint the very essential musical examples in this book. Because of space limitations, only brief copyright information is given following the first appearance of each composition; full acknowledgments are provided here.

Permission to reproduce excerpts from the following works has been granted by Associated Music Publishers, Inc., international copyrights secured, all rights reserved:

Ives, Fourth Symphony (Ex. 9-12), copyright © 1965.

Ives, Piano Sonata No. 2 (Exx. 9-9, 9-10, 9-11), copyright © 1937 (renewed).

Ives, Sonata for Violin and Piano, No. 4 (Exx. 9-3, 9-4b), copyright © 1942 (renewed).

Mahler, Tenth Symphony (Ex. 3-11), edited and revised by Otto A. Jokl, copyright © 1951 (renewed).

Permission to reproduce excerpts from the following works of Schoenberg has been granted by Belmont Music Publishers, Pacific Palisades, CA 90272:

Erwartung (Exx. 4-6, 4-7, 4-8)

Die Glückliche Hand (Ex. 4-10)

Die Jakobsleiter (Exx. 4-11, 4-12, 4-13)

Second String Quartet (Exx. 4-1, 4-2)

A Survivor from Warsaw (Ex. 11-8)

Op. 11/III (Ex. 4-5)

Permission to reproduce excerpts from the following works of Bartók has been granted by Boosey & Hawkes, Inc.:

Duke Bluebeard's Castle (Ex. 8-6), © copyright 1921 by Universal Edition, copyright renewed; copyright and renewal assigned to Boosey & Hawkes, Inc. for the U.S.A.

Fourteen Bagatelles, Op. 6 (Exx. 8-3, 8-4), new version © copyright 1950 by Boosey & Hawkes, Inc., copyright renewed.

The Miraculous Mandarin (Exx. 8-10, 8-11, 8-12), © copyright 1925, by Universal Edition, copyright renewed; copyright and renewal assigned to Boosey & Hawkes for the U.S.A.

Second Sonata for Violin and Piano (Ex. 8-13), © 1923 by Universal Edition, copyright renewed; copyright and renewal assigned to Boosey & Hawkes for the U.S.A.

String Quartet No. 1 (Ex. 8-5), used by permission of Boosey & Hawkes, sole agents for Kultura in the U.S.A.

String Quartet, No. 2, Op. 17 (Exx. 8-8, 8-9). © copyright 1920 by Universal Edition, copyright renewed; copyright and renewal assigned to Boosey & Hawkes for the U.S.A.

Violin Concerto No. 1 (Exx. 8-1, 8-2), © copyright 1946 by Hawkes & Son (London) Ltd, copyright renewed.

An excerpt from Hindemith, Op. 18/VI (Ex. 11-1), © B. Schott's Söhne, Mainz, 1922, © renewed, all rights reserved, is used by permission of European American Music Distributors Corporation, sole U.S. and Canadian agent for B. Schott's Söhne.

Permission to reproduce excerpts from the following works has been granted by European American Music Distributors Corporation, sole U.S. and Canadian agent for Universal Edition, Vienna, all rights reserved:

Bartók, Five Songs (Ex. 8-7), © copyright 1961 by Universal Edition (London); U.S. copyright 1958 by Victor Bator, Trustee, Béla Bartók estate, copyright assigned to Universal Edition (London); © copyrights renewed.

Berg, Three Pieces for Orchestra (Ex. 3-7c), copyright 1923, copyright renewed; second version (composed 1929) copyright 1954, copyright renewed.

Berg, *Lyric Suite* (Exx. 6-9, 6-10, 6-11, 6-12), copyright 1927, copyright renewed.

Berg, *Wozzeck* (Exx. 6-4, 6-5, 6-6, 6-7, 6-8a), full score copyright 1926, copyright renewed; pocket score copyright 1955, copyright renewed.

Krenek, *Orpheus und Eurydike* (Ex. 11-4), copyright 1925, copyright renewed.

Krenek, Symphony No. 2 (Ex. 11-3), © copyright, 1924, 1952.

Mahler, "Der Tambourg'sell" (Ex. 3-2).

Webern, Op. 3/I, "Dies ist ein Lied" (Ex. 5–1), copyright 1921, copyright renewed.

Webern, Op. 5/I (Exx. 5-2, 5-3), copyright 1922, copyright renewed.

Webern, Op. 6 (Exx. 5-4, 5-5, 5-6), © copyright 1956, © copyright renewed.

Webern, Op. 13 (Exx. 5-10b, c, d), copyright 1926, copyright renewed.

Webern, Op. 14 (Exx. 5-11, 5-12), copyright 1924, copyright renewed.

Weill, *Der Protagonist* (Ex. 11-2), copyright 1926, copyright renewed; English translation (by Lionel Salter), copyright 1978.

An excerpt from Webern, "O sanftes Glühn der Berge," copyright © 1964, 1968 by Carl Fischer, Inc., New York, international copyright secured, all rights reserved, is reprinted by permission of the publisher.

Expressionism in Twentieth-Century Music

CHAPTER ONE

Twentieth-Century Expressionism:
Its Nature, Background, and Language

> Humanity is deprived of its soul, nature is de-
> humanized. . . . Mankind cries for his soul; the
> whole time is a cry of need. Art also cries out,
> deeply into the depths it cries for help, for the
> spirit: that is Expressionism.
>
> Hermann Bahr (1916)

Expressionism gives primacy to the emotions. It is an explosive, subjective awareness of anxiety, sordidness, and disorder beneath surface order, well-being, and beauty. It is manifested among artists by a compulsive sense of responsibility to confront truth at all costs, and thus to save
humanity from spiritual decay. Expressionism is a radical art, searching for
its sources not in the conventional and commonplace but in the primal: in
primitive art or in explorations of the psyche. While other manifestations of
early twentieth-century modernism also seek their roots in the primitive,
expressionism is unique in its reliance on instinct, rather than technique or
rational processes, to deal with its materials.[1] Arnold Schoenberg articulated
better than any other composer the expressionist view of art: "Art belongs
to the *unconscious!* One must express *oneself!* Express oneself *directly!* Not
one's taste or one's upbringing, or one's intelligence knowledge or skill. Not
all these *acquired* characteristics, but that which is *inborn, instinctive.*"[2] In a
similar vein, Bartók wrote: "All my music is in the first place a matter of
feeling and instinct. Do not ask me why I have written thus and not otherwise. I can give only one answer to this: I wrote the way I felt."[3]

Another unique aspect of expressionism, differentiating it from other types
of modernism, is that it is an embodiment primarily of artists' attitudes toward
society and the individual, and only secondarily their attitudes toward art
itself. In their anger at the encrustations of bourgeois culture, which hid truths
and suppressed individuality, artists opposed such manifestations of the art-
for-art's-sake principle as Impressionism, *Jugendstil* (or *art nouveau*), and, in
America, the prevailing genteel tradition. They rejected realism and Naturalism, for surface imitations did not satisfy their need to probe for more pro-

found meaning. They hoped to capture the "thing-in-itself," the essence of experience. Anton Webern wrote,

> I want the thing itself. The reality of a work of art is no symbol, no imitation either of outer or inner Nature. It doesn't imitate the pulse of the heart. It is its own self; it has its own pulse. Otherwise everything would be an imitation in relation to something. Perhaps that's so: This *something* is God. Only I don't like the word imitation.[4]

Similarly, Charles Ives claimed,

> The fabric of existence weaves itself into a whole. You cannot set art off in the corner and hope for it to have vitality, reality, and substance. There can be nothing "exclusive" about a substantial art. It comes directly out of the heart of experience of life and thinking about life and living life.[5]

This bias toward humanism in expressionism rejected such rational processes as weighing, testing, balancing, and formulating, and put faith instead in the integrity of the individual's unconscious or intuitive sense of form and coherence.

"Expressionism has always occurred when a man held the roots of things in his hand," wrote an important early spokesman for literary expressionism, Kasimir Edschmid. He called expressionism an *Übernational* (supranational) art, and mentioned Grünewald, Shakespeare, and Strindberg as examples of artists whose creativity was concerned with eternal significance in the same way.[6] An expressionist impulse can be found in such differing composers of extreme emotional compulsion as Don Carlo Gesualdo (ca. 1560–1613), whose late madrigals use chromaticism, extreme dissonance, and abrupt texture changes to exploit every mood of love-obsessed texts; Carl Philipp Emanuel Bach (1714–88), whose keyboard fantasies employing chromaticism, surprising shifts in texture, strange modulations, and abrupt accents are expressively related to early Romantic literary *Sturm und Drang* (storm and stress); and Beethoven (1770–1827), whose later music attained an extraordinarily probing self-expression, marked by an almost improvisatory freedom of form and a transcendent inwardness.

While some scholars have limited the definition of expressionism to German movements in visual and literary arts before World War I, others, like Herbert Read, a critic and an authority on modern art, find that expressionism can be thought of as "a permanent basic element in all art which the times seem to have brought to the surface."[7] Read claims that " 'expressionism' is a fundamentally necessary word, like 'idealism' and 'realism,' and not a word of secondary implications like 'impressionism.' *It denotes one of the basic modes of perceiving and representing the world around us.*"[8] Recent scholarship seems to have accepted the international scope of expressionism, as arguments continue over specific definitions, movements, and artists.[9]

Although the phenomenon of expressionism is focused in Central Europe during the decade before World War I, a good part of its impetus came from outside Germany and Austria, as did the word itself, which arose out of the painting of the French Fauves.[10] In music, expressionism was not confined to Germany and Austria, but appeared wherever composers shared the same spirit and preoccupations. It erupted in works of Ives and Ruggles in America, Bartók in Hungary, in some of the Russian works of Stravinsky, as well as in the commonly recognized Austrians and Germans Schoenberg, Berg, Webern, and—in a second wave—Krenek, Weill, and Hindemith. While these widespread occurrences derive from similar sociological and psychological necessities, it is clear that musical expressionism did not take the organized form of a movement, as it did, for example, in the community of *Die Brücke* (The Bridge) artists in Dresden and later Berlin, from 1905 to 1913, or in the literary circles formed around activist periodicals such as *Der Sturm* (Storm) and *Die Aktion* (Action) in Berlin, beginning in 1910–11.

Expressionism in music presents a close chronological parallel to its appearance in the other arts. Ives's unprecedented, highly subjective *Unanswered Question* and his "In the Cage," written in 1906, followed by a year the founding of *Die Brücke*. In Stockholm, in 1908, Strindberg opened the Intimate Theater, for which he wrote his expressionist Chamber Plays; during the same year, Schoenberg, Webern, and Bartók produced their first revolutionary works based solely on individual "feeling for form," as Schoenberg put it.[11] In 1909, Kokoschka produced his Viennese cabaret readings—concerning his struggle with the female sex—and his first expressionist play, *Mörder, Hoffnung der Frauen* (Murderer, Hope of Women); the same year there was an extraordinary outpouring of expressionist compositions by Schoenberg, Webern, Berg, Bartók, and Ives. By 1913 the *Blaue Reiter Almanac* (by the Blue Rider group of Munich) and Reinhard Johannes Sorge's *Der Bettler* (The Beggar), the first German Expressionist play, had been published; and such epoch-making expressionist compositions as Schoenberg's *Pierrot lunaire;* Webern's Six Bagatelles, Op. 9, for String Quartet; Berg's Altenberg Lieder, Op. 4; Stravinsky's *Petrushka* and *Rite of Spring;* Bartók's opera, *Duke Bluebeard's Castle,* and the "Allegro Barbaro" for piano, had all been written. Ives's *Concord Sonata* was composed in 1911–15, and Berg's *Wozzeck* was conceived and begun in 1914.

World War I shook inner artistic convictions, so that post-1918 expressionist compositions emulated the prewar creative explosions, but not always with similar spiritual fire. In music, as in the visual and literary arts, the "second wave" of expressionists produced more politically engaged works during expressionism's brief postwar vogue. By 1923, with the spiritual bankruptcy attending drastic devaluation of currencies and failures of social reforms, composers sought greater balance and control. In music, the fifteen years in which expressionism flourished then gave way to new formulas of constructivism, and an emphasis on technique again replaced the instinctive.

What provoked the alienation, anxiety, rebellion against authority or convention, and the need to reassess all values which produced expressionist art? As Oswald Spengler wrote in *The Decline of the West* (in 1911, at the time of the rise of expressionism), "World-fear is assuredly the most creative of all prime feelings."[12] Many expressionist artists came from the comfortable, complacent middle class, yet they felt the strongest premonitions of catastrophe, as tensions which had been building during the nineteenth century came to the surface. With rapid industrialization and urbanization, severe oppression of workers and consequent socialism, as well as the accelerating pace of technological advance, the demands of human spirit, feelings, and imagination had been ignored and repressed in favor of materialist values.

Like other expressionist artists, most expressionist composers were caught up in socialist idealism. As early as 1878 Gustav Mahler—then a music student in Vienna—became a lifelong friend of Victor Adler, the subsequent founder of the Austrian Socialist party. In 1905, although he was by then fighting controversy as director of the Court Opera, Mahler joined with passionate feeling in the Socialist party's immense May Day demonstration of the brotherhood of workers.[13] Schoenberg served as a conductor for workers' choral societies near Vienna in the years 1895–1900, although this activity brought little income to the needy composer, who had resigned from his clerkship in a bank in order to pursue his career in music.[14] In 1910, Schoenberg planned in detail a Volkskonservatorium (People's Music School), of which Webern and Berg were to be co-directors, in Vienna.[15] After the collapse of the Habsburg regime in 1918, the Austrian Socialist Democratic party appointed Anton Webern conductor of an amateur men's chorus in Mödling (near Vienna). He sustained this activity with much greater satisfaction than he experienced from his professional conducting of operetta and opera in provincial theaters. In 1921, his success with the Workmen's Symphony Concerts, founded by the Social Democratic party to bring culture to the working classes, established his reputation as a conductor.[16] Béla Bartók began his important investigations into folk music in 1905, recording songs from peasants in remote areas before technological advances in communications further corrupted unique folk characteristics, which were already deteriorating because of the railroad. In 1907 Charles Ives began a distinguished and innovative career in life insurance, based on passionate advocacy of the common man. He bypassed the commercial aspects of the business, and he himself never sold insurance. Instead, he trained his agents in the principles and philosophy of the Concord Transcendentalists. He calculated the amount an individual's share in the country's wealth should be, and rather than become many times a millionaire, he returned his own excess to his business, and to music. His strenuous opposition to big financial interests, which Ives felt caused war, brought on a heart attack in 1918, which crippled the remainder of his creative life.[17]

Nineteenth-century scientific positivism and materialism had destroyed much religious belief; between 1895 and 1905, a series of discoveries in radioactivity, atomic structure, and Einstein's Special Theory of Relativity invalidated conceptions—dependable since Newton—about the solidity of the universe. Expressionist painter Wassily Kandinsky voiced the fear caused by these ruptures in belief and proposed the solution for the artist: "Men of learning . . . cast doubt on that very matter which was yesterday the foundation of everything, so that the whole universe is shaken. . . . When outer supports threaten to fall, man turns his gaze from externals in onto himself."[18] Indeed, Kandinsky wrote in a letter to Schoenberg in 1911, *"self-perception . . . is the root of the 'new' art, of art in general, which is never new, but which must only enter into a new phase—'Today!' "*[19]

The generation of expressionists was the first to make use of the symbols and methods of psychoanalysis. The Viennese composers not only knew of but had personal connections with theories of Freud and his disciples: Mahler met with Freud in Holland, in 1910, to discuss his marital crisis; Berg consulted Freud in 1908 in an attempt to cure his asthma; Webern underwent psychoanalysis with Alfred Adler in 1913, soon after Adler's break with Freud's circle. The "inner necessity"[20] so many expressionist artists followed is closely related to the new primacy of psychology.[21]

Freud emphasized the role of the father at the very time the young generation of expressionists felt most keenly the repression of natural instincts, youth's daring, and lust for life by their authoritarian elders, whose thoughts focused only on the fetishes of security and material "substance."[22] Overwhelming anger and rebellion against the father and figures of authority was a frequent expressionist theme (particularly in influential expressionist plays, such as Walter Hasenclever's *Der Sohn*, published in 1914). Stravinsky's expressionist compositions *Petrushka* and *The Rite of Spring* reflect his hatred for the St. Petersburg musical establishment, of which his father had been an important member. Stravinsky later recalled that he had written *The Rite* in order to send all authority figures, including his family, "to hell."[23] Webern's psychoanalysis, at the high point of his expressionist phase, dealt with his subservient yet antagonistic relationship to authority figures, who included his employers, Schoenberg, and his own father.

On the other hand, Freud felt that the death of one's father was "the most important event, the most poignant loss, of a man's life."[24] The father's death, when Schoenberg was seventeen, Berg fifteen, Bartók seven, and Ives twenty, caused a rupture, or created a sense of anxiety, crucial to the development of each composer. Exorcism of such personal crises could only be achieved through a music which was radically new. Ives expressed grief for his loss by evoking in his music scenes, memories, and thoughts shared with his parent, yet ever extending his father's musical radicalism.

Expressionist music was often either secretly or overtly concerned with difficulties in relations between the sexes. Emergence from long-standing sexual repression and hypocrisy took various psychologically painful and often confusing forms in the opening years of the twentieth century, at the same time that Freud was applying psychoanalysis to the free associations and dreams of women patients suffering from hysteria. Otto Weininger, who recognized that "never since human history began have we heard of female psychology," stated the misogynist view that woman is nonmoral—a phallus worshiper incapable of love—in his widely read book, *Sex and Character* (1903).[25] Weininger's view of the soullessness of women was shared in Strindberg's plays dealing with battles between the sexes for personal dominance. Frank Wedekind, like Strindberg a playwright of cardinal importance to musical expressionism, also held a misogynist view. His Lulu is amoral; she represents the elemental conflict of sex with bourgeois society. New attitudes toward sex were of major concern to Schoenberg, Bartók, and Berg in particular. In 1905 Bartók wavered on the then radical question of sexual equality in a letter to his mother from Paris:

> Women should be accorded the same liberties as men. Women ought to be free to do the same things as men, or men ought not to be free to do the things women aren't supposed to do—I used to believe that this should indeed be so for the sake of equality. However, after giving the subject a great deal of thought, I have come to believe that men and women are so different in mind and body that it may not be such a bad idea after all to demand from women a greater degree of chastity. These matters are too intimate to write about in detail.[26]

Berg expressed his advanced views on sexuality in a 1907 letter to an American girl, Frida Semler:

> Wedekind—the really new direction—the emphasis on the sensual in modern works!! . . . I believe it is a good thing. At last we have come to the realization that sensuality is not a weakness, does not mean a surrender to one's own will. Rather is it an immense strength that lies in us—the pivot of all being and thinking. (Yes; all thinking!) In this I am declaring firmly and certainly the great importance of sensuality, for everything spiritual. Only through the understanding of sensuality, only through a fundamental insight into the "depths of mankind" (shouldn't it rather be called the "heights of mankind"?) can one arrive at a real idea of the human psyche.[27]

It is typical of the expressionist sensibility to stress the importance of the spiritual, even when breaking the bonds of earlier sexual mores. These questions frequently resulted in personal crises, which in turn generated important creative work. In the year of Berg's letter, 1907, Schoenberg withdrew into depression. He neglected his marriage to such an extent that Mathilde Schoenberg deserted the family, her lover (expressionist painter Richard Gerstl) subsequently took his own life, and Schoenberg himself contemplated suicide.[28] These events catalyzed his breakthrough into expressionist composition and resulted in what can almost be called a doctrine of musical expressionism: the statement (for his 1912 diary) that "the most wonderful thing about music is that one can say everything in it, so that he who knows understands everything; and yet one hasn't given away one's secrets—the things one doesn't admit even to oneself."[29]

Much expressionist music is confession. Philosopher and music critic Theodor Adorno calls expressionism "loneliness as style."[30] At the outset of his composing career, in the same letter quoted above, the 24-year-old Béla Bartók expressed typical expressionist loneliness to his mother:

> I am a lonely man! I may be looked after . . . and I may have friends . . . yet there are times when I suddenly become aware of the fact that I am absolutely alone! And I prophesy, I have a foreknowledge, that this spiritual loneliness is to be my destiny. I look about me in search of the ideal companion, and yet I am fully aware that it is a vain quest. Even if I should ever succeed in finding someone, I am sure that I would soon be disappointed.[31]

Given the profundity of the life-problems facing this generation of psychologically aware artists, their creativity was a means of transcending the reality they saw around them. Conventional religion was not a solution, for expressionists were among the most ardent of Nietzsche's followers. His writings exhorted them to overcome all difficulties in a new morality of self-reliance (influenced by the thought of Emerson[32]). Bartók lectured a young woman friend:

> What!! You are rebuking me for being a pessimist?!! *Me,* a follower of Nietzsche?!! *Each must strive to rise above all: nothing must touch him; he must be completely independent, completely indifferent. Only thus can he reconcile himself to death and to the meaninglessness of life.*[33]

Many aspects of Nietzsche's thought reverberate in expressionist works in all the arts; chief among them was the personal necessity for revaluation of all values. Expressionists also found a creative solution to Schopenhauer's pessimism in advocacy of the Dionysian, irrational, creative force, which annihilates the appearance of beauty in a search for truth, over the Apollonian spirit, which is against instinct and therefore life-undermining. Nietzsche exalted the individual and the artist in *Thus Spake Zarathustra* (1884). Only by overcoming pain and terror through truth in art could one attain affirmation. "One must still have chaos in one, to give birth to a dancing star," Nietzsche wrote in the Prologue to *Zarathustra*.[34] While his atheism was problematical for many expressionists, their concept of "inner necessity," the basis of their creativity, came from his thought. The spiritual preoccupied them, often leading to mysticism. Schoenberg, discussing with Kandinsky the integrating importance of "the soul" to the rendering of inner vision in a work of art, expresses the experience of the spiritual as *unfassbar* (ungraspable), incapable of solution:

> We must become conscious that there are puzzles around us. And we must find the courage to look these puzzles in the eye without timidly asking about "the solution." It is important that our creation . . . mirror the puzzles with which we are surrounded, so that our soul may endeavor—not to solve them—but to decipher them . . . for the puzzles are an image of the ungraspable. An imperfect, that is, a human image. But if we can only learn from them to consider the

ungraspable as possible, we get nearer to God, because we no longer demand to understand him.[35]

Rudolf Steiner, the founder of Anthroposophy, whose understanding of religion, art, and science drew both Kandinsky and Schoenberg to his ideas, stated clearly the spiritual challenge expressionist artists felt as they faced societal, psychological, and philosophical problems in the first years of the twentieth century:

> I experienced so deeply the contrast between what I saw as the plain truth, and the views generally held, that this experience overshadowed all else at the turn of the century. . . . I felt deep pain, for I believed that I recognized destructive powers everywhere opposing cultural progress. . . . It seemed to me that the turn of the century must bring new spiritual light to humanity. A climax had been reached in the exclusion of the spirit from man's thinking and willing. A complete change in direction in humanity's evolution seemed an absolute necessity.[36]

A complete change in direction demanded a transcendent art. Wilhelm Worringer, the earliest art historian in the field of expressionism, provided a theoretical basis for the new "psychology of style."[37] In 1906 he wrote that in times of unease and terror man resorts to emotive distortions, then to abstraction in his creative efforts, in order to control, master, and transcend his primal fears and the chaotic phenomena of the outer world. This type of creation involves an instinctive, elemental necessity, without the intervention of the intellect, and is the only way in which man can find rest from outer confusion. Worringer found past examples of this transcendental urge toward abstraction in Oriental and primitive art, in Egyptian art, and particularly in northern, linear Gothic art, climaxing in Holbein and Dürer. Although his thesis, published in 1908, was opposed by art historians, it was widely influential among artists. Taking their own spiritual influences from primitive and folk art, artists of *Die Brücke*[38] used the angularity of the woodcut (see Ills. 1-1, 1-2, and 1-3, and Color Plate I); *Der blaue Reiter* artists[39] emphasized the expressive power of line and color (frontispiece, Color Plate II, and Ill. 1-4); and the Viennese painters (Egon Schiele, Oskar Kokoschka, and Richard Gerstl[40]) used distortion and the grotesque—all to express personal visions of the atmosphere of impending catastrophe (Ills. 1-5, 1-6, and 1-7).

Kokoschka, whose early expressionist portraits were remarkable in their psychological perception, wrote, "Before the War people lived in security yet they were all afraid. . . . I painted them in their anxiety and pain" (Ill. 1-8).[41] When Kandinsky was asked if his explosively violent, ominous *Composition #7* (Color Plate III), painted in 1913, was a foreboding of World War I, he answered, "I had no premonition of that. But I knew that a terrible struggle was going on in the spiritual sphere, and that made me paint the picture."[42]

Ill. 1-1. Ernst Ludwig Kirchner, *Street, Berlin*, 1913. Oil on canvas, 47½ x 35 ⅞". Museum of Modern Art, New York.

Ill. 1-2. Emil Nolde, *Prophet*, 1912. Woodcut, 12 ⅝ x 8 ¾". Los Angeles County Museum of Art, M.82.288.239. The Robert Gore Rifkind Center for German Expressionist Studies.

Ill. 1-3. Emil Nolde, *Dancer*, 1913. Color lithograph, 20 ⅞ x 27 ⅛". Los Angeles County Museum of Art, M.82.288.232. The Robert Gore Rifkind Center for German Expressionist Studies.

Ill. 1-4. Wassily Kandinsky, *Lyrisches*, 1911. Oil on canvas, 94 x 130 cm. Museum Boymans-van Beuningen, Rotterdam. Copyright 1992, ARS, New York.

Ill. 1-5. Oskar Kokoschka, *The Bride of the Wind*, 1914. Oil on canvas, 181 x 220 cm. Kunstmuseum, Basel.

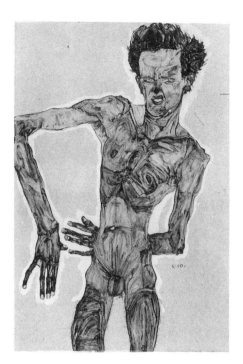

Ill. 1-6. Egon Schiele, *Self-portrait*, 1910. Pencil and tempera. 558 x 369 mm. Albertina, Vienna.

Ill. 1-7. Richard Gerstl, *Laughing Self-portrait*, 1908. Oil on canvas, 40 x 30 cm. Österreichische Galerie, Vienna.

Ill. 1-8. Oskar Kokoschka, *Hans Tietze and Erica Tietze-Conrat*, 1909. Oil on canvas, 30 ⅛ x 53 ⅝″. The Museum of Modern Art, New York, Abby Aldrich Rockefeller Fund.

Both Worringer and the Viennese writer Hermann Bahr (whose critical interest in turn-of-the century avant-garde movements caused him to be one of the earliest writers on expressionism) agreed that there must be a new way of seeing "with the eye of the spirit."[43] The new language of art should shock its audience into active participation, for the artist was now the activator rather than the echo of the world.[44] Herbert Read later recognized the explosive nature of expressionism as an

> outward release to some inner pressure, some internal necessity. . . . Such a release of psychic energy is apt to lead to exaggerated gestures, to a distortion of natural appearances that borders on the grotesque. . . . In the type of art which is specifically expressionism, the form of expression is nearest to the source of feeling.[45]

He made a further point which is particularly important to our discussion of expressionism in music: "Expressionism . . . tries to depict, not the objective facts of nature, nor any abstract notion based on these facts, but the subjective feelings of the artist."[46] Expressionist art, literature, and music are filled with subjective meaning and are neither fully objective nor fully abstract.[47] Rather, expressionism is an urgent emotional phase which constitutes a transition from the objective to the abstract.

It is easiest to perceive this phenomenon in the visual arts. In Kandinsky's expressionist paintings, mountain images gradually become protective, massive triangular shapes; a tree or church tower is expressed as a strongly spiritual vertical accent; people become suppliant, bent, motivic elements; horse and rider are reduced to a lyrical arc. When Kandinsky's fully abstract style is reached in his Bauhaus period (in the 1920s), these motifs are pure geometric shapes, and we are no longer certain of the subjective feelings connected with them (Ills. 1-9, 1-10, and 1-11).

In music, the linguistic realm of twentieth-century expressionism lies between the abandonment of tonality and composers' adoption of formulations (also in the 1920s) such as symmetrical constructions and the twelve-tone system. For example, instead of using the language of tonal harmony for tension and repose, in the twelve-tone system the composer constructs a fixed consecutive order—or row—out of the twelve possible pitches of the chromatic scale, none of which have priority. If tonality (the objective) offers a system of laws suggested by the overtone series in nature, and if the twelve-tone system (the abstract) offers a virtual dictatorship by the composer, it is the anarchic (subjective) area in between which is the linguistic area of expressionist music. Neither objective nor abstract, this music is governed by expressive necessity. Within this unsystematized area one possibility is the complete avoidance of tonal function, which came to be called *atonality,* and which Schoenberg, Berg, and Webern later recognized as a developmental stage on the road to the twelve-tone system. Another possibility is Stravinsky's *bitonality,* or the imposition of a second tonality on a first. In his derivations from peasant music Bartók often uses *bimodality.* A further possibility is *polytonality* (the simultaneous layering of several keys), which Ives uses to express the shifting flow of nature and human events, or the existence of an all-pervasive spiritual presence hovering above the realities of nature. In all these cases, it is the *expressive meaning* within the music which demands the particular use of the tonal materials available. Although the seeds of procedures eventually developed in the later constructivist stage are sown, fully formulated abstraction is not yet reached.

Because the expressionist phase is turbulent and developmental, generally at its most acute in the early maturity of each composer considered, it is extremely difficult to sustain. This problem can be seen in the extraordinarily reductive brevity of some expressionist works and in the relatively short but intensely productive period of expressionism in composers' lives. Expressionism ignores boundaries between means and modes of expression. Various nonexpressionist styles and techniques, such as Impressionism and aspects of constructivism, appear within many expressionist compositions, just as in the visual arts (see frontispiece). No security is provided by any particular exterior method; Schoenberg calls attention to "elimination of the conscious will" in expressionism.[48]

In accord with its humanistic nature, expressionism is prone to paradox and dichotomy: a prime example is the conflict of emotionalism with the urge toward the abstract. Others are the confrontations of chaos and form (particularly in Berg's operas), of heart and brain (in Schoenberg and Webern), and

Ill. 1-9. Wassily Kandinsky, *Murnau Landscape,* 1909. Oil on board, 26 ¼ x 37 ¼". Richard S. Zeisler Collection, New York. Copyright 1992 ARS, New York.

Ill. 1-10. Wassily Kandinsky, *Composition IV,* 1911. Oil on canvas, 38 ⅛ x 43 ¾". Kunstsammlung Nordrhein-Westfalen, Düsseldorf. Copyright 1992 ARS, New York.

Ill. 1-11. Wassily Kandinsky, *Composition VIII*, 1923. Oil on canvas, 55 ⅛ x 78 ¾". Solomon R. Guggenheim Museum, New York. (Photo by Robert E. Mates.) Copyright 1992 ARS, New York.

of archaisms (or the vernacular) and artifice (in Stravinsky, Bartók, and Ives). Another is the ambivalence between direct, truthful communication and the need to shelter the secret self.

There are no fixed norms of technique and style in musical expressionism, although one can find "dialects"—stylistic traits—affected by national origin. As the composer seeks the roots of his consciousness or expresses private meanings in his works, he forms his own language of personal musical symbols combined with preexistent ones. For all these reasons, expressionism is as difficult to define stylistically in music as it is in the other arts. However, some general and particular stylistic characteristics are common to many works. Arnold Schering was the first music historian to attempt to clarify these attributes. In an extended article entitled "The Expressionist Trend in Music" (1919), he recognized the international implications of expressionism's central spiritual point of view, but he noted that composers were not united on how to reach the new musical ideal. He felt that the impulse had its European beginnings when Liszt gave up sonata form for program music. But, Schering continued, in expressionism there is no program, nothing "outer." All forms are individual, allowing "improvisation in the highest sense." Free form is used to symbolize inner life. Musical content therefore is concerned with the "incalculable exultations of the soul": experiences on the border between the conscious and the unconscious. In contrast with musical Impressionism (which is concerned with mood, not emotion), in expressionism, Schering wrote, conflicting emotions of ecstasy, anxiety, fear, and visionary mysticism are set up by a storm and result in turbulent creation.[49]

In many ways expressionism seems to be an attitude rather than a style. Yet some general observations can be made on stylistic manifestations of expressionism in the various elements of music. These can also be closely related to expressionistic characteristics in art and literature. Distortion and the grotesque play an important role in depicting psychological states, whose meaning, while intensely felt, must remain hidden. Expressionism marks the end of the nineteenth-century concept of program music, as exemplified by the Strauss tone poems. While the new music is never without content, there is no longer a literary program, or narrative, for the personal and psychological content of expressionist music is not expressed in a linear way. This new attitude allows the composer to emphasize "his own visionary form, the poet in himself, direct musical expression," as Schoenberg wrote in a criticism of the "second-hand poetry" of Liszt's program music.[50]

In expressionism, form is the embodiment of content. As Kandinsky wrote, "form is the outer expression of the inner content."[51] Schoenberg defined "expressionism" (a term he and other composers as well as other artists and writers at first found difficult to accept) as "the *art of the representation of inner occurrences.*"[52] Texted works or ballets and pantomime with scenarios constitute the major part of the expressionist musical repertoire. Since composers tended to use texts (or scenarios) which corresponded to their urgent psychological needs, they contain important clues to underlying content (or subtext). Texted works can also illumine the inner content of purely instrumental works written in the same time period.

Expressionists rejected the restrictions of conventional form. For example, the Expressionist poet Ernst Stadler wrote: "Form wants to oppress and stifle me/But I desire a vast expansion of my being."[53] Expressionist music is not necessarily formless. Form is not rationalized but can be intuited by the composer. Schoenberg spoke of trusting one's "feeling for form," which allowed one to "serenely abandon oneself to one's imagination, without theories."[54] His unpredictable, constantly changing forms are similar to the free association Freud was using in psychoanalysis to replace the earlier procedure of hypnosis.[55] Strindberg applied this dreamlike approach to dramatic form in 1902. The description of form in his *A Dream Play* (produced in 1907) is analogous to some expressionist musical forms:

> In this dream play, as in his former dream play *To Damascus,* the Author has sought to reproduce the disconnected but apparently logical form of a dream. Anything can happen; everything is possible and probable. Time and space do not exist; on a slight groundwork of reality, imagination spins and weaves new patterns made up of memories, experiences, unfettered fancies, absurdities, and improvisations. The characters are split, double and multiply; they evaporate, crystallize, scatter and converge. But a single consciousness holds sway over them all—that of the dreamer.[56]

Forms were often improvisatory; an example is the second movement of Ives's Fourth Symphony, which presents a succession of seemingly unconnected images with a minimum of linear structure. Ives, like Schoenberg, had a concept of "organic" form, which was profoundly rooted in his interpretation of meaning in nature.

The variation principle became the favored device of expressionist composers, in their almost obsessive desire not to repeat. Truthfulness to psychological flux required avoidance of cadences and often led to open-ended forms. The extreme of open-ended form is the phenomenon of "conceptual" music: large, uncompleted works, such as Schoenberg's *Die Jakobsleiter* and *Moses und Aron*, forerunner Scriabin's *Mysterium*, and Ives's *Universe Symphony;* these compositions contemplated enormous ethical and religious questions and defied their composers' efforts to finish them.

There is a typically expressionist dichotomy between this expansiveness and the tendency to aphoristic compression, in which a concentration of thematic material reduces the music almost to silence. Webern's extremely reduced instrumental works in this vein can be compared to the effort in expressionist poetry and drama to exaggerate the emotive significance of words, until a single word assumes the full meaning of the sentence it replaces, and the silence between words is filled with reverberation. The following example, a poem by August Stramm, is called "Patrouille" (Patrol):

Die Steine feinden	The stones are hostile
Fenster grinst Verrat	Window grins betrayal
Äste würgen	Branches strangle
Berge Straücher	Mountain bushes
blättern raschlig	leaves rustling
Gellen	A scream
Tod	Death.[57]

The tension achieved in musical melody, through abrupt shifts in direction, wide intervals, and extremes of range, produces an effect of modern unease or alienation similar to that conveyed by the jagged treatment of line in paintings and woodcuts of the *Die Brücke* artists. Melodic symmetry (along with all other manifestations of symmetry, for that matter) is avoided, as being inconsistent with the lack of balance in inner life. Likewise, literal repetition and periodic structure are rejected for not reflecting the spirit of the times. Schoenberg called this asymmetrical melodic style "musical prose" (a term also used in similar ways by Wagner and Ives).[58] Indeed, Schoenberg and Webern came close to athematic writing at this time, but eventually rejected the concept. In 1932 Webern remembered:

As we gradually gave up tonality an idea occurred to us: "We don't want to repeat, there must constantly be something new!" Obviously this doesn't work, it destroys comprehensibility. At least it's impossible to write long stretches of music in that way.[59]

In this period of experiment, Webern and Schoenberg began to build their melodic languages on intervallic cells which may have embodied personal symbolic meaning. Bartók used a similar approach to melody, deriving symbolic cells from folk music as well as creating them himself. Stravinsky (particularly in *Petrushka*) and Ives (in many works) quoted colloquial or popular melodic material, with the intention of cutting directly through an intervening layer of musical gentility to the listener's psyche. By employing recognizable tunes or motives, grotesquely distorted or surprisingly juxtaposed, a composer could evoke a particular psychological response. In expressionist music, counterpoint regains a predominant role, after having been subordinate to harmony in late-Romantic and Impressionist music. Simultaneity is a prime characteristic of expressionism;[60] contrapuntal writing allows the composer to express several levels of consciousness simultaneously. The unique ability of music to state the progressive flow of thought at the same time that it deals with various depths and sources of thought is extraordinarily useful to the expressionist. For Mahler, the contrapuntal layering of remembered sounds of nature, peasant dances, and military bands serves as an ideal of polyphony[61] akin to Ives's strata of remembered sounds and tunes from country holidays and religious camp meetings. In the works of Schoenberg and Berg, contrapuntal layering frequently represents psychological layering.[62] Although *strict* counterpoint was not characteristic of expressionist music, paradoxically, the Viennese composers eventually turned to rigorous contrapuntal devices to establish unity in the atonal context, in order to prevent structural chaos. Thus canon, fugue, and passacaglia appear in Schoenberg's expressionist work *Pierrot lunaire* (1912), pointing the way toward the greater abstraction of the twelve-tone system which was to come.

Rhythm in expressionist music is characterized by unpredictable asymmetry, reflecting the discontinuity of both outer and inner modern life. Bartók and Stravinsky use shifting, violently syncopated accents and motoric rhythms to invoke their primitive sources as well as to shock European gentility. Obsessively repeated rhythmic motives in their works provide structure as well as build tension. Constant expressive rubato is particularly exploited by Webern (who goes so far as to intend its use in rests!) in order to portray psychological flux. Ragtime and jazz rhythms and gestures are employed by Ives and Hindemith to convey urban pace and tumult.

An unprecedented liberation of harmonic language from the remaining restrictions of tonal harmony is achieved by expressionist composers. Chords become unclassifiable aggregations of notes, often built on intervals previously stated melodically. Schoenberg wrote, "every chord is created and placed under compulsion, the compulsion of a creative need."[63] His radical treatment of harmonic language extends traditional practices to the point of the emancipation of dissonance and release from tonality. Very often, extreme expressive intensity may be compressed into a single chord, just as in literary expressionism one word may be the carrier of powerful emotions. The unique chord which occurs when the Sage kisses the earth in Stravinsky's *Rite of Spring* is an example.

Early in his composing career Ives was compelled to use a dissonant language because of his subject matter: "In the outward life of the old settlers, pioneers and Puritans, there was . . . inward beauty, but a rather harsh exterior. Music to express this must, before all else, be something in art removed from physical comfort."[64] In his devotion to the Transcendentalists, Ives constantly sought "ear and mind stretching."[65]

Although the expressionist composer's need to achieve simultaneity often leads to extremely dense textures, there is no melodic and harmonic "filler," which was so characteristic of late nineteenth-century music. This elimination of the ornamental corresponds to the new functional simplicity achieved by the Viennese architect Adolf Loos, a friend and patron of Schoenberg during the early years of expressionism. Musical textures may be extremely discontinuous, as unpredictable emotional impulses cause frequent changes in the general pattern of sound. Paradoxically, a kind of emotional stasis, or sense of fixation, is often achieved by the use of ostinato-dominated textures.

There is an extraordinary registral expansion in the use of the orchestra and of individual instruments. It is as if the release of inner pressure demands extremes of both range and dynamics. The extensive use of new instrumental techniques (such as flutter-tongue, glissandi, playing with the wood of the bow, and playing near the bridge) is another outgrowth of these expressive demands. Webern used these new techniques in a very intense way in the original versions of instrumental pieces and orchestral songs written between 1909 and 1918, toning them down considerably when he revised the works for publication in the altered musical climate of the 1920s' "New Objectivity."

Although tonal beauty is no longer the goal in expressionist music, color is of the utmost importance as an expressive means. Thus a melody may be fragmented into a succession of different tone colors as in *Klangfarbenmelodie* (tone color melody). New acoustical effects (in Schoenberg's *Die Jakobsleiter* and in Ives's Fourth Symphony and *The Housatonic at Stockbridge*) also expand expressive dimensions into a transcendental realm.

A reemphasis on the human voice was natural to the humanistic concerns of expressionist composers, and much of the music examined in this study is vocal. In some cases (such as in some of Ives's instrumental works and in the finale of Berg's *Lyric Suite*), the text is set but not sung; it underlies the feeling, or meaning, germinal to the composition. The traditional boundaries of vocal technique are continually extended in range, dynamics, and tone production in response to psychological pressures. The *Ur-schrei,* or primal scream, which appears in expressionist literature and the visual arts as well as in music (see Color Plate IV), is perhaps the most extreme outlet for emotional stress.[66] Although primarily a vocal phenomenon, the *Ur-schrei* can appear instrumentally as well, as it does in the first of Webern's Five

Pieces for String Quartet, Op. 5 (1909). Perhaps the most important extension of vocal technique in musical expressionism is *Sprechgesang* (half spoken, half sung, often referred to as *Sprechstimme*), which provides not only
new possibilities of vocal timbre but also a shockingly direct communication
with the listener.

Musical symbolism plays an important role in expressionist music, where
a melodic motive, a harmony or a series of harmonies, a rhythmic pattern or
a tone color, even a tonality or a combination of tonalities may denote an
idea or an emotion. Whereas a leitmotif often deals with an external action
or object (a sword, a fire, a kiss), in expressionism a musical symbol deals
with an inner occurrence. Expressionist composers made use of the accumulated meaning of musical symbols from earlier periods in an urgent desire for
direct and unambiguous communication, as if to compensate for having sacrificed comprehensibility in such elements of music as harmony and form.
However, if (as is frequently the case) an expressionist composer's musical
symbolism is new and highly personal, it may reflect a typical ambivalence:
the desire to communicate but at the same time to maintain one's secrecy (see
Schoenberg's statement above, p. 6). By extensive use of personal, private
musical symbolism, a composer may actually create a secret language, difficult to penetrate.[67]

Arnold Schering wrote in 1919 that a "music psychology" would have
to be invented to show the connection between soul-life and artistic work in
expressionist music.[68] The composer Elliott Carter felt that expressionist music "must be analyzed in terms of its musical-expressive character . . . to
discover the way an atonal work is constructed technically *in order* to make
its musical-expressive point."[69] Perhaps Jan Maegaard comes closest to the
heart of the matter when he writes: "It is inherent in the spiritual attitude of
expressionism that formal devices should not be clearly recognizable from the
sounding surface of the music; for expressionism is to a large extent an ad-
venture into the subconscious."[70] These three writers imply in different ways
that the understanding of expressionist music will *not* be reached primarily
by way of rational analysis, but by a search for meaning in which our intuition (aided by a knowledge of the composers and their milieu) must play a
large role.

Expressionism is often seen as the last and most extreme manifestation
of Romanticism. But expressionism is a part of early modernism, reflecting
the twentieth century's painful separations from nature and communal values. While the Romantic artist concentrated on the most beautiful moments
of inner life, the expressionist was under compulsion to express truthfully its
ugliness as well. While Romantic composers extended musical form and tonal
harmony to their limits, expressionists definitively shattered these unifying
concepts, which represented outmoded illusions. For expressionists there was
no longer the security of a common musical language; both form and harmony became matters of the most difficult individual struggle.

Expressionism differs from the main trend of other modernist movements toward impersonality, coolness, and constructivism. In expressionism, the arts are freely intermixed, not separate and self-referential. The message or content is paramount, not the medium or form. Expressionism's opposition to art-for-art's-sake shunned the technical manipulation of surface elements in favor of self-revelation and spiritual openness. Schoenberg observed, in 1911, "Is technique a cause, or an effect, a by-product? Expressive content wishes to make itself understood; its upheaval produces a form." In order to teach art, he continued,

> Belief in technique as the only salvation would have to be suppressed, and the urge for truthfulness encouraged. . . . For . . . in the real work of art everything gives the impression of having come first, because everything was born at the same moment. Feeling is already form, the idea is already the word.[71]

Although expressionism shares with other manifestations of modernism the tendency toward the abstract, it is not elitist in intent and remains centered on the individual. Like Italian and Russian Futurism, it is dynamic and seeks to activate humanity, but it reacts to the speed and machinery of modern life with anxiety, rather than embracing it as do the Futurists.

A fiery, brief, meteoric eruption, musical expressionism is an often undervalued aspect of modernism. Expressionist compositions, written under emotional compulsion, helped bring about a revolution in musical language which was the outward manifestation of an expansion of spirit, individualism, and ethical stance. The body of expressionist music played a crucial liberating role in the further development of modern music.

Select Bibliography

Adorno, Theodor Wiesengrund. *Philosophy of Modern Music.* Trans. A. Mitchell and W. Blomster. New York: Seabury, 1973.

Bahr, Hermann. *Expressionismus.* Munich: Delphin, 1920.

Bradbury, Malcolm, and McFarlane, James, eds. *Modernism: A Guide to European Literature, 1890–1930.* London: Penguin, 1976.

Brinkman, Richard, ed. *Expressionismus: Internationale Forschung zu einem internationalen Phänomen.* Stuttgart: Metzler, 1980.

Cardinal, Roger. *Expressionism.* London: Paladin, 1984.

Carter, Elliott. "Expressionism in American Music." *Perspectives of New Music* 4/2 (Fall–Winter 1965): 1–13.

Däubler, Theodor. *Der neue Standpunkt.* Leipzig: Insel Verlag, 1916.

Dube, Wolf-Dieter. *The Expressionists.* London: Thames and Hudson, 1972.

Edschmid, Kasimir. *Frühe Manifeste: Epochen des Expressionismus.* Reprint, Hamburg: Wegner, 1957.

Gay, Peter. "How the Modern World Began." *Horizon* 15/2 (Spring 1973): 10–15.

Hahl-Koch, Jelena, ed. *Arnold Schoenberg/Wassily Kandinsky: Letters, Pictures and Documents.* Trans. John C. Crawford. London and Boston: Faber, 1984.

Janick, Allen, and Toulmin, Stephen. *Wittgenstein's Vienna*. New York: Simon and Schuster, 1973.

Kandinsky, Wassily. *Concerning the Spiritual in Art* (1911). Trans. M. T. H. Sadler. Reprint, New York: Dover, 1977.

———, and Marc, Franz, eds. *The Blaue Reiter Almanac* (1912). New Documentary edition. Ed. Klaus Lankheit, trans. H. Falkenstein, M. Terzian, and G. Hinderlie. Reprint, New York: Viking, 1974.

Kokoschka, Oskar. *Schriften*. Ed. H. M. Wingler. Munich: Langen/Müller, 1956.

———. *My Life*. Trans. David Britt. London: Thames & Hudson, 1974.

McGrath, William. *Dionysian Art and Populist Politics in Austria*. New Haven: Yale University Press, 1975.

Miesel, Victor. *Voices of Expressionism*. Englewood Cliffs, NJ: Prentice-Hall, 1970.

Nietzsche, Friedrich. *Complete Works*. Ed. Oscar Levy. New York: Russell, 1964.

Pfeffer, Rose. *Nietzsche: Disciple of Dionysus*. Lewisburg, PA: Associated University Presses, 1972.

Pickar, Gertrud Bauer, and Webb, Karl Eugene, eds. *Expressionism Reconsidered* (Houston German Studies). Munich: Fink, 1979.

Raabe, Paul, ed. *Expressionismus: Der Kampf um eine literarische Bewegung*. Zurich: Arche, 1965; reprint, 1987.

———, ed. *The Era of German Expressionism*. Trans. J. M. Ritchie. Woodstock, NY: Overlook, 1974.

Read, Herbert. *The Meaning of Art*. Rev. ed. London: Faber, 1972.

Ritchie, James MacPherson, ed. *German Expressionist Drama*. Boston: Hall, 1976.

Rognoni, Luigi. *The Second Vienna School: Expressionism and Dodecaphony*. Trans. R. W. Mann. London: Calder, 1977.

Der Ruf: ein Flugblatt an junge Menschen. Vienna: Akademische Verband für Literatur und Musik, 1912–13.

Samuel, Richard, and Thomas, R. Hinton. *Expressionism in German Life, Literature and the Theatre (1910–24)*. Philadelphia: Saifer, 1971.

Schering, Arnold. "Die expressionistische Bewegung in der Musik." In *Zur Einführung in die Kunst der Gegenwart*. Leipzig: Seemann, 1919.

Schorske, Carl E. *Fin-de-siècle Vienna: Politics and Culture*. New York: Knopf, 1980.

Selz, Peter. *German Expressionist Painting*. Berkeley: University of California Press, 1957.

Sokel, Walter. *The Writer in Extremis: Expressionism in Twentieth Century German Literature*. Palo Alto: Stanford University Press, 1959.

Strindberg, August. Preface to *A Dream Play*. In *Six Plays of Strindberg*. Trans. Elizabeth Sprigge. New York: Doubleday, 1955.

Der Sturm. Berlin: 1910–32.

Waissenberger, Robert. *Vienna, 1890–1920*. New York: Rizzoli, 1984.

Weininger, Otto. *Sex and Character*. Trans. anon. London: William Heineman, 1906.

Weisstein, Ulrich, ed. *Expressionism as an International Literary Phenomenon*. Paris: Didier, and Budapest: Akadémiai Kiadó, 1973.

Werenskiold, Marit. *The Concept of Expressionism: Origin and Metamorphoses*. Trans. R. Walford. Oslo: Universitatsforlaget, 1984.

Whitford, Frank. *Oskar Kokoschka: A Life*. New York: Atheneum, 1986.

Willett, John. *Expressionism*. New York: McGraw-Hill, 1970.

Wörner, Karl H.; Maunzen, Walter; and Hofmann, Will. "Expressionismus," *Musik in Geschichte und Gegenwart* III. Ed. Friedrich Blume. Kassel: Bärenreiter, 1954.

Worringer, Wilhelm. *Abstraction and Empathy: A Contribution to the Psychology of Style* (1908). Trans. M. Bullock. New York: International Universities Press, 1953.

———. *Form in Gothic* (1912). Trans. Herbert Read. London: G. P. Putnam, 1927.

Zweig, Stefan. *The World of Yesterday*. New York: Viking Press, 1943.

CHAPTER TWO

Forerunners I:
Wagner and Strauss

> Music's message to our ear is of the selfsame
> nature as the cry sent forth to it from the depths
> of our own inner heart.
>   Richard Wagner (1870)

It is difficult today to realize fully the dominant role which the music dramas and ideas of Richard Wagner (1813–83) played in the German-speaking countries during the late nineteenth and early twentieth centuries. Performances of his music dramas were frequent during the formative years of the expressionist composers—Schoenberg later remarked that he had heard each of Wagner's works twenty to thirty times in his youth[1]—and Wagner's aesthetic and political theories, expressed in his voluminous writings, were also taken seriously in many circles. Clubs were formed in German and Austrian cities to promote Wagner's music, aesthetic theories, and Pan-Germanic ideals. (In 1877, the young Gustav Mahler joined one of these, undeterred by the anti-Semitism of some of Wagner's writings.) The foundation of the first Wagner Society had coincided with that of the German Empire in 1871, and, for better or worse, Wagner's music was strongly identified with German nationalism from that time on.[2]

In his prose writings, Wagner left several accounts of the aims of his operatic reform. Rejecting the operatic conventions of his day, such as the use of numbers (arias for vocal display, choruses, and so on), Wagner postulated a new type of music drama in which the Aristotelian unities of time and space would be replaced by the unity of expressive content.[3] This unity could only be achieved by combining the functions of poet and composer in one person, thus bringing about the true *Gesamtkunstwerk* (total work of art).[4]

In the belief that music should be unfettered by the laws of logical thought, Wagner abandoned historical plots after his early opera *Rienzi* (1840) and turned for his subjects to myth and legend, which he felt better exhibited "inner soul-motives."[5] Just as he wished his music to be liberated from rational thought and his texts to be free of the complexities of historical plot, he felt himself, in the Utopian socialism of his earlier years, to be the prophet of the new classless society, in which barriers to the "spontaneity of individual dealings" would disappear and feeling would dominate reason.[6] In this society, theatrical performances would be partly ritual in nature, as in ancient Greece—a concept contributed by Nietzsche during his friendship with Wagner.

To provide a theoretical basis for the texts of his dramas, Wagner looked back on man's primitive state, in which vowel sounds, combined with melodic inflection and gestures, were the vehicles of emotion. According to this theory, consonants were then gradually added for more specific meaning, and language as we know it evolved. Wagner wished to return to these primitive roots and to achieve a new kind of emotional speech through compression and alliteration.[7] The musical settings of these texts would follow their meaning rather than their meter, thus producing a "musical prose" in which square structure would vanish and be replaced by a "sublime irregularity" like that of Shakespeare. Integrated with gesture and orchestral comment, this musical prose would produce a "fixed mimetic and musical improvisation" in the same work.[8] The orchestra would present "motives of foreboding" and "motives of remembrance" (i.e., leitmotifs), whose "play of repetition" would furnish a unity of form which the composer felt had hitherto been lacking in opera.[9]

These ideas, in essays written between 1851 and 1871, clearly show Wagner's tendency toward expressionism. The predominance of content over form and of emotion over meaning, the *Gesamtkunstwerk* concept, a Utopian view of the future of art and society, compression of the text, use of musical symbolism, and a striving toward asymmetry and spontaneity were all to become features of expressionism early in the twentieth century.

In both his music and his ideas, Wagner was strongly influenced by Beethoven, Berlioz, and Liszt. He viewed Beethoven as the composer who helped free music from conventional form and melodic style,[10] allowing it "to seek the deepest wisdom . . . in a tongue his reason did not understand."[11] In his highly subjective interpretation, Wagner saw the C-sharp minor Quartet, Op. 131, as a portrayal of a day in Beethoven's inner life.[12] He also felt that many of the late works approached "fixed improvisations."[13] The last movement of Beethoven's Ninth Symphony, with its introduction of the human voice, held a particular fascination for Wagner, and he returned to it repeatedly in his writings.[14] With that movement, he wrote, Beethoven had expanded the resources of music enormously by integrating the "clear and definite" emotion of the human voice with the "wild, unfettered elemental feelings" represented by the instruments.[15]

Wagner is sometimes guilty of making Beethoven the mouthpiece for his own views, and his detailed programmatic interpretations of various works would scarcely be acceptable in our day. Nevertheless, Wagner was perceptive in realizing the quasi-improvisatory character of parts of the late works and the widening of expressive possibilities through greater formal diversity which Beethoven brought to music. He was also able to grasp the epochal significance of the choral movement of the Ninth Symphony as a principal precursor of his own *Gesamtkunstwerk.**

Hector Berlioz (1803–69) was the founder of nineteenth-century program music and the first to use the *idée fixe,* the inspiration for the leitmotif as later used by Liszt and Wagner. In its essence, program music shows the nineteenth century's leaning toward fusion of the arts, since it attempts to express the content of a work of art from another medium (such as a poem or a picture) in terms of music. Although Wagner himself composed little program music, he was profoundly influenced by the loosening of musical form and the new possibilities for content which this kind of music presented. The leitmotif and the techniques of thematic transformation to which it was subjected by Berlioz became essential elements in Wagner's mature music dramas. In Berlioz's *Symphonie Fantastique* (1830), one of the transformations of the *idée fixe* is in fact a deformation in regard to both orchestration and rhythm, and thus an early instance of the conscious use of the grotesque, which was to influence Liszt, Strauss, Mahler, and the expressionist composers who followed them (Exx. 2-1a and b).

Ex. 2-1. Berlioz, *Symphonie fantastique.* a. I, mm. 72–79, flute and violin I only; b. V, mm. 22–25, clarinet only.

Franz Liszt (1811–68), who was a great champion of both Berlioz and Wagner, continued the development of the tone poem in works that are often experimental in orchestration and harmony; his chromaticism and use of novel harmonies, such as the augmented triad, were crucial to the formation of Wagner's mature style. Rapidly changing textures, often used by Liszt in the interpretation of the program (as in Ex. 2-2), eventually became an important ingredient of expressionist music.

In view of the many ideas in Wagner's prose writings which clearly anticipate expressionism, we must ask ourselves whether the music dramas of his maturity are in fact expressionist. The answer must be a qualified no. In the main, these works are the definitive embodiment of late nineteenth-century Romanticism in their penchant for size (comparable to the novels of

---

*The Finale of Beethoven's Ninth was also the forerunner of the symphonies of Berlioz, Liszt, and Mahler in which the voice is introduced. In his Second String Quartet (1907–1908), Schoenberg carries this tendency a step further by bringing the voice into the framework of the string quartet for the first time.

Ex. 2.2. Liszt, *Hamlet*, mm. 173–78.

Dickens and Tolstoy), in their materialism—of which the giant Wagnerian orchestra is but one manifestation—and in their romantic nationalism. Nevertheless, passages in Act III of *Tristan und Isolde* (1859) and in *Parsifal* (1882) go far to anticipate expressionist musical drama.

Wagner emphasizes human emotion throughout *Tristan,* simplifying the plot and compressing the text in order to stress the psychology of the characters,[16] and making use of a musical language which is very often highly chromatic and expressive. However, to portray the wounded, feverish Tristan as he awaits Isolde in Act III, Wagner composed music which passes beyond the musical Romanticism of the rest of the work and becomes expressionist. For the specific portrayal of Tristan's delirium, Wagner uses chromatically rising augmented triads, accelerando, and crescendo, in passages which derive from Liszt and were to have great influence on Strauss, Schoenberg, and Berg (Ex. 2-3).

TRISTAN. Glaring and deceptive, the day's countenance wakes my brain to delusion and madness!

Ex. 2-3. Wagner, *Tristan und Isolde*, III, mm. 399–404.

At the climax of a second extreme passage (mm. 747–836), Tristan's curse of the love potion which has caused him to lose his senses ("verflucht sei, furchtbarer Trank") is followed by a *ff* orchestral outburst which combines three leitmotifs (marked a., b., and c. in Ex. 2-4) in a highly dissonant texture. Theodor Adorno, one of the few writers to grasp the connection between Wagner and expressionism, has written that "the fever sections of the third act of *Tristan* contain that black, uncouth, jagged music that does not so much underlay the vision as unmask it."[17]

Ex. 2-4. Wagner, *Tristan und Isolde*, III, mm. 835–36.

In 1859, Wagner wrote that Amfortas, one of the principal characters in his planned *Parsifal*, "is my Tristan of the third act with an unthinkable intensification."[18] Thus the composer makes clear that he intends to cultivate situations of extreme and long-lasting psychological tension in *Parsifal*—a point of view which was to have important consequences in the operas of Strauss and Schoenberg. Although *Parsifal* is often dramatically static, and its music as a whole lacks stylistic unity, this work of Wagner's old age contains long passages of his most radically emotional music.

While the extreme passages which depicted Tristan's delirium had been relatively brief, two of the principal characters in *Parsifal* continually endure a state of almost unrelieved torment. Amfortas, king of the knights who guard the Holy Grail, has earlier been seduced by Kundry. He feels both terrible mental guilt and extreme physical pain; he was stabbed by the sorcerer Klingsor with his own holy spear during the encounter with Kundry and the wound will not heal. Kundry, whom Wagner created by fusing two widely differing characters in Wolfram von Eschenbach's *Parsival*, is at once a holy messenger and a temptress under Klingsor's spell. She is a creature of extreme psychological conflicts, which Wagner exploits to the full. He was influenced by the Indian idea of reincarnation in his creation of Kundry; the libretto makes clear that she has existed throughout history under different names. Thus Klingsor summons Kundry in Act II: "Your master calls you, nameless one, primal fiend, rose of hell!/Herodias you were, and what else? Gundryggia there, Kundry here!" Kundry is less an individual than a universal human type. She foreshadows Wedekind's Lulu—also a composite—and the many unnamed characters of expressionist opera and drama.

Act II, set in Klingsor's magic castle, contains extended passages in which both music and text are extremely demanding. Invoked by the sorcerer, Kundry awakens with a "ghastly scream," followed by a "howl of lamentation, falling off from greatest intensity to anxious whimpering."[19] Trying to find speech, she sings the following lines in "hoarse and disjointed tones," her individual words set off by rests:

Ach!—Ach!—
Tiefe Nacht . . .
Wahnsinn . . . O!—Wut . . .
Ach! Jammer! . . .
Schlaf . . . Schlaf . . .
Tiefer Schlaf! . . . Tod!

[Oh!—Oh!—/Deep night . . . /Madness . . . Oh!—Rage . . . /Oh! Misery! . . . /Sleep . . . Sleep . . . /Deep sleep! . . . Death!]

This passage anticipates the fragmented, nongrammatical style of expressionist poetry and also shows the influence of Schopenhauer's theory of dreams, which Wagner discussed in his essay "Beethoven":

> From the most terrifying of these clairvoyant dreams we wake with a *scream*, the immediate expression of the anguished will. . . . Now if we take the Scream in all the diminutions of its vehemence, down to the gentler cry of longing, as the root element of every human message to the ear . . . then we have less cause to wonder at its immediate intelligibility than at an *art* arising from this element.[20]

Wagner's emphasis on the scream is particularly significant in that the *Urschrei* (primal scream) was to become an important symbol to expressionist composers, writers, and visual artists (see Color Plate IV, *The Scream* by Edvard Munch).

Later in Act II Kundry reappears in the role of temptress, and her central encounter with Parsifal takes place. As she kisses him, Parsifal suddenly feels a "tearing pain" in his heart, which he first thinks comes from his remembrance of Amfortas's guilt and suffering. At the words "Amfortas!—Die Wunde!" (Amfortas!—The wound!; see Ex. 2-5), the highly dissonant motive of the curse on both Kundry and Amfortas reappears. A dissonant chord, tutti and *ff* (a diminished-seventh chord with an added minor ninth above its bass), forms the first part of the motive; it remains unresolved except in the voice part. The second part of the motive is a wildly descending arpeggio identified with Kundry's hysterical laughter. Rejected by Parsifal, Kundry launches into a dramatic monologue which far surpasses even Parsifal's in dramatic intensity. She tells him the basis of all her suffering: she saw Christ on the cross and laughed at him (Ex. 2-6). The fragmented nature of both the text and its setting in this passage are thoroughly expressionist, as is also the use of extreme intervals and range in the voice part. The rest of Kundry's monologue (to m. 2075) is characterized by constant, rapid changes of tempo, texture, and leitmotif, which combine to produce a penetrating psychological portrait of Kundry, as she is repeatedly torn between sin and repentance.[21] In her obsessive hysteria, Kundry is the direct ancestor of both Strauss's Elektra and the Woman of Schoenberg's *Erwartung*.

Ex. 2-5. Wagner, *Parsifal*, II, mm. 994–99.

Ex. 2-6. Wagner, *Parsifal*, II, mm. 1175–83.

Of necessity, the musical language of this scene becomes disconnected. Such a broken, asymmetrical texture, presenting contrasting "affects" in close juxtaposition, does indeed have precedents in earlier opera; the orchestrally accompanied recitatives of Mozart are an example, and Beethoven even carried this operatic procedure into instrumental music.[22] But *Parsifal* marks a very significant historic moment; as Adorno has written:

> The grandiose disintegration of musical language, that—like Kundry's expressionistic stammering—disassociates itself into disconnected expressive impulses, threatens the harmonic structure. . . . For the first time the sound, many-layered and broken, becomes emancipated and responsible [only] to itself.[23]

Parsifal contains the most radical realizations of Wagner's theories of musical prose and fixed mimetic and musical improvisation. Wagner is the pivotal figure of nineteenth-century music, who not only presents the culmination of Romanticism but also anticipates expressionism in many important ways. Beyond his theories and his neoprimitive textual innovations, Wagner's experiments in musical prose, rapid texture change, extreme dissonance, and new vocal techniques, in order to be directly responsive to the ever-changing emotions of the human psyche, constitute the initial steps toward creation of an expressionist style in music. In the following generations, Richard Strauss and Arnold Schoenberg were to develop this style to its ultimate limits.

> Don't play it like gentlemen, but like raging beasts!
> Richard Strauss (at a rehearsal of *Elektra*, 1910)

Richard Strauss (1864–1949) continued and intensified the nascent expressionism we have seen in parts of Wagner's *Tristan* and *Parsifal*. Although Strauss's compositional career lasted more than 60 years, his influence on expressionism is virtually limited to two works, the one-act operas *Salome* (1905) and *Elektra* (1908). In these operas his pragmatic approach to composition, his choice of texts which emphasize extreme psychological states, and his sensitivity to the growing malaise in the society around him led Strauss to develop an expressionist musical style. Some elements of this style (discontinuous textures and large melodic leaps) are further developed from Wagnerian tendencies. Others, such as rapid vocal declamation and extreme, prolonged and unresolved dissonance, originate in Strauss. This complex of stylistic features makes *Salome* and *Elektra* the most important source of operatic expressionism.

Strauss grew up in Munich in a highly musical, rather bourgeois environment. His meeting, at the age of 21, with Alexander Ritter, a musician from Wagner's circle and the composer of two operas which were well known at the time, influenced Strauss's future development profoundly:

Before I met him, I had been brought up exclusively on Haydn, Mozart and Beethoven, and I had just been through the stage of Mendelssohn, Chopin, Schumann and Brahms. I owe to Ritter alone the fact that I came to understand Liszt and Wagner; it is he who showed me the importance, in the history of the art, of the writings and works of these two masters. It is he who, by dint of years of lessons and affectionate advice, made me a musician of the future and put me on the path along which I can now walk independently and alone. It was he who initiated me into the ideas of Schopenhauer.[24]

Four years after this meeting, the programmatic symphonic poems which were to make Strauss the most influential German composer of his generation began to appear.

Expressionism is largely absent from the tone poems, but in *Ein Heldenleben* (1898), where Strauss casts himself in the autobiographical role of the Nietzschean "superman," the battle scene ([49]–[75] of the miniature score, anticipated at [42]), with its aggressive dissonances and innovative layering of themes and textures, foreshadows the orchestral experiments of *Salome* and *Elektra*. Romain Rolland, the French musicologist who was both an admirer and a discerning critic of Strauss, has described the strong audience responses this passage provoked at its premiere:

I saw people shudder when they heard it, suddenly rise to their feet, and make violent and unconscious gestures. I myself experienced the strange intoxication, the dizziness of this heaving ocean; and I thought then that, for the first time in thirty years, the Germans had found their poet of victory.[25]

Rolland, in fact, links Strauss to Nietzsche and the Kaiser as a major embodiment of the aggressive spirit of the new German empire. Just as Wagner was a prime representative of that empire at its formation, Strauss, who made no secret of his love of the "Teutonic fortissimo" in this period,[26] is seen by Barbara Tuchman as an appropriate embodiment of the German empire at its period of greatest power.[27]

Signs of malaise were already apparent amid the pomp and power of turn-of-the-century Germany, however. The publication of Krafft-Ebing's *Psychopathia Sexualis* (1886) influenced German dramatists and foreshadowed the trials of intimates of the Kaiser for homosexuality in 1907–1909. Playwrights like Hauptmann, and especially Wedekind and Strindberg in his early years, stressed morbid subject matter. Rolland was concerned that Strauss was joining forces with this decadent "Berlin brotherhood" and could feel in his conducting the "morbid excitement" and the "malady hidden beneath the power and the military stiffness."[28] It is not surprising that the works of the French Symbolist writers (sometimes also called Decadents, particularly in reference to the more extreme manifestations of the movement) found a ready response in Germany. (Indeed, the influence was reciprocal, as there was a cult for Wagner's music among the Symbolists.) Oscar Wilde's play *Salomé* (published in 1893), written in French and strongly influenced by the Symbolist style of Maeterlinck, shared in this response. The Symbolists regarded Salome and her mother, Herodias, as perfect incarnations of the fatal, man-destroying woman, and this is their role in Wilde's drama. Another strong factor in the play is the exotic aestheticism introduced by Théophile Gautier in the 1830s and continued by Gustave Flaubert.[29]

Strauss saw Max Reinhardt's Berlin production of Wilde's *Salomé* in 1903 and decided to set the text in its original form (as Debussy had done with Maeterlinck's *Pelléas et Mélisande*), although with extensive cuts.[30] Because he had visited Egypt in 1892, Strauss knew his music could supply the "true oriental color and scorching sun" which the play demanded. He later wrote that "the needs of the moment inspired me to truly exotic harmonies, which sparkled like taffeta, particularly in the strange cadences."[31] Strauss's technique of descriptive and psychological tone painting, developed in his symphonic poems, now responded to Wilde's colorful and elaborate language; the extremes of the plot (the debauched Herod and the prophet Jochanaan live in such different worlds that there can be little communication between them) both motivated and justified the use of extreme musical means.

Although Salome and Herod are governed by their sexual obsessions throughout the opera, it is in Herod, whose character is unrelieved by positive traits, that we have a fully worked-out portrait of an individual unbalanced by debauchery and passion for his step-daughter, Salome. Among the most striking passages in the opera are those in which Herod suffers hallucinations. At [164] of the score, he imagines that a cold wind is passing over him. (We know from an earlier passage that this wind comes from the powerful—though imaginary—wings of the angel of death [90].) Strauss portrays this wind with a rapidly moving chromatic scale against slower chromatically moving diminished-seventh chords (Ex. 2-7). By introducing chromatic movement at two differing speeds, Strauss took the chromatic procedures of Liszt and Wagner (see Ex. 2-3) an important step further and provided a model for famous passages in Schoenberg's *Erwartung* and Berg's *Wozzeck*. As the passage continues, leitmotifs identified with Herodias and Jochanaan are superimposed on the chromatic scales in a much freer and less clearly tonal manner than would have occurred in Wagner.

Ex. 2-7. Strauss, *Salome*, 2 mm. before [169], violins and violas only.

In a similar but more extended "mad scene," which occurs later ([233]–[242]), Herod first feels cold, then hot (brass sforzandos before [237]), and demands to have water poured over his hands (Ex. 2-8). This passage is a good example of the discontinuity of musical texture which we have seen developing in Liszt's tone poems and Wagner's *Parsifal;* such discontinuity was very soon to become a prime feature of Schoenberg's musical expressionism.

HEROD. This rustling is frightful. It is a chill wind. But no, it
is not cold, - - - it is hot. Pour water over my hands.

Ex. 2-8. Strauss, *Salome,* 1 m. before [236]–m. 3 of [237].

The score abounds in "progressive" details of all sorts, including tone clusters (as at [355]), whole-tone scales ([255]), extreme vocal leaps (2 mm. before [300]), purposefully distorted declamation (3 mm. before [250], 3 mm. before [362]), and many passages in which the harmony and orchestration were daring for their time. All these new elements derive from Strauss's direct and undogmatic approach to the text. It is significant that Strauss later attributed the novel introduction of bitonality in *Salome* to the necessities of the drama: "The wish to characterize the *dramatis personae* as clearly as possible led me to bitonality, since the purely rhythmic characterization Mozart uses did not appear to me sufficient to express the antithesis between

Herod and the Nazarene."[32] The vocal style is a rapid, disjunct, and often fragmented *parlando,* which far surpasses the pace of Wagner's declamation and verges at times on melodrama (i.e., spoken text with musical accompaniment). In *Erwartung* and *Wozzeck,* the speed of Strauss's most rapid, melodramatic passages becomes the norm, causing events and emotions to pass with sometimes cinematic swiftness.

Alban Berg was one of the many young people "whose only luggage was a piano score" of *Salome*[33] when he arrived in Graz to attend its first performance in Austria in 1906. (Mahler and Puccini were also in the audience.) Berg was so strongly affected by the work that he attended six more performances in Vienna the same year.[34] Our examination of Berg's *Wozzeck* will show how many features of Strauss's work were carried over and developed by the younger composer.

Late in 1903, Strauss saw the Berlin stage production of Hugo von Hofmannsthal's *Elektra,* directed by Max Reinhardt, who had also directed Wilde's *Salomé.* Strauss once again created an opera out of a successful completed play, though he did make certain cuts and changes in consultation with the playwright. Hofmannsthal (1874–1929), an important figure in modern Austrian literature, was subsequently to provide the libretti for many of Strauss's operas. When he wrote his play in 1903, he had read Freud and Breuer's 1895 *Studies in Hysteria.* He added Elektra's crazed dance of triumph, which ends in her collapse and death, to Sophocles' tragedy. Hofmannsthal's version of *Elektra* is one of the first works of art in which psychoanalytical findings are used consistently.[35] Indeed, after the opera's first Vienna performance, in 1909, Hofmannsthal and Strauss were criticized in the press for reducing Elektra's psychology to an "insuperably perverse instinct," thereby sacrificing both the tragic impulse of the drama and its ethical values.[36] Even more than Salome, the character Elektra is dominated from beginning to end by an obsession: to avenge the death of her father, Agamemnon, by causing the death of his murderers—his wife, Clytemnestra, and her lover, Aegisthus.

Strauss's *Elektra* (composed in 1906–1908 and first performed in 1909) has a dark, larger-than-life quality; it continues and extends the extreme idiom of his *Salome* in order to portray the "grotesque unhinging of a human mind."[37] The fin-de-siècle exoticism of the earlier opera gives place in *Elektra* to a work which Strauss himself says is "even more intense in the unity of structure and the force of its climaxes."[38] The length and difficulty of Elektra's role contribute to the monumental quality of the work.

Elektra's great scene (which occurs after a brief opening expository passage for the maids of the household) establishes this monumental feeling. Without preliminary warmup, Elektra launches into a long monologue, which passes from lonely despair, as she recalls the circumstances of her father's murder, to exaltation, as she anticipates the triumphal dance that will follow her revenge. Strauss uses a highly dissonant, unresolved bitonal chord (E major/D-flat major) as the main musical symbol of Elektra, her hatred, and her incipient madness (Ex. 2-9a). The idea of using a particular chord as a psychological or dramatic symbol has antecedents in the "Tristan" chord (Ex. 2-9b) and in the highly dissonant chord in *Parsifal* which symbolizes Amfortas' suffering and guilt (see Ex. 2-5).

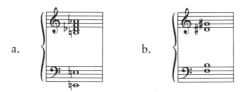

a.   b.

Ex. 2-9. a. Strauss, "Elektra" chord; b. Wagner, "Tristan" chord.

Strauss, however, goes far beyond Wagner, in that the "Elektra" chord is a real "emancipated dissonance" (to borrow Schoenberg's later term), which does not call for a tonal resolution. It therefore becomes a musical "object" which the composer can transpose freely, or even put into chromatic parallels (Ex. 2-10). Strauss here surpasses the chromatic procedures he had used in *Salome,* for the chord he now uses is a freely invented one, rather than a diminished-seventh chord (see Ex. 2-7). Since the "Elektra" chord, a symbol of the character's reigning obsession, returns obstinately at many points in the monologue, it serves as a musically unifying factor as well. Both Schoenberg's *Erwartung* and Berg's *Wozzeck* were influenced by this kind of procedure.

Ex. 2-10. Strauss, *Elektra,* 1 m. before [27]–m. 2 of [27], orchestra only.

When the word "blood" occurs in the text of Elektra's monologue, Strauss responds with a clear change of musical texture. For instance, at the words "as from overturned pitchers, the blood will flow out of the bound murderers," he introduces rapid chromatic parallels in strings and winds. The first beat of each measure is a transposition of the "Elektra" chord (Ex. 2-11). This passage clearly foreshadows Schoenberg's *Erwartung,* in its flexibility of texture change and in the prominence given to the depiction of "blood," which was to become an important expressionist symbol in itself.

Following Elektra's monologue, the entrance of her sister, Chrysothemis, provides relief from tension, though the latter's long aria anticipating marriage and motherhood (in clearly tonal E-flat major and waltzlike $\frac{3}{4}$ time, starting at [75]), is so complete a contrast as to be stylistically incongruous. The brighter mood ends suddenly at [114], as muted trumpets and trombones, *ff,* sound the "Elektra" chord. Four measures later, the strings take

Ex. 2-11. Strauss, *Elektra*, 3 mm. before [49], orchestra only.

over the chord, stating it in short, percussive off-beat thrusts, much as Stravinsky was later to do with a similar bitonal chord in *The Rite of Spring* (see Exx. 2-12a and b). Both passages symbolize threat and fear.

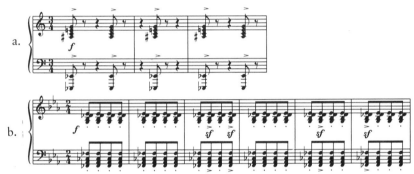

Ex. 2-12. a. Strauss, *Elektra*, mm. 5–7 of [114], orchestra only; b. Stravinsky, *Rite of Spring*, mm. 1–6 of [13].

Queen Clytemnestra enters, and, in the climax of the opera, she confronts Elektra. The scene includes Clytemnestra's long monologue describing her recurrent dream, a passage in which Strauss felt he had reached "the uttermost limits of harmony, psychological polyphony . . . and the receptivity of the modern ears."[39] In her dream monologue ([178]–[200]), Clytemnestra confides to Elektra that she is plagued by fearful nightmares, which she tries unsuccessfully to banish by the sacrifice of animals. But her nights continue to be tormented by an indefinable terror, a "something" which "crawls between day and night" ([186]). This "something" is musically portrayed as a motive in contrabassoon and tubas, rising in ever-larger intervals beneath long-held chords whose dissonance is unresolved throughout the passage (Ex. 2-13). The enormous intervals, unresolved dissonance, and the emotion of nameless terror are all strikingly similar to Schoenberg's *Erwartung*, which was written in 1909, a year after Strauss completed his opera.

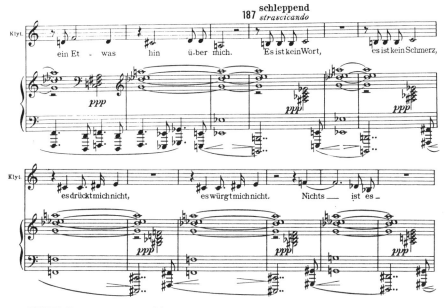

CLYTEMNESTRA. A Something creeps over me. It is not a word, it is not a pain, it does not oppress me, it does not choke me. It is nothing - - -

Ex. 2-13. Strauss, *Elektra*, 3 mm. before [187]–m. 9 of [187].

In another highly significant passage, which occurs as Elektra recognizes Orestes, Strauss verges on atonality for a dozen measures ([144a]–[146a]). This passage is an early instance of simultaneity in musical expressionism; the many-layered polyphony expresses the differing emotions which surge through Elektra's psyche at this crucial juncture of the drama (Ex. 2-14).

Even a brief examination of *Salome* and *Elektra* shows that these operas contain most of the essential features of the operatic expressionism of Schoenberg and Berg. Like Wagner, Strauss uses texts which stress morbid psychology in order to inspire and justify the use of extreme musical means. In the case of Strauss, these include unresolved dissonance and daring, highly differentiated orchestration. Under the influence of the spoken drama, he introduces a rapid *parlando* (sometimes disjunct and distorted), which allows events and emotions to occur much more swiftly than in previous operas. Most important, he draws on Wagner's musical prose and the procedures of program music to create highly discontinuous textures. These lead to "free association forms"[40] and enable the composer to mirror the rapidly changing psychological states of his characters.

Nevertheless, *Salome* and *Elektra* are not truly expressionist works because they frequently veer toward a lush, late-romantic style. His pragmatic attitude toward composition enabled Strauss to respond freely and imagina-

Ex. 2-14. Strauss, *Elektra*, mm. 1–4 of [144a].

tively to stimuli in his libretti, but it also resulted in stylistic incongruities like the Chrysothemis aria mentioned above. Though the composer could absorb and reflect the tensions of his time in his music, his creations were not the result of an overwhelming need to express his own inner emotions, as would be the case with a truly expressionist composer.

In view of his crucial contributions, one may ask why Strauss has not received greater credit as a pioneer of musical expressionism.[41] One explanation is that he had no lasting commitment to musical innovation and, in fact, turned his back on it permanently in *Der Rosenkavalier* (1910).[42] A personal reason, however, was perhaps equally responsible for his failure to gain credit as a "father of the new music." Stuckenschmidt, in his Schoenberg biography, gives a detailed chronicle of Strauss's friendship with Schoenberg, beginning in 1902, and the financial and professional help the older composer extended to the younger.[43] However, Strauss was unable or unwilling to understand Schoenberg's free atonal music. When Schoenberg was awarded the Mahler Fund in 1912, Strauss remarked, "I believe it would be better if he shovelled snow, rather than filling up sheets of music paper with scribbling,"[44] even though he actually approved giving the prize to Schoenberg. Strauss's insulting words reached Schoenberg's ears through Alma Mahler, and their friendship was definitively broken off. Since until the 1950s, the authors of much of the writing about Schoenberg and Berg were closely identified with the Second Viennese School, it is not surprising that the influence of Strauss received little mention. Nevertheless, he deserves to be recognized as a crucial figure in the development of operatic expressionism.

Select Bibliography

GENERAL

Praz, Mario. *The Romantic Agony.* Trans. Angus Davidson. 2d ed. London and New York: Oxford University Press, 1951.

Salzman, Eric. *Twentieth-Century Music: An Introduction.* 2d ed. Englewood Cliffs, NJ: Prentice-Hall, 1974.

Schopenhauer, Arthur. *The World as Will and Representation.* 2 vols. Trans. E. F. J. Payne. Indian Hills, CO: Falcon's Wing, 1958.

Wickes, Lewis. "Schoenberg, *Erwartung,* and the Reception of Psychoanalysis in Vienna until 1910/1911." *Studies in Music* 23 (1989): 88.

WAGNER

Adorno, Theodor. *Versuch über Wagner.* Berlin: Suhrkamp, 1952.

———. *Moments musicaux.* Frankfurt: Suhrkamp, 1964.

Mann, Thomas. *Essays of Three Decades.* Trans. H. T. Lowe-Porter. New York: Knopf, 1947.

Stein, Jack M. *Richard Wagner and the Synthesis of the Arts.* Detroit: Wayne State University Press, 1960.

Wagner, Richard. *Richard Wagner an Mathilde Wesendonck.* 2d ed. Ed. Wolfgang Golther. Berlin: Duncker, 1904.

———. *Richard Wagner's Prose Works.* 8 vols. Trans. William Ashton Ellis. New York: Broude Brothers, [1966].

STRAUSS

Del Mar, Norman. *Richard Strauss.* 2 vols. New York: Free Press of Glencoe, 1962.

Mann, William. *Richard Strauss: A Critical Study of the Operas.* New York: Oxford University Press, 1966.

Myers, Rollo, ed. *Romain Rolland/Richard Strauss Correspondence.* Berkeley and Los Angeles: University of California Press, 1968.

Strauss, Franz; Strauss, Alice; and Schuh, Willi, eds. *A Working Friendship: The Correspondence between Richard Strauss and Hugo von Hofmannsthal.* Trans. Hanns Hammelmann and Ewald Osers. New York: Random House, 1961.

Strauss, Richard. *Der Strom der Töne trug mich fort: Die Welt um Richard Strauss in Briefen.* Ed. Franz Grasberger. Tutzing: Schneider, 1967.

———. *Recollections and Reflections.* Ed. Willi Schuh. London and New York: Boosey & Hawkes, 1973.

CHAPTER THREE

Forerunners II:
Mahler and Scriabin

> My music is *"lived."* What attitude should those
> take to it who do *not* "live," who feel no breath
> of the rushing gale of our great epoch?
> Gustav Mahler (1895)

Although, as we have seen, only a few of the works of Wagner and Strauss are important to the development of expressionism in music, the compositions of Gustav Mahler (1860–1911) intermittently exhibit expressionist traits throughout his comparatively short career as a composer. However, Mahler's evolving expressionism is constantly at odds with his affinity to Viennese classicism and to the romanticism of Schubert and Schumann. His entire output can, in fact, be seen as a struggle to integrate the demands of an urgent and highly personal content with those of classical and early-romantic form.

Mahler was raised in Moravia (then a province of the Austro-Hungarian Empire), where he was exposed to the folk and military music which were to influence his compositions profoundly. The most important part of his formal education took place in Vienna in 1875–80. Significantly, it was not limited to music but also included courses at the University of Vienna in ancient literature, the history of Greek art, and the history of philosophy.[1]

During the years 1880–97, his growing career as an opera conductor led Mahler from humble to increasingly important positions in the Austro-Hungarian Empire and in Germany. Not surprisingly, the many moves this involved intensified his lifelong feelings of alienation; during these years he repeatedly identified himself with the Wandering Jew.[2]

The period 1897–1907, when Mahler was director of the Vienna Court Opera, marked the climax of his public career. He used the power of his position to bring the Vienna Opera to a high state of musical and dramatic excellence (see chapter 10), and he was idolized by the younger and more progressive members of the Viennese public. Nevertheless, he often railed against the "dreadful, consuming life" of the theater,[3] which allowed him time to compose only during brief summer vacations.

Ill. 3-1. Gustav Klimt, Beethoven Frieze, "The Sufferings of Weak Humanity" (Mahler in knight's armor), detail from Panel I, *Longing for Happiness,* 1902. Österreichische Galerie, Vienna.

For his last four years (1907–11), Mahler had to live with the knowledge of his heart disease and approaching death. No longer director of the Vienna Opera, he again led the life of a semi-exile, alternating between winter months spent conducting in New York and summer sojourns in Europe. This period was marked by intense creativity (*Das Lied von der Erde* [The Song of the Earth], the Ninth Symphony, the unfinished Tenth Symphony) and by extreme states of mind. As Mahler wrote to Bruno Walter early in 1909,

> I am experiencing so infinitely much now (in the last eighteen months), I can hardly talk about it. How should I attempt to describe such a tremendous crisis? I see everything in such a new light—am in such a state of flux, sometimes I should hardly be surprised to find myself suddenly in a new body. . . .[4]

The expressionist elements in Mahler's creative works come directly out of his personality and strong expressive needs. Like Wagner before him, and Schoenberg, Webern, Kokoschka, and Kandinsky in the generation following,

Mahler sometimes expressed himself in the written word as well as in music. He wrote both text and music for the early song cycle *Lieder eines fahrenden Gesellen* (Songs of a Wayfarer, 1884),[5] impelled by his unhappy love affair with the singer Johanna Kassel in 1884. The cycle's autobiographical origin confirms Mahler's statement that *"only when I experience* something do I compose, and only when composing do I experience!"[6] Like a true expressionist artist, Mahler draws on his own emotional life in the cycle, rather than mirroring nature or the emotions of others.

Though he never again wrote the complete text for one of his works, Mahler made important revisions and additions to the texts of the finales of the Second Symphony and *Das Lied von der Erde*. Even as Beethoven rearranged Schiller's ode "To Joy" in the Finale of the Ninth Symphony, Mahler changed these texts so that they would better meet his expressive needs. He makes this clear in an 1897 letter: "in the last movement of my Second I simply had to go through the whole of world literature, including the Bible, in search of the right word . . . and in the end I had no choice but to find my own words for my thoughts and feelings."[7] Thus Mahler used only the first two stanzas of Klopstock's "Resurrection" ode in the Finale, providing the bulk of the text (the final 23 lines) himself.[8] The tone of the music becomes notably more intense and subjective at the point where Mahler's own text begins ("O glaube, mein Herz" [O believe, my heart]).[9]

Even when he set the texts of others, Mahler frequently felt a strong psychological identification with the poems he chose. He changed the title of the *Wunderhorn* poem "Verspätung" (Delay) to "Das irdische Leben" (Earthly Life) to make it clear that he saw the mother's repeated withholding of bread from her starving child as an allegory of human destiny: "everything that one most needs for the growth of spirit and body . . . is withheld—as with the dead child—until it is too late."[10] In a similar way he identified himself as a conductor with St. Anthony preaching to the fishes in the song "Des Antonius von Padua Fischpredigt," convinced that his carefully prepared opera performances would go "in one ear and out the other" of his thoughtless audiences.[11] The 1901 Rückert song "Ich bin der Welt abhanden gekommen" (I am lost to the world) is perhaps the most significant instance in which Mahler made a song the carrier of his own feelings. He told Natalie Bauer-Lechner simply, "It is my very self."[12] The final words, "I live alone, in my Heaven, in my song," express perfectly the composer's longing for release from his "dreadful, consuming existence" as director of the Vienna Opera, which caused his feelings of alienation: "All my senses and emotions are turned outward. I am becoming more and more a stranger to myself."[13]

Mahler's unfulfilled wish for a retired life is closely linked to his longing for the transcendental—a "yearning for what is beyond the things of this world,"[14] for that " 'other world,' in which things no longer fall apart in time and space."[15] It is not by chance that the violins' ending phrase in the song (Ex. 3-1) is marked "verklärt" (transfigured).

Ex. 3-1. Mahler, "Ich bin der Welt abhanden gekommen," last 6 mm., violin I only.

Throughout his life, Mahler was subject to rapid and extreme changes of mood. In spite of its youthful, high-flown language, an early (1879) letter vividly portrays his characteristic gamut of emotions:

A great deal has been going on since I last wrote. But I can't tell you about it. Only this: I have become a different person; whether a better one, I don't know, anyway not a happier one. The greatest intensity of the most joyful vitality and the most consuming yearning for death dominate my heart by turn, very often alternate hour by hour—one thing I know: I can't go on like this much longer! When the abominable tyranny of our modern hypocrisy and mendacity has driven me to the point of dishonoring myself, when the inextricable web of conditions on art and life has filled my heart with disgust for all that is sacred to me—art, love, religion—what way out is there but self-annihilation? Wildly I wrench at the bonds that chain me to the loathsome, insipid swamp of this life, and with all the strength of despair I cling to sorrow, my only consolation.—Then all at once the sun smiles upon me—and gone is the ice that encased my heart, again I see the blue sky and the flowers swaying in the wind, and my mocking laughter dissolves in tears of love. Then I *needs must* love this world with all its deceit and frivolity and its eternal laughter.[16]

Such extreme variations of mood apparently influenced Mahler's conducting style, which was characterized by rhythmic fluctuations and violent dynamic contrasts.[17] In his own music, the need to express such drastically differing states of mind caused Mahler to go far beyond the usual boundaries of artistic expression for his day.

The macabre, ironic slow movement of the First Symphony (1884–88) presents a clear-cut challenge to nineteenth-century ideas of what was beautiful or appropriate to the concert hall. A distorted version of the well-known round "Frère Jacques" ("Bruder Martin" in German) forms the principal material of the movement. The round is transformed into a funeral march in the minor mode and orchestrated in a purposely grotesque way. In order to obtain a "strangely eerie and unusual" effect, Mahler places various instruments (such as the solo, muted contrabass, which opens the movement) in ranges where they can play only "with effort" and with a "forced tone."[18] The second section of the movement introduces material of intentional vulgarity. A Slavic-sounding tavern theme is interrupted by marchlike material, marked "mit Parodie" and assigned to the strident timbre of two E-flat clarinets. The rhythmic accompaniment is provided by strings *col legno* (with the wood of the bow), a rare technique for the period, and a bass drum with attached Turkish cymbals, to be played by one musician, as in a military band. Like the march music itself, this last orchestral detail derives from memories of military music in the provincial town of Iglau, where Mahler spent his early youth.

After a brief return to the initial funeral march material, the movement passes almost without transition to an ineffably lyrical, Schubertian folk melody quoted from the final song of *Lieder eines fahrenden Gesellen*. This rapid change from the vulgar to the sublime matches the tendency toward emotional extremes in Mahler's character and foreshadows the expressionists' love of stark, almost cinematic contrasts. All the expressionist characteristics of this movement—distortion in melody and orchestration, purposeful vulgarity, and the rapid shifts in character—can be traced to Mahler's intense need for emotional communication. By the use of such extreme artistic means, Mahler could bypass conventional artistic expectation and have direct access to his listener's psyche.

But how are we to interpret the movement's content? In 1900, Mahler offered a revealing explanation:

> A funeral procession passes by; all the misery and all the sorrow of the world strikes our hero with its biting contrasts and its dreadful irony. The Bruder Martin funeral march must be imagined played by a cheap band; it draws near, takes shape, and disappears. . . . In the midst of all this, all the coarseness, the mirth, and banality of the world are heard in the sound of a Bohemian village band, together with the hero's terrible cries of pain. . . . After a wonderful interlude, the funeral procession returns and a soul-piercing "gay tune" is heard.[19]

The appearance of the vulgar, "banal" music at the moment of greatest emotion can be related to a childhood experience which Mahler later recounted to Freud: He ran out of the house when his parents were having a stormy quarrel and came upon an organ grinder playing "Ach, du lieber Augustin." Mahler felt that thereafter he was always subject to such absurd interruptions at moments of deep emotional creation.[20]

The orchestral song "Der Tambourg'sell" (The Drummer Boy, 1901) provides a striking instance of Mahler's taking a popular genre, such as the military funeral march, and reshaping it to his own expressive purposes. In the text (from *Des Knaben Wunderhorn* [The Youth's Magic Horn]), a drummer boy who is about to be hanged (perhaps for desertion) poignantly bids farewell to his fellow soldiers and to nature. At the beginning of the song, Mahler employs a simple tonic-dominant progression typical of military music (Ex. 3-2a); later, just before the drummer boy mentions the gallows from which he will soon hang, the progression is distorted and intensified by the lowering of the fifth degree in both chords (Ex. 3-2b).

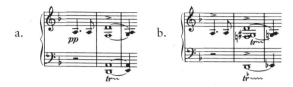

Ex. 3-2. Mahler, "Der Tambourg'sell." a. mm. 5–6; b. mm. 31–32. Used by permission of European American Music.

Somber orchestration (the upper strings are omitted) and extreme performance instructions add to the song's effect: at various points the voice part is marked "with horror," "with very raised voice," "doleful," and "with a broken voice." But perhaps the song's most powerful feature is the sinking down to C minor (the song begins in D minor), which anticipates the drummer boy's final farewell to nature ("Good night, you marble stones, mountains, and little hills"). In an orchestral interlude, Mahler slackens the original slow tempo of the song still more and adds the depth of covered bass drum and tam-tam to the covered military drum used at the beginning of the song. A melody in the English horn plumbs a depth of depression that music had perhaps never reached before, recalling Mahler's comment that this song and his *Kindertotenlieder* (Songs on the Death of Children) were so "terribly sad" that "he felt sorry for himself that he should have had to write [them], and felt sorry for the world that would have to hear them one day."[21] "Der Tambourg'sell" is strongly expressionist in its distorted harmony (as in Ex. 3-2b), its use of extreme vocal means, and its tendency toward open form (it does not return to the original key). The song relates to the composer's socialist sympathies as well. Like Berg's *Wozzeck,* it makes known the fate of a hapless individual crushed by society's total indifference.

To express his feeling of aversion to the "dreadful hubbub of voices in 'this day and age' " and the "terrible treadmill of the opera-house,"[22] Mahler recurrently used a particular type of rapid, circling *perpetuo mobile* movement. Adorno has interpreted such movements as an image of the Hegelian "verkehrten Weltlauf" (senseless running of the world).[23] Two songs from *Des Knaben Wunderhorn*, "Das irdische Leben" and "Des Antonius von Padua Fischpredigt," both written in 1893, are the earliest examples of this genre. As Mahler was composing the latter song, he was simultaneously adapting it to serve as the Scherzo of the Second symphony (1894), heightening many details of the orchestration in the process and providing a new orchestral climax near the end of the movement. His programs for the Scherzo help explain the movement's psychological content:

When you awaken from this melancholy dream [the preceding Andante moderato] and must return to life's confusion, it can easily happen that the ceaseless agitation, the meaningless bustle of life, seems to you unreal, like dancing forms

in a brightly lit ballroom: you watch them from the darkness and from a distance, so that you cannot hear the accompanying music! And so life seems without meaning, a fearful nightmare from which you awaken with a cry of horror
[1895].

To someone who has lost himself and his happiness, the world seems crazy
and confused, as if deformed by a concave mirror. The Scherzo ends with the
fearful scream of a soul that has experienced this torture [1896].[24]

The image of the concave mirror is particularly significant in view of the
role played by distortion in expressionism. Mahler's reference to the "cry of
horror" upon awakening from a "fearful nightmare" recalls Wagner's Scho-
penhauer-influenced description of the scream as the "immediate expression
of the anguished will" (quoted on p. 28) and confirms the importance of the
scream as an expressionist symbol. The third movement of the Ninth Symphony, entitled "Rondo-Burleske," is a much later example of such a
perpetuo mobile movement. It was originally dedicated to "my brothers in
Apollo" (i.e., Mahler's fellow composers) because of its contrapuntal skills.
However, its tone owes more to Dionysus than to Apollo, since its contrapuntal elements are constantly combined, varied, and fragmented, with ever-
changing orchestration and in rapidly shifting tonal contexts. Particularly as
the movement draws to a close, while increasing in tempo, contrapuntal combination and ceaseless activity become the unmistakable expressions of a manic,
feverish state of mind.

At the other extreme from Mahler's purposeful use of the ugly, grotesque, and distorted as musical expressions of deep depression and alienation, stands a work like the Eighth Symphony (1906), which clearly shows
the composer's yearning for transcendence. The Eighth is a basically optimistic, even ecstatic work, which combines settings of the medieval Latin hymn
"Veni, Creator Spiritus" and the final scene of Part II of Goethe's *Faust*. By
a "violent, superhuman assertion of will," utterly negating "reason and moderation,"[25] Mahler was able to achieve a transcendental integration of texts
in widely differing languages and styles. (Schoenberg planned to attempt
something similar six years later in his unfinished "Symphony for soloists,
chorus and orchestra" of 1914–15, using texts by Dehmel and Tagore and
from the Bible.[26]) According to a conversation between Mahler and the music
critic Richard Specht,[27] the entire symphony was sketched in three weeks. On
18 August 1906, Mahler wrote to Mengelberg: "I have just finished my
Eighth—it is the grandest thing I have done yet—and so peculiar in content
and form that it is really impossible to write anything about it. Try to imagine the whole universe beginning to ring and resound."[28] Mahler could scarcely
have provided a clearer key to his cosmic intention in the work. In his conversation with Specht, Mahler goes on to say that he had never previously
"worked under such compulsion: it was like a lightning vision—the whole
stood before my eyes immediately, and I only needed to write it down, as
if it had been dictated to me."[29] Thus the composer stresses the role of

the subconscious in his creation, as he had previously in his Third Symphony.*

Like *Parsifal,* which also combines various musical styles, Mahler's Eighth is partially ritualistic in nature. Even though this work is not intended to be staged, the fact that Mahler retained—in the final movement—all of Goethe's stage directions indicates that he was thinking in dramatic, spatial terms. In 1921, Paul Bekker rightly perceived that the aim of the Eighth, motivated by the composer's "all-embracing, messianic love of humanity," was to reach beyond the limits of the concert halls to the "Community of Man." To this broad community, Mahler revealed a new art, "beyond the social and intellectual borders, an art that once again touched the elemental impulses of the emotions."[30] Thus this symphony, which Mahler said was "a present bestowed upon the nation," is another expression of his socialist sympathies; it can be compared in its communicative purpose to the more outgoing and political expressionist plays, such as Georg Kaiser's *Gas* (1918) and Ernst Toller's *Masse Mensch* (1920).

It is in the large, outer movements of his symphonies that Mahler's struggle to integrate highly subjective content with the demands of symphonic form becomes most intense. The Finale of the Second Symphony (1894) is particularly important because it is the first major movement in which Mahler introduces the human voice. Its vast, 471-measure instrumental introduction presents a bewildering variety of tempos and themes, which are difficult to analyze successfully according to classical formal precepts. Like Kundry's monologue, but on an infinitely larger scale, the introduction anticipates expressionist music in its rapid and unexpected alternation of affects. The composer admitted that the movement was "altogether dramatic":

> Here, all is motion and occurrence. The movement starts with the same dreadful death cry which ended the Scherzo. And now, after these frightening questions, comes the answer, redemption. To begin with, as faith and the church picture it: the day of judgement, a huge tremor shakes the earth. The climax of this terrifying event is accompanied by drum rolls. Then the last trump sounds. The graves burst open, all creatures struggle out of the ground, moaning and trembling. Now they march in mighty processions: rich and poor, peasants and kings, the whole church with bishops and popes. All have the same fear, all cry and tremble alike because, in the eyes of God, there are no just men. As though from another world, the last trump sounds again. Finally, after they have left their empty graves and the earth lies silent and deserted, there comes only the long-drawn-out note of the bird of death. Even he finally dies.

---

*In writing the first movement of the Third, Mahler had felt himself to be "nothing but an instrument on which the universe plays" (letter to Anna Mildenburg, 29 June 1896, Henry-Louis de La Grange, *Mahler,* vol. 1, pp. 368–69), a statement which is remarkably close to Stravinsky's comment on *The Rite of Spring:* "I am the vessel through which the *Sacre* passed" (Igor Stravinsky and Robert Craft, *Expositions and Developments* [New York: Doubleday, 1962], p. 169). These comments, and Webern's frequent claims that his music had been dictated to him, reflect the expressionist tendency to draw directly from the subconscious.

What happens now is far from expected: no divine judgement, no blessed and no damned, no Good and Evil, and no judge. Everything has ceased to exist. Soft and simple, the words gently swell out: "Rise again, yes rise again, wilt thou, my dust, when rest is o'er."[31]

The instrumental introduction can be conceived as an enormously expanded version of the introduction of the last movement of Beethoven's Ninth, containing both cyclic flashbacks to the earlier movements of the symphony and material to be used in the final choral section. (Mahler had in fact hesitated to write the movement, since he was concerned that it would be taken as a superficial imitation of Beethoven.[32])

The composer's aim in this Finale is to communicate to the listener in the most direct and persuasive fashion the extremes of anxious fear and transcendental ecstasy. To do this, Mahler virtually abandons the formal traditions of the symphony, drawing instead on his operatic experience (as is apparent in the frequent use of off-stage brass and percussion) and relying on a dramatic type of continuity achieved through multiple contrasts of texture, character, and tempo. These frequent contrasts are in themselves a potent musical symbol of anxiety.

We have already called attention to Mahler's special concept of polyphony (see p. 18). He told Natalie Bauer-Lechner that the mingled sounds of barrel organs, military band, and male choir, all rhythmically independent and coming from different directions, represented for him an ideal of counterpoint.[33] Not counterpoint in the classic sense, but a simultaneous layering of varied and conflicting themes, such as we have already seen in Wagner and Strauss (Exx. 2-4 and 2-14). In the Finale of the Second Symphony, such simultaneous contrast is employed when off-stage brass enters against an extension of the "sighing" or grief motive (modeled on *Parsifal*), giving rise to a momentary counterpoint of meters (Ex. 3-3). (Mahler's note to the conductor explains that the brass entry must not disturb the lyrical line of the cellos and bassoon: "the author has in mind here, more or less, a scarcely perceptible music, fragments of which are brought over by the wind.") In another striking instance of simultaneity, in which the song of the "bird of death" mingles with the trumpet and horn calls of the last judgment, Mahler combines differing tempi in an even freer way, indicating rhythmic simultaneities by means of vertical lines (Ex. 3-4).

Beginning about the time of the Fifth Symphony, extreme musical characteristics begin to appear in Mahler's compositions which specifically foreshadow the Viennese expressionism of Schoenberg, Berg, and Webern. Traits such as violence of expression, intense subjectivity, dense texture, dissonant counterpoint, and large melodic leaps have led some writers to characterize Mahler's middle period as constituting an "expressionist phase" in his music;[34] however, we believe that instances of expressionism occur throughout Mahler's works. For the three purely instrumental symphonies of his middle

Ex. 3-3. Mahler, Second Symphony, V, mm. 342–44.

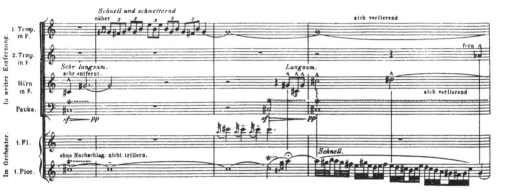

Ex. 3-4. Mahler, Second Symphony, V, mm. 464–67.

period (the Fifth, 1902; the Sixth, 1904; and the Seventh, 1905), Mahler no longer supplies programs. (He had become increasingly reluctant to do so during the 1890s.) However, it would be a mistake to assume that this represents a turning away from emotional and psychological content; on the contrary, Mahler distances himself from Straussian materialism in order to achieve an even more untrammeled subjectivity. As he wrote in 1904: "If one wants to compose, one must not want to paint, write poetry, describe. But *what* one composes is, after all, only the whole man (i.e. man feeling, thinking, breathing, suffering)."[35] Earlier, Mahler had written that his need to write music began where words are no longer adequate, "on the plane of *obscure* feelings, at the gate that opens into the 'other world.' "[36] A bit of mystery should remain, "even for the creator!"[37]

The formal problem inherent in the last movement of the Second Symphony becomes much more severe in the gigantic Finale of the Sixth, since there is neither a text nor a detailed program to aid in coherence. Alma Mahler wrote that the "tragic" Sixth was closest to Mahler's "inmost heart." She reported his agitation and sobbing after its dress rehearsal and gave the following description of the Finale: "It is the hero, on whose head fall three blows of fate, the last of which fells him as a tree is felled."[38] These three blows of fate are symbolized by the three hammer strokes called for in the score. (Significantly, Mahler removed the third hammer stroke from the score after the premiere.[39]) In an uncanny way, they prophesied the three misfortunes that were to befall the composer three years later, in the summer of 1907: the death of his daughter Maria Anna, his discovery of his own heart condition, and his departure from the Vienna Opera.[40] Similarly, Mahler's completion of the *Kindertotenlieder* in 1904 antedated his daughter's death by three years. It is difficult to explain such "coincidences" except in terms of an extreme psychological sensitivity, amounting almost to second sight—a faculty highly valued by the younger expressionists.*

It is not only the extreme length of the Finale (822 measures) which makes it one of Mahler's most difficult to understand. The difficulty is compounded by the movement's tendency toward the perpetual development and recasting of materials. What Mahler said in reference to the Fifth Symphony is equally true of the Sixth and Seventh: "it is kneaded through and through, till not a grain of the mixture remains unmixed and unchanged."[41] In keeping with Adorno's view that Mahler's form is "novelistic,"[42] Erwin Ratz, in his excellent analysis of this movement, sees the long struggle between exposition elements in the development as leading to a catastrophe (symbolized by the second hammer blow), which can only be followed by a new beginning—a developmental recapitulation which is in fact a complete rethinking of the material.[43]

In the development, the life-or-death struggle between the movement's main march theme, a. , and what Ratz calls the "annihilation theme," b. (see Ex. 3-5), is so drawn out and vehement (the marking "everything with brutal strength" appears), that the listener may well get lost in the form. As Schoenberg wrote in his 1912 speech on Mahler, it is in such passages that "gigantic structures clash against one another: the architecture crumbles."[44] This sprawling movement, which marks the extreme point of Mahler's struggle to integrate traditional symphonic form with highly personal content, ends in an unmistakable note of despair. It is significant that during the height of expressionism, Schoenberg, Berg, and Webern no longer attempted this sort of integration, but wrote sets of pieces for orchestra rather than symphonies.[45]

---

*The popularity of Theosophy, with its emphasis on the occult, may have increased the value intimations of supernatural insight had for the expressionists. (The Theosophical Society was founded in America in 1875 by Helena Blavatsky, and the movement was at the height of its influence in Europe around the turn of the century.) Oskar Kokoschka is one who claims to have had second sight. (See Kokoschka, *My Life,* trans. David Britt [London: Thames & Hudson, 1974], pp. 42, 51, 78.)

Ex. 3-5. Mahler, Sixth Symphony, IV, mm. 453–56.

In the song "Ich bin der Welt abhanden gekommen" Mahler introduced a type of generative melody, which, like an opening flower, unfolds organically from a two-note motive (Ex. 3-6a). The same type of melody reappears in his Ninth Symphony (Ex. 3-6b); it is also used by Berg in the Altenberg Songs, Op. 4 (1912), and in Three Pieces for Orchestra, of 1914 (Ex. 3-6c).

Ex. 3-6. a. Mahler, "Ich bin der Welt abhanden gekommen," mm. 1–5, English horn only; b. Mahler, Ninth Symphony, I, mm. 18–21, violin I only; c. Berg, Three Pieces for Orchestra, I, mm. 16–19, violin I only (Copyright 1923, 1954 by Universal Edition A.G., Vienna).

Mahler's use of rhythmic symbols (in the works of his middle and late period) was also important to Berg. These include not only the three hammer blows in the Finale of the Sixth Symphony but also the rhythmic pattern which occurs repeatedly in that movement (Ex. 3-7a). Another rhythmic pattern—perhaps inspired by the irregular beating of Mahler's diseased heart[46]—is used at important formal points in the first movement of the Ninth (Ex. 3-7b). When this pattern recurs "mit höchster Gewalt" (with greatest power) at the climax of the movement, Berg sees it as a clear symbol of death.[47] In the last of the Four Songs, Op. 2 (1908–10), and the first of the Three Pieces for Orchestra (Ex. 3-7c), Berg uses similar emblematic rhythmic patterns. In his opera *Wozzeck*, yet another pattern is employed not only for dramatic symbolism, but as the basic constructive element of Act III, scene 3 (Ex. 3-7d). In the use of such symbolic rhythmic patterns, as in so many other aspects of his music, Berg's debt to Mahler was considerable, and it remained so throughout his career.

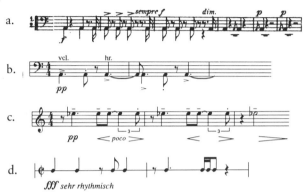

Ex. 3-7. a. Mahler, Sixth Symphony, IV, mm. 9–14, timpani I and II only; b. Mahler, Ninth Symphony, I, mm. 1–2, cellos and horn only; c. Berg, Three Pieces for Orchestra, I, mm. 9–12, trombone I only; d. Berg, *Wozzeck*, III/3, mm. 114–15, bass drum only (Copyright 1926, 1955 by Universal Edition A.G., Vienna).

The works of Mahler's late period, beginning with the symphonic song cycle *Das Lied von der Erde* (1907–1909), share many features with those of the Viennese expressionist composers. One of the most novel of these traits is a rudimentary serialism present in *Das Lied*. In accord with the work's oriental texts (seven poems from Hans Bethge's free translation and adaptation of Chinese poetry, *Die chinesische Flöte*), Mahler used melodies of pentatonic character throughout the work. A three-note motive derived from the pentatonic scale (A–G–E) becomes the work's chief unifying device (Ex. 3-8a–f). In free anticipation of later serial practice, the motive is used not only in its original form (O—Exx. 3-8a and b), but in inversion (I—Ex. 3-8c), retrograde (R—Ex. 3-8d), and retrograde of the inversion (RI—Ex. 3-8e), as well as in chordal form (Ex. 3-8f).[48] These procedures closely approximate Schoenberg's manipulations of three-note patterns in works of the 1908–1909 period, such as the George Songs, Op. 15, and *Erwartung*.[49]

In several passages of *Das Lied von der Erde*, Mahler uses recitative-like musical prose in both the voice and the instruments, which are related to one another in very free counterpoint. Thin, widely spaced textures convey a feeling of immobility and *angst* (Ex. 3-9). Such attenuated textures occur frequently in Schoenberg and, particularly, in Webern.

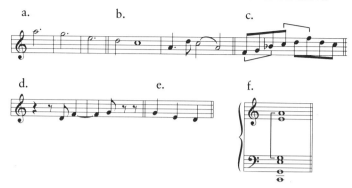

Ex. 3-8. Motives from Mahler, *Das Lied von der Erde.*

he evening descends on all the valleys with its shadows, which are
ull of coolness.

Ex. 3-9. Mahler, *Das Lied von der Erde,* VI, mm. 22–26.

Mahler's late works also show an increased use of musical symbols. One
of the most striking is an ostinato alternating between notes a third or a fifth
apart (Ex. 3-10). Mahler first used this symbol in the fourth movement of the
Third Symphony, a setting of a text by Nietzsche. In both cases, the text
makes clear that the ostinato symbolizes sleep, night, or (by extension) death.
The voice part of Ex. 3-10 contains an older musical symbol, the three-note
figure consisting of an ascending and a descending half-tone, which had pre-

viously been used by such composers as Josquin des Près and Bach to signify supplication, sorrow, and suffering. The second two notes of this motive are identical with the even more widely used "sighing motive," a descending legato half-tone.[50] The use of such musical symbols in the atonal works of Schoenberg *(Erwartung)* and Berg *(Wozzeck)* was to constitute an important element of continuity between tonal and atonal music.

Ex. 3-10. Mahler, *Das Lied von der Erde,* II, mm. 78–79.

For the extraordinary conclusion of *Das Lied,* Mahler changes and expands the text. In its original form, it reads

Never more shall I wander far abroad,—
My foot is weary, weary is my soul;
The earth is everywhere the same,
And endless, endless the white clouds . . .

Mahler's much longer adaptation of these lines introduces the idea of death very specifically, but it also concludes with a transcendental vision not present in the original poem:

Where do I go? I leave, I'm going to the mountains.
I seek peace for my lonely heart.
I journey to my homeland, to my resting place.
Never more shall I wander far abroad.
My heart is quiet, waiting for its hour.
Everywhere the dear earth
Blossoms in springtime and burgeons again!
Everywhere and evermore the blue distance beckons,
Evermore . . . Evermore . . .[51]

His musical setting of this text is in fact not an ending at all, but a transcendental evanescence, stressing the ethereal colors of celesta, mandolin, and harp, and continuing, not with a triad, but with the pentatonic sound C–E–G–A, to which the voice part's final D adds a diffuse quality. The last six measures are marked "completely dying away." Such open-ended conclusions are typical of expressionism, appearing in works of Schoenberg (*Erwartung* and *Die glückliche Hand*), Berg *(Wozzeck),* and Ives (second and fourth movements of the Fourth Symphony).

The opening Adagio of the unfinished Tenth Symphony (1909–10) is Mahler's most expressionist work. Harmonically and linearly, it is the one that is closest in style to Schoenberg and Berg. The movement's climax is a highly dissonant tutti chord (containing nine of the twelve possible tones), carefully built up and long-sustained (Ex. 3-11). Though the chord is constructed in thirds, and can thus be thought of as the dominant of the F-sharp major chord four measures later, its effect is exactly like that of the unresolved and unresolvable dissonances used by Schoenberg and Berg in their atonal works.

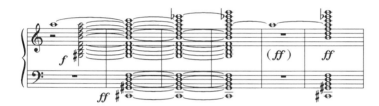

Ex. 3-11. Mahler, Tenth Symphony, I, mm. 203–208. Edited and revised by Otto A. Jokl. Copyright © 1951 (renewed) by Associated Music Publishers, Inc.

Mahler's crucial contributions to expressionism can be viewed as complementary to those of Richard Strauss. Strauss developed many important features of musical expressionism in response to the extreme libretti of *Salome* and *Elektra,* whereas Mahler, in a more typically expressionist mode, turned texts into vehicles for his own emotions. Strauss's main contribution is to the melodramatic, almost hysterical aspect of expressionism; although melodrama is not lacking in Mahler, his music inclines more to expressionism's spiritual, transcendental side. Both these divergent components were to be of great importance to the next generation of composers.

It is not surprising to find that Mahler's music experienced a major vogue during the brief popular emergence of expressionism immediately following World War I—a period which coincided with the equally short ascendance of left-wing elements in Germany. In 1920, a large Mahler festival was held in Amsterdam. In the same year, the young conductor Hermann Scherchen, in an article in the expressionist yearbook *Die Erhebung* (The Uprising), praised Mahler (who had died in 1911) as the ideal musical representative of expressionism. Scherchen connected Mahler's love for all humanity with idealistic hopes for the formation of a new society:

> Mahler expresses his soul's yearning for the deep memories which unite mankind, sounds the song of his love for *all* that exists. . . . Music, which, so long as it paid attention to its "worthiness," had become ever more a means of pleasure for the chosen, the gourmet, now suddenly includes in its domain nature sounds, elemental images, seeks to press everything human to its heart in direct simplicity.[52]

The need to communicate deeply personal emotion led Mahler to surpass conventional limits of length and mood and to stress the extremes of the grotesque and transcendental in his compositions. Even his partial turning-away from program music (beginning with the Fifth Symphony) is related to his wish to achieve a still more personal expression. Paul Bekker wrote that man becomes subject instead of object from that work on.[53] In the longer movements of Mahler's symphonies, the ascendance of content over form—typical of expressionism—threatens formal coherence, while the simultaneous layering of divergent musical materials is present from time to time throughout his compositions. The works of his middle and late periods show many technical features of expressionist music, including large melodic leaps, highly dissonant counterpoint, and perpetual variation. In view of its wealth of expressionist features, only the strong survival of classicism and romanticism in Mahler's music keep it from being fully expressionist.

> The purpose of music is revelation.
> Alexander Scriabin

Although Alexander Scriabin (1872–1915) was of the same generation as Schoenberg, his widely liberating influence demands his inclusion in the list of forerunners. Scriabin's thought and music present many similarities to expressionism. His egocentricity was shaped by Nietzsche's ideas, but this influence was subsequently modified by Theosophy, which became the dominating force in Scriabin's "doctrine," an irrational collection of mystical thought from many sources. His composing was controlled by compulsion; experience must be conjured up spontaneously from within and translated into music. Although there was a considerable French influence in his music, Scriabin was strongly opposed to the passivity of Impressionism. To the contrary, his entire creative thrust was to change the world through his art. His ideas in the synthesis of the arts were the most far-reaching and the most closely connected with the philosophy of spiritual salvation. The expressionist idea of unity in multiplicity appears in his music as the identity of harmony and melody: "The melody [is] a disintegrated harmony, and harmony a compacted melody."[54] Some of his other innovations related to expressionist music are the condensation of forms, rejection of tonality, and use of mystic musical symbols.

Scriabin was close to the spirit of his times; Boris Pasternak felt that Scriabin personified the triumph of Russian culture.[55] Martin Cooper notes that because the Russian intelligentsia were denied activity in political and social affairs, prerevolutionary thinkers and artists turned with hysterical intensity to irrational, mystical, and unnaturally "other-worldly" fields of interest.[56] The desire by Scriabin to restore to music its ancient magical powers is a peculiarly Russian attitude, which he extended to his concept of music as the materialization of the occult. His mystical attitude anticipates such expressionist works as Schoenberg's *Die Jakobsleiter,* the original versions of Webern's Bagatelles for String Quartet (later Op. 9) and Pieces for Orchestra (later Op. 10), and Webern's play, *Tot.* Scriabin exceeded the egocentricity of even the expressionists. He not only believed that by the most thorough self-analysis he would be able to explain—and therefore compose—the cosmos, but also felt himself to be the Messiah of the coming salvation through his own music.

Scriabin was raised by three adoring female relatives (his aunt, grandmother, and great-aunt); some have claimed that his upbringing contributed to the effeminacy and egocentricity he showed in later life. His widely admired piano playing was characterized by great delicacy. As his friend Konstantin Balmont, a Russian Symbolist poet, remarked: "When Scriabin plays, there is no piano, only a beautiful woman. He is making love to her."[57] Sensuality is a basic motivating force in much of Scriabin's music.

The period in Scriabin's life and work most relevant to expressionism begins in 1903. At this time his music was becoming both more complex and more subsidiary to ideas.[58] Scriabin resigned from the Moscow Conservatory (where he had taught since 1898) and gradually abandoned his wife and four children in favor of a mistress, who encouraged his philosophical obsessions. For the next six years he lived in Italy, Switzerland, and Belgium in comparative poverty, developing his Messianic "doctrine," a mixture of concepts deriving chiefly from Johann Gottlieb Fichte, Schopenhauer, and Theosophy.[59] His notebooks of 1904–1905 give the most vivid idea of Scriabin's search for ecstasy:

> I am, and there is nothing outside of me. I am nothing, I am all. I am one, and within me is multiplicity . . . I am fire. I am chaos . . . I create the world by the play of my mood, my smile, my sigh, my caress, anger, hope, doubt. . . . I am the creative ascent that tenderly caresses, that captivates, that soars, destroying, revivifying . . . I am God! I am the blossoming, I am the bliss, I am all-consuming passion, all engulfing, I am fire enveloping the universe, reducing it to chaos. . . . The growth of human consciousness is the growth of the consciousness of geniuses. . . . There is only one consciousness. That is mine.[60]

These Dionysian pronouncements foreshadow the egocentric thinking of the German expressionists. The statement that "the growth of human consciousness is the growth of the consciousness of geniuses" is remarkably similar to Schoenberg's later dictum that "the laws of the nature of a man of genius are the laws of the humanity of the future."[61] Like the expressionists, Scriabin saw his art as an active force whose aim was to change humanity.

Also like many expressionists, Scriabin found it necessary to impart his message through means other than the art in which he was trained. He considered himself as much a writer and thinker as a composer at this time. His major orchestral work of the period, the widely influential *Poème de l'extase* (1905–1908), was preceded by his 300-line poem of the same title.[62] The music he wrote while living in Western Europe reflects the influences of Wagner, Franck, Debussy, and the Decadent writers. Its luxuriant sensuality and orgiastic climaxes made it a sensation among younger Russian composers. During these years Scriabin advanced rapidly toward a highly individual style characterized by complex dominant harmonies, which are usually not resolved.

In 1908 Serge Koussevitsky arranged to subsidize Scriabin's work for five years, so that the composer could begin work on his *Mysterium*, a gigantic *Gesamtkunstwerk*. This enabled him to return to Russia in 1909, where he closely studied progressive trends in the Moscow art, dance, and theater worlds for use in his developing concepts. His highly individualistic mode of composition was integrally related to mystical ideas. Scriabin asked his biographer Sabaneiev, "How can you express mysticism with major and minor? How can you convey the dissolution of matter, or luminosity?"[63]

Like Kandinsky, Scriabin was gifted with synaesthesia, the ability to visualize colors along with musical sounds. At this time he became obsessed by a theory of correspondences developed out of the theosophical idea of opposing but equal forces (creation and dissolution) active in the universe. His goal of ecstasy was to be achieved by the balance of these forces.[64] All things, however dissimilar, are related by "vibrations" (a concept from Theosophy also embraced by Kandinsky). For Scriabin, a way to express the unity of all things was through the identity of harmony and melody. For his concept of balanced opposing forces he found a musical equivalent in the relationship of highly unified, often static harmony to constant thematic transformation and textural change.

The large symphonic poem *Prometheus* ("Poem of Fire," Op. 60, 1908–10) exemplifies the interdependence of Scriabin's music and his mystical ideas. The orchestral score includes a part for the "color-organ," which had recently been invented by Scriabin's friend Alexander Mozer. This visionary synthesis of colored light and music was ahead of its time; Scriabin did not live to experience his *Prometheus* performed with adequate lighting. The work was originally to have formed a section of the final *Mysterium*. Both the chorus (which enters near the end) and the audience were to have been robed in white, in accord with the ritual nature of the work. In another aspect of synthesis, the chorus's abstract vowel sounds correspond to various colors.[65]

The music of *Prometheus* is characterized by multiple changes of texture and mood. In contrast to the work's episodic nature, its melody and harmony are consistently derived from a six-note scale, its corresponding chord, and their transpositions (Ex. 3-12). The chord is in fact a form of dominant harmony, a $V^{13}_{5\flat}$ (the lowered fifth is notated enharmonically as an augmented fourth), rearranged in a series of augmented, diminished, and perfect fourths. Scriabin called it "synthetic"; other writers have referred to it as the "mystic" or "Prometheus" chord. It usually retains its dominant sound, but at times Scriabin rearranges it so that it no longer sounds like a dominant. A notable instance occurs at the opening of the work, in which a transposition of the chord appears in inversion in a low register and has the effect of a tone cluster. Except for the F-sharp major triad which ends the work, the "Prometheus" chord, in its many forms, is never resolved; it moves instead to transpositions and rearrangements of itself, often by means of tritone root progressions. Thus the chord is no longer treated as a functioning harmony demanding resolution, but becomes a musical "object," like Strauss's "Elektra" chord. The effect of Scriabin's harmony is basically static, in contrast to the numerous changes of tempo, orchestration, and character and the continuous thematic transformation.

Ex. 3-12. Scriabin, *Prometheus* scale and chord.

The two most reliable sources for the underlying plot of this one-movement symphonic poem are the program notes written by Leonid Sabaneiev for the 1911 Moscow premiere and the numerous character indications Scriabin put in the score to clarify his expressive intent. Sabaneiev's program notes, authorized by Scriabin, state:

> Prometheus, Satanas and Lucifer all meet in ancient myth. They represent the active energy of the universe, its creative principle. The fire is light, life, struggle, increase, abundance and thought. At first, this powerful force manifests itself wearily, as languid thirsting for life. Within this lassitude then appears the primordial polarity between soul and matter. The creative upsurge or gust of feeling registers a protest against this torpor. Later it does battle and conquers matter— of which it itself is a mere atom—and returns to the original quiet and tranquility . . . thus completing the cycle. . . .[66]

The symphony begins with the idea of Chaos (marked "foggy"); the orchestra represents "the Cosmos as it was before Karma, before lives had been lived and deeds accumulated predestination."[67] After themes representing the Creative Principle, the Will, and the "dawn of human consciousness" have been introduced, there is a major section corresponding to the "languid thirsting for life" mentioned in the program notes. Expressive designations make clear the highly charged sensuality of this passage ("languorous"; "voluptuously, almost with pain"; "with delight"; "with intense desire"; and others). A battle episode follows, expressing the conflict brought about by "the primordial polarity of soul and matter." Marked "with defiance, bellicose" and "stormy," it leads to the work's first large climax. An even greater climax (marked "victorious") later expresses the victory of the soul over matter. In keeping with Scriabin's idea that the work of art could "dematerialize" the world, the prestissimo coda (marked "winged, dancing" and "vertiginous") portrays the final dance of disintegrating atoms.

In accord with the Theosophists' emphasis on esoteric meanings, Scriabin makes use of some obscure musical symbolism in *Prometheus*, such as the downward leap of a minor ninth to portray "the descent of spirit into matter."[68] However, he also employs more familiar musical symbols, such as the descending half-step "sighing" figure, signifying sadness or suffering (at "voluptuous, almost with pain," solo violin part).

In the years 1911–14 other compositions by Scriabin—Piano Sonatas Nos. 6–10 and the Five Preludes, Op. 74—show an increase in expressionist traits. In these works he continues to expand his use of scales and equivalent chords, adding notes to both, until, in the musical sketches for the unfinished "Prefatory Action" (intended to introduce his *Mysterium*), he writes chords containing all twelve chromatic tones.[69] As Scriabin's harmonies become ever more complex, the sense of tonality disappears, and its place is taken by an increasingly strict serial organization of melody and harmony. As George Perle has written, Scriabin "may be considered the first to exploit serial procedures systematically as a means of compensating for the loss of traditional tonal functions."[70] Like the expressionists, Scriabin arrived at his "secret harmonies" intuitively, under extreme psychic pressure.[71] He considered his reinforcement of the upper partials of the overtone series a physical manifestation of the astral world.[72] As tonality disappears in Scriabin's music, the final cadence is often replaced by an evanescence comparable to the "non-endings" in the atonal works of Schoenberg and Berg (Ex. 3-13).

Ex. 3-13. Scriabin, Sonata No. 7, last five mm.

A famous pianist in his day, Scriabin was known for the feeling of improvisation in his playing. His late sonatas have the same improvisatory quality, although they are actually strictly constructed. They are condensed to a one-movement form, with a dramatic progression of psychological and spiritual states and moods. Thematic transformation and constant texture change contrast with the static harmony. The programmatic content present in Scriabin's earlier music is gradually replaced by delineation of spiritual states; music becomes a materialization of the occult. Interest in the demonic, which Scriabin showed in *Prometheus,* continues. Particularly in the Sixth and Ninth Piano Sonatas (1911 and 1912–13), his aim is to disturb the public with "a hypnosis of apparitional rhythms."[73] In the Sixth Sonata (Ex. 3-14), the words "fear springs up" appear in the score as constant rhythmic motion is interrupted by *ff* dissonant chords and mysterious low repeated sonorities.

Ex. 3-14. Scriabin, Sonata No. 6, mm. 110–25.

Scriabin's last piano pieces, the aphoristic Preludes, Op. 74 (1914), show great economy of musical material. Op. 74/1 is based melodically on the motive of two ascending half-steps. This prelude is marked "painful, tearing," and its most striking feature is the melody's hesitant, tortured ascent from E-sharp to E-natural a diminished octave higher, over a harmonic texture of unrelieved dissonance (Exx. 3-15a and b). Here, the composer has removed all self-indulgence from his music and expresses emotion with searing directness.

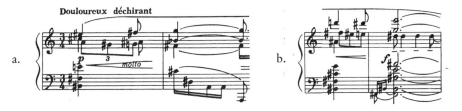

Ex. 3-15. Scriabin, Op. 74/1. a. mm. 1–2; b. mm. 11–12.

Scriabin seeks to affect the listener actively, even cataclysmically. Like the expressionists, he turned away from the concept of art-for-art's-sake, though his ideals of destruction and recreation through art lack the ethical component present in much expressionist thought. Scriabin is also expressionist in that his music and ideas show complete egocentricity; Rollo Myers writes that Scriabin's expressionism is "the outcome of an ultra-subjective . . . approach to art in which the nature of inner experience determines to a large extent the objective form in which the work will be cast and the appropriate technique."[74] In that his need for personal expression leads him to develop a new, highly individualized musical language, Scriabin closely parallels Arnold Schoenberg. The two composers abandoned tonality at about the same time, but Scriabin preceded Schoenberg by more than a decade in the development of a new compositional principle to replace it. However, there is undeniably a side of Scriabin which is not expressionist—his refined and decadent sensuality, with its hothouse atmosphere and highly sensuous evocations of nature.

Although Scriabin was considered a leading modern composer in the period just before World War I (particularly in Russia and England), his reputation declined greatly in the 1920s. Until very recently historians have been inclined to ignore or underestimate his influence on later composers. Stravinsky's relationship to Scriabin, which contained elements of admiration and imitation as well as rebellion, was important to his development. Scriabin's influence is clear in Stravinsky's Piano Études of 1908 and in *The Firebird*, 1910. While planning *The Rite of Spring* and composing his Symbolist cantata, *Zvezdoliki*, in July 1911, Stravinsky was "playing only Debussy and Scriabin," he wrote to Florent Schmitt.[75] In October 1913, after the cataclysmic premiere of *The Rite* and his subsequent illness, Stravinsky traveled with Scriabin from Russia to Clarens, Switzerland. Scriabin played his last piano sonatas for Stravinsky, who admired them and immediately purchased the Sixth and Seventh.[76]

Alban Berg's music shows the influence of Scriabin in its harmonic practice, orchestration, and gestures.[77] Schoenberg and his circle were well aware of Scriabin's music; the Russian composer's Fourth and Seventh Piano Sonatas were played at the first concert of Schoenberg's Verein für musikalische Privataufführungen (Society for Private Musical Performances) on 29 December 1918.[78] In New York, Charles Ives and his young friend Elliott Carter attended private performances—which may have started as early as 1916—of Scriabin's piano works by Katherine Ruth Heyman.[79] The *Blaue Reiter* expressionists were interested in Scriabin's rejection of art-for-art's-sake and his consequent notion of the artist as an active force in the universe, as well as in his novel ideas of synthesis. Kandinsky and Marc published a major article on *Prometheus* in the 1912 *Blaue Reiter Almanac*. Thus, Scriabin was in no way an isolated figure. However, it was his misfortune to be so much in tune with his pre–World War I era, its elements of decadence, and its mystical interests, that his importance as a musical innovator and as a liberating influence on other composers has yet to be fully recognized.

Select Bibliography

MAHLER

Adorno, Theodor. *Mahler: Eine musikalische Physionomik*. Frankfurt: Suhrkamp, 1960.
Bauer-Lechner, Natalie. *Recollections of Gustav Mahler*. Ed. Peter Franklin, trans. Dika Newlin. Cambridge: Cambridge University Press, 1980.
Bekker, Paul. *Gustav Mahlers Symphonien*. Berlin: Schuster and Loeffler, 1921.
Blaukopf, Herta, ed. *Mahler's Unknown Letters*. Trans. Richard Stokes. London: Gollancz, 1986.
Blaukopf, Kurt. *Gustav Mahler*. Trans. Inge Goodwin. New York: Praeger, 1973.
La Grange, Henry-Louis de. *Mahler*. Vol. 1. New York: Doubleday, 1973.
———. *Gustav Mahler: Chronique d'une vie*. Vol. 2, Paris: Fayard, 1983; Vol. 3, Paris: Fayard, 1984.
Mahler, Alma. *Gustav Mahler: Memories and Letters*. 3d ed. Ed. Donald Mitchell, trans. Basil Creighton. Seattle: University of Washington Press, 1975.
Mahler, Gustav. *Selected Letters*. Ed. Knud Martner, trans. Eithne Wilkins, Ernst Kaiser, and Bill Hopkins. London: Faber, 1979.
Mahler-Werfel, Alma. *Mein Leben*. Frankfurt: Fischer, 1960.
Mersmann, Hans. "Gustav Mahlers 'Lied von der Erde.' " *Melos* 2/7 (1 May 1921): 131.
Mitchell, Donald. *Gustav Mahler: The Early Years*. 2d. ed. Rev. and ed. Paul Banks and David Matthews. London and Boston: Faber, 1980.
———. *Gustav Mahler: The Wunderhorn Years*. Berkeley and Los Angeles: University of California Press, 1980.
———. *Gustav Mahler: Songs and Symphonies of Life and Death*. Berkeley and Los Angeles: University of California Press, 1985.
Newlin, Dika. *Bruckner, Mahler, Schoenberg*. 2d rev. ed. New York: Norton, 1978.
Scherchen, Hermann. "Das neue Führertum in der Musik." *Die Erhebung*. Vol. 2. Ed. Alfred Wolfenstein. Berlin: Fischer, 1920.
Schönberg, Arnold et al. *Gustav Mahler*. Tübingen: Wunderlich, 1966.

Stefan, Paul, ed. *Gustav Mahler: Ein Bild seiner Persönlichkeit in Widmungen.* Munich: Piper, 1910.

Walter, Bruno. *Gustav Mahler.* Trans. Lotte Walter Lindt. New York: Schocken, 1974.

SCRIABIN

Baker, James Marshall. "Alexander Scriabin: The Transition from Tonality to Atonality." Ph.D. diss., Yale University, 1977. 2 vols.

Bowers, Faubion. *Scriabin: A Biography of the Russian Composer.* 2 vols. Tokyo and Palo Alto: Kodansha International, 1969.

———. *The New Scriabin: Enigmas and Answers.* New York, St. Martin's Press, 1983.

Kelkel, Manfred. *Alexandre Scriabine: Sa vie, l'ésoterisme et le langage musical dans son oeuvre.* Paris: Honoré Champion, 1978.

Myers, Rollo H. "Scriabin: A Reassessment." *The Musical Times* 1367 (January 1957): 17.

CHAPTER FOUR

Arnold Schoenberg

> The true composer writes a novel and unusual
> new harmony only in order to express the new
> and unheard-of which moves him. The new sound
> is an instinctively discovered symbol, proclaim-
> ing the new man who expresses himself in it.
>
> Arnold Schoenberg (1911)

During his expressionist period, Schoenberg (1874–1951) asserted that he had "broken through every restriction of a bygone aesthetic,
. . . obeying an inner compulsion, which is stronger than any up-bringing,
. . . obeying the formative process which, being the one natural to me, is
stronger than my artistic education." [1] Schoenberg abandoned the prevailing
conception of art-for-art's-sake in favor of involvement with the human condition:

> Art is the cry of distress uttered by those who experience at first hand the fate
> of mankind. Who are not reconciled to it, but come to grips with it. Who do not
> apathetically wait upon the motor called "hidden forces," but hurl themselves in
> among the moving wheels, to understand how it all works. Who do not turn
> their eyes away, to shield themselves from emotions, but open them wide, so as
> to tackle what must be tackled. Who do, however, often close their eyes, in order
> to perceive things incommunicable by the senses, to envision within themselves
> the process that only seems to be in the world outside. The world revolves within—
> inside them: what bursts out is merely the echo—the work of art. [2]

Schoenberg's expressionist period began with his Second String Quartet (1907–
1908), came to a peak with such works as the operas *Erwartung* (1909) and
Die glückliche Hand (1910–13), and closed with the unfinished oratorio *Die
Jakobsleiter* (1915–22).[3] His expressionist works were preceded by many in
a post-Romantic style, the best known being the string sextet *Verklärte Nacht*
(Transfigured Night, 1899). The expressionist works were followed, starting
in 1921, by a large body of twelve-tone compositions marking a return to a
more objective style of composition.

Around 1911, when Schoenberg was articulating his expressionist beliefs (particularly in the original version of *Harmonielehre*), he felt that this new art was the product of creative compulsion: "I believe art is born of 'I must,' not 'I can.'"[4] The composer should be guided by intuition, not intellect or theory, in creating art that "on its highest level . . . concerns itself exclusively with inner nature."[5] Initially, the content of Schoenberg's new art arose from psychological necessity. Over the course of time, however, his increasing desire to communicate his transcendental yearnings became predominant, and, in *Die Jakobsleiter* it replaced his earlier self-absorption. This art is one in which the message is more important than the medium (*what* is said rather than *how*); during this period Schoenberg's painting, essays, and libretti also helped satisfy his overriding compulsion to express himself.

Unprecedented freedom is the hallmark of Schoenberg's expressionist music; he made compositional decisions "only by feeling, by feeling for form. Every chord that I set down corresponds to a compulsion; the compulsion of my necessity for expression."[6] These urges led to the emancipation of dissonance and to atonality. Schoenberg avoided literal repetitions, tending at times toward athematic writing. He used rapidly changing textures and extreme means in instrumentation and melodic writing. As he explained his radical ideas to Ferruccio Busoni:

> My only intention is: to have *no* intention!
>
> No formal, architectural, or other artistic intentions (except perhaps of capturing the mood of a poem), no aesthetic intentions—none of any kind; at most this:
>
> To place nothing inhibiting in the stream of my unconscious sensations. Not to allow anything to infiltrate which may be invoked either by intelligence or consciousness.[7]

It may seem paradoxical that Schoenberg, the foremost exponent of expressionism in music, should have been born and come to maturity in Vienna, a city which, in spite of its great musical traditions, was extremely conservative in its politics, in the hierarchical structure of its society, and in its reluctance to accept new developments in the arts. Nevertheless, his central role in bringing musical expressionism to its climax was a consequence not only of the nature of his character and creativity and of certain forces inherent in the development of Western music (notably the progressive weakening of tonality from *Tristan* on), but also of the particular milieu of which he was a part.

Schoenberg's father, who had moved to Vienna from his birthplace in Slovakia, has been described as an anarchistic wit and a freethinker,[8] while his mother, who came from a very musical Prague family, was pious and conservative. The family belonged to the lower middle class and ran a shoe store. They had no piano, but Arnold learned to play the violin as a child and, according to his sister, began to compose at age ten.[9] Probably the earliest opportunities for him to hear music publicly performed were at band concerts in his neighborhood. When Arnold was seventeen, his father died; this was the first of several traumas Schoenberg had to endure. (His father's death on New Year's Eve so affected Schoenberg that throughout his life he refused to celebrate on the last evening of the year.[10]) He had to leave the Realschule and take a post as a bank apprentice, but after four years he left the bank, and he supported himself as a musician from then on.

Schoenberg must have felt the ferment below Vienna's placid surface as the conservative upper-middle class lost political power in the 1890s to new, more extreme mass movements: on the left, the Social Democrats; on the right—and intensely anti-Semitic—Pan-Germanism and Christian Socialism. All three movements were in revolt against reason and law.[11] The growing anti-Semitism in the 1890s must have increased Schoenberg's sense of alienation; like Mahler's conversion to Catholicism in 1897,[12] Schoenberg's turn to Protestantism in 1898[13] may have been caused by the wish to find acceptance in a society becoming increasingly hostile to Jews.

The artistic life of fin-de-siècle Vienna was marked by the pervasive aestheticism of the *Jugendstil* (the German counterpart of *art nouveau*), as manifested in the Secession movement in the visual arts (founded in 1897). The hothouse climate of this Austrian aestheticism was "an expression of [bourgeois] civilization, an affirmation of an attitude in which neither ethical nor social ideals played a predominant part."[14] The 1908–1909 expressionist works of Schoenberg and his Viennese contemporary Oskar Kokoschka (1886–1980) signaled a revolt against this aestheticism. With these works, they initiated a new phase in the arts, marked by the destruction of traditional norms and the beginning of a new, radically different sensibility. Rejecting the professed values of their society, Schoenberg and Kokoschka created new musical and visual languages to proclaim "the universality of suffering."[15] Kokoschka's play, *Mörder, Hoffnung der Frauen* (Murderer, Hope of Women), directed by its author at the garden theater of the Internationale Kunstschau in July 1909,[16] and his poster and illustrations for the play inaugurated his expressionism in these media (see Ill. 4-1 and chapter 10). The two artists respected each other throughout their lives. A later letter from the composer to the painter recalls that they had both been members of the same intellectual circle.[17] The members of this radical-intellectual circle, drawn together in reaction to the stuffiness of Vienna's cultural and political establishment, were to have a significant influence on the epoch-making changes in Schoenberg's musical style around 1908.

Early in the 1890s, the composer and conductor Alexander von Zemlinsky introduced Schoenberg to the intellectual and artistic group centered on Karl Kraus and Peter Altenberg, which met at the Café Griensteidl (nicknamed "Café Megalomania"). Even at this early period, the "wild and energetic" young Schoenberg was known for his "witty and pert replies" and the "paradoxes which he tossed about"[18]—a mental liveliness doubtless inherited from his father. In spite of his limited formal education, Schoenberg was a great reader and was passionately interested in ideas.[19] We may as-

Ill. 4-1. Oskar Kokoschka, *Pietà*, poster for the Kunstschau theater, 1909. Color lithograph, 46 ½ x 30″. Museum of Modern Art, New York.

sume that he took part in wide-ranging discussions with other members of the circle, probably dealing with politics and philosophy as well as the arts.

Schoenberg idolized the satirist and polemicist Karl Kraus for his devotion to truth, as well as for the epigrammatic ruthlessness of his writing style, and was influenced by both. The composer's initial literary efforts (in 1909, in response to the vituperative newspaper criticism of his music) were strongly Krausian in tone and style. He acknowledged this influence in the copy of his *Harmonielehre* he presented to Kraus: "I have learned more from you, perhaps, than a man should learn, if he wants to remain independent."[20]

The poet and essayist Peter Altenberg, a consummate stylist who had the ability to create a mood or a scene in a minimum of words, swayed Schoenberg (and Webern) toward aphoristic brevity. The architect and writer Adolf Loos, another key figure of the Viennese avant-garde, expressed his aversion to useless decoration in his 1908 lecture "Ornament und Verbrechung" (Ornament and Crime). Schoenberg shows a similar point of view when he avoids any sort of harmonic or contrapuntal "filler" in his atonal works, though both are found in his post-Romantic compositions. Loos, who believed the function of the artist to be "to shake us out of our complacency,"[21] was a friend and patron to both Kokoschka and Schoenberg during the early years of the twentieth century.[22]

Personal crisis also played a crucial role in impelling Schoenberg toward expressionism. Poverty was a constant problem, as he attempted to support himself and his family by orchestrating other composers' music and by teaching. On the occasions when his atonal music was performed, it was usually met by the noisy disapproval of a large part of the audience and by mocking reactions in the press.[23] This hostile treatment, perhaps more violent and sustained than that accorded any other composer in history, caused lasting feelings of persecution and embitterment in Schoenberg.

He met Mahler in 1904, and their increasingly close friendship gave Schoenberg a degree of artistic and material support. Mahler's departure from Vienna in 1907 was a serious blow to the younger composer, and with the loss of this important father-figure, Schoenberg began to experience spiritual and psychological unrest. He became absorbed in painting, seeking isolation from the realities of life. His alienation brought on a marital crisis,[24] and during the summer of 1908 his wife, Mathilde, left him in order to live with the expressionist painter Richard Gerstl. (Gerstl had become acquainted with the Schoenbergs in 1907 and had given the composer some painting instruction.) Mathilde came home after a short time, and Gerstl committed suicide in November. After her return, Mathilde was depressed and taciturn,[25] and Schoenberg himself had thoughts of suicide and made a very pessimistic "Outline for a Will." This document vividly reveals the tortured state of Schoenberg's mind following Mathilde's unfaithfulness:

> I see myself obliged . . . to write down my *last will*, as preparation for some voluntary actions which I intend at this time. . . . Whether it would be my body that gave way, or my soul—I do not feel the difference—but I have a presentiment of dissolution. . . .
>
> I have wept, acted like a desperate man, have made decisions and rejected them, have had ideas of suicide and nearly carried them out, have dashed from one senselessness to another—in a word, I am completely torn to pieces.

In his desperation, Schoenberg attempts to rationalize away the pain he feels:

> I deny the fact that my wife betrayed me. She didn't betray me, for my imagination long since made clear to me everything she did. My power of presentiment constantly saw through her lies and suspected her crimes long before she herself thought of committing them. And I only trusted her because I saw as lies what she gave me as facts. . . .

Finally, he comes to the realization that he has never really known or understood Mathilde:

> The soul of my wife was so alien from mine that I could not arrive at either a truthful or a dishonest relationship with her. We never really spoke with one another—i.e., communicated—we just talked. . . .

I was remote from her. She never saw me and I never [saw] her. We never knew each other. Also, I don't even know what she looks like. I cannot bring her likeness to mind. Perhaps she doesn't exist at all. Lives only in my imagination. . . .[26]

Schoenberg's extreme reaction to his wife's temporary absence may have been even more painful because it recalled the earlier traumatic loss of his father. It was during and immediately after his marital troubles in 1908 that Schoenberg took his final steps into atonality and the extremes which characterize his expressionist music. Like that music, the "visions" the composer painted during the period following Gerstl's death give evidence of an extraordinary state of mind. They are among the most remarkable documents of early expressionism (Ill. 4-2).

Ill. 4-2. Arnold Schoenberg, *Red Gaze,* 1910. Oil on pasteboard, 32 x 25 cm. Städtische Galerie im Lenbachhaus, Munich. Collection Lawrence and Ronald Schoenberg and Nuria Schoenberg Nono.

A compelling parallel can be drawn between this experience of Schoenberg's, with its accompanying stylistic change, and that of August Strindberg, a writer revered by Schoenberg and his circle. Strindberg's autobiographical novel, *Inferno,* describes the years (1894–96) of his personal crisis, which bordered on madness. His writing changed, after this experience, from naturalism to expressionism, particularly in his dramas; his works are frequently referred to as either pre- or post-*Inferno.* As with Schoenberg and Strindberg, a mental crisis also preceded an important stylistic change in the work of Wassily Kandinsky. After suffering a nervous breakdown in Paris in 1907,[27] the painter, like Schoenberg, felt the need to "change instruments" by writing poetry and stage works. By 1910 he produced his first semi-abstract, expressionist paintings and drawings. Just as the effect of personal crisis on such artists as van Gogh, Munch, and Kafka led to expressionist tendencies, so must it be recognized that many of the composers who produced a truly expressionist mode in their creative work had first to undergo extreme personal, psychological suffering before reaching the kind of communion with their deepest psyches that seems necessary to expressionism.

The most important musical influences on Schoenberg's turn to expressionism were Wagner, Strauss, and Mahler. It was Zemlinsky, whom Schoenberg met in 1893 through their mutual involvement with workers' choruses,[28] who opened his mind to the influence of Wagner and provided his only real instruction in theory and composition. In a 1909 interview, Schoenberg acknowledged the importance of Wagner's music to his advance toward atonality ("after I became a Wagnerian—then the rest of the development came rather fast"), and mentioned specifically Wagner's "short motives, with their possibility of changing the composition as quickly and as often as the least detail of mood requires."[29] The influence of Strauss's *Salome* and *Elektra*, though not often acknowledged by Schoenberg, was also of great importance. Strauss's discontinuous textures, rapid and distorted *parlando*, and daring treatment of melody, harmony, and orchestration all helped to form Schoenberg's expressionist idiom.

Mahler's influence can be seen in Schoenberg's turn toward a leaner, more astringent, and more linear texture. This change occurs in the Chamber Symphony, Op. 9 (1906), the final large-scale work of Schoenberg's tonal period. It reflects his changing attitude toward the music of Mahler: up to 1904, Schoenberg seems to have been concerned lest the older composer influence his own development unduly. However, a letter he wrote to Mahler after the Vienna premiere of Mahler's Third Symphony, on 12 December 1904, shows a total change in attitude:

> I must not speak as a musician to a musician if I am to give any idea of the incredible impression your symphony made on me: I can speak only as one human being to another. For I saw your very soul, naked, stark naked . . . I saw the forces of evil and good wrestling with each other; I saw a man in torment struggling towards inward harmony; I divined a personality, a drama, and *truthfulness*, the most uncompromising truthfulness.[30]

Schoenberg's Second String Quartet, Op. 10 (written in 1907–1908 and dedicated to Mathilde), is of particular importance and fascination, since its four movements show the composer at different stages of his development toward expressionism. The opening movement, written largely in 1907, is still post-Romantic and clearly tonal. The two middle movements were written during the height of the crisis in Schoenberg's marriage.[31] His state of mind is reflected in the Scherzo's scurrilous black humor (including the introduction of the Viennese street song "Ach, du lieber Augustin, alles ist hin" [Oh my dear Augustin, everything's lost[32]]—the same tune which had confronted Mahler at a moment of great emotional trauma) and in the extreme emotionalism of Stefan George's text and its setting in "Litanei" (third movement). The finale, a setting of George's "Entrückung" (Rapture), was the last movement completed and the only one notated without a key signature. Though its tonic is F-sharp major, it includes long stretches of music which are in fact atonal.

In the fall of 1907 Schoenberg discovered the poetry of Stefan George (1868–1933), whose works both he and Webern would frequently set.[33] The poems Schoenberg set in his Second Quartet came from a time when George had abandoned his earlier aestheticism and wrote visionary poetry in which he himself played the role of seer and prophet: "I am but a spark of the holy fire/Only a rumbling of the holy voice."[34] George's poetry, although strict in form, is often intensely emotional, like Schoenberg's music. The composer seems to have felt the need for a formal counterbalance to his own extreme expressive impulses. He found this not only in the formalism of George's poetry but also in the musical forms he used in his settings of that poetry: variation form in the setting of "Litanei" and—more freely—sonata form in "Entrückung." In spite of the use of these forms Schoenberg makes frequent changes in the music in order to express the content of the text. Thus, at the climax of his setting of "Litanei" (Ex. 4-1), a poem which expresses the cry of anguish of a wanderer seeking spiritual solace, the last two lines ("Take from me earthly love,/Grant me thy happiness!") are expressed by changes in dynamics (from *fff* to *p*) and harmonic tension (extreme dissonance to consonance), accompanied by a dramatic break in texture and a downward leap of two octaves and a minor second in the voice (an even larger leap than Kundry's in Act II of *Parsifal,* which may have inspired it—see Ex. 2-6). In passages like this, Schoenberg uses George's text as a vehicle for expressing his own emotional crisis.

"Entrückung," the text of the final movement, is the vision of a transcendental experience. Objects well known to the narrator begin to lose their accustomed aspect, and he gives himself over to a state of divine ectasy:

> I climb over fearful chasms
> I feel as if, beyond the last cloud,
> I swim in a sea of crystal brilliance—[35]

The text matches Schoenberg's own transcendental tendency and his vision of himself as a prophet of the New. More specifically, there is an integral relationship between the other-worldly visions in "Entrückung" and Schoenberg's advance into atonality in the introduction and development section of the movement. The atonal opening sets the mood perfectly for the first line of the poem: "Air from another planet floats around me," (Ex. 4-2). A statement by Schoenberg in 1932 supports the view that George's poem helped

Ex. 4-1. Schoenberg, Second String Quartet/III, mm. 63–68. Used by permission of Belmont Music Publishers, Pacific Palisades, CA 90272.

him break the bounds of tonality: "I found help where music always finds it when it has reached a crucial point in its development. . . . [I was] assisted by feelings, insights, impressions and the like, mainly in the form of poetry."[36]

Schoenberg's next major work, *Fifteen Poems from "Das Buch der hängenden Gärten"* [The Book of the Hanging Gardens] *by Stefan George,* Op. 15 (1908–1909), marks a further advance into the realm of expressionism. This song cycle represented a major line of demarcation for Schoenberg, as expressed in his program note for the 1910 premiere of the songs: "With the George Songs I have succeeded for the first time in approaching an ideal of expression and form that has hovered before me for years."[37] In his text, George portrays the narrator's love for a mysterious, beautiful woman, his rising passion for her, its consummation, and love's eventual ending. Like Schoenberg's works of the 1908–1909 period, George's cycle of poems is the product of a period of emotional crisis which brought on an important stylistic change. Between 1892 and 1896, George went through a stressful, ultimately unsuccessful love relationship with Ida Coblenz (who later married Richard Dehmel), a young woman from a wealthy family who loved oriental

Ex. 4-2. Schoenberg, Second String Quartet/IV, mm. 1–2.

things. The elaborate garden of the family's estate in Bingen is the model for the garden in George's poems, just as Ida herself is the source of the priestess-like woman in the cycle. Although George keeps strictly to the form of lyric poetry in *The Book of the Hanging Gardens,* the content of the poems Schoenberg set is at the extreme of what could be expressed in that form. The poems represent the point at which George turned away from his youthful art-for-art's-sake aestheticism and began to develop the new, visionary style of his later years.[38]

Schoenberg is able to respond to both the exotic nature descriptions and the strong emotions in the text, but he far surpasses George in power and directness of expression. The song cycle's vocal line, written for soprano but often pitched in a low, sensuously breathy range, is mostly a syllabic *parlando* which avoids symmetrical phrases and contains elements of distortion. The fabulously colorful piano accompaniment changes textures often in response to stimuli in George's poems. The songs consistently avoid literal repetition of entire sections of music; repetition always occurs in varied form or altered order. Schoenberg's frequent use of inconclusive "non-endings" enhances the dramatic continuity between the songs. Tonality appears occasionally, but it is no longer the governing force it was in the Second String Quartet.

The short period between May and October 1909 was marked by an extraordinary burst of creativity in Schoenberg. Writing under strong compulsion, he swiftly completed the three works which define his expressionism in its purest and most intense state:

Five Pieces for Orchestra, Op. 16
1. "Premonitions" (finished 3 May 1909)
2. "The Past" (finished before 15 June 1909)
3. "Colors: Summer Morning by a Lake" (finished 1 July 1909)
4. *"Peripeteia"* (finished 17 July 1909)
5. "The Obbligato Recitative" (finished before 11 August 1909)
Piano Piece, Op. 11/3 (finished 7 August 1909)[39]
Erwartung, opera, Op. 17 (27 August–4 October 1909)[40]

"Premonitions," the first of the Five Pieces for Orchestra, expresses a very high state of emotional tension. Its opening section incorporates the multiple, often unpredictable changes of affect (tempo, dynamics, orchestration) which we have seen in the dramatic works of Wagner and Strauss, and which serve Schoenberg as a potent symbol of *angst*. In the longer, more continuous second section of "Premonitions," extremes of orchestration and the dense layering of melodic and chordal ostinati convey a feeling of almost unbearable psychic stress (Ex. 4-3). The movement ends with a non-cadence characteristic of Schoenberg at this time: two ostinati simply break off abruptly.

In "Premonitions," Schoenberg seeks emotional truth rather than conventional beauty. Its dense concentration enables him to pack great intensity of emotion into a small time-span. The extremes of orchestration, rapidly changing textures, and tendency toward open, centrifugal form all contribute to the movement's expressionism. "Premonitions" is highly unified in spite of its many changes of character. It illustrates Schoenberg's comment that "the work of art is like every other complete organism. It is so homogeneous that every detail reveals its truest, inmost essence. When one cuts into any part of the human body, the same thing comes out—blood."[41]

The second piece, "The Past," exemplifies Schoenberg's lyric gifts, both in its long-lined, arching opening melody and in its second theme, characterized by Webern as "unendlich zart" (infinitely tender).[42] This theme is presented in the soloistic, highly differentiated orchestration typical of Schoenberg during his expressionist period. The theme's multiple, intertwined statements at subtly differing speeds produce an unforgettably dreamlike effect (Ex. 4-4). Ostinato plays an important part in "The Past," just as in "Premonitions." Here, however, ostinati seem to express the immobility of a state of trance. "The Past" is the complete opposite of "Premonitions," and not only in its title: this movement embodies the hypnotically dreamy, introspective side of expressionism.

The third piece, to which Schoenberg gave the title "Colors: Summer Morning by a Lake," is the only movement of Op. 16 which is impressionist rather than expressionist. By means of reorchestrations of a slowly changing chord, which are intended to occur imperceptibly, Schoenberg's concept of *Klangfarbenmelodie* (melody of sound colors) is given material realization.

Ex. 4-3. Schoenberg, Op. 16/I, mm. 78–86. © 1952 by Henmar Press, Inc. Reprinted by permission of C. F. Peters Corporation.

Starting from the premise that pitch is a dimension of tone color, Schoenberg writes in *Harmonielehre,*

> if it is possible to produce structures, which we call melodies, from tone colors differentiated by pitch . . . then it must also be possible to set up such successions out of the sound colors of the other dimension (which we call simply sound

Ex. 4-4. Schoenberg, Op. 16/II, mm. 23–27. Reprinted by permission of C. F. Peters Corporation.

colors), whose relationship to one another operates with a kind of logic fully equivalent to that logic which we find in pitch melodies.[43]

The dense, constant harmonies of Op. 16/III, only occasionally relieved by fugitive melodic fragments, produce a brooding, almost oppressive effect.

The stasis of "Colors" is contradicted in the fourth piece, entitled *"Peripeteia"* (the Greek term for a sudden reversal of circumstances). The multiple changes of affect which occurred in the opening section of "Premonitions" become the governing principle of the entire piece in *"Peripeteia"*: violent and lyrical materials alternate throughout, and the final climax is reached partly by shortening the length of the alternating sections.

The last of the five pieces, "The Obbligato Recitative," is characterized by an "endless melody," which constantly flows from one instrument to another, thus providing another kind of realization of Schoenberg's *Klangfarbenmelodie* concept.[44] This piece summons up rhythmic patterns typical of the Viennese waltz: in spite of its often densely contrapuntal texture, it moves toward its two climaxes with compelling élan. The composer's 1912 diary tells us that here Schoenberg used "free form" in order to "express the inexpressible,"[45] thus providing an early glimpse of the longing for transcendence which became increasingly characteristic of him. In its avoidance of literal repetition, symmetrical phrasing, and thematic development, the "endless melody" shows a strong tendency toward athematic writing. By avoiding melodic repetition, Schoenberg hoped to equal in melodic freedom the harmonic freedom he had achieved in atonality, and thus to reflect the spontaneous, unstructured life of the psyche. The "endless melody" contains short elements which are repeated in varied form (notably the descending minor second and the rhythmic pattern $\frac{3}{8}$ ♪♪.♪♩ | with which it opens). Nevertheless, the repetition is treated in such a way that a melody of great plasticity and spontaneity results.

Just after completing *"Peripeteia"* and very close in time to the composition of "The Obbligato Recitative," Schoenberg wrote the third of the Three Piano Pieces, Op.11, one of his most radically expressionist works. In this often violent piece, the multisectional structure of *"Peripeteia"* and the athematic tendency of "The Obbligato Recitative" are combined and pushed to such extremes that the composer seems on the very brink of foregoing rational control of his creation. Here, more than in any other instrumental work, Schoenberg approaches a spontaneous, "free association" form. The music consists of a large number of short, highly contrasting sections, often not connected by transitional material (Ex. 4-5). (Schoenberg later wrote that he learned at this period "to link ideas together without the use of formal connectives, merely by juxtaposition."[46]) In this extreme instance, only his intuitive "feeling for form" saves the work from incoherence, as some of the musical materials of the earlier groups do recur in recognizable—though not exact—form.

For his next work, the monodrama *Erwartung* (Expectation), Schoenberg asked during the summer of 1909 for a very specific libretto from his younger acquaintance, the poet and recent medical graduate Marie Pappenheim.[47] With its use of free association, her libretto reflects a knowledge of psychoanalysis which she may well have gained from her older brother, Martin Pappenheim, who became a prominent Viennese psychiatrist, one of the few professors at the University of Vienna to teach Freud's theories and methods.[48] *Erwartung* thus marks an important point of contact—even if indirect—between Schoenberg's music and Freud's explorations of the unconscious. The Vienna premiere of Strauss's *Elektra* in March 1909 probably provided the final impetus for the composition of *Erwartung*, since both the central character in Hofmannsthal's drama and the Woman in *Erwartung* are dominated by a single psychological obsession throughout. But Pappenheim's libretto for *Erwartung* goes much further than Hofmannsthal's for *Elektra* in its stream of consciousness monologue, which often consists of fragmentary, disconnected phrases. Schoenberg made deletions in the libretto to get away from any literal plot in order to concentrate on the Woman's emotional states.

His marital difficulties had aroused his interest in feminine psychology, making him aware, in a most painful way, of his previous ignorance in that area: "The soul of my wife was so foreign to me that I could not arrive either at a truthful or a dishonest relation with her. . . . We never knew each other." *Erwartung*'s libretto relates to Mathilde's experience, since it consists exclusively of the ever-changing thoughts and emotions of the opera's single character, the Woman, as she searches the woods at night for her lover. Schoenberg wished "to portray how, in moments of fearful tension, the whole of one's life seems to flash again before one's eyes."[49] This desire for the utmost concentration in presenting conflicting emotions is typical of the expressionist urge toward simultaneity.[50]

As in Strindberg's expressionist plays, the central character of *Erwartung* is unnamed, in order to stress that she is a universal human type. Also, cer-

Ex. 4-5. Schoenberg, Op. 11/III, mm. 1–10. Used by permission of Belmont Music Publishers, Pacific Palisades, CA 90272.

tain crudities of subject matter, reminiscent of early expressionist theater (and particularly of Kokoschka's *Mörder, Hoffnung der Frauen*), appear, as, in the final scene, when the Woman caresses and kisses her dead lover. (Whether this actually happens, or whether the Woman only *imagines* finding her lover's corpse, is left ambiguous because of Schoenberg's deletions from the libretto.)

In a 1912 article, Webern aptly describes the music of *Erwartung*:

The score of this monodrama is an unheard-of event. In it, all traditional form is broken with; something new always follows according to the rapid change of expression. The same is true of the instrumentation: an uninterrupted succession of sounds never before heard. There is no measure of this score which fails to show a completely new sound-picture . . . and so this music flows onward . . . giving expression to the most hidden and slightest impulses of the emotions.[51]

More than any other work, *Erwartung* epitomizes expressionism in music. In its kaleidoscopic probing of the Woman's mind, the monodrama is the freest and most spontaneous of all Schoenberg's major works, the short score having been completed in just sixteen days.[52] Written at the borderline of conscious control, *Erwartung* is profoundly effective as a work of art.

A letter Schoenberg wrote to Busoni when he was about to begin the monodrama clarifies his musical aims:

> I strive for complete liberation from all forms, from all symbols of cohesion and of logic. Thus, away with "motivic working out." . . . And the results I wish for: no stylized and sterile protracted emotion. People are not like that. It is *impossible* for a person to have only *one* sensation at a time. One has *thousands* simultaneously. And these thousands can no more readily be added together than an apple and a pear. . . . And this variegation, this multifariousness, this *illogicality* which our senses demonstrate, the illogicality presented by their interactions, set forth by some rising rush of blood, by some reaction of the senses or the nerves, this I should like to have in my music. It should be an expression of feeling, as our feelings, which bring us in contact with our subconscious, really are, and no false child of feelings and "conscious logic."[53]

Schoenberg later wrote to Kandinsky that he sought nothing less than the "elimination of the conscious will in art."[54] One consequence of this is his avoidance of exact musical repetition in *Erwartung*.

Sudden changes of musical texture are frequent in Schoenberg's monodrama. There is often alternation between lyricism, as the text expresses the Woman's tender thoughts, and unexpected outbreaks portraying her returning anxiety. The highly broken texture accompanying the words "I am afraid" (Ex. 4-6) is used by Schoenberg in the opera to symbolize *angst*.

The almost completely syllabic setting follows the spoken inflections of the text, reflecting the influence of the rapid Straussian *parlando* of *Salome*, but with increased elements of hysterical distortion. Only occasionally (largely in the final, aria-like section of the work) does a more expansive and sustained vocal line appear. As in the orchestral pieces, Op. 16, Schoenberg makes considerable use of ostinato in *Erwartung*, to build excitement, to represent motion, or to portray various aspects of nature. In Ex. 4-7, for instance, the brief mention of "the crickets, with their love song," motivates a short-lived ostinato in celesta and tremolo strings (to be played near the bridge). As frequently happens in the score, an objective element (the ostinato) is layered with a subjective one (the clarinet melody which appears above, marked *sehr zart* [very tenderly]). Just as Schoenberg uses active ostinati to convey the idea of movement, he employs long-sustained chords to portray the idea of motionlessness. (See, for example, mm. 126–28, at the words

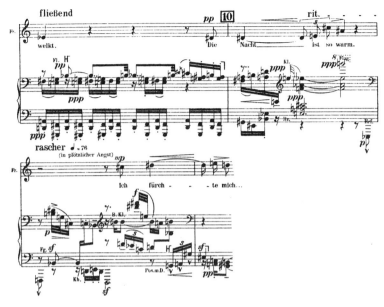

THE WOMAN. The night is so warm. (in sudden fear) I am afraid . . .

Ex. 4-6. Schoenberg, *Erwartung*, mm. 9–11. Used by permission of Belmont Music Publishers, Pacific Palisades, CA 90272.

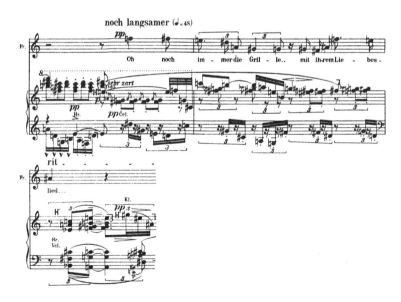

THE WOMAN. Oh, still the crickets . . . with their love song . . .

Ex. 4-7. Schoenberg, *Erwartung*, mm. 17–19.

"Auf der ganzen langen Strasse—nichts Lebendiges . . . und kein Laut" [On the whole, long street—nothing living and no sound].)

The text of *Erwartung* ends on an ambiguous and inconclusive note: "THE WOMAN (crying out in delight): Oh, you are there . . . (going in the direction of something) I searched. . . ." Rather than cadencing after these words, the music evaporates into thin air by means of the Straussian device of chromatic voices moving against each other at varying rates of speed (see Ex. 2-7). The centrifugal nature of this conclusion epitomizes the open-ended quality of the entire work (Ex. 4-8).

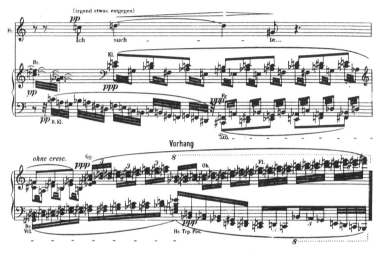

THE WOMAN. (going towards something) I searched . . .

Ex. 4-8. Schoenberg, *Erwartung*, mm. 425–26.

What are the elements which promote coherence within the extremely fluid context of *Erwartung*'s atonality and constant texture change? Schoenberg himself offered the most important clue to its structure when he acknowledged, in an article written toward the end of his life, the text's decisive influence on the works of his expressionist period:

> [After 1908] I discovered how to construct larger forms by following a text or poem. The differences in size and shape of its parts and the change in character and mood were mirrored in the size and shape of the composition, in its dynamics and tempo, figuration and accentuation, instrumentation and orchestration. Thus the parts were differentiated as clearly as they had formerly been by the tonal and structural functions of harmony.[55]

The key to understanding the music of *Erwartung* is Schoenberg's endlessly flexible and imaginative response to the emotions and images present in the text and the actions it implies.[56] The drama plays a decisive role in determining the form of *Erwartung*. It has six major climaxes, which subdivide the music;[57] three are followed by full pauses,[58] and another is used to end scene 3.[59] Most of them occur at important dramatic points, such as when the Woman experiences a powerful shock; for example, in scene 4, there is one when she discovers, or imagines that she discovers, that the body under the bench is her lover's. The lyric passages[60] in *Erwartung* also provide an element of recurrence. Like the major climaxes, they depend on the dramatic text. Their often more stable texture provides relief from the constant, restless changes of orchestration, dynamics, and rhythm so characteristic of Schoenberg's monodrama.

In spite of the extreme freedom of the music, leitmotifs and musical symbolism play an important role in *Erwartung*. Although both are used in an almost "subconscious" way, as an element in Schoenberg's spontaneous response to the text, they show his will toward concrete and specific communication with his audience. Perhaps the most important leitmotif is the rising figure D–F–C-sharp, motive a. in Ex. 4-9. The textual situations in which it appears indicate that it refers to the lover and his shocking fate. Two other three-note motives, b. and c., related to motive a. and to each other, are also important in the score.[61] Their lyrical character and the contexts in which they appear associate them with the love and tenderness of the Woman for her lover.

Ex. 4-9. Motives from Schoenberg, *Erwartung*.

Schoenberg's use of musical symbols in *Erwartung* not only provides an important link with musical tradition but also enhances the communicative power of the work. Certain key words and concepts, such as "Nacht" (night), "Mond" (moon), and "Blut" (blood), motivate a particular musical texture.[62] The use of the "night" symbol by Mahler, Schoenberg, and, later, Berg is a significant element of continuity between tonal and atonal music. In *Erwartung,* the concept of night consistently calls forth a low-pitched ostinato, which alternates between two notes (see Ex. 4-6, where the Woman's words "The night is so warm" are preceded by such an ostinato in harp and bassoon). The source of the musical symbol for "night" can be traced to the fourth movement of Mahler's Third Symphony (1895)—the work which had made such a deep impression on Schoenberg in 1904. Mahler later used the same type of ostinato in *Das Lied von der Erde* in connection with the idea of night, sleep, or death (see p. 53 and Ex. 3-10).

The mention of "moon" or "moonlight" in *Erwartung* usually motivates a tone color of harp combined with celesta. (See, for instance, mm. 16–17 and 318–19.) This symbolic tone color was also to be used later by Berg in *Wozzeck*.[63] The concept of flowing blood gives rise to a texture of undulating chromatic figures and string tremolos reminiscent of Strauss's treatment of the same word in *Elektra*.[64] Other, more traditional musical symbols, such as the two-note sighing figure and the related three-note sadness motive, also appear, saturating the texture at the point where a stage direction calls for the Woman to sob.[65]

In spite of a degree of sectionalism and the use of leitmotifs and musical symbolism, the score of *Erwartung* is remarkable above all for its probing of a character's mind. The Woman is actually psychoanalyzed through music.[66] Schoenberg accomplishes this tour de force by means of complete emotional involvement and a music unprecedented in its freedom and originality.

Five Pieces for Orchestra, Op. 16, the piano piece Op. 11, No. 3, and *Erwartung* together constitute the most extreme phase of Schoenberg's expressionism; his hypersensitive psychological state following his marital trauma of 1908 is reflected in the overriding concern with the expression of emotion (what Schoenberg called "inner nature") in these works. Their new harmonic language is atonal and totally chromatic. They show a strong tendency toward "athematic" writing, though this could more accurately be termed a loosening of thematic construction, since the theoretical aim of nonrepetition is never fully reached. Musical textures are extremely changeable in all the works; in Op. 16 and *Erwartung* this textural flexibility is carried out partly by a highly differentiated approach to orchestration. All three compositions show Schoenberg's remarkable originality in finding and quickly bringing to maturity an expressionist mode, a new musical language capable of portraying the human psyche with unheard-of freedom, audacity, and sensitivity.

During the next two years (1910–11), Schoenberg produced only two short compositions, perhaps because he was preoccupied with the writing of *Harmonielehre,* but also because he needed a respite after his great burst of creative activity in 1909. Continuing poverty also hampered his composing during these years, and the early death of Mahler (18 May 1911) depressed him. In August 1911 Schoenberg sustained another personal crisis when he had to flee to Bavaria and then to Berlin to escape the threats of a deranged neighbor.[67] The two works of 1910–11 (Three Pieces for Chamber Orchestra—the third is unfinished; and Six Little Piano Pieces, Op. 19) are the most aphoristic in his entire output and come the closest to total nonrepetition. At times they resemble Webern's music; Schoenberg later complained to Alma Mahler "how greatly he suffered under Webern's dangerous influence, and that he needed all his strength to evade it."[68]

By the end of June 1910, Schoenberg had completed the libretto for his second opera, *Die glückliche Hand* (The Lucky Hand).[69] This text is an attempt to come to terms, on a symbolic level, with the painful memory of his marital crisis and with the difficulties of his life as an artist. Although he had composed and orchestrated *Erwartung* in six weeks, it took Schoenberg over three years to finish the music of *Die glückliche Hand*.[70] The delay may well have been due to the conflict between the work's autobiographical, confessional nature and his wish to maintain his privacy (see the quotation from his 1912 diary, p. 6). While Schoenberg could easily have resolved this conflict in a purely instrumental work, the personal implications in a work with text by its composer were inescapable.

As the drama opens, the Man is consumed by the desire for earthly happiness, symbolized by a catlike monster crouching on his back. The Woman he loves leaves him for a well-dressed gentleman. In a workshop, the Man easily creates a beautiful artifact, but jealous fellow workers threaten him. His emotional and artistic problems converge in an overwhelming crescendo of inner anxiety. The drama ends unresolved: from above, the Woman pushes an immense boulder, which crushes him and is transformed into the consuming catlike monster of the opening.

The "lucky hand" of the title symbolizes both the Man's artistic successes (with it, he creates the diadem) and the disastrous failure of his emotional life (it deludes him into imagining he still possesses the Woman). The threatening artisans in the workshop may represent jealous fellow composers or, more probably, the music critics, most of whom attacked Schoenberg unmercifully at this period.

There are many links between Schoenberg's libretto and early expressionist drama. In its autobiographical nature and concentration on a single central character (the Woman and the Gentleman are only mimed roles), the libretto antedates the expressionist "Ich-Drama" (I-drama).[71] The sparsity of the Man's words anticipates the dramas of August Stramm. The form resembles the mirror construction and loosely related scenes of Strindberg's autobiographical play *To Damascus*. The Man and Strindberg's Unknown One share the faculty of second sight; both are successful artists but failures in their emotional lives.

The music of *Die glückliche Hand* is similar to *Erwartung* in its constant reflection, by means of extreme contrasts, of the changing emotional states of the characters. Schoenberg consistently employs particular tone colors for the opera's main characters. He uses his own instrument, the cello (and by extension, the other bass instruments of the orchestra), to represent the Man. The Woman is represented by the solo violin and the light and shimmering colors of flutes, piccolo, celesta, and harp (in the upper register). She is also associated with an actual leitmotif (see m. 36 of Ex. 4-10).

Like Schoenberg's other works of 1910–11, the music of *Die glückliche Hand* is extremely compressed. The Man's musical response to his first, supernatural awareness of the Woman's presence surpasses anything in *Erwartung* in its abbreviated intensity. At the instant of the Man's awareness (m. 37), the Woman's tone colors and leitmotif are replaced by an extremely wide-ranging phrase in the celli (Ex. 4-10). Another aspect of the work's compressed expressivity is an increased tendency toward the layering of disparate materials, giving rise to a typically expressionist simultaneity. Schoenberg later wrote that in *Die glückliche Hand* "a major drama is compressed into about twenty minutes, as if photographed with a quick-motion apparatus."[72] The complete avoidance of musical transitions between scenes and episodes gives the work an almost cinematic quality, and we know that Schoenberg welcomed the idea of a possible film of *Die glückliche Hand*.[73]

Ex. 4-10. Schoenberg, *Die glückliche Hand*, mm. 35–39. Used by permission of Belmont Music Publishers, Pacific Palisades, CA 90272.

The 21 melodramas of *Pierrot lunaire* were commissioned by the actress Albertine Zehme. They were completed in 1912, when Schoenberg was still striving to finish *Die glückliche Hand*. *Pierrot lunaire* constitutes the most famous work of Schoenberg's expressionist period. The formally strict texts were chosen by Zehme (they were written in French by Albert Guiraud and translated into German by Otto Erich Hartleben) and reflect the idea of art-for-art's-sake—an attitude antithetical to expressionism.[74] Schoenberg responded to their variety of stimuli both as an expressionist and as an increasingly conscious constructivist.

Schoenberg had first used *Sprechgesang* (speech-song, with exact rhythm and pitch inflection notated) in *Gurre-Lieder* (1900; completed in 1911). In *Pierrot* the treatment is often distorted and hyperemotional. Although this work was a commission, Schoenberg continued to be driven to create by inner necessity; according to his 1912 diary, the sounds of the ninth melodrama, "Prayer to Pierrot," were a "bestially direct expression of sensual and spiritual impulses—almost as if everything were directly transmitted."[75] Schoenberg's settings of the gruesome texts of *Pierrot*'s central section (for example, "Red Mass," No. 11, and "The Crosses," No. 14) are formally free and emotionally violent. Some of the other melodramas (such as "Parody," No. 17, and "The Moonfleck," No. 18) use strict contrapuntal devices, which foreshadow Schoenberg's later development of twelve-tone technique.

The last completed works of Schoenberg's expressionist period are the Four Orchestral Songs, Op. 22 (1913–16). The second and third songs are settings of religious poems by Rilke; Schoenberg's choice of these texts reflects his increasing turn to spirituality during the war years:[76]

> When one's been used . . . to clearing away all obstacles . . . by means of one immense intellectual effort . . . for a man for whom ideas have been everything [the war situation] means nothing less than the total collapse of things, unless he has come to find support, in ever increasing measure, in the belief in something higher, beyond . . . what I mean is—even without any organizational fetters— religion. This was my one and only support during these years—here let this be said for the first time.[77]

Schoenberg's struggle for spirituality is traceable as far back as his settings of C. F. Meyer's "Friede auf Erden" in 1907 and George's "Litanei" in 1908. It had become even more evident in the text he wrote in 1910 for the choruses which address the Man in *Die glückliche Hand:* "Once again you give yourself up to the sirens of your thoughts, thoughts that roam the cosmos, that are unworldly, [yet you] thirst for worldly fulfillment."[78]

Between 1911 and 1915, Schoenberg was preoccupied with writing a large, spiritually oriented work combining heterogeneous texts. Perhaps his model was Mahler's Eighth Symphony, which had been premiered with great success in 1910. He seems to have floundered in his search for texts and his effort to find an appropriate form. In his spiritual quest, he was much influenced by Balzac's religious novel, *Séraphîta* (1835), which is a fictional popularization of the ideas of Emanuel Swedenborg (1688–1772). (The ideas in *Séraphîta* preoccupied Berg and Webern as well: Webern was reading the book in 1910, and in 1912 Berg planned to end a "large symphonic movement" with the singing of words from the novel.[79])

Schoenberg's personal friendship with Kandinsky, which began in 1911, probably also contributed to his increasing interest in spiritual matters. As Kandinsky's *Concerning the Spiritual in Art* attests, the artist was well acquainted with theosophical and, particularly, anthroposophical ideas.[80] Theosophical concepts of reincarnation and Karma (correcting mistakes and rising toward perfection in a series of lives) became part of Schoenberg's thinking.

Schoenberg considered setting either Strindberg's *Jacob Wrestling* or a section of Balzac's *Séraphîta*,[81] or even combining the two,[82] but he rejected these ideas and asked the poet Richard Dehmel to write a text for an "oratorio" he was planning. Its content was to show how

> modern man, having passed through materialism, socialism and anarchy, and, despite having been an atheist, still having in him some residue of ancient faith (in the form of superstition), wrestles with God . . . and finally succeeds in finding God and becoming religious . . . learning to pray![83]

Dehmel refused to write a text to order for Schoenberg and sent instead his *Schöpfungsfeier* (Celebration of Creation). In 1912–14, Schoenberg planned to incorporate portions of Dehmel's poem into a large-scale "Symphony for soloists, mixed chorus and orchestra," which was also to use texts by the Indian mystical poet Rabindranath Tagore, from the Bible, and by Schoenberg himself.[84] In his plan for the symphony, Schoenberg gave the final movement the heading "The Faith of the 'disillusioned one,' " and between 18 January 1915 and 26 May 1917, he wrote his own text for it, entitled *Die Jakobsleiter* (Jacob's Ladder).[85] He later abandoned the idea of a symphony and came to conceive of *Die Jakobsleiter* as a large independent oratorio in two parts. (A portrait of the composer by Egon Schiele depicts Schoenberg's deep, penetrating gaze and strained demeanor during this wartime period. See Ill. 4-3.)

The text of *Die Jakobsleiter* is an important document in Schoenberg's spiritual development. His earlier highly subjective, psychological expression-

Ill. 4-3. Egon Schiele, *Portrait of the Composer Arnold Schoenberg*, 1917. Gouache, watercolor and black crayon, 45.7 x 29.2 cm. Private collection, courtesy Galerie St. Etienne, New York.

ism is largely replaced by a messianic, almost didactic tone, showing Schoenberg's desire to influence the thinking as well as the emotions of his fellow men. (Expressionist drama as a whole underwent a similar development during the same years; *Die Jakobsleiter* has been compared to the "proclamation drama" of the expressionists' second decade.[86])

After the opening chorus, which reflects human experience in all its emotional variety, the archangel Gabriel calls on individuals who believe that they have come nearer to salvation by their actions. (Here Schoenberg draws on the Eastern idea of Karma, as these individuals are on various steps of the ladder toward perfection.) All of them are found wanting by Gabriel except the Chosen One, who seems to represent Schoenberg himself, in his role as martyr of the New Art and prophet of a New Humanity. Announced by Gabriel, the Chosen One speaks:

> I should not come nearer, for I lose thereby.
> But I must, it seems, go into the thick of things,
> although my Word remains uncomprehended.[87]

The idea of reincarnation is expressed as the Dying One (given to a woman's voice) ascends to heaven, and then, like Indra's Daughter in Strindberg's *A Dream Play,* descends again to earth to begin a new life. The ascension episode is carried over from Schoenberg's earlier plan to adapt Balzac's *Séraphîta.*

In the second half of the oratorio text, which Schoenberg did not set to music, both God and Gabriel gave advice to humanity. Schoenberg again expresses the idea of the material versus the spiritual, but to this concept is now added that of positive religion: "Learn to pray: for he who prays has become one with God."[88] The text ends with the combined prayers of the "main chorus," the "chorus from above," and the " chorus from below."

Although Schoenberg's stylistic concept in the music of *Die Jakobsleiter* is broadened to include both traditional elements of harmony and form and strong intimations of twelve-tone technique, the work is essentially expressionist. First and foremost, it is the product of a strong inner necessity, although its creation arises out of a spiritual rather than a psychological crisis. Writing and composing during World War I, Schoenberg saw nothing less than the end of culture and civilization as he knew them[89]—the "total collapse of things." Only in the metaphysical realm could hope be found.

Schoenberg began writing the music of *Die Jakobsleiter* in June 1917 and worked on it sporadically until 1922, but it was destined to remain incomplete.[90] Exterior circumstances were partly responsible: Schoenberg was called into the army and served from 19 September to 7 December 1917.[91] Following his release, the chaos attending the collapse of the Austro-Hungarian war effort was scarcely conducive to composition, and Schoenberg soon became absorbed in his Society for Private Musical Performances, founded in November 1918. All the same, inner factors must also be considered in

Schoenberg's failure to complete *Die Jakobsleiter*. The work was in a sense superseded by his rapid development of twelve-tone technique, and the depiction of static scenes of bliss at the end of the text may have presented a problem in light of his evolving musical style.

Instead of constantly changing texture and character, as in *Erwartung*, the music of *Die Jakobsleiter* falls into much bigger sections. However, it still expresses the general emotion of the text with undiminished vehemence. The implicit aim of reaching and influencing humanity is reflected in the extensive use of *Sprechgesang*, as being more comprehensible than singing. Schoenberg's harmonic language is broadened to include many triads, sometimes used singly, but more often layered to produce complex dissonances. To unify the sprawling work, Schoenberg makes extensive use of a six-note motive whose tones may be reordered and used vertically; the use of such a motive is one of the early steps toward twelve-tone technique.[92]

In spite of the many intellectual concepts expressed in the text, the music is urgently emotional from the opening of the orchestral introduction, where an increasing density of overlapping ostinati leads quickly to a climax (m. 11). The massive opening chorus is notable for its expressionist simultaneity: at certain points, three texts of contrasting emotional content are heard at the same time (as at mm. 104–24).

By basing the main themes on a six-note unordered set, Schoenberg provides a certain degree of unity in this work, but the music of *Die Jakobsleiter* by no means shares the constructivist rationalism of his early twelve-tone compositions. Even the evolving twelve-tone method has its spiritual side, as Schoenberg confirms in a late essay, where he likens the perception of a tone row (in no matter what form) to "Swedenborg's heaven (described in Balzac's *Séraphîta*)," where "there is no absolute down, no right or left, backward or forward."[93]

In keeping with the aim of the work to instruct mankind, Schoenberg's music becomes at times a powerful means of artistic or social criticism. One telling instance occurs in the aria of One Who Is Called. At the words "I have unhesitatingly subordinated meaning to form," there is an unmistakably Straussian triadic passage (mm. 203–206). Here Schoenberg criticizes Strauss's retreat from musical innovation in *Der Rosenkavalier*. Earlier, in the opening chorus, the Gently Yielding Ones, who "take things as they come," are joined by the whole chorus in the words "Oh, but how nicely one can live in filth." (Schoenberg marks the passage "very 'lyrical,' beautifully sung.") With the obvious introduction of waltz rhythms in this episode (see mm. 138–41), Schoenberg is clearly ridiculing the complacency of the Viennese, as Karl Kraus does in his play *Die letzten Tage der Menschheit* (The Last Days of Humanity), written about the same time.[94]

It is, however, the transcendental portions of the work which are most musically memorable. The first of these (mm. 332–59) begins as Gabriel introduces the Chosen One. *Sprechgesang* is replaced by singing, and the wordless humming of the chorus forms a background reminiscent of the string harmonies accompanying the recitatives of Jesus in Bach's St. Matthew Passion. The choral parts are saturated with parallel thirds.

The last of the individuals to appear is the Dying One, which is assigned to the unusual timbre of a high woman's voice performing the *Sprechgesang* in a deep range. Like Wagner's Kundry, the Dying One has lived "a thousand lives." As the soul begins to take flight, swooping lines with enormous skips create a remarkably fluid texture (mm. 557–630). From this point on, the music of *Die Jakobsleiter* becomes an unparalleled expression of mystical feelings. At m. 565 the Dying One, now identified as the Soul, wordlessly sings a version of the six-note row in a magnificently arching and ethereal form. She is supported by a chorus of high women's voices, *pppp*, and by "flying" figures in the orchestra (Ex. 4-11).

This kind of texture prevails until the "Great Symphonic Interlude" begins, at m. 602. The uncompleted interlude, which represents the dying Soul's

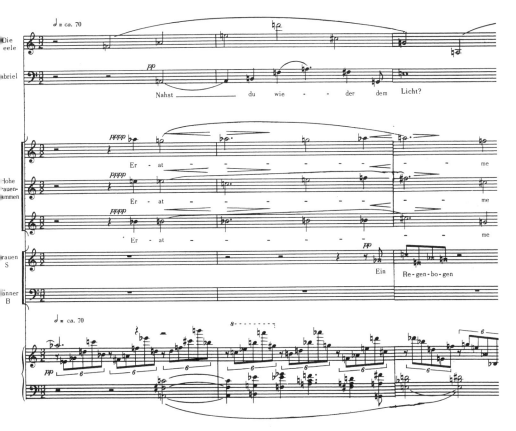

GABRIEL. Do you approach the light once more?

Ex. 4-11. Schoenberg, *Die Jakobsleiter*, mm. 565–67. Used by permission of Belmont Music Publishers, Pacific Palisades, CA 90272.

ascent to heaven and union with God before its descent to earth to begin a new life, is the most extraordinary manifestation of Schoenberg's mystical transcendentalism. To portray the meeting of higher and lower realms of existence, the composer employs four distant orchestral groups, two of which are to be placed higher than the main body of performers. At certain points, he specifies that the distant orchestras are not to enter on particular beats, "but should be brought in in fluctuating rhythm outside of the meter."[95] His aim here is to represent the "dissolution of matter and the liberation of the spirit" (Ex. 4-12).[96] The dramatic situation in which this device occurs, its concept of layering, and the use of lines to indicate approximate points of entry and correspondence are reminiscent of the last movement of Mahler's Second Symphony (see p. 48 and Ex. 3-4). This is true in spite of important differences, both theological (resurrection in Mahler versus reincarnation in Schoenberg) and musical (tonality in the earlier composer, atonality in the later).

Ex. 4-12. Schoenberg, *Die Jakobsleiter,* mm. 643–44.

Although Schoenberg did not intend to end *Die Jakobsleiter* at the point where it breaks off, he could hardly have provided a more appropriate finish for his oratorio (and for his expressionist period as a whole). The final passage is an ethereal, imitative trio between two wordless soprano voices (one in the distance, one above) and solo violin, accompanied by a high, wordless female chorus. As the 700-measure fragment of *Die Jakobsleiter* ends, only the two soprano soloists remain, representing the dying Soul and its reincarnation. Truly, Schoenberg has here "expressed the inexpressible" (Ex. 4-13). In his 1912 lecture on Mahler, Schoenberg wrote: "There is only one content, which all great men wish to express: the longing of mankind for its future form, for an immortal soul, for dissolution into the universe—the longing of this soul for its God."[97] These words could be applied even more appropriately to the Schoenberg of *Die Jakobsleiter*.

Ex. 4-13. Schoenberg, *Die Jakobsleiter*, mm. 697–700.

With this oratorio, Schoenberg came to the end of the body of expressionist works he began in 1908. Although he created a musical language which drew on Wagner, Strauss, and Mahler, these compositions were radically new in melody, harmony, form, and orchestration. The inherent conflict between Schoenberg's strong emotional intuition and his powerful musical intellect was resolved largely in favor of emotion and instinct. Schoenberg was able to probe his creative subconscious and produce a series of works unequaled in the freedom with which the human psyche is portrayed in sound. Although, by its very nature, this expressionism, which stretched music to the farthest limits of coherence, could not be long sustained by Schoenberg (or, indeed, by any other composer), its emergence inaugurated a new era in music as important as the "new music" of 1600.

Select Bibliography

Arnold Schönberg Gedankausstellung 1974. Ed. Ernst Hilmar. Vienna: Universal, 1974.
Arnold Schönberg Gesammelte Schriften. Ed. Ivan Vojtech. Frankfurt: Fischer, 1976.
Auner, Joseph. "Schoenberg's Aesthetic Transformations and the Evolution of Form in *Die glückliche Hand.*" *Journal of the Arnold Schoenberg Institute* 12/2 (November 1989): 103.
Beaumont, Antony, trans. and ed. *Ferruccio Busoni: Selected Letters.* London and Boston: Faber, 1987.
Berg, Alban, et al. *Arnold Schönberg.* Munich: Piper, 1912.
The Berg-Schoenberg Correspondence: Selected Letters. Ed. Juliane Brand, Christopher Hailey, and Donald Harris. New York and London: Norton, 1987.
Boretz, Benjamin, and Cone, Edward T., eds. *Perspectives of Schoenberg and Stravinsky.* Rev. ed. New York: Norton, 1972.

Christensen, Jean M. "Arnold Schoenberg's Oratorio 'Die Jakobsleiter.'" Ph.D. diss., UCLA, 1979. 2 vols.

Crawford, John C. "The Relationship of Text and Music in the Vocal Works of Schoenberg, 1908–24. Ph.D. diss. , Harvard University, 1963.

———. *"Die glückliche Hand:* Schoenberg's *Gesamtkunstwerk. Musical Quarterly* 60/4 (October 1974): 583.

———. *"Die glückliche Hand:* Further Notes." *Journal of the Arnold Schoenberg Institute* 4/1 (June 1980): 68.

Dümling, Albrecht. *Die fremden Klänge der hängenden Gärten: Die öffentliche Einsamkeit am Beispiel von Arnold Schönberg und Stefan George.* Munich: Kindler, 1981.

Journal of the Arnold Schoenberg Institute. Los Angeles, 1976–.

Kallir, Jane. *Arnold Schoenberg's Vienna.* New York: Galerie St. Etienne/Rizzoli, 1984.

Maegaard, Jan. *Studien zur Entwicklung des dodekaphonen Satzes bei Arnold Schoenberg.* 2 vols. Copenhagen: Hansen, 1972.

Mauser, Siegfried. *Das expressionistische Musiktheater der Wiener Schule.* Regensberg: Bosse, 1982.

Meyerowitz, Jan. *Arnold Schönberg.* Berlin: Colloquium, 1967.

Neighbour, Oliver. "Schoenberg." In *The New Grove Second Viennese School.* New York and London: Norton, 1983. Pp. 1–85.

Payne, Anthony. "Schoenberg's *Jacob's Ladder." Tempo* 75 (Winter 1965–66): 21.

Reich, Willi. *Arnold Schoenberg: A Critical Biography.* Trans. Leo Black. New York: Praeger, 1971.

Rosen, Charles. *Arnold Schoenberg.* New York: Viking, 1975.

Rufer, Josef. *The Works of Arnold Schoenberg.* Trans. Dika Newlin. London: Faber, 1962.

Schönberg, Arnold. *Harmonielehre.* Leipzig and Vienna: Universal, 1911.

———. *Berliner Tagebuch.* Ed. Josef Rufer. Frankfurt: Propyläen, 1974.

———. *Style and Idea.* Ed. Leonard Stein. Trans. Leo Black. Berkeley: University of California Press, 1984.

Schorske, Carl E. *Fin-de-siècle Vienna: Politics and Culture.* New York: Knopf, 1980.

Smith, Joan Allen. *Schoenberg and His Circle: A Viennese Portrait.* New York: Schirmer Books, 1986.

Stefan, Paul. *Das Grab in Wien: Eine Chronik 1903–11.* Berlin: Reiss, 1913.

Stein, Erwin, ed. *Arnold Schoenberg Letters.* Trans. Eithne Wilkins and Ernst Kaiser. Berkeley: University of California Press, 1987.

Stephan, Rudolf, ed. *Bericht über den 1. Kongress der Internationalen Schönberg-Gesellschaft, 1974.* Vienna: Lafite, 1978.

———. *Bericht über den 2. Kongress der Internationalen Schönberg-Gesellschaft, 1984.* Vienna: Lafite, 1986.

Stuckenschmidt, H. H. *Schoenberg: His Life, World and Work.* Trans. Humphrey Searle. New York: Schirmer Books, 1978.

Wellesz, Egon. *Arnold Schoenberg.* Trans. W. H. Kerridge. London: Dent, 1925.

Wörner, Karl H. *Die Musik in der Geistesgeschichte: Studien zur Situation der Jahre um 1910.* Bonn: Bouvier, 1970.

CHAPTER FIVE

Anton Webern

I only want to express, all my life, without interruption, that which fills my soul. I do not want
anything else.

Anton Webern (1910)

No composer was closer to Schoenberg than Anton Webern (1883–1945) in the expressionist period before and during World War I. Naturally, there are strong reverberations from Schoenberg's ideas in Webern's work, but Webern's own expressive needs were so compulsive, his style so unique, that, as Adorno aptly put it, "Webern pursues to its furthest extreme the subjectivism which Schoenberg first released."[1] This fact is difficult to appreciate fully. Webern encountered great resistance getting his music published, and he expunged many expressionist characteristics when his works finally began to appear in the 1920s, for by then the climate of musical thought had altered to embrace the "new objectivity." However, unpublished manuscripts (among them presentation copies to Schoenberg) show Webern's full intent in his expressionist period when these works were written. His correspondence, particularly with Berg and Schoenberg, allows glimpses of the intense subjectivity that engendered his works in the decade 1908–18.

Webern's character in his years of early maturity was compulsive in the extreme, and often severely self-defeating. While his most profound goal was to create, his psychological dependence on and continuing desire to be near Schoenberg often meant sacrificing this goal. This, along with his difficulties facing the realities of making a living, resulted in severe depressions and psychosomatic illness. Personal crises prompted his compositions in this period. The years 1911–13, his most difficult period of nervous breakdown and psychoanalysis, were particularly fruitful in expressionist works.

In July 1912, Webern was caught in a theater position he loathed. He was in deepest despair about his inability to compose, and he was lamenting the loss of the Carinthian family estate, where he had found the isolation, serenity, and flood of childhood memories which enabled him to compose. In the midst of his distress he wrote a startling confession to Berg: the force behind the George Songs (composed in 1908–1909; published in 1921 and 1923 as Opp. 3 and 4), the Five Movements for String Quartet (1909; published in 1922 as Op. 5), the Six Pieces for Orchestra (1909; published in 1961 as Op. 6), and the quartet and orchestra pieces he had written in 1911 (published in Opp. 9 [1924] and 10 [1923]) was his persistent and increasing grief over the death of his mother in 1906, when he was 23 and still a student of Schoenberg's in Vienna.[2] On the other hand, revelations in letters to Berg and Schoenberg about the composition of the Rilke Orchestral Songs of 1910 (published in 1926 as Op. 8), and perhaps also the Violin Pieces written the same year (published in 1922 as Op. 7), indicate that these works may have stemmed from Webern's personal crisis when his cousin Wilhelmine, whom he had loved since 1905, conceived their first child.[3] Their marriage, forbidden by the Catholic Church and disapproved of by both families, took place in a civil ceremony on 22 February 1911, six weeks before the birth of the child.

"Tell me, how do you approach composing?" Webern wrote to Berg in his confessional letter of 12 July 1912. "With me it is thus: an experience dwells in me so long, until music results, with a very definite relationship to this experience. Often right down to details."[4] In these very details, during Webern's expressionist period, one can see the growth of a personal symbolic language, derived from ideas Webern received from Mahler at their first meeting, in 1905. Since Webern's tragic death in 1945, interest in the constructivist aspect of his music has disregarded his compulsive, intuitive, and extremely emotive expressive desires, which continued as a part of his character even after Webern had turned, in 1922, to the technique of strict canon and subsequently to the "law" (as he called it) of the twelve-tone method.

Webern's expressionist period begins, as does Schoenberg's, with settings of texts by Stefan George (1908–1909), reaches an extreme point in the quartet and orchestral works of 1911–13, tends toward abstraction in the Georg Trakl settings (1917–21) and the sacred songs of Op. 15 (1917–22), and ends when Webern returns to a preoccupation with strictest canonic principles in the songs on Latin religious texts of Op. 16 (1924). The expressive immediacy of text is of utmost necessity to his meaning in this period. In his instrumental music Webern reduced and crystallized the new language and gesture he found in his songs. This process led (in Opp. 5 and 9 for string quartet, Op. 7 for violin and piano, Op. 10 for orchestra, and Op. 11 for cello and piano [1914]) to pieces of the most extreme brevity, which in itself seemed to alarm him . Webern continually attempted to write longer, fuller pieces and to ward off the implications of his tendency toward abstraction.[5] His expressionist attitude is typified in a remark to Schoenberg in 1910: "Tell me, can one at all denote thinking and feeling as things entirely separable? I cannot imagine a sublime intellect without the ardor of emotion."[6] In 1912 he wrote to Schoenberg, "Music is probably philosophy itself."[7]

In secondary school Webern showed no particular ability in mathematics and physics. But his precise, meticulous personality thrilled with profound and perpetual wonder at the perfect structures he found in nature, particularly in wildflowers. Webern's father, Carl, remembered in his obituary as "a noble, selfless man, an old Austrian official of iron industry,"[8] achieved a distinguished governmental career in mining and agriculture, which necessitated many changes of residence for his young family. Although the family visited the Preglhof (a 500-acre family estate east of Klagenfurt in Carinthia) only for Easter and the summer months, this peaceful farm became Anton's most important home. Webern's mother was musical and well schooled in piano. She gave her son his first piano lessons and encouraged his rapidly expanding musical interests, while his father did not understand the music profession and remained skeptical of Anton's musical gifts. Nevertheless, during his school years in Klagenfurt Webern studied piano and theory and played the cello in a local orchestra. In 1904 he won permission from his parents to study musicology at the University of Vienna, in spite of his father's desire that he study botany and take on management of the Preglhof.[9]

The conflicts in Webern's situation as the only son and heir to the estate of an ennobled family increased after his mother's death in 1906. By then his father had reached the pinnacle of his career as chief of the Department of Mining in the empire's Ministry of Agriculture, but his declining health resulted in his retirement in 1909. From this time on it was necessary that Webern support himself by coaching and conducting operettas in provincial opera houses. In such situations he felt "like a criminal even collaborating in this hell-hole of mankind."[10] (Although he was not trained as a conductor, from early in his career he harbored high ambitions to conduct masterworks.) Between 1908 and 1918—the year Webern withdrew from theater work to live near Schoenberg in Mödling—he obtained eight different theater positions, sometimes fleeing his tasks in abhorrence almost immediately, and never remaining longer than eight months. During periods of unemployment he was sustained by a monthly allowance from his father, given with dire warnings about the future instead of the total approval and acceptance he had earlier received from his mother.

Webern's expressionist outlook was shaped by his years (1904–1908) as Schoenberg's pupil and by Schoenberg's extraordinarily individualistic approach to teaching at that time. In a 1912 article Webern described how Schoenberg "demands above all . . . that [his pupils'] work should spring from a need to express themselves," and to that end "He pursues with greatest energy every trace of the personality of his pupils, attempts to deepen it. . . . [This is] an education that teaches one to find the utmost in oneself." For ultimately, Schoenberg taught, a teacher cannot give a pupil the most important thing—"the courage and the strength of attitude, so that everything he looks at becomes extraordinary as a result of the way he looks at it."[11]

Webern's further testimony about Schoenberg as a composer gives glimpses into the subjective attitudes shared in Schoenberg's intimate circle in those years:

> The experiences of his heart become tones. Schoenberg's relationship to art is rooted exclusively in expressive necessity. His emotion is of flaming ardor; it creates completely new values of expression, and therefore needs new means of expression. Content and form are not to be separated.[12]

In 1911 Schoenberg wrote in his *Harmonielehre* that "compulsion exerted by my expressive needs" shaped his "feeling for form."[13] The expressive compulsion Webern absorbed from Schoenberg reached beyond music to all areas of his life. Particularly in his expressionist years the unity of life and art, content and form, were matters of the greatest idealism and integrity to him. Schoenberg called Webern "the spiritual leader" among his pupils; "a very Hotspur in his principles, a real fighter, a friend whose faithfulness can never be surpassed, a real genius as a composer."[14] Erwin Stein, with Webern one of the earliest Schoenberg pupils, remembered Webern's uncompromising character and tenacity in pursuing his musical ideals. "Ecstasy was his natural state of mind," wrote Stein; his compositions should be understood as "musical visions."[15] Eugene Lehner, violist of the Kolisch Quartet, recalled Webern's spending twenty minutes of rehearsal describing a single pause, with such a transfigured face of burning, breathless excitement, such an incredible demand for accuracy and exactness, that no performer took this unique approach less than seriously.[16] Oskar Kokoschka, for whom Webern expressed "gigantic sympathy,"[17] painted Webern in 1914 as a wild-haired radical, emphasizing his high forehead and somewhat melancholy expression. Drawings in 1917 and 1918 by Egon Schiele show great intensity in Webern's eyes and brow and the tight precision of his mouth (see Ills. 5-1 and 5-2).

Webern held broad intellectual interests and attitudes. His university doctorate encompassed art history as well as musicology. He was deeply interested in philosophical studies. His letters from the expressionist period chronicle his excited reading of the advanced or influential thinkers of his time, such as Strindberg (from 1908, when Webern began collecting his works), Maeterlinck, Rilke, Weininger, Kraus, Altenberg, Dehmel, Balzac, Bergson, Baudelaire (a gift from Berg in 1911), Swedenborg, Wedekind, Trakl, and Goethe. Webern's approach to these authors was often avid to an extreme, and his letters show close connections between his reading and his composing.

Webern may have confided his most passionate interests only to a select few, for contradictions abound in his aquaintances' reports of his intellectual attitudes. Hans Swarowsky, who studied with both Schoenberg and Webern, described Webern as "wonderfully naive" and "completely unintellectual."[18]

Ill. 5-1. Oskar Kokoschka, *Portrait of Anton von Webern*, 1914. Oil on canvas, 63.3 x 48.2 cm. Private collection, courtesy Galerie St. Etienne, New York.

Ill. 5-2. Egon Schiele, *Portrait of Anton von Webern*, 1917. Charcoal, 47 x 29 cm. Private collection, courtesy Galerie St. Etienne, New York.

Felix Greissle, Schoenberg's son-in-law, recalling Webern's mountain dialect and his peasantlike, slow movements and thought, said Webern was never "Viennese."[19] Nevertheless, as he had lived intermittently in the city since 1902, Webern's attitudes were strongly conditioned by many of the Viennese influences we recognize in Schoenberg's development. Karl Kraus's and Adolf Loos's desire to eliminate all ornamental or extraneous detail for the sake of truth in art was pursued further by Webern than by Schoenberg. Peter Altenberg's pithy, deeply felt prose poems inspired Webern to such an extent that he called himself "the Altenberg of Music."[20] He was very proud of the genius produced in Austria, in spite of recognizing that its philistinism and provincialism repeatedly defied genius.

Of all the influential figures in his background, none inspired Webern more than Gustav Mahler. Swarowsky says that Mahler was the real father-figure to whom Webern's heart was given and whose loss was a lasting sorrow.[21] Webern often wrote about Mahler in letters to his closest confidants. At the time of Mahler's death he wrote to Schoenberg that for years he had thought of Mahler every day.[22] He had a mystical feeling about Mahler's music. In 1913 Webern wrote to Schoenberg " My most decided impression of [Mahler's Fourth Symphony], as with all works of such elevated nature, is: this is dictated. And I could die of love and reverence for him who is so endowed by a higher grace."[23]

Webern kept a diary of the most important events in his life. On 4 February 1905 he wrote in his "beloved book" of the first time he was "in the immediate influence of a great personality," after hearing a Vienna *Lieder-abend* which included Mahler's *Wunderhorn-*, *Kindertoten-*, and *Rückert Lieder*. Almost every word Mahler spoke at the reception after the concert remained in Webern's memory. Indeed, what was noted in his diary entry remained uppermost in his composing thereafter, particularly Mahler's notion that the model in composition should be nature:

> Just as in [nature] everything developed out of the primal cell—through plants, animals and humans up to God, the highest being—so also in music a large tone structure should develop out of a single motive in which the kernel of everything which will one day come into being is contained.*

Mahler further remarked that "variation is the most important factor of musical work," an idea of crucial importance to the Viennese School. His lyricism appealed to Webern, who felt himself to be, above all else, a lyrical composer.[24]

In 1906 Webern distinguished himself with his doctoral dissertation in musicology, an introduction to and edition of Heinrich Isaac's *Choralis Constantinus II*. He was particularly drawn to the Netherlander's "deeply personal" expressivity and investigated Isaac's bold deviations from conventional early sixteenth-century contrapuntal practice to achieve this. Webern pointed out freely handled dissonances, revealed in duos "of the greatest inwardness," and found wonderful an effect when, after a pause, the soprano enters on a high pitch and sweeps downward, "as from heaven"—an effect he himself carried to utmost extremes in his own vocal compositions.[25]

The Stefan George settings of 1908–1909 show Webern's developing atonal style. Webern was following Schoenberg's lead in the choice of poet in this case (Schoenberg's Second String Quartet had been premiered in December 1908; his *Book of the Hanging Gardens* was being composed at the same time that Webern was writing his George songs), but the meaning Webern extracts from the George texts is entirely different from Schoenberg's. With one exception, the texts of Opp. 3 and 4 (as they are published) are poems of mourning. Many of them are chosen from *The Seventh Ring*, published by George in 1907, after his own personal crisis following the death of a gifted teen-aged poet he deeply admired. Webern converts these statements of extreme grief and tender memories of earlier happiness into a memorial to his own mother. His musical language springs from the emotional essence of the poems rather than from the formal rhyme and meter George uses.

In his Op. 3, Webern sets George's entire cycle except for the last poem, which ends: "You do not care"; Webern evidently could not associate these

---

* Goethe's *Farbenlehre*, in which this idea of the primal cell originates, became (after the outbreak of World War I) a sort of bible for Webern, as he continued his own quest for the essential musical unity in diversity which Mahler was seeking.

words with the memory of his mother. The first song, "Dies ist ein Lied für dich allein," is the most intimate of all:

This is a song for you alone:
Of childish folly,
Of pious tears . . .
Through morning gardens it rings
Lightly lilting.
Only to you
Would it seem to be
A touching song.[26]

The vocal melody is reduced to short phrases, separated by rests and ritards. Within each phrase Webern creates an expressively flexible speech-rhythm by the gentle interpolation of triplets and dotted rhythms characteristic of his vocal writing in this period.[27] The vocal range is relatively limited, the dynamics consistently quiet. The range of emotion is so subdued that the middle phrase of the song, "Through morning gardens it rings/ Lightly lilting" seems an ecstatic, floating outburst (Ex. 5-1). The sixths in the piano, which introduce this moment, evoke tenderest warmth, as do the thirds accompanying the voice. Thirds and sixths—the intervals most reminiscent of tonality—when traced in Webern's subsequent expressionist works, gain a symbolic meaning most probably connected with the memory of his mother's love.

Ex. 5-1. Webern, Op. 3/I, "Dies ist ein Lied," mm. 5–7. Copyright 1921 by Universal Edition; copyright renewed.

"Dies ist ein Lied" shows the expressive concentration of Webern's atonal style. The formal structure (ABA) is almost hidden, as are underlying tonal concepts.[28] The musical line is frequently broken by rests, and hints of contrapuntal imitation invest melodic fragments with extra meaning. Single chords, endowed by duration and dynamics with a sense of repose, lose their sense of dissonance, while it is the consonant harmonies—thirds and sixths—which move restlessly. Above all, Webern's reductive tendency is seen in this song. It has twelve measures—36 beats. At the metronome marking of 60 quarter notes per minute, the song would last about half a minute. But Webern's rubato technique, characterized here by the use of ritard and fermata, seems intended to draw out the time between phrases, giving each considerable expressive weight. (No metronome markings appear in Webern's carefully copied final manuscripts of this period. There is evidence that his sense of time—and the relation of musical gesture to time in his brief compositions—was unrealistic; when preparing programs of his songs, Webern would give durations vastly longer than the actual length of the pieces to be performed.[29]) Whereas Schoenberg's "Entrückung," the setting of the George poem which forms the last movement of his Second Quartet, is a passage outward to unknown realms, Webern's George songs—and the development of his atonal style—are profoundly introspective.

In 1908 Webern was intimately involved in Schoenberg's personal crisis, acting as an intermediary to bring Mathilde Schoenberg (who resented him ever afterward) back to her young children and husband. Although nine years separated them in age, after this event a bond of trust and constant communication between Schoenberg and Webern grew into an important relationship of mutual influence. The reverberations of crisis in Schoenberg's works of this period seem to have released in Webern his own deeply personal creative need.[30] Webern's music of the period 1909–13 pursues even further than does Schoenberg's the ideas expressed in Schoenberg's revealing correspondence with Busoni in August 1909. In an essay written in 1951 about Webern, Schoenberg remembered "immediately and exhaustively" sharing new ideas with him—and his irritation that "Webern immediately uses everything I do, plan or say, so that . . . I haven't the slightest idea who I am."[31] Webern himself recalled this period, and the process of rejecting tonality, "As if the light had been put out! . . . At the time everything was in a state of flux—uncertain, dark, very stimulating and exciting, so that there wasn't time to notice the loss."[32]

Schoenberg's new ideas clearly affected Webern's works in the summer of 1909, particularly the Five Movements for String Quartet (published as Op. 5) and some orchestral movements later published as Six Pieces for Orchestra (Op. 6). The quartet movements carry the reductive tendency seen in "Dies ist ein Lied" to a new extreme. In these terse movements Webern derives as much as possible from each motive, in practical application of the "kernel" notion Mahler had expressed in 1905. The first movement of Op. 5 is a compressed sonata allegro. Thematic material is telescoped to the briefest intervallic cells, chordal gestures, and fragmented phrases. The dramatic relationship between strong, aggressive material (mm. 1–6) and tender, lyrical material (mm. 7–13) is so concentrated, and passes so swiftly, it can only be grasped by careful study (see Ex. 5-2). The tension set up by the opening cry-like motive (an ascending augmented octave in cello and second violin), the nervous sixteenth notes which follow, and the gasping, dissonant chords of mm. 5 and 6 convey a psychological impression of extreme anxiety. The cry reappears throughout the movement, transposed, inverted, and built into chords. The lyrical material (somewhat slower in tempo) makes use of melodic and harmonic major and minor thirds and sixths, creating (at m. 9 *sehr zart* [very tender]) the greatest possible contrast to the previous anguish. (Here love and reassurance are evoked by the warmth of thirds and sixths, as in "Dies ist ein Lied.") The psychologically dramatic essence of sonata form is used to express emotional memory in the most intense, most distilled way. As Schoenberg expressed the new style to Busoni: "Away with harmony as cement or bricks of a building. Harmony is *expression* and nothing else. . . . Away with pathos! Away with protracted ten-ton scores. . . . Music must be *brief*. Concise! In two notes: not built, but *'expressed.'!!*"[33]

Along with exaggerated extremes in dynamics, Webern uses such string techniques as harmonics, tremolo, plucking, and bowing on the bridge or with the wood of the bow. They are employed not just as radical techniques—which they were at the time—but to heighten the drama, particularly in the development section (mm. 14-44). Here the juxtaposition of contrasting materials, with rapid and violent changes of dynamics and tempo, produce an atmosphere of inner conflict which is resolved by a sudden change of texture as the lyrical elements return. The recapitulation (beginning at m. 44) restates the original materials in a new way, as had the closing section of "Dies ist ein Lied." "Think what your themes and motives have lived through in between!" was the psychological attitude of the expressionists toward recapitulation.[34] After the final appearance of the lyrical material (thirds and sixths, *fff, noch breiter,* at m. 50), the C–C sharp cry, now more like a scream, continues as a miniature coda to the end, gradually losing strength and subsiding from *sfff* to *ppp*. The silent horror of the open ending leaves the psychological conflict of the movement unresolved (Ex. 5-3).

Six Pieces for Orchestra (published as Op. 6) were written "to supplement what was said in the string quartet," Webern told Schoenberg.[35] Schoenberg's Five Pieces for Orchestra, Op. 16, had been completed only months before Webern's orchestral pieces were written, and there is definite influence, but only of a general nature. Webern takes up the technique of *Klangfarbenmelodie,* which Schoenberg had used. The focus on orchestral color is also a common element, but as Erwin Stein said, while Webern may have had *manner* in common with Schoenberg, the *matter*—the particular emotional necessity—is very personal to Webern.[36] When Schoenberg was about to conduct the first performance of Webern's Six Pieces for Orchestra in 1913, Webern wrote him in detail what he had in mind while composing

Ex. 5-2. Webern, Op. 5/I, exposition, mm. 1–13. Copyright 1922 by Universal Edition; copyright renewed.

Ex. 5-3. Webern, Op. 5/I, mm. 52–55, first violin.

the pieces, confessing he had "talked to no one about it as yet." The first piece expresses his frame of mind while in Vienna, "sensing the disaster" of his mother's death from diabetes, yet always maintaining the hope that she was alive. The second is the fulfillment of this premonition, as he was on the train ride from Vienna to Carinthia. The third is the tenderest representation of Erika, a variety of heather which Webern gathered in a favorite spot to lay on his mother's bier. The fourth is the funeral march:

> Even today I do not understand my feelings as I walked behind the coffin to the cemetery. I only know that I walked the entire way with my head held high, as if to banish everything lowly all around. I beg you to understand me properly— I am myself trying to gain clarity about that peculiar state.

The fifth piece recalls the "miraculous" evening after the funeral, when Webern went with his cousin Wilhelmine to straighten the flowers on the grave. The final piece expresses the feeling of his mother's presence: "I saw her friendly smile, it was a blissful feeling that lasted moments." Three years after the calamity, he wrote his Six Pieces for Orchestra while living at the family estate; he returned to the grave each day at dusk, in late summer, the season of her death.[37]

Mahler's "Tragic" Sixth Symphony—which his wife called the most completely personal of his works—had been performed in Vienna in January 1907.[38] Webern had attended the rehearsals and undoubtedly knew Zemlinsky's piano edition of 1906. In the original version of his 1909 orchestral pieces, Webern was inspired to use Mahlerian orchestral forces, yet maintain a transparent, intimate quality. In 1928 Webern condensed the extravagant instrumentation to make the work more practical to perform. This revision was published in 1956, and in 1961 the original version was published, making it possible to see the differences in Webern's musical attitudes between 1909 and 1928. In the later version, instrumental colors and drama were sacrificed by the elimination of many instruments: two flutes (one of them an alto flute), two English horns (to which special themes had been assigned in the first and fifth movements), two clarinets, two trumpets, a harp, two timpani, and the "Whip." Two measures were cut from the work. The title *marcia funebre* disappeared from the fourth piece. Metronome markings—absent from Webern's manuscripts of his expressionist period—appeared, and most expressive markings were altered. Certain subjective expressions, such as *äusserst zart* (extremely tender), were replaced by more objective indications. In 1928 the classical ideal was in Webern's mind. Upon finishing his revision he wrote to Berg, it "looks like an old Haydn score."[39]

In the revision, however, the expressive intent of the work is not altered. In the first movement of Mahler's Sixth Symphony there is a moment during the development section when—in a sudden and unexpected textural shift—cowbells and celesta, over tremolo strings, sound as if from a distance. For Mahler this effect evoked "the wanderer on the highest peaks, who hears only the cowbells as the last earthly sounds"—for him a symbol of absolute aloneness.[40] Although Webern does not use actual cowbells in Op. 6, the fourth piece, a funeral march, makes profoundly expressive use of the same kind of effect. Over a very soft bass drum roll, at a very slow tempo, tam-tam and deep bells of unspecified pitch ring very softly, as from distant churches, in irregular quarter-note rhythm (Ex. 5-4). Irregularity of rhythm is found throughout the fourth piece. Fragments of melody appear off the beat and continue in irregular syncopation against the inexorable, slow quarter-note beat. Chains of varying chords, or obsessively repeated chords, also appear against the beat. These rhythms create an impression of difficulty in breathing, of almost impossible progress under the burden of crushing weight. The dissonant harmonies are built on minor seconds—an idea developed from the Op. 5 String Quartet. Hesitant melodic fragments, torn by rests, are built on small intervals (seconds and thirds), which constantly turn back on themselves. One exception to these nervous rhythmic and melodic characteristics is a rhythmically regular, somber low trumpet theme in minor seconds and a minor third. (In his expressionist works Webern seems to develop a personal syntax of melodic intervals as his solution for the loss of tonal functions.) The extraordinary drawn-out climax of the movement begins with a snare drum roll *(ppp),* one measure after the trumpet phrase. At the close, chords build in the brass and woodwinds to a nerve-shattering, unforgettable force (Ex. 5-5).[41]

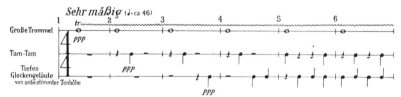

Ex. 5-4. Webern, Op. 6/IV, mm. 1–6. © Copyright 1956 by Universal Edition A.G., Vienna; © copyright renewed.

In 1933 Webern stated that because he "aimed at an always changing mode of expression," there is no thematic connection between the Six Pieces for Orchestra.[42] However, at the time of their composition he described them to Schoenberg as a "cycle."[43] If the technique of perpetual variation—the principle of nonrepetition so prevalent in expressionism—is taken into account, there is one motive which serves as a unifying, symbolic factor in all except the funeral march of Op. 6. This motive appears to be inspired by the Mahlerian notion of the "kernel," out of which the larger structure grows. It is characterized by falling fifths or sixths, and although the intervals, pitch,

Ex. 5-5. Webern, Op. 6/IV, mm. 37–40.

dynamics, and rhythm are varied with each statement, it is possible to hear in the metamorphoses of the motive the changing inner feelings of personal loss (Ex. 5-6). While this illustration shows the impossibility of presenting tidy analyses of expressionist music representing psychological states, it is helpful to remember Webern's desire—cited on p. 2—for "the thing itself. The reality of a work of art is no symbol, no imitation." [44] His use of this motive may show "the thing itself": the painful, enduring but changing grief Webern attempted to capture and express.

Other expressionist techniques abound in Op. 6. The layering of simul-

Ex. 5-6. Webern, Op. 6, the "loss" motive.

taneous subconscious fears, hopes, memories, and feelings is expressed in ostinati of great rhythmic complexity.[45] A sudden presence of tenderly expressed thirds and sixths, reminiscent of the ecstatic moment cited in "Dies ist ein Lied," appears in the first piece, mm. 2 and 3, in the violas and cellos. Twisting, struggling small-intervalled melodies (like those noted in the fourth movement) conclude the first movement on a chord of minor seconds. The second piece is filled with rhythmic tension, bizarre instrumental effects, extremes of range, and brief premonitions of the funeral march, and it ends on a grotesque-sounding chord (all instruments in the highest parts of their ranges, muted trumpets and clarinets trilling) which uses all the notes of the chromatic scale. A recollection of a children's song makes a brief, nostalgic appearance in the third piece (in flute, horn, and glockenspiel, mm. 5–6). Instrumental color is of extreme importance throughout the work, and there is particular emphasis on solo characteristics. The tension and melancholy of the entire work is peculiarly Webern's. Op. 6 and his other works of 1909 (many of the George songs, the Five Movements for String Quartet, Op. 5) show a mature mastery of his expressive needs and materials only a year after the completion of his studies with Schoenberg.

Webern's composing continued to be dominated by compulsions, on the one hand expressing ever further his inner necessity, on the other reaching for an "ever-increasing conquest of the material."[46] The exceptions Webern noted in his 1912 letter to Berg about the origins of his composition—the Violin Pieces (Op. 7), and the Two Orchestral Songs (Op. 8) on texts of Rilke—coincide with his personal crisis of the summer of 1910. As his relationship with his cousin Wilhelmine intensified and both families became strongly opposed to their marriage, Webern found at the ecstatic ending of Rainer Maria Rilke's *The Notebooks of Malte Laurids Brigge* two song texts, framed in a silently tense atmosphere, about the difficulty and lonely aspects of loving. He dropped work on sketches for an opera and reported to Berg: "The [Rilke] poem compelled me, for it corresponded so completely to my thoughts. I composed it and orchestrated it quickly."[47] This haste was unusual for Webern, who ordinarily composed very slowly, believing that time must be allowed to understand what was "dictated" to him.[48]

After the couple was married in a civil ceremony in February 1911, Webern's troubled theater career gave him little time to compose. Even worse, for a time the young Weberns were not welcome at the Preglhof (Ill. 5-3), the composer's haven for creative work.[49] In these difficult years Webern frequently endeavored to move his family close to Schoenberg, whose world represented "loftiness of spirit" to him.[50] Wherever Webern was between 1910 and 1913, much of his time was devoted to tasks for Schoenberg. He sought professional and financial help for the beleaguered older composer, made trips to hear his works, made piano arrangements of his orchestral works, and wrote articles about him.

Mahler's death in May 1911 was a deep blow to Webern, who thought constantly about Mahler, his similarly frustrating theater career, and his transcendent music. Webern tried, at Schoenberg's suggestion, to write an essay on Mahler, but confessed himself too timid when writing. After the birth of Anton and Wilhelmine's child in the spring of 1911, their parents recognized their union, and Webern returned that summer to the Preglhof. There he began an outpouring—not concluded until 1913—of string quartet and orchestral movements. Selections from these were later titled Bagatelles, Op. 9 (published in 1924), and Five Pieces for Orchestra, Op. 10 (published in 1923). With these string quartet and orchestral pieces (along with Opp. 7 and 11), Webern's urge to expressive compression reached such extremes that the next

Ill. 5-3. The Preglhof, the Webern family's summer home. Photo by Dorothy L. Crawford, 1989.

step would have been silence. This attitude toward brevity is akin to that of Webern's ascetic contemporary the Viennese philosopher Ludwig Wittgenstein, whose critique of verbosity in metaphysics led him to claim about his enigmatic and tersely stated *Tractatus Logico-Philosophicus* (published in 1921), "Where many others today are just gassing, I have managed in my book to put everything firmly in place by being silent about it."[51] For Webern, who, like Wittgenstein, was strongly influenced by Karl Kraus, art had to be ethical. The casting off of all that is impure and the striving for God were always deeply connected with his composing, which he wanted to be "good. I mean good also in other respects [than the purely artistic]."[52]

Four of Webern's 1911–13 string quartet pieces were intended as a "Second String Quartet." (They were published as movements 2, 3, 4, and 5 of the Bagatelles, Op. 9). In them Webern extends coloristic string techniques for expressive purposes. He makes such frequent use of harmonics, bowing on the fingerboard and at the bridge, pizzicato, tremolo, and ostinati using these effects that an often dry, tense sound results, and a normally bowed fragment of melody, even with extreme intervals, assumes a new expressive strength by contrast. Rhythms are set against each other in unusual relationships so that independence of voices is much greater than in the Op. 5 pieces for string quartet (Ex. 5-7). In 1932 Webern said about these quartet pieces that he wrote out the chromatic scale and crossed off individual notes as he composed: "I had the feeling that when the twelve notes had all been played the piece was over. . . . It sounds grotesque, incomprehensible, and it was incredibly difficult. The inner ear decided."[53] He did not mention this at the time to Schoenberg, but later told him, "I never knew what to do after the twelve tones."[54]

Ex. 5-7. Webern, manuscript of third movement from "Second String Quartet," 1911 (later Op. 9/III), as reproduced in *Der Ruf* IV (May 1913).

Webern wrote seven orchestral pieces during the summer of 1911 (two were later published as the first and fourth pieces of Op. 10). They are also aphoristic and make use of heightened color images. At the time of their composition he described them to Schoenberg as chamber pieces with changes of colors in sixteenth and 32d notes. The fourth piece of Op. 10 consists of only six measures, with a melody passing from voice to voice in *Klangfarbenmelodie* style, the final gesture of which (marked *wie ein Hauch* [like a breath]) is reminiscent of the "loss" motive of the Op. 6 orchestra pieces. Indeed, for a later performance Webern titled the piece "Remembrance." Instrumental colors are delicate and include celesta, mandolin, and harp.

During the relatively happy and fruitful summer of 1911, Webern was reading Bergson, Strindberg, and Balzac. The previous summer he had read Balzac's *Séraphîta;* in July 1911, he sent a quotation from Balzac to Schoenberg: "Are not religion, love, and music the three-fold expression for one and the same thing, for the need for expansion which torments every noble soul? These three parts all mount up to God who resolves all earthly agitations."[55] In this period Schoenberg, Berg, and Webern were all caught up in a Swedenborgian quest for values, which is further articulated in the work of Balzac and Strindberg. (These ideas are strongly reflected in the three Viennese composers' projects in synthesis of the arts [*Gesamtkunstwerk*], which are discussed in chapter 10.)

After considerable efforts on Schoenberg's part, Webern received an offer of a job during his creative summer of 1911. The position—in Prague as assistant to conductor/composer Alexander Zemlinsky (Schoenberg's brother-in-law)—offered relative financial security but allowed no time for composing. Reluctant to take the position, Webern emphasized the strength of his conviction to Schoenberg: "If I do not sense how something works within me, how something new originates and is born, then I do not exist."[56] Hoping to continue composing, Webern refused the position and moved his family to Berlin to live near Schoenberg, who had fled Vienna that summer. "Above everything," wrote Webern, "I would like to be with you."[57] In atonement for his seeming lack of gratitude, he began work on an essay about Schoenberg and asked to make more piano reductions of his works.

In November 1911 Webern attended the first performance of Mahler's *Das Lied von der Erde,* conducted by Bruno Walter in Munich. Webern found the event overwhelming and referred to it again and again in his correspondence with Schoenberg, who was too busy in Berlin with his teaching and the publication of *Harmonielehre* to attend. Webern also shared the experience with Berg. Webern expected from the music "the most wonderful things there are; something so marvelous that it has never existed," and he was not disappointed. "It is like the passing-by of life—better than life—in the soul of one who is dying. The work of art condenses, dematerializes; the factual evaporates, the idea remains—that is what these songs are like."[58]

In his ecstatic letters to Berg about *Das Lied von der Erde,* Webern could be describing his own compositional aims. He finds "the summit of music" in the second movement, "Der Einsame im Herbst." About a solo passage for cello in this movement he writes, "Have you thought what happens when you hear that? What is this *unnameable?* I have something that orients me; of course, nothing is explained by it. I believe in God." "This quiet, gentle, lovely relationship," in the fourth movement depicting young love, reminds him: "I have felt [love] only so, never otherwise; that is, also otherwise, namely sadly—yes, Berg, one can't speak of that. It could make you pass away, die." The sound of the contrabassoon in the fifth movement is "certainly the most mysterious that ever was. I would have liked best to give up the ghost." He writes of the final movement: "I often think, should one be allowed to hear this? Do we deserve it? But there is this: To die for it, that we may deserve it. Reach into our hearts, out with the muck, upwards. 'Lift up your hearts' says the Christian religion. So Mahler lived, so Schoenberg. There is remorse, there is longing."[59]

These comments express not only Webern's reverence for Mahler's music but also his mounting creative frustration. In 1912 Webern produced no compositions. His life in Berlin—with the exception of two Mahler pilgrimages[60]—was almost totally occupied with Schoenberg's affairs. Publishers rejected Webern's work. At performances of his music the audience laughed. His father found his son's music "too nervous" for his tastes. Unable to maintain the family estate or to count on Anton's supervision of it, Carl von Webern sold the Preglhof. (With income from this sale Webern published some of his music privately, including the Six Pieces for Orchestra [1909], which he numbered at that time "Op. 4.") Financial need now forced Webern to accept a theater post at Stettin, but as summer came, longing for the Preglhof overwhelmed him. He wrote to Berg of his misery in the theater, while trying to put a somewhat better face on it for Schoenberg. He sank into deepest depression and illness. While reading Strindberg's *To Damascus,* Webern wrote to Schoenberg that his insomnia, headaches, and nervous weakness were the kind of punishment Strindberg had suffered. He managed to travel to Berlin for the premiere of *Pierrot lunaire,* which made a tremendous impression on him, but it also reminded him how unproductive he had been. He fell into increasing difficulties with the theater authorities. He wrote to Schoenberg that he could not conduct the incompetent theater orchestra if he was not in the right mood.[61] His wife was again pregnant, and his psychosomatic symptoms became acute.

Webern was granted a sick leave from the Stettin theater and went alone to a sanatorium on Semmering, a mountain resort outside Vienna, where he remained for two months. During this time his wife gave birth in Stettin to their second child. Separation from his family caused him "to suffer so terribly, as if it were a crime . . . . Never again in my life will I do this. I could perish for longing."[62] Immediately after his release Webern experienced the shocking riot of 31 March 1913, which aborted a concert at the Vienna Musikverein. Webern's Six Pieces for Orchestra, Schoenberg's First Chamber Symphony, and Berg's Altenberg Songs had been on the program. (This outburst of virulent hostility against the Viennese composers rivaled the scandal accompanying the premiere of Stravinsky's *Sacre du Printemps* in Paris two months later.)

Trying to recover from his nervous collapse at his wife's family home in Styria during the summer of 1913, Webern wrote three expressionist poems of intense longing: "Leise Düfte" (Gentle fragrances), "O sanftes Glühn der Berge" (Oh gentle mountain radiance), and " Schmerz, blick immer nach Oben" (Pain, glance ever upward). The three poems evoke varied images of his mother, with stream-of-consciousness associations: evening, blossoms, mountain heights, tenderness, pain of loss. He immediately began composing a "Third String Quartet," using the last of these poems as a central vocal movement. On 3 June he wrote to Schoenberg that he hoped to gain enough strength to carry out this plan, which had been in his mind for a long time.[63] Three weeks later the three very short quartet movements were finished. Webern made a final copy and sent it to Schoenberg, who replied that he wanted them performed in Berlin in the autumn.

In July, the sudden death of his favorite nephew shattered Webern's hypersensitive nerves yet again. Ill and exhausted, Webern wrote to Berg, "I can hardly recognize myself, what is wrong with me, where I am, where I belong." He sent the poem he had just set for voice and string quartet to Berg, recalling Strindberg's suffering:

> One must go through a lot as the years accumulate, and what Strindberg says is the truth, and the most important commandment: one foot here, the other "there." "Work but pray." Only thus is it possible to bear life. So one gradually strips off all lies. One sees everything differently, sadness alone reconciles, assuages. . . . The meaning of my life is only fulfilled in productivity. . . . It is a necessity I must obey.[64]

At the end of July Webern's troubles came to a head. Facing another new theater position (again obtained through the good offices of Zemlinsky) to begin in Prague the following Monday, yet feeling too weak to take it on, Webern wrote a desperate letter to Schoenberg on Thursday, 31 July 1913: "What shall I do now? I beg you, what shall I do?"[65] Wilhelmine wired Schoenberg about Webern's incapacity for work. Schoenberg wired back that Webern should consult a nerve specialist, and not go to Prague. Further diagnosis and advice convinced Webern to try the "Freud-method," not with Freud but with Dr. Alfred Adler, who had broken with Freud's theories on the sexual basis of neuroses and had left the Vienna Psychoanalytical Society in 1911.[66] Webern's case fit easily into ideas Adler had developed in 1912, of Individual Psychology, in which he found that maladjustment is caused by feelings of inferiority and consequent unconscious compensation through exaggerated striving for personal superiority. Treatment with Adler lasted for three months (August–October 1913), during which time Webern remained in Vienna while living in his imagination in the mountains.[67] Because he believed that his indispositions (insomnia, weakening of the powers of perception, pains in the limbs, digestive difficulties) were not self-produced but were inflicted by his circumstances, Webern at first felt antipathy to psychoanalysis. (He wrote to Schoenberg, "I can always quit.") Gradually he became convinced of Adler's analysis and revealed to Schoenberg his entire case history: his timidity and exaggerated sensitivity since childhood; his desire to surpass his older sister; and his striving for perfection, which resulted in a fear of making decisions. Through his new awareness of his body's ability to produce illness whenever he met resistance, he came to recognize his nervous attacks as "tricks" that allowed him to withdraw from competition or masked his inability to meet his own unrealistic standards.[68] He felt so convinced of the efficacy of his treatment that he was shocked by Karl Kraus's attack on psychoanalysis in *Die Fackel*.[69] Adler explained that the attack (based on Kraus's attitude that psychoanalysis is the mental illness for whose therapy it mistakes itself[70]) pertained only to Freud's method and outlined for Webern his (Adler's) differences with Freud's thought.[71]

Toward the end of his psychoanalysis (October 1913), feeling "almost excellent," Webern suggested to Schoenberg that all three of his string quartets be included in the Berlin performance, for "these three groups [of pieces] *belong together as to content,* and I would therefore like them always to be played in sequence. I have combined them into one opus."[72] This he called "Op. 3," Nos. 1 (later Op. 5), 2, and 3 (later the Bagatelles, Op. 9). The final movement of the "Third String Quartet" ("Op. 3, No. 3/III," later the sixth movement of the Bagatelles), he explained to Schoenberg, is

> the incomprehensible state after death. I come more and more to the absolute belief in these things: heaven and hell. But not in the transferred sense: hell on this earth, a condition in this life. No, really only after death. However, I would not like to separate the "here" from the "beyond." Not at all.[73]

The text of the center movement of this "Third Quartet" is the shortest of Webern's three expressionist poems:

Schmerz, immer	Pain, always
Blick nach oben	Glance to the mountains
Himmelstau	Heaven's dew
Erinnerung	Memory
Schwarze Blüten	Black blossoms
Auf Herz, aus	On heart, gone
Mutter	Mother[74]

This vocal movement is so quiet as to be almost unperformable as written (see Ex. 5-8). The voice part makes use of *Sprechstimme* for two words, "immer" (always), and "Erinnerung" (memory). "Himmelstau" (heaven's dew) is sung pianissimo, descending almost two octaves, from G-sharp above the staff to B-flat below. The string quartet is required to play harmonics—with mutes—on the bridge, with the wood of the bow, creating such hushed dynamics as to be "barely audible" (the expressive indication for the voice at "Schwarze Blüten"), until the two-note phrase "Auf Herz" (On heart). This vocal interval (a major ninth) demands a sudden crescendo, but the string sound is choked by the special effects. The silences surrounding the single note on the word "aus" (gone), and the vocal decrescendo from fortissimo to pianissimo speak total loss. The expression of the final word, "Mutter," is to be sung as a sigh, hesitatingly (*zögernd,* a frequent expressive indication in Webern's manuscripts of this period, which is omitted in the published works of the 1920s). In this piece, composed in 1913, Webern's obsession with death is so deeply felt that it communicates itself best in the imagination; the composition itself makes almost unperformable demands.

Toward the end of his sessions with Adler, Webern sent Schoenberg another poetic evocation of maternal spirit, the text "O sanftes Glühn der

Ex. 5-8. Webern, second movement of "Third String Quartet," 1913, "Schmerz, blick immer nach Oben," last 5 mm. Courtesy of The Pierpont Morgan Library, New York, Lehman Collection.

Berge," as he returned to work on the series of chamber orchestra pieces begun in 1911.

O sanftes Glühn der Berge—	Oh gentle mountain radiance—
Jetzt sehe ich Sie wieder.	Now I see her again.
O Gott so zart und schön,	Oh God, so tender and beautiful,
Gnadenmutter, in Himmelshöhn.	Mother of Grace, in heaven.
O neige Dich, o komme wieder . . .	Oh come down, return again . . .
Du grüsst und segnest—	You greet and bless—

Der Hauch des Abends	The breath of evening
nimmt das Licht—	takes the light—
Ich seh's nicht mehr,	I see it no more,
Dein Liebes Angesicht.	Your beloved face.[75]

The shortness of his recently completed quartet pieces was embarrassing, Webern wrote Schoenberg. The pieces for chamber orchestra were to be "much longer."[76] A vocal setting of this text was to occupy a central position in the orchestral cycle. This movement has the sparest of instrumental textures, with all attention focused on the barely accompanied vocal part. The dynamic indications are extremely quiet ("like a sigh," "echo-tone," "hardly audible," etc.), and again there are two instances of whispered or very softly uttered *Sprechstimme*. The orchestral instruments are muted. The trumpet must trill, "like a sigh," *ppp* on B below the staff. Cowbells—as from a distance—appear for one intense and brief moment as a gesture of blessing, accompanied by rolls on timpani and bass drum. The rhythmic notation of this moment appears on the page like a triangle, a mystic symbol perhaps signifying the appearance and swift disappearance of a vision[77] (see Ex. 5-9). Webern had written to Schoenberg the previous summer, "Often a quite soft, tender radiance, a supernatural warmth falls upon me—this comes from her, my mother."[78]

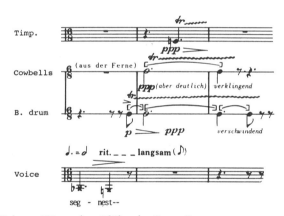

Ex. 5-9. Webern, "O sanftes Glühn der Berge," 1913, mm. 24–26. Copyright © 1964, 1968 by Carl Fischer, Inc., New York.

This visionary experience is expanded in *Tot* (Dead), a play Webern wrote at the same time, in which he exorcised his grief over the death of his nephew. On 30 October 1913, he wrote to Schoenberg about the successful completion of his psychoanalysis. In the same letter he described the play: he had conceived it in a "sudden inspiration" and wrote the first half of it in one sitting.[79] *Tot* portrays an autobiographical mystical progress, influenced by Balzac's *Séraphîta,* Strindberg's *To Damascus,* and Swedenborg's *Vera Reli-*

gio, from which Webern quoted a long passage. Berg was enthusiastic about the play; Schoenberg found it "wonderful" but was critical of the long quote from Swedenborg.[80]

What became of these visionary creative works completed in 1913, during and shortly after the period Webern was in psychoanalysis? He sent his stage work to Schoenberg as soon as it was finished, in the beginning of November 1913. During the same month he sent Schoenberg a fair copy of the "Third Quartet" ("Op. 3, No. 3"), including its song, "Schmerz, blick immer nach Oben."[81] For Christmas 1913 he sent Schoenberg a gift copy of four recently completed orchestral pieces, numbered "Op. 6," with the song "O sanftes Glühn der Berge" as the third one.[82] The musical works met with unqualified approval from Schoenberg, who planned immediately for their performances in Berlin—none of which took place. Webern's enthusiasm for composing to his own poems lasted through spring 1914. On 2 May Webern sent Schoenberg settings of "Leise Düfte" (another of his 1913 poems) and "Die Einsame" (a translation by Hans Bethge from the Chinese) for mezzo-soprano and orchestra—in a fair copy numbered "Op. 7."[83] Hans and Rosaleen Moldenhauer surmise that when Webern composed "Die Einsame" in 1914, he extracted "O sanftes Glühn der Berge" from the cycle of four orchestral pieces ("Op. 6") in order to form separate collections of purely orchestral pieces and orchestral songs.[84] For a performance in the 1919–20 season of the Society for Private Performances in Vienna, Webern selected five orchestral pieces from the compositions of 1911–13 and assigned titles to them, "to indicate the feelings that ruled him" while composing them.[85] The orchestra pieces were published in 1923, minus the revealing vocal movement, as Five Pieces for Orchestra, Op. 10.[86] In 1926, Erwin Stein, aware that the 1913 orchestra pieces were contradictory to the "advanced" mode of the day, listed and interpreted their titles to give a brief glance into Webern's "spiritual sphere":

    I. Urbild (Archetype) "something of humanity which is not of this world";
    II. Verwandlung (Transformation) "incarnation";
    III. Rückkehr (Return) "death";
    IV. Erinnerung (Remembrance);
    V. Seele (Soul) "childlike daydreaming, playing, naughty, innocent."

One could describe the pieces as lyric aphorisms, Stein wrote, and exhorted the listener to differentiate the slightest tone.[87] In 1924, the 1911–13 string quartet pieces (until then numbered "Op. 3, No. 2" and "Op. 3, No. 3") were combined for publication as Six Bagatelles, Op. 9. The vocal movement ("Schmerz, blick immer nach Oben") was omitted, metronome markings were added, and there were many alterations of color, expressive indications, and time durations, to suit the new attitudes of the 1920s.

These works, along with his psychoanalysis, freed Webern from much of his obsessive grief for the past. He drew nearer to his father, who had previously been a distant authority figure to him, and—as his father expressed fondness for music for cello, Webern's boyhood instrument—wrote the Three Little Pieces for Cello and Piano (published in 1924 as Op. 11) for his parent's birthday in the spring of 1914. Memories of painful emotions continued to be a source for his compositions, but now at a somewhat more objective distance.

Two of the poems chosen for what became the Op. 13 Orchestral Songs may reflect Webern's anguished separation from his young family while at the Semmering sanatorium in the course of his 1913 nervous breakdown. "Die Einsame" (Lonely Girl; composed in the winter of 1914)[88] and "In der Fremde" (In a foreign Land; sketched in 1915 and completed in 1917, after his war service) are a musical homage to Mahler. Both are Chinese texts from Hans Bethge's translation, the source of Mahler's texts for *Das Lied von der Erde*.[89] They contain verbal images very similar to images in the second and the final movements of the Mahler work. Although Webern makes no attempt to use pentatonic material for oriental atmosphere—as Mahler does—there are references to Mahler's motivic material. One of the clearest makes use of the symbolic ascending and descending half-step motive (the setting of the words "My heart is tired," illustrated on p. 54) signifying supplication, sorrow, suffering. This motive also appears in Mahler's second song at a textual reference to weeping (Ex. 5-10a). Webern uses the symbol similarly in his second song (Ex. 5-10b). Further, Webern uses this motive of suffering in the opening measures of both of these sorrowful songs (Exx. 5-10c and d).

Webern's military career in World War I was as conflicted and complex as his professional life had been. His attitude at the outbreak of hostilities was one of intense chauvinist excitement, which changed in a matter of months. On 26 November 1914 Webern wrote to Schoenberg,

> My first astonishment over this unbelievable excitement, my submission to it have completely changed into feelings of pain over that which now happens in every moment. I can no longer believe that which I believed so securely at the beginning: that after this war all will become cleaner and better than it was before.[90]

Early in the war Webern was shocked to learn of the death, on 3 November 1914, of the Austrian expressionist poet Georg Trakl, at the age of 27. Trakl had taken his own life in a military hospital during the Austrian war against Russia. Webern told Schoenberg that he had been deeply impressed by Trakl's poetry when *Der Brenner* had published some of his poems the previous fall. Reading Trakl's first volume again, Webern now found these poems "totally wonderful."[91] In the same month, as he reported to Schoenberg, Webern attended a lecture in Vienna by Karl Kraus, who announced that in this barren time he would be heard no longer.[92] Feeling disillusioned yet anxious to be involved in the war, Webern studied Schoenberg's *Erwartung* and *Pierrot lunaire* while waiting impatiently for military assignment.[93]

Ex. 5-10. a. Mahler, *Das Lied von der Erde*/II, m. 109; b. Webern, "Die Einsame," Op. 13/II, mm. 17–22; c. Webern, "Die Einsame," Op. 13/II, mm. 3–6, voice only; d. Webern, "In der Fremde," Op. 13/III, mm. 4–5, voice only. (Exx. 5-10 b, c, d, copyright 1926 by Universal Edition; copyright renewed.)

Webern pressed for and achieved induction in February 1915, but he soon applied to the ever-helpful Zemlinsky for a position in Prague, so that he might be released from duty in the infantry in the fall of 1915. While Webern was waiting for his release, Schoenberg was inducted. Furloughed with Zemlinsky's help, successfully installed in Prague, but overcome with guilt at his release, Webern got himself back into the military, without Zemlinsky's knowledge, and returned to his division in February 1916. He was finally dismissed from service because of poor eyesight in December 1916.

The first of the Op. 13 songs, "Wiese im Park" (Lawn in the Park), to a text by Karl Kraus, is a composition Webern tried to work at during his army duty. It was completed in June–July 1917 and gives a wistful backward glance at prewar attitudes. The first words, "How timeless I feel," set the tone of the song, which has rich, warmly felt vocal phrases on the words "And this was my land" and "It must be Sunday, and everything is ringing blue." The Viennese waltz is unmistakable in the sunnier parts of the song, which describe a green-mirrored swan, bluebells, and an Admiral butterfly. But the colors turn war-torn gray in the final pessimistic phrase: "A dead day opens its eyes. / And everything remains so old." Youthful idealism, so much a part of Webern's earlier expressionism, ceases with this song.

Before his induction Webern began settings of Trakl's poetry. Trakl had seen his poems published only in 1913 and 1914, the last two years of his short, alcohol- and drug-ridden, desperate life. The images of his poetry make much use of color, evoke nature, and are strongly lyrical, even when horrifying. Trakl omits all the words which do not express his inner meaning, leaving an emotional condensation and a willful, lawless use of syntax which must have held great fascination for Webern. In the period 1915–21 he attempted sixteen settings of Trakl's difficult poetry. All but seven remained fragments, showing that Webern's infrequent wartime composing was a time of experimentation.[94]

Six of the completed Trakl songs, published in 1924 as Op. 14, further reject the exuberantly colored instrumental techniques and profoundly emotional declamation which Webern had used in his earlier songs. Now taking Schoenberg's *Pierrot* as his model, Webern's style changed.[95] Walter Kolneder remarks that the development from Six Pieces for Orchestra, Op. 6, to the Trakl Songs, Op. 14, is "a path from color to black and white drawing."[96] (Expressionist visual artists found their strongest, most immediate means of expression in woodcuts, lithographs, and other graphic media. Compare Ill. 5-4 and Color Plate IV.)

In Webern's Trakl Songs, lines and shapes replace color. The vocal line is more arbitrarily angular; an instrumental vocal style results, replacing the purely declamatory earlier style. The vocal line becomes equalized with the other instruments. In the summer of 1917, as he was working on the Trakl settings, Webern wrote to both Berg and Schoenberg that he felt a new clarity, concentration, and confidence: "Now I am writing quite differently. . . . Homogeneous sounds, in part long themes, altogether something entirely dif-

Ill. 5-4. Edvard Munch, *The Scream,* 1896. Lithograph, 13 ¹⁵/₁₆ x 10″. Museum of Modern Art, New York, Matthew T. Mellon Fund. Copyright Munch Museum, Oslo.

ferent from before the war."[97] This new style is evident in the final song of Op. 13, Trakl's "Ein Winterabend" (A Winter Evening; completed in July 1918 and reworked in 1922), and separates it from the others of Op. 13. In the Op. 14 Trakl Songs, few instruments are used, they are less contrasting in color, and there is greater emphasis on a densely wrought polyphony (Ex. 5-11). With the greater emphasis on counterpoint comes a cooler, more objective attitude, which Webern counters by the extremes of pitch and dynamics of his vocal writing (Exx. 5-12a and b). Both of these phrases, with descents from the heights on the words "blue" and "heaven," are reminiscent of Webern's enthusiasm for expressive moments in Heinrich Isaac, when, after a pause, the soprano enters on a high pitch and sweeps downward, "as from heaven."

Webern asked Schoenberg for a copy of the score of *Pierrot lunaire* in December 1914; thereafter he often expressed his interest in and debt to that

Equally mute the nameless one follows

Ex. 5-11. Webern, Op. 14/IV, "Abendland III," mm. 4–5. Copyright 1924 by Universal Edition; copyright renewed.

Beneath the round Heaven glides the Fisherman softly

The blue of my eyes has (faded)

Ex. 5-12. Webern, Op. 14. a. I, "Die Sonne," mm. 13–15, voice only; b. V, "Nachts," mm. 1–3, voice only.

work. Through the influence of Schoenberg's contrapuntal style in *Pierrot*, Webern gradually returned to strict canonic writing in the final song of Op. 15 and all the songs of Op. 16, and the more purely intuitive phase of his composing was over. In Opp. 14-15, although such musical devices as linear distortion, rhythmic complexity, and contrapuntal layering contribute to stylistic contortion, the "seismographic registration of traumatic shock" is no longer—as, in Adorno's view of expressionism, it should be—"the law of the form of the music."[98]

For Webern, Schoenberg's revelation of the twelve-tone method, in February 1923, was at first difficult to assimilate. Felix Greissle remembers Webern "waiting for some intuitive sign in the whole matter."[99] But Schoenberg's attitudes had changed: "I hear that the young call their music 'psychological' music. . . . Nowadays I make a point of keeping my ideas at a decent distance from the feelings accompanying them."[100] Indeed, his introduction to Webern's Bagatelles, penned in 1924, contains important references to the new classical distance:

> While the brevity of these pieces is their eloquent advocate, such brevity stands equally in need of advocacy. Think what self-denial it takes to cut a long story so short. A glance can always be spun out into a poem, a sigh into a novel. But to convey a novel through a single gesture, or felicity by a single catch of the breath: such concentration exists only when emotional self-indulgence is correspondingly absent.[101]

Although his music changed in keeping with the New Objectivity, throughout the remainder of his life Webern retained some of the attitudes of his expressionist period. After discovering the sketch books which encompass all Webern's works from Op. 17 to Op. 31, his biographer Hans Moldenhauer wished to correct assumptions about the abstract nature of Webern's creative impulse:

> Many regard his compositions as the epitome of nonassociative essays in the domain of tones. . . . What has not been known is the fact that preparatory sketches of Webern's purely instrumental works also contain numerous indications of specific associations underlying the musical ideas. These sources of inspiration revolve around the two great poles of his world: his family and nature. . . . He approached each work with definite visions and corresponding emotions, and not as an abstruse mathematician operating from a kind of notational drafting board.[102]

Throughout his composing career Webern continued to consider his work—much as he had the work of the artists he most admired—to be "dictated" and to have ethical value. He expressed this to Schoenberg as early as 1912, upon hearing a performance that convinced him he was on the right path: "On such occasions, I sense all the more distinctly how little I myself am responsible should I really produce something good. I am only the instrument of a higher power. Myself, I am nothing."[103]

Select Bibliography

Adorno, Theodor Wiesengrund. "Berg and Webern, Schoenberg's Heirs." *Modern Music* 8 (January–February 1931): 29–38.

Beiträge Österreichische Gesellschaft für Musik 1972/73: Webern Kongress. Kassel: Bärenreiter, 1973.

Berg, Alban, et al. *Arnold Schönberg.* Munich: Piper, 1912.

Eimert, H., and Stockhausen, K., eds. *Die Reihe 2: Anton Webern.* Trans. L. Black and E. Smith. Vienna: Universal, 1975.

Griffiths, Paul. "Anton Webern." In *The New Grove Second Viennese School.* New York: Norton, 1983.

Hilmar, Ernst, ed. *Anton Webern Festschrift.* Vienna: Universal, 1983.

Kolneder, Walter. *Anton Webern: An Introduction to His Works.* Trans. H. Searle. Berkeley: University of California Press, 1968.

———. *Webern: Genesis und Metamorphosis eines Stils.* Vienna: Lafite, 1974.

Maegaard, Jan. "Some Formal Devices in Expressionistic Works." *Dansk Aarbog for Musikforskning* 1 (1961): 69–75.

Moldenhauer, Hans, compiler, and Irvine, Demar, ed. *Anton Webern Perspectives.* New York: Da Capo, 1978.

Moldenhauer, Hans, and Moldenhauer, Rosaleen. *Anton von Webern: A Chronicle of His Life and Work.* New York: Knopf, 1979.

Perle, George. *Serial Composition and Atonality: An Introduction to the Music of Schoenberg Berg, and Webern.* 6th ed., rev. Berkeley, Los Angeles, and Oxford: University of California Press, 1991.

Reich, Willi, ed. *Anton Webern: Weg und Gestalt in Selbstzeugnissen und Worten der Freunde.* Zurich: Arche, 1961.

Roman, Zoltan. *Webern: Annotated Bibliography.* Detroit: Studies in Music Bibliography, 1983.

Schoenberg, Arnold. *Style and Idea.* Ed. Leonard Stein, trans. Leo Black. Berkeley: University of California Press, 1984.

Searle, Humphrey. "Conversations With Anton Webern." *Musical Times* 81 (October 1940): 405–406.

Smith, Joan Allen. *Schoenberg and His Circle: A Viennese Portrait.* New York: Schirmer Books, 1986.

Stein, Erwin. "Fünf Stücke für Orchester von Anton Webern." *Pult und Taktstock* 5/6 (May–June 1926): 109–10.

Swarowsky, Hans. *Wahrung der Gestalt.* Ed. Manfred Huss. Vienna: Universal, 1978.

Webern, Anton. *The Path to the New Music.* Ed. Willi Reich, trans. Leo Black. London: Universal, 1975.

Wildgans, Friedrich. *Anton Webern.* Trans. E. T. Roberts and H. Searle. London: Calder and Boyars, 1966.

CHAPTER SIX

Alban Berg

> There is a bit of me in [Wozzeck's] character,
> since I have been spending these war years just
> as dependent on people I hate, have been in
> chains, captive, resigned, in fact humiliated.
>
> Alban Berg (1918)

In the public mind, Alban Berg's highly successful opera *Wozzeck* is the work which perhaps best exemplifies musical expressionism. Berg, who composed his first opera toward the end of the expressionist period, built on the earlier achievements of musical expressionism to create a work which was, and is, accessible to a larger public. With the wide, although brief, popularity of expressionism following World War I, the time was ripe for a work like *Wozzeck*, and Berg, by virtue of his particular background, gifts, and training, was perfectly suited to be its creator.

Alban Berg (1885–1935) was born into a prosperous Viennese family. At an early age he showed signs of aesthetic sensibility and varied (but as yet unfocused) artistic gifts combined with a pronounced tendency toward sensuality. On the negative side, he was lazy and lacked discipline. He was also plagued by asthma. As a child, Berg drew and painted.[1] Though an indifferent student, he was a great reader, and, like Schumann, at first he wanted to be a poet.[2] His description of a 1904 storm at his family's country estate in Carinthia shows his talent for the dramatic and his gift with words, which later proved helpful in his operatic adaptations of Büchner and Wedekind:

> There were eight of us at dinner—it was very dark round about, only here and there uncannily bright; for bright, flashing lightning cleft the cloudy sky and bathed the lake in garish blue. The foliage around us rustled weirdly—and our lamps were like flares in a storm; lightning flashed over the landscape again, like a glowing whip. In the distance a peal of thunder, and a red glow crept up behind the mountains and climbed—and grew, up into the clouds, that shone hideously and threw down their purple glow to be reflected in the lake.[3]

Berg's childhood love of drama was furthered by his family's governess/housekeeper, who arranged for him and his siblings, Charly and Smaragda, to participate in play readings, "living pictures" (a kind of pantomime), and short scenic presentations with music for the family's guests on special occasions. The children learned arias and duets for these performances.[4] Later, during his adolescent years, Berg profited from the rich artistic ambience of turn-of-the-century Vienna by going to the opera, the theater, or a concert almost every night.[5] Through his sister, Smaragda, who was widely known and admired in Bohemian artistic circles, he met Peter Altenberg, Gustav Klimt, and Karl Kraus.[6]

In this period, Berg's favorite authors were Ibsen, Nietzsche, Strindberg, Wilde, and Wedekind.[7] His preference for the last two, in particular, was linked to his interest in sensuality as "a force within us" and "a tendency found in all new art," praise of which is found repeatedly in Berg's letters of the early 1900s.[8] Along with this emphasis on sensuality, which reflected the new sexual attitudes voiced by Freud, Weininger, and Kraus, Berg idealistically defended "the pure reality of the spirit" against "the brutal materialism of ordinary life"[9] and insisted that "prostitutes of the spirit," who "sully themselves for money," are not much better than actual prostitutes.[10]

As a youth Berg was so lazy that, in spite of his intellectual gifts, he more than once asked a friend to write his school essays for him.[11] One instance of his lack of self-discipline is the length of a letter—64 pages—he wrote to a friend in 1906 about Ibsen's *A Doll's House*.[12] Consistent with the adolescent Berg's traits of irresponsibility and sensuality is his fathering of an illegitimate child in 1902, with Marie Scheuchl, a peasant girl employed by his family.[13]

Young Berg explored music literature by accompanying his older brother, Charly, in lieder and playing piano four-hands with Smaragda. By 1904, Mahler had become one of his "living ideals,"[14] and in a letter of 1907 Berg calls Strauss "the greatest of living composers."[15] Probably through Smaragda, Berg also learned to admire the music of Debussy and Ravel.[16]

Like many another fin-de-siècle youth, there was something of the "infirm Tristan" in the handsome, aesthetic Berg,[17] who bore a marked resemblance to Oscar Wilde. Always in uncertain health, Berg admitted to the father of his fiancée, Helene Nahowski, that he was "highly strung, excitable and extremely sensitive."[18] At the same time he was resourceful and energetic in his rebuttal of her father's criticisms, and he persevered through a difficult, if highly romantic, four-year courtship of Helene, finally marrying her in 1911.

When Schoenberg accepted him as a pupil in the fall of 1904, the nineteen-year-old Berg was in many ways an unformed dilettante. This determined the character of their relationship in the early years—a relationship that was more intense and problematical than that between Webern and Schoenberg. Schoenberg became a father-figure to Berg (who had lost his own father in 1900), not only influencing his music by putting him through studies which included a rigorous course of counterpoint, but also criticizing his character, dress, and writing style.[19] Schoenberg supplied the discipline which Berg vitally needed to develop his character, but Berg paid a price for it in the tensions produced by his filial relationship to Schoenberg. The published correspondence shows Berg subservient and even obsequious to his teacher during the prewar period, but he nevertheless maintained independent literary tastes and was more open to other musical influences (notably that of Debussy) than was Schoenberg. The formal part of Berg's studies ended in 1911, though Berg often discussed his compositions with Schoenberg in the years that followed. During and after the composition of *Wozzeck* (1915–21), Berg took great pains to maintain his musical independence, while remaining loyal to his teacher.

Schoenberg found the songs Berg initially submitted to him to be "in a style between Hugo Wolf and Brahms,"[20] but recognized "that music was to [Berg] a language, and that he really expressed himself in that language" with "overflowing warmth of feeling."[21] The *Seven Early Songs* (1905–1908), with their long Wagnerian phrases and richly chromatic harmony, give a good idea of Berg's neoromanticism, as does the one-movement Piano Sonata, Op. 1 (1908). The tonally ambiguous French sixth chord (which can also be treated as a dominant with lowered fifth) appears frequently in these early works. Berg's preference for this Scriabin-like sound—which continues in his atonal and twelve-tone compositions—is certainly linked to the sensual side of his nature.

Berg's evolution from neoromanticism to expressionism is clearly evident in Four Songs, Op. 2 (1909–10). As with the movements of Schoenberg's Second String Quartet, each of the Op. 2 songs grows more advanced in style. The final song, which is Berg's first atonal composition, arrives at expressionism.

For the texts of the last three songs of Op. 2, Berg shows his literary independence from the Schoenberg circle by choosing three poems from *Der Glühende* (The Fervent One), by Alfred Mombert (1872–1942). Published in 1896, these poems were radically new for their time in form and content,[22] combining free verse with a personal, mystical vision in a way that closely anticipates expressionism. The text of the last song resembles Schoenberg's *Erwartung* in its portrayal of feminine desire:

> The breezes are warm,
> Grass sprouts on sunny meadows,
> Hark! the nightingale warbles.
> I want to sing:
> High above in the gloomy forest
> The cold snow melts and glitters,
> A girl in a gray dress leans on the damp trunk of an oak,
> Sick are her tender cheeks,
> Her gray eyes shine feverishly through dark, giant tree trunks.
> "He has still not come—

He leaves me waiting . . ."
She died!
One dies, while the other lives:
That makes the world so deeply beautiful.

Musically, as well, the song resembles *Erwartung*. New, highly dissonant harmonies predominate, as Berg uses his more customary whole-tone and dominant complexes only toward the end of the song. The asymmetrical *parlando* of the voice part, with its wide skips, matches Mombert's free verse. Frequent changes of texture and tempo are related to the expression of textual details, such as "the nightingale warbles," "I want to sing," and the "glittering" of the snow. The entire song leads up to a highly operatic climax at the words " 'He has still not come—/He leaves me waiting . . .' " (Ex. 6-1). Schoenberg's pupil Karl Linke, in the earliest article on Berg's and Webern's music (1912), wrote perceptively that "whereas, in Webern, the complexes of feeling are concentrated inwards," in this song by Berg "catastrophes of the soul are discharged outward with elemental force."[23] Extreme dynamics and constant accelerandi and ritardandi heighten the climax, while a double glissando (upward on black notes, downward on white) shows Berg's inventiveness in exploring new instrumental means for the sake of maximum dramatic effect. The climax is followed by what is clearly a Mahlerian death rhythm in the left hand (mm. 18–20). In this apparently spontaneous and uninhibited song, in which constructive devices are little in evidence, Berg has used drastic means to move close to the essence of expressionism.

For about two years after completing his String Quartet, Op. 3 (1910), Berg lacked time to compose. He was working on piano reductions of Franz

Ex. 6-1. Berg, "Warm die Lüfte," Op. 2/IV, mm. 15–20.

Schreker's opera *Der ferne Klang,* Schoenberg's *Gurre-Lieder,* and the last two movements of Schoenberg's Second String Quartet. In a letter of January 1912, Schoenberg suggested that Berg "let poetry lead one back to music" and write some orchestral songs.[24] Berg chose to set the "picture-postcard texts" of Peter Altenberg, the eccentric Viennese poet and "Socrates of the coffee-house." Berg was personally acquainted with him through both Smaragda, to whom the poet had written more than a hundred letters, and Helene, who was the object of two touching love poems and a bittersweet prose sketch by Altenberg.[25] In the last, entitled "Bekanntschaft" (Acquaintance), Berg himself appears (unnamed) as the "noble youth," who ironically wins Helene by following Altenberg's own advice.

The five picture-postcard texts Berg used for his Op. 4 are aphoristic impressions sent by the poet to his female friends.[26] In the first and last Berg makes the texts even shorter by setting only the first stanza or paragraph. The text of No. 1, "Snowstorm," reads:

> Soul, how much more beautiful you are, and more profound,
> after snowstorms − − −.
> You have them too, like nature − − −.
> And over both, a gloomy haze still lingers, though
> the clouds have already dispersed.[27]

In his elaborately orchestrated Altenberg Songs Berg complements the free verse with an asymmetrical and atonal musical prose of his own, and he responds fully to Altenberg's empathetic grasp of feminine psychology. The large orchestra depicts the forces of nature rising to a great climax; both a snowstorm and a crescendo of feminine eroticism are probably intended. Ernst Krenek has described the passage as a "Wirrnis" (entanglement, confusion);[28] its texture can be compared to the dense nets of lines in some of Kokoschka's drawings of this period. At the beginning of the song, six ostinati, all of different lengths, create a constantly changing, highly coloristic pattern. As the ostinati move upward toward a *fff* climax,[29] an espressivo generative melody, constructed like that in the first movement of Mahler's Ninth, is introduced.[30] (The premiere of Mahler's work, which Berg attended in June 1912, just before beginning work on the Altenberg Songs, made a profound impression on him, which was expressed in a letter to Helene.[31]) The climax is followed by a harmonically clearer passage—stressing altered dominants—during which the voice enters. These harmonies, along with the voice's initial humming and short melodic decoration on the word "schöner" (more beautiful), emphasize the sensual character of the passage. However, at the words "You have [storms] too, like nature," a second, more violent and broken crescendo begins to build, culminating in a climax at m. 29. (In the letter just mentioned, Berg wrote that in Mahler's Ninth "the tenderest passages are followed by tremendous climaxes like new eruptions of a volcano."[32]) The two great climaxes have the effect of dividing the work into two large sections.[33] In the evanescent coda (from m. 29 on), fragmentary motives "disperse" above and below a three-note pedal in the harmonium, E–B–F, which represents the text's "gloomy haze."

The vocal line, which tends toward a *parlando,* is sometimes expressionistically extreme. Frequent changes of color and texture in the orchestra reflect every shade of meaning in the text. Each of the five Altenberg Songs is highly individual in mood and construction, yet the songs are unified by strong and subtle cyclic connections. Berg's frequently daring and innovative orchestration is amazingly successful, particularly since the songs were his first orchestral score.

The first performance of the second and third songs, under Schoenberg's direction (Vienna, 31 March 1913—the same program on which Webern's Op. 6. was premiered), was interrupted by a riotous demonstration. (It is hard to understand why Schoenberg chose to perform the two songs least capable of standing on their own, rather than the longer first and fifth.) The traumatic effect of this reception on Berg was increased by unfavorable newspaper reviews and by Schoenberg's own harsh criticisms. Even before the concert, Schoenberg wrote to Berg pointing out the "rather too obvious desire to use new means" in the songs and questioning the "organic interrelationship between these means and the requirements of expression."[34] More criticism from Schoenberg—probably concerning both the Altenberg Songs and Berg's next work, the aphoristic Four Pieces for Clarinet and Piano, Op. 5—followed when Berg visited his teacher in Berlin in June 1913. Schoenberg seems to have disapproved of the shortness of these more recent works, finding them so brief as to exclude any possibility of extended thematic development. He also reproached Berg for indolence and recommended that he write a suite of character pieces for orchestra.[35] Schoenberg's criticisms plunged Berg into a morose state, with a lack of confidence which lasted until 1915. For a time, he was unable to decide between writing a large one-movement symphony and the "gay suite" which Schoenberg had suggested.

After beginning work on Three Pieces for Orchestra, Op. 6 (1913–15), Berg was deeply impressed by his first hearing of Schoenberg's Five Pieces for Orchestra in 1914. However, it is Mahler's influence that is paramount in Berg's orchestral pieces. (Some years later, Adorno, who was Berg's pupil, commented, on seeing the March, that "it must sound as if Schoenberg's orchestral pieces and Mahler's Ninth Symphony were played at the same time."[36]) In his Op. 6, Berg comes to terms with the problem of writing a lengthy atonal symphonic work—which neither Schoenberg nor Webern had achieved at this period. As in the Altenberg Songs, there are multiple cyclic connections between the movements: one example is the ingenious foreshadowing, at the climax of the first movement ("Präludium," mm. 37 and 45), of two important themes which will appear in the second ("Reigen").

Although "Präludium" and "Reigen" are remarkable for their warmth of feeling, it is in the March that we find Berg's expressionism in its most extreme form. The composer left no record as to what inner feelings were connected to the March. He wrote to Helene on 13 July 1914, while at work on the movement, that "one feels terribly shy about baring one's innermost feeling, even if one has already done so in the music."[37] George Perle finds the March, which was completed in the weeks following the assassination at Sarajevo (which precipitated World War I), an ideal expression of the feeling of doom and catastrophe stemming from that event.[38] Adorno likens it to the poems of the expressionists Georg Heym and Georg Trakl, which conjure up the approaching war.[39] To this outer tension must certainly be added Berg's inner turmoil over his relationship to Schoenberg. Still feeling the effects of Schoenberg's criticisms, Berg was often depressed and unsure of himself while composing the March:

> Even if I'm absolutely determined for once to avoid "the tears" it will probably not be the march of an upright person marching cheerfully, but rather at best— in which case it would at least be a "character piece"—the "March of an Asthmatic," which I am and, it seems to me, will remain forever.[40]

The work is close to chaotic in its inexhaustible contrapuntal density and constant thematic metamorphosis. It resembles the Finale of Mahler's Sixth Symphony in the way it pushes musical coherence to its limits. Since a march normally connotes order, this threatened breakdown of control has a particularly disturbing effect on the listener. A feverish, hectic mood is apparent even in the opening measures, which combine four different march motives (Ex. 6-2). This nervous quality is rarely absent, even in the brief lyrical episodes of the movement.[41]

The climax of the movement is a tutti of tremendous contrapuntal complication. It combines whole-tone and chromatic runs with arching lines in piccolos, clarinets, and upper strings. These arching lines are derived from one of the movement's main themes, first introduced in m. 5. They coalesce in enormous downward leaps, against which three hammer blows—surely inspired by the Finale of Mahler's Sixth—are heard. The passage shown in Ex. 6-3, which can be compared to the most extreme climaxes of *Erwartung* or *Die glückliche Hand*, is perhaps the high point of Berg's expressionism.

As early as 1912, Schoenberg suggested that Berg write something for the stage, possibly based on Strindberg.[42] In May 1914, Berg attended the first performances of Georg Büchner's play *Wozzeck*[43] at the Vienna Residenzbühne. He was so affected by this work that he immediately decided to set it to music,[44] although he was still in the midst of Op. 6 and was not to complete "Reigen" until August 1915. A friend later reported that after the performance of the play Berg "was deathly pale and perspiring profusely. 'What do you say?' he gasped, beside himself. 'Isn't it fantastic, incredible? . . . Someone must set it to music.' "[45] Thus it was an actual theatrical performance which made Berg decide on *Wozzeck*, just as had been true for Strauss in the cases of *Salome* and *Elektra* some ten years earlier. Since Berg did not finish the short score of his opera until 1921, his adaptation and

III. Marsch

Ex. 6-2. Berg, Op.6/III, mm. 1–4.

Ex. 6-3. Berg, Op. 6/III, mm. 123–29.

Ex. 6-3 (cont.).

setting of *Wozzeck* benefited from a long, if much interrupted, period of gestation.

Although it survives only in fragmentary form, the play *Wozzeck* is the masterpiece of the short-lived, politically radical German playwright and scientist Georg Büchner (1813–37). In a loose collection of scenes, whose order remains a matter of dispute, Büchner tells the story of the simple and harassed soldier Wozzeck, the unfaithfulness of his common-law wife, Marie, Wozzeck's increasing mental derangement, and his murder of Marie. The plot is a free version of actual events which occurred in Leipzig in 1821, and the delusions voiced by Wozzeck in the play are partly based on surviving reports of his mental examination by a Privy Councillor, Dr. Clarus.[46] In its unsentimental concision, emphasis on psychological states, apparently loose construction, and grotesquerie, as well as in the way its characters often do not communicate, but talk "past" one another, Büchner's *Wozzeck* is an uncanny anticipation, by almost one hundred years, of expressionist theater. It is not by chance that it was first performed and became popular during the expressionist era.

In his revision of Büchner's play, which he based primarily on a 1913 edition,[47] Berg reduced the number of scenes from 25 to fifteen, divided into three acts of five scenes each. He tightened and clarified the action of the play and, in one case, adroitly combined three of Büchner's scenes into one (Act II, scene 5).[48] He also added numerous stage directions throughout. One of these, the direction for a sunset, occurs when Wozzeck, gathering sticks in a field with his friend Andres, suddenly envisions the setting sun as "A fire! It rises from earth to heaven and falls with a tumult like trombones" (Act I, scene 2, mm. 290–95). This added stage direction is expressionist in character and shows Berg's capacity, so important to an opera composer, to imagine in three dimensions: "The sun is about to set. Its last sharp ray bathes the horizon in the most glaring sunlight, which is suddenly followed (with the effect of deepest darkness) by twilight, to which the eye gradually becomes accustomed." Like Edvard Munch, who perceived sunset as a scream passing through nature,[49] Berg usually portrays nature as threatening.[50] His dramatic revisions and additions, which were accomplished as he wrote the music, rather than before, are evidence of his literary skills and the visual and dramatic sense of a born man of the theater.

Berg's own experiences as a common soldier in the Austrian army (from 1915 to 1918) slowed his work on the opera, but they also caused him to identify deeply with the soldier Wozzeck. The snoring of the soldiers in the barracks at Bruck an der Leitha, where Berg was sent for training in the fall of 1915, inspired the chorus of snoring in Act II, scene 5. His encounter later that year with a sadistic army doctor (who made fun of his patients and threatened to send them to the front) must certainly have enriched the portrait of the military doctor for whom Wozzeck serves as a guinea pig (Act I, scene 4; Act II, scene 2).[51]

In an important letter to Webern, dated 19 August 1918, Berg discussed his theatrical and musical intentions for *Wozzeck,* at a point when the opera was still in its formative stages:

> It is not only the destiny of this poor man, exploited and tormented by *everyone,* that touches me so deeply, but also the unheard-of mood of the individual scenes. The connections of four or five scenes in *one* act by means of orchestral interludes naturally tempted me as well. (You will find something similar in Maeterlinck-Debussy's "Pelléas!")
>
> In accordance with the diversity of these individual scenes, I have also conceived of a great variety in their musical form. Thus, for example, normal opera scenes with thematic working out, then those *without* any thematic structure, in the manner of *Erwartung* (understand me rightly: no stylistic imitation, but only in respect to form!), song forms, variations, etc. So far I have finished composing one scene, and hope to finish another large one while I am still here. Both are in the style of the *Pierrot melodramas.*[52]

This letter makes clear that the musical forms Berg chose for his opera—five character pieces for Act I, a five-movement symphony for Act II, and five inventions for Act III[53]—were not picked arbitrarily, but were suggested by the drama and mood of the individual scenes. The forms, which were not meant to be perceived by the audience,[54] were never so strict as to inhibit sudden changes of musical texture for dramatic reasons. One such change is motivated by the sunset, described in the stage direction quoted above, and Wozzeck's visionary response to it (Ex. 6-4). The stasis of the previous passage (Wozzeck's words are "It is curiously still . . . it makes you want to hold your breath") makes the following orchestral explosion (reminiscent of *Erwartung*) very effective. The fact that the passage is based on two of the three chords Berg chose as the structural underpinning of the scene[55] in no way conflicts with his response to the text.

To point up the drama, and as an additional reinforcement of the structure of his opera, Berg uses a network of leitmotifs which is much more fully realized than in *Erwartung,* or even in Strauss's *Salome* and *Elektra.* Most of these motives are identified with individuals, but one of the most prominent, associated with Wozzeck's words "Wir arme Leut" (We poor people—words which are themselves a verbal leitmotif in Büchner), expresses the plight of oppressed humanity everywhere (Ex. 6-5).

Berg was resourceful in overcoming the difficulty of evoking popular forms and styles without sacrificing musical consistency. This was done, as he says in a 1929 lecture on *Wozzeck,* by the use of

> symmetrically built periods and phrase structures, harmonies that are based on thirds (or, more especially, fourths), and melodic patterns in which an important role is played by the whole tone scale and the perfect fourth. . . . So called "polytonality" is another such means of creating a harmonically primitive music.[56]

Ex. 6-4. Berg, *Wozzeck*, I/3, mm. 283–87.

He likens the polytonal dissonance of the slow Ländler which introduces the scene at the Inn (Act II, scene 4) to the effect produced at a fairground when the listener hears several pieces in different keys simultaneously[57]—a description which echoes Mahler's statement of his ideal of counterpoint.[58] Like Mahler's use of popular music in the slow movement of his First Symphony, Berg's polytonal Ländler is not at all gay, but produces an effect of oppressive morbidity.

Simultaneities of various kinds are indeed the outstanding features of the scene at the Inn, which Berg found the most difficult of the opera to complete.[59] As the troubled, jealous Wozzeck observes Marie dancing with her new lover, the Drum Major, the distorted popular music of the onstage band mingles and competes with the orchestra in the pit. Wozzeck's torment becomes ever more severe, and his singing, supported by the main orchestra, is pitted against a waltz played by the onstage band, giving rise to polymetric conflict ($\frac{3}{4}$ versus $\frac{3}{2}$). (See Ex. 6-6.)

Act III, which portrays the catastrophes of Marie's murder and Wozzeck's subsequent suicide, is the briefest and tightest of the opera. Here, the

Ex. 6-5. Berg, *Wozzeck*, I/1, m. 136, voice only.

musical devices Berg uses to structure the individual scenes are at once the most novel, the most audible, and the closest to the drama, and the musical interludes between the first four scenes are so brief as to lend the action an almost cinematic swiftness. (According to the expressionist theorist Theodor Däubler, such intense rapidity is itself an important characteristic of expressionism.[60]) The second scene, Wozzeck's murder of Marie, is called an "invention on one note" by the composer. The note B, constantly held or repeated in a great variety of ranges and orchestral colors, plays a crucial role in building the suspense leading up to the killing. Berg's inspiration for this device may well have come from *Salome,* where Strauss had used long-held

WOZZECK. It is red before my eyes.

Ex. 6-6. Berg, *Wozzeck,* II/4, mm. 673–77.

trills to increase the tension preceding the deaths of Jochanaan and Salome herself.[61] The music which accompanies Marie's death is perhaps the supreme example of expressionist simultaneity (Ex. 6-7). Her final scream for help, as she is stabbed, is a high B, followed by a two-octave downward leap, and a low B continues in the timpani throughout the passage. Against this, six motives associated with Marie are fleetingly presented, like a dying per-

Ex. 6-7. Berg, *Wozzeck*, III/3, mm. 103–108.

son's view of her whole life. As Berg later wrote, "the most important images of her life pass through her mind distorted and at lightning speed."[62] Motives a. and d. are identified with the Drum Major, the cause of Marie's downfall; motive b. is from her lullaby (Act I, scene 3); motive c. is from her "jewel scene" (Act II, scene 2); motive e. is Marie's "bemoaning her wretched life"; and motive f. represents Marie's waiting, which ends in her death. As Wozzeck flees, the "rushing" motive associated with him is heard (g.). The influence of *Erwartung* on this passage is notable. Marie's cry for help is on the same word and the same note as the Woman's in Schoenberg's opera (mm. 190-93), and it ends with a similar downward leap; Berg's motive e. is the same as motive c. of *Erwartung*,[63] and the two alternating pitches of motive f. had been used as a musical symbol of night or death by Schoenberg in *Erwartung* and by Mahler before him.[64]

The brief transition which follows is probably the opera's most famous passage (Act III, mm. 109-21). Between two great orchestral crescendos on the single note B, the obsessive rhythmic pattern (called "principal rhythm" by Berg), which dominates the following Tavern scene, is introduced.[65] To Berg's biographer Mosco Carner, the principal rhythm symbolizes Wozzeck's guilt.[66] In a drastic contrast, the full orchestra, playing *fff*, is suddenly replaced by a single out-of-tune piano on stage playing a wild and distorted polka in the obsessive rhythm. For the Tavern scene, in which the blood on Wozzeck's hand and elbow betrays his guilt, Berg wanted only a "minimum of realism . . . sufficient for the scene of an action which passes before the spectator's eyes like an apparition—scarcely reality anymore. It is also *composed* in that way."[67]

Scene 4, in which Wozzeck drowns while trying to dispose of the knife with which he killed Marie, is an "invention on a six-note chord." The idea of basing an entire scene on a single chord and its transpositions owes much to Strauss's *Elektra*;[68] the influence of his *Salome* can also be seen in the motive for "das Messer" (the knife). (See Exx. 6-8a and b.) There is a marked similarity between the passage which accompanies Wozzeck's drowning and the ending of *Erwartung*.[69] Both are based on the chromatic movement of

SALOME. Now strike, now strike, Naaman, now strike, I tell you . . .

Ex. 6-8. a. Berg, *Wozzeck*, III/4, mm. 222–24, voice and timpani only; b. Strauss, *Salome*, [306], mm. 1–3.

chords against each other at different speeds. However, Berg reduces Schoenberg's prodigal layering of different speeds and chords to one chord (that on which the scene is based) and no more than two speeds at one time. Thus Berg, writing *Wozzeck* toward the end of the expressionist era, simplifies and crystallizes Schoenberg's more spontaneous procedures. As the scene ends, there is another similarity to *Erwartung*: at the Captain's words "Uncanny! The moon is red, the mist gray," Berg introduces the harp and celesta, the tone colors used by Schoenberg to symbolize the moon in his opera.

Berg regarded the extended interlude which follows Act III, scene 4 as an epilogue to Wozzeck's suicide, "a confession of the author who now steps outside the dramatic action on the stage. . . . An appeal to Humanity through its representatives, the audience."[70] For this broad appeal to Humanity, which goes far beyond Büchner's dispassionate, almost clinical treatment of his characters, and which is typical of the later stages of expressionist drama, Berg writes tonal music. As often happens when he returns to tonality, the music becomes Mahlerian in character. For example, in the climactic middle section of the interlude, a montage of motives from the opera leads to a chord containing all twelve tones (Act III, m. 364). This chord is then treated as a dominant of the following return to the interlude's tonic, D minor—a procedure strikingly close to Mahler's in the Adagio of the Tenth Symphony.[71] The great emotional warmth of the interlude increases the chilling effectiveness of the brief final scene, in which Marie's son, riding his hobby-horse in front of her house, cannot take in the news of her death; he finally rides gaily off after a group of children who are going to see Marie's corpse.

In *Wozzeck*, carrying out the functions of an "ideal director,"[72] Berg was able to draw on his strong theatrical and visual talents to create a total work of art, in which all the elements of the stage are pressed into the service of the drama. He was careful not to let Schoenberg see this work as he was composing it, and *Wozzeck* marks the point when Berg freed himself from his teacher's domination. Musically, the opera is a brilliant synthesis of the influence of Schoenberg (whose *Sprechgesang* plays a major and varied role in the work), Strauss, Mahler, and, to a lesser extent, Debussy and Franz Schreker. If the expressionism of *Wozzeck*—mitigated as it is by formal construction and elements of tonality and popular music—seems less pure than that of *Erwartung,* it must be kept in mind that Berg, motivated by the spirit typical of the later expressionists, was anxious to reach out to a larger audience than Schoenberg did in his earlier opera. Nevertheless, the two works are remarkably similar in psychological aim. Berg himself felt that his music "follows the man Wozzeck into the abyss which he sees opening before him." Its function is the "representation and illumination of the unconscious"; the opera is "naked inwardness, made transparent by the interpretive power of music."[73]

Berg's next work was the Chamber Concerto for piano, violin, and thirteen wind instruments (1923–25), which shows a transitional stage in the gradual adoption of twelve-tone technique.[74] Berg, who felt that Schoenberg's initial twelve-tone works lacked warmth,[75] was able to accomplish this transition without drastic changes of style or loss to the immediacy of his expression. Like his Three Pieces for Orchestra, Op. 6, Berg's Chamber Concerto is not absolute music. It has, in fact, both a public program and a private one.[76] The public program, Berg explained in an "Open Letter" to Schoenberg (which was printed in the periodical *Pult und Taktstock* in 1925),[77] celebrates the friendship of Schoenberg, Webern, and Berg himself, along with some of Schoenberg's disciples, who are portrayed in the set of variations in the first movement. Berg only hints at the secret program of the second movement—an Adagio—in his "Open Letter": "I can tell you, dearest friend, that if it became known how much friendship, love, and a world of human and spiritual references I have smuggled into these three movements, the adherents of program music—should there be any left—would go mad with joy."[78] This program concerns Mathilde Schoenberg, whose death occurred on 18 October 1923, while Berg was at work on this movement. The duality of the public and secret programs is a manifestation of his complex personality, which relished such dichotomies. *Wozzeck* had already shown the apparent contradictions between tonal and atonal writing, and between dramatic spontaneity and strict underlying musical construction.

In the "Open Letter" Berg explains that the Adagio of the Chamber Concerto is in an arch form. At the midpoint (between mm. 360 and 361) the music retrogrades, causing the entire movement to become a palindrome. (This palindrome is strict only in part, as when mm. 283-310 are retrograded in mm. 411-38. Otherwise, the subsections of the first half of the movement recur in reverse order in the second half.) The original subtitle was "Liebe" (love), and below this Berg wrote the letters *Ma* in a sketched outline of the movement. Another outline sketch shows that he derived one of the important themes of the movement from the letters of Mathilde's name.[79] Quotations of the "Melisande" theme from Schoenberg's *Pelleas und Melisande* also play an important role. They connect the fictional love triangle between Melisande, Pelleas, and Golaud with the real-life tensions between Mathilde, Richard Gerstl, and Schoenberg.[80] Berg's allusive web is further tightened by a Mahlerian fate motive (a fixed rhythmic pattern which first appears in m. 297) and by a death-knell motive of twelve repeated C-sharps, which overlaps the moment when the music reverses itself. By the interaction of these motives, Berg expresses both the tragedy of Mathilde Schoenberg's life and the struggle leading up to her death, which occurs at the exact midpoint of the Adagio.

Berg used palindromic writing throughout his career in order to convey deeply subjective meanings. This can be seen in *Wozzeck,* where the palindrome which frames Act I, scene 1[81] reflects the Captain's obsession with time and eternity as well as the circular nature of his conversation with Wozzeck. In the concert aria *Der Wein* (1929), the palindrome in the setting of the second of Baudelaire's poems portrays the lovers' ascent to the climax of erotic bliss and subsequent falling away from it. In the opera *Lulu* (1929–35), the Film Music between scenes 1 and 2 of Act II retrogrades at m. 687, marking not only the exact midpoint of the opera but the beginning of Lulu's steep decline. All these disparate palindromes reflect the artist's wish to make musical and emotional events "unhappen."[82] They also show Berg's realization of the uselessly cyclical nature of human experience and the fatalism it engenders.[83]

For the *Lyric Suite* (1925–26), Berg chose a row whose definite harmonic implications enhanced its expressive possibilities. Its first four notes form a major-seventh chord on F, and its last four, enharmonically, one on B (Ex. 6-9). Beyond this, he based only certain parts of the *Lyric Suite* on twelve-tone technique: the first movement, the opening and closing sections of the third, the two trios of the fifth, and the entire sixth movement. Even in these sections, he made modifications in the row from movement to movement.

Ex. 6-9. Berg, tone row of *Lyric Suite*. Copyright 1927 by Universal Edition; copyright renewed.

As he was beginning the work, Berg described it to Webern as "more lyric than symphonic in character";[84] Adorno, going further, calls it a "latent opera."[85] In his own analysis, Berg wrote that the work aims at "intensification of mood" and (more cryptically) that the row is changed from movement to movement as if "suffering a fate."[86] The highly affective titles show increasing polarization of mood and tempo. As the work progresses, each pair of movements evidences greater extremity of contrast, and there is no return to the moderation which characterizes the beginning:

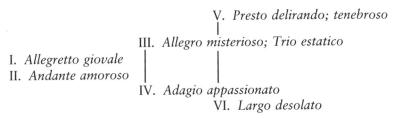

The work was the outcome of a specific emotional experience of the composer. A completely new psychological dimension of the *Lyric Suite* was revealed by documents which came to light in 1976 and 1977.[87] George Perle discovered a printed study score of the *Lyric Suite,* copiously annotated by Berg, which it made clear that the entire work was conceived (in the composer's words) as a "little monument to a great love"—for Hanna Fuchs-Robettin, sister of Franz Werfel. A study by Douglass Green of the composer's sketches and manuscript of the *Largo desolato* shows that Berg based the movement on Stefan George's translation of Baudelaire's poem "De Profundis Clamavi." The sketches indicate that during the composition Berg considered making an actual vocal setting of the Baudelaire poem; however, his final decision, based on discretion or practicality, was to write a purely instrumental setting, but one which follows the text line by line.

Berg met Hanna, the wife of a wealthy industrialist, when he stayed with the Fuchs-Robettins in Prague in May 1925. The occasion of his visit was a performance of the *Three Fragments from Wozzeck* under Zemlinsky's direction. Letters from Berg to his wife express his exhilaration at the recognition he was finally receiving, as well as his delight in the luxury and warm friendliness of the Fuchs-Robettins' home.[88] These factors, along with his hyperromantic, sensual nature, may have made him susceptible to a love affair with Hanna, which began (as the annotated score shows) on this visit.

Although it is light in character and, according to Berg's annotations, "gives no hint of the tragedy to follow,"[89] the first movement introduces two important symbolic elements. It stresses the notes and keys F and B (in German, H), Hanna Fuchs's initials, and it is 69 measures long, or three times 23, the number Berg regarded as having great personal significance for him. All the movements of the *Lyric Suite* correspond in length to multiples of 23 measures or ten (Hanna's number). The second movement *(Andante amoroso)* is a rondo; its three themes correspond (according to Berg's annotations) to Hanna herself (the opening lyric theme in the first violin), to her son, "Munzo," and to her daughter, Dorothea (nicknamed "Do-Do," and represented by a repeated figure of two C's in the viola [m. 56]).

Following the tender charm of the second movement, the tone darkens in the scherzo with trio *(Allegro misterioso),* which Berg prefaces with the twice-underlined date, 20 May 1925 (the sixth day of his visit to Prague), and the words "everything was still a mystery to *us.*" He interchanges notes 4 and 10 of his original tone row (transposed to start on B-flat) in order to obtain B-flat–A–F–B (in German, B–A–F–H), his initials and Hanna's, which then appear very frequently (in various orders) throughout the scherzo sections. Muted and mostly *pp,* a multitude of different types of bowing and pizzicato pass by with phantasmagorical rapidity, in a densely contrapuntal texture. A sudden *ff* in violins I and II (marked "ausbrechend" [bursting out] by Berg in the printed score) introduces the *Trio estatico,* with its enormous, expressionist leaps in all instruments (Ex. 6-10). The first four notes in the violins are a statement of the B–A–F–H motto. Berg wrote in the words "but repressed, still with mutes" above the trio. The fact that the strings, although *ff,* are muted increases the tension of the moment of avowal or recognition which is portrayed. The return of the scherzo section appears in shortened, retrograde form; the words "Forget it" are written above it. Berg's inscription explains the psychological significance of his use of palindrome: the scherzo's reversal symbolizes his temporary wish to "take back" the avowal which has just been made, to unlive the moments which have just passed.

Ex. 6-10. Berg, *Lyric Suite,* III, mm. 70–73.

The fourth movement *(Adagio appassionato)* is the emotional core of the work. In its central section, a broadly phrased love duet between viola and violin I (the two parts are marked "I" and "You" by Berg), leads to a quotation from Zemlinsky's *Lyrische Symphonie* (viola, mm. 32–33). Its text (not given in the printed score) is "You are my own, my own." The coda of this movement, "wholly ethereal, spiritual, transcendental" (according to Berg's annotations), is followed by the *Presto delirando,* which

> can only be understood by one who has the foreboding of the horrors and pains which are to come—of the horrors of the days with their racing pulses . . . of the painful *tenebroso* of the nights, with their darkening decline into what can hardly be called sleep.

Two musical images stand out in this violent, obsessional movement: the duplet figures, which represent the "racing pulses" and "insane, rapid heartbeat" (Ex. 6-11a), and the long glissandi in all instruments, over which Berg wrote "delirium without end" (Ex. 6-11b).

Ex. 6-11. Berg, *Lyric Suite*, V. a. mm. 329–39; b. mm. 411–14.

Important as the above revelations are, it is in the last movement that the discoveries are most crucial to any true understanding of Berg's expressive, musical intentions. Of the form of the movement, the composer wrote simply that it is "cantabile throughout".[90] Its phrasing, changes of character, and climaxes are in fact fully comprehensible only with detailed knowledge of the way the music was intended to fit the text. As his letters show, Berg had felt a close spiritual identification with Baudelaire's poetry ever since he discovered it in 1910.[91] In the French poet's sonnet "De Profundis Clamavi" (Out of the Depths, I Cried), Berg found an ideal expression of his own feeling of desolation on parting from Hanna and realizing the impossibility of their relationship.

> To you, you sole dear one, my cry rises
> Out of the deepest abyss in which my heart has fallen
> There the landscape is dead, the air like lead
> And in the dark, curse and terror well up.
> . . . .
> I envy the lot of the most common animal
> Which can plunge into the dizziness of a senseless sleep
> So slowly does the spindle of time unwind![92]

In the annotated score Berg gave to Hanna, he indicated his setting of the entire text. Usually, the texted line doubles one of the instruments, but in a few cases, the composer synthesized a new vocal part from the instrumental texture (mm. 19 and 31).[93] In setting the third and fourth lines of Baudelaire's poem Berg closely follows the meaning of the text. While the third line ("There the landscape is dead, the air like lead") is marked *non*-vibrato" in violin I and *col legno* (with the wood of the bow) in the other instruments, the fourth line ("And in the dark, curse and terror well up") brings a change to "molto vibrato" in violin I, an enormous increase in rhythmic activity, and a wildly descending accelerando passage in voice and instruments (Ex. 6-12). In the setting of the last line ("So slowly does the spindle of time unwind"), the even, legato, and almost uninflected unwinding of the row forms in voice and instruments is a perfect expression of the poetic meaning. The texture is progressively reduced as violin II, cello, and violin I drop out, leaving only the viola, which alternates between two notes a third apart—the Mahlerian symbol of sleep, night, and death. In the annotated score, Berg marks this "dying away in love, yearning and grief. . . ." Like many another expressionist conclusion, the ending stretches on into nothingness.

The secret program of Berg's *Lyric Suite* demonstrates how much the composer drew on the deepest levels of his emotional life in order to create his music. In spite of the numerological and twelve-tone aspects of the work, expressionism continues to predominate. Indeed, the discoveries concerning the *Lyric Suite* and the Chamber Concerto suggest that it is unwise to assume that any of Berg's expressionist instrumental works are "pure" music; no analysis of them is complete without considering the possibility of a psychological or programmatic basis.

Douglas Jarman has suggested that, like the Chamber Concerto, Berg's final instrumental work, the Violin Concerto (1935), also has a secret as well as a public program.[94] The work is dedicated to the memory of Manon Gropius, the nineteen-year daughter of Alma Mahler and Walter Gropius, who

There is the landscape dead, the air like lead and
Dort ist die Gegend tot, die Luft wie Blei und

in the dark, curse and terror well up.
in dem Finstern Fluch und Schreken wallen.

Ex. 6-12. Berg, *Lyric Suite*, VI, mm. 17–20.

had recently died. Berg himself said that in the first part he sought to translate aspects of the young girl's character into musical terms, while the second part represents the catastrophe of her death and its spiritual resolution. The private program, on the other hand, has been interpreted by Jarman to recapitulate Berg's own emotional life, with musical and numerological references to Hanna Fuchs-Robettin, to Marie Scheuchl (the mother of his illegitimate daughter), and to Berg himself. If this deeper level of meaning is accepted, the Violin Concerto can be heard as a requiem for Berg as well as for Manon Gropius.

For his second and last opera, *Lulu*, Berg combined two related plays by Frank Wedekind (1864–1918): *Erdgeist* (Earth Spirit, published in 1894) and *Die Büchse der Pandora* (Pandora's Box, published in 1902).[95] Berg first became enthusiastic about Wedekind when he read *Erdgeist* in 1904,[96] but he was probably more impressed when, as a member of an invited audience, he attended the private premiere of *Die Büchse der Pandora* put on by Karl Kraus in Vienna on 29 May 1905, and by Kraus's speech introducing the play.[97]

The two Lulu plays were originally written as one "monster tragedy" by Wedekind.[98] In *Erdgeist*, the first play, Lulu, who embodies the elemental power of female sexual instinct, causes the death of three successive husbands (the Medical Specialist; the Painter; and the wealthy, powerful Dr. Schön) by her complete, almost innocent, amorality. The second play, *Die Büchse der Pandora,* was attacked by German censors and was seldom produced in Wedekind's lifetime. In this more lurid and grotesque sequel, which Kraus calls a "fever dream," Lulu loses her position in society and ends up as a prostitute in London, where she is murdered by one of her clients, Jack the Ripper. In his adaptation, Berg recombines the two plays, cutting the text by about two-thirds.[99] The love relationships between Lulu and Dr. Schön, and Lulu and Schön's idealistic son Alwa, are accentuated. (Berg identifies himself with Alwa, making him a composer instead of a playwright, as he was in Wedekind's original.) Berg's most important contribution—perhaps suggested by Kraus's description of Lulu's fate as the world avenging itself for its own guilt[100]—is to have Lulu's three clients at the end of the opera portrayed by the same singers who took the roles of her admirers—the Medical Specialist, the Painter, and Dr. Schön—in Acts I and II. This adds great depth to the final tragedy; it also allows for a large-scale recapitulation in the final scene.

The music of *Lulu* is written completely in twelve-tone technique. The individual characters have their own rows (all derived from the opera's principal row), which serve as the basis for themes and leitmotifs identified with each character. In spite of Berg's use of twelve-tone technique, there are more and longer tonal passages than in the freely atonal *Wozzeck*.[101] As in Berg's earlier opera, classical forms are present (sonata, rondo, and variation), but their sections are interspersed with other materials. Though few specifically vocal forms were used in *Wozzeck*, these forms are important throughout

Lulu, perhaps most of all in the three large operatic ensembles of Act III, scene 1 (beginning in mm. 26, 231, and 564). Lulu's part is operatic in a bel canto, coloratura style. The influence of neoclassicism is also widely apparent—the recurrent "circus music" introduced in the Prologue (mm. 9–15) could almost have been written by the Stravinsky of the 1920s and 30s—and popular jazz of the same period plays a considerable role.

With this abundance of new stylistic elements, it is inevitable that expressionism plays a less pervasive role than it had in *Wozzeck.* Nevertheless, many passages are still strongly expressionist. One of the most striking is the "Monoritmica" of Act I, scene 2 (mm. 666–842). As Dr. Schön informs the Painter of Lulu's background and his own continuing relationship with her, the Painter becomes increasingly desperate and finally commits suicide in an adjoining room. Berg's musical treatment of the scene develops from the "invention on a rhythm" (*Wozzeck,* Act III, scene 3), but in *Lulu* the dramatic tension is increased even more by making the entire passage (largely in $\frac{5}{4}$) a grand accelerando passing through eighteen progressively faster tempi. The sense of ever-mounting tension is furthered by the extensive use of melodrama and *Sprechgesang,* and by a stretto of the ostinato rhythm for the percussion section alone (mm. 748–86).

It is the lyrical passages of the opera, however, which make the greatest impression on the listener. It is almost as if Berg returns to his early neoromantic roots in this work. But the neoromanticism of *Lulu,* like that of Mahler's Tenth, is so intense as to be itself expressionistic. The music transforms the story of Lulu into the apotheosis of Berg's own sensuality—sensuality so heightened as to lead to irrationality and chaos.

As Mozart does in *Così fan tutte,* Berg, in *Lulu,* humanizes a plot of ambiguous emotional tone with music of real and deep feeling. To do this, he draws once again on the deepest levels of his own emotional life—perhaps identifying Lulu with Hanna Fuchs.[102] In a moving letter to Hanna, written in October 1931, Berg laments that his continuing love for her has forced him to become a "double," or "play-acting," person. His "exterior layer" might seem to be enjoying happy domesticity with his wife, Helene, and "might be fulfilled for a time with the joys of motoring, but could never be able to compose *Lulu.*"[103]

After 1910, once Berg had absorbed Schoenberg's teachings, his style remained remarkably consistent. New elements (twelve-tone technique was perhaps the most important) did not cause abrupt stylistic changes, but were smoothly integrated into a complex which continued to include the previous elements as well. Berg benefited enormously from his knowledge of Schoenberg's seminal, pioneering expressionist works (in particular, *Erwartung,* Five Pieces for Orchestra, and *Pierrot lunaire*), but his stylistic frame of reference was much wider than Schoenberg's, and he remained open throughout his compositional career to influences beyond the Viennese circle. The comparative inclusiveness of Berg's music helped the public to accept it, as did his highly developed literary tastes and theatrical sense.

Berg's expressionism is governed from beginning to end by a strong inner necessity of feeling, a necessity which has as its two most important aspects sensuality and an affinity for catastrophe (love and death). His sensuality has its roots in neoromanticism and *Jugendstil,* and it finds its characteristic expression in lyrical melodic lines and elaborate dominant and French sixth harmonies. At its strongest, the sensuality Berg expresses borders on emotional chaos. The importance of catastrophe, which Karl Linke commented on as early as 1912, is connected in Berg's music with the deep impressions made by Mahler's "tragic" Sixth Symphony and death-haunted Ninth. The catastrophe may actually lead to death (as in Op. 2, No. 4; *Wozzeck;* and *Lulu*) or may be emotional in nature (the finale of the *Lyric Suite*). Though the sensuality of Berg's music and its tendency toward chaos and catastrophe would seem to work against any sort of abstract construction, Berg had a unique ability to draw on apparently irreconcilable elements of his nature—his extreme emotionalism and his penchant for meticulous constructivism—in order to create music of great power and unity.

Select Bibliography

Adorno, Theodor. *Berg: Der Meister des kleinsten Übergangs.* Frankfurt: Suhrkamp, 1977.
———. *Alban Berg: Master of the Smallest Link.* Trans. Juliane Brand and Christopher Hailey. Cambridge and New York: Cambridge University Press, 1991.
Alban Berg 1885–1935. Ausstellung der Österreichischen Nationalbibliothek 23. Mai bis 20. Oktober 1985. Vienna: Österreichischen Nationalbibliothek and Universal Edition, 1985.
Berg, Alban. *Briefe an seine Frau.* Munich and Vienna: Langen und Müller, 1965.
———. *Letters to His Wife.* Ed. and trans. Bernard Grun. New York: St. Martin's Press, 1971.
Berg, E. A. *Der unverbesserliche Romantiker: Alban Berg 1885–1835.* Vienna: Österreichischer Bundesverlag, 1985.
———, ed. *Alban Berg: Leben und Werk in Daten und Bildern.* Frankfurt: Insel, 1976.
The Berg-Schoenberg Correspondence: Selected Letters. Ed. Juliane Brand, Christopher Hailey, and Donald Harris. New York and London: Norton, 1987.
Blaukopf, Kurt. "Autobiographische Elemente in Alban Bergs *Wozzeck.*" *Österreichische Musikzeitschrift* 9/2 (May 1954): 156.
Carner, Mosco. *Alban Berg: The Man and the Work.* London: Duckworth, 1975.
DeVoto, Mark. "Alban Berg's Picture Postcard Songs." Ph.D. diss., Princeton University, 1966.
———. "Alban Berg's 'Marche Macabre,' " *Perspectives of New Music* 22 (Fall–Winter 1983/Spring–Summer 1984): 386.
Green, Douglass. "Berg's De Profundis: The Finale of the *Lyric Suite.*" *International Alban Berg Society Newsletter* 5 (June 1977): 13.
Hilmar, Ernst. *Wozzeck von Alban Berg.* Vienna: Universal, 1975.
Hilmar, Rosemary. *Alban Berg: Leben und Wirken in Wien bis zu seinen ersten Er-*

folgen als Komponist. Wiener Musikwissenschaftliche Beiträge 10. Vienna: Böl-haus, 1978.

Jarman, Douglas. *The Music of Alban Berg.* Berkeley and Los Angeles: University of California Press, 1979.

———. *Alban Berg: Wozzeck.* Cambridge and New York: Cambridge University Press, 1989.

———, ed. *The Berg Companion.* Boston: Northeastern University Press, 1990.

Keller, Hans. "The Eclecticism of *Wozzeck.*" *Music Review* 12/4 (November 1951): 309 and 13/2 (May 1952): 133.

Klein, Rudolf, ed. *Alban Berg Symposion Wien 1980: Tagungsbericht. Alban Berg Studien,* 2. Vienna: Universal, 1981.

Krenek, Ernst. "Marginal Remarks re *Lulu.*" *International Alban Berg Society Newsletter* 9 (Fall 1980): 10.

Perle, George. "The Secret Program of the *Lyric Suite.*" *International Alban Berg Society Newsletter* 5 (June 1977): 4.

———. *The Operas of Alban Berg.* Vol. 1: *Wozzeck.* Berkeley and Los Angeles: University of California Press, 1980.

———. *The Operas of Alban Berg.* Vol. 2: *Lulu.* Berkeley and Los Angeles: University of California Press, 1985.

Rauchhaupt, Ursula von. *Schoenberg, Berg, Webern: The String Quartets. A Documentary Study.* Trans. Eugene Hartzell. Hamburg: Deutsche Grammophon Gesellschaft, 1971.

Redlich, H. F. *Alban Berg: Versuch einer Würdigung.* Vienna: Universal, 1957.

———. *Alban Berg: The Man and His Music.* New York: Abelard-Schumann, 1957.

Reich, Willi. "Aus unbekannten Briefen von Alban Berg an Anton von Webern." *Schweizerische Musikzeitung* 93/2 (1 February 1953): 50.

———. *Alban Berg.* Trans. Cornelius Cardew. New York: Vienna House, 1974.

Seabury, Frida Semler. "1903 and 1904." *International Alban Berg Society Newsletter* 1 (December 1968): 5.

Stein, Jack M. "From *Woyzeck* to *Wozzeck:* Alban Berg's Adaptation of Büchner." *Germanic Review* 47 (May 1972): 168.

———. "*Lulu:* Alban Berg's Adaptation of Wedekind." *Comparative Literature* 26/3 (Summer 1974): 223.

CHAPTER SEVEN

The Problem of Expressionism in Stravinsky

> We cannot consider *Sacre* as Russian, nor even Slavic—it is more ancient and pan-human. This is the natural festival of the soul. This is the joy of love and self-sacrifice, not under the knife of crude conventionality, but in exuberance of spirit, in connecting our earthly existence with a Supreme.
>
> Nicholas Roerich (1930)

No early twentieth-century work has been perceived as so Dionysian in spirit or so anarchic in effect as *Le Sacre du Printemps* (The Rite of Spring). While most of Igor Stravinsky's oeuvre is distinctly anti-expressionist, and while most of the products of Diaghilev's ideals of *Gesamtkunstwerk* were not expressionist, *The Rite,* with strong foreshadowings in its predecessor, *Petrushka,* is generated by inner necessities and social forces clearly related to expressionism. Its musical language embodies many—if not all—of the linguistic changes of expressionism. *The Rite of Spring* is a work of universal meaning, the roots of which lie in the collective unconscious rather than in the individual psyche. On the other hand, in *Petrushka,* the puppet's prison is the dark cell of his very human soul.

The collaborative genesis of both works provided a context of demands, freedoms, and memory which provoked expressionist explosions from Stravinsky, yet his later denials of the importance of these collaborations pose difficulties. His meteoric fame, his exile from Russia, and his subsequent adoptions of Western musical styles confuse any view of his early maturity. Further, much of his literary self-explanation was written in collaboration with or "through other people."[1] As Mikhail Druskin has pointed out, Stravinsky's personality was a complex of opposed forces.[2] It is necessary to examine them in order to attempt an understanding of his compositional aims in his collaborative works.

Ultimately, Stravinsky (1882–1971) himself felt that the place of his birth was the most important fact in his life.[3] It was in the oral tradition of Russian peasant music, the directly expressive naivete of Mussorgsky, and the uninhibited tonal vocabulary of Scriabin that Stravinsky found sources for his own revolutionary language. Yet he denied these sources for much of the rest of his life. Perhaps noticing the beginning of this tendency, Debussy (who had lived and worked in Russia) wrote to Stravinsky in 1915, "You are a great artist. Be with all your strength a great Russian artist. It is so wonderful to be of one's country, to be attached to one's soil like the humblest of peasants!"[4]

Petrushka (1910–11) and *The Rite of Spring* (1911–12) come from a deep awareness of revolutionary turmoil in turn-of-the-century Russia. In his *Poetics* of 1939, while denying that he should have ever been considered a revolutionary, Stravinsky admits that the works of this pre–World War I period "appeared at a time characterized by profound changes that dislocated many things and troubled many minds. . . . The changes of which I speak effected a general revision of both the basic values and the primordial elements of music."[5] During his neoclassical retreat from revolution, much was denied by Stravinsky that has later come to light, particularly with the publication of his memories in conversations with Robert Craft, memoirs of Stravinsky's collaborators, the recovery of the sketches and choreographic notations of *The Rite,* and the revival of Nijinsky's choreography by the Joffrey Ballet.

Stravinsky's recollections of his childhood in Russia stress loneliness, fears, and personal alienation: "The real answer to your questions about my childhood is that it was a period of waiting for the moment when I could send everyone and everything connected with it to hell."[6] Always small in stature, frequently ill, a middle son with three vigorously healthy brothers, often taunted not only by his own family but by his five older cousins as well, Stravinsky developed a deep resentment toward humiliation: "I cannot abide it when others look down on me from their superior height."[7] He feared his father, the leading bass of St. Petersburg's Imperial Opera, who was renowned for his extraordinary acting ability and his fine singing of 66 operatic roles. The elder Stravinsky had a temperament, a capacity for iron-clad discipline and hard work, and performance nerves which made the family home tremble.[8] Igor seems to have felt only a sense of duty toward his mother, whom he considered cold and egotistical. Although starving for affection, he was not able to open his heart to his younger brother Gury because "in my innermost being I feared, notwithstanding our mutual affection, that there would be misunderstandings which would have deeply wounded my pride."[9] School was a hated torture, sports were not allowed because of his frailty, and St. Petersburg winters meant long incarceration in the suffocating environment of the family apartment. While his father practiced, rehearsed, and met with important people, Igor spent his time in the room he shared with Gury, which he later likened to Petrushka's cell.[10] The most wonderful event of every year of his childhood was "the violent Russian spring that seemed to begin in an hour and was like the whole earth cracking."[11] The dramatic breaking of ice on the St. Petersburg canals augured release to the relative freedom of the family estate in the countryside each summer.

As a child, Stravinsky was given piano lessons and became adept at both sightreading and improvisation. He devoured his father's opera scores and spent five or six nights a week at rehearsals of the Imperial Opera in the Marinsky Theater. Stravinsky's introduction in the summer of 1902 to the Rimsky-Korsakov family and circle, through his friends Andrey and Vladimir, sons of the composer, was the important beginning of his own artistic life. Rimsky-Korsakov agreed to teach Stravinsky orchestration privately if he would continue training in harmony and counterpoint from Rimsky's students. Stravinsky had a strong antipathy to any kind of pedantic routine. He was a fierce enemy of the Petersburg Conservatory ("that horrible musical prison"[12]), where he felt the growth of his compositional technique was restrained.[13] After his father's death, at the end of 1902 (when Stravinsky was twenty), he rebelled against his childhood surroundings, "adopted" the Rimsky-Korsakovs as a more congenial family, and later remembered being at Rimsky's home almost every day of 1903–1905. There he encountered many important composers, conductors, and virtuosi.[14] However, his family did not encourage him to continue in music but guided him instead into the study of law. Stravinsky received his law degree in 1905, and in 1906 he married his cousin Catherine, who had been his best friend since he was ten.

During this period Stravinsky entered "liberal" circles, through an uncle, the only relative who encouraged his aspirations as a composer. Uncle Ielatchitch was a passionate musical amateur and an outspoken admirer of Mussorgsky. Mussorgsky had died of alcoholism the year before Stravinsky's birth, but Stravinsky seemed to cling to those who had known and valued his untrained but "genuinely intuitive" genius.[15] He later remarked that "the milieu in which Mussorgsky's powers developed was wholly alien to the attitudes and tastes of the official [St. Petersburg] musical world at that time."[16] In 1893 Rimsky-Korsakov had revised Mussorgsky's *Boris Godunov*, and in the Rimsky household contempt for Mussorgsky's alleged sins against art remained high. In this atmosphere Stravinsky's aptitude for contradicting attitudes developed:

> Uncle Ielatchitch's house was just around the corner from Rimsky's and I would often go from one to the other, finding it difficult to keep a balance between them. . . . At that time, being influenced by the master who recomposed almost the whole work of Mussorgsky, I repeated what was usually said about his "big talent" and "poor musicianship," and about the "important services" rendered by Rimsky to his "embarrassing" and "unpresentable" scores.[17]

In the period of simmering revolutionary turmoil during the unpopular Russo-Japanese war (1904–1905), exposure to his Uncle Ielatchitch's advanced intellectual circle revealed to Stravinsky that the mind of his father-figure Rimsky was "closed to any religious or metaphysical idea" and permitted no philosophical discussion.[18] Stravinsky gives only a few clues to his own philosophy at this time, but quietly espoused the Russian revolution,[19] admired Gorky and Strindberg, and hero-worshipped Dostoevski.[20] He also wished for "music that would satisfy the ideals of my growing mind, as Rimsky's was failing to do."[21]

Other musical influences asserted themselves. Scriabin, ten years older, whom Stravinsky often encountered at Rimsky's house, was one of those the supersensitive younger composer felt to be condescending. Scriabin was "better grounded in counterpoint and harmony than most of the Russians"[22] and began to have a sudden and considerable vogue among Petersburg avant-garde circles in 1905. For a time, Stravinsky professed enthusiasm for Scriabin's music and respect for his mystical beliefs, but admiration turned to antipathy shortly after the older composer's death in 1915.[23] A source of bitter contention between Stravinsky and his mother was her continued adoration of Scriabin's music.[24] The direct influence of Scriabin's asymmetrical rhythmic patterns, one of the preoccupations of his Piano Etudes, Op. 42, of 1903, shows in Stravinsky's 1908 Piano Etudes (Exx. 7-1a and b). Scriabinesque passages occur in *The Firebird* (1910), and there is evidence that, in the period of composing *Zvezdoliki* and *The Rite*, Stravinsky studied Scriabin's music closely.[25]

Ex. 7-1. a. Scriabin, Piano Etudes, Op. 42, No. 8 (1903), mm. 1–2; b. Stravinsky, Piano Etudes, Op. 7, No. 1 (1908), mm. 1–3.

In the fertile period of 1911–12, when Stravinsky was looking for "the creation of new forms,"[26] Mussorgsky's musical language and attitude toward form were important to him. The influence of Russian speech inflections and such important peasant characteristics as the use of medieval modes, irregular or "defective" modes, and abrupt modulation from one mode to another appear in Mussorgsky's melodies and are also used by Stravinsky. ("Variable" scales found in Russian folk tunes are important ingredients of Stravinsky's simultaneous major/minor melodic and harmonic practices.[27]) Stravinsky was clearly interested in Mussorgsky's starkly abrupt harmonizations (which

Rimsky-Korsakov recomposed). They are "very close to what is to be found in the native music of Russia," according to M. D. Calvocoressi, the first to fully investigate and analyze Mussorgsky's musical sources.[28] Mussorgsky boldly used the powerful expressive device—considered ugly by his contemporaries but later adopted by Stravinsky—of parallel harmonic movement derived from the rude, archaic method of peasant harmonization. His rhythms made use of asymmetrical, changing meters peculiar to peasant song. In exploiting this material Mussorgsky was seeking "terseness and vividness in expression and characterization"[29]—an escape from formalism to a true depiction of "the subtlest traits of human nature, as manifest in individuals and in the masses."[30]

Stravinsky had a strong interest in new tendencies, which brought him into contact with Diaghilev's vanguard review, The World of Art (Mir Iskusstva, 1898–1904), and the related chamber concerts of the Evenings of Contemporary Music. There, the quartets and songs of Debussy and Ravel, as well as music of d'Indy, Brahms, and Reger, were performed along with works by Russian composers.[31] The extraordinary freshness of Debussy's music appealed strongly to Stravinsky. This discovery was an indirect reinforcement of Mussorgsky's influence, for Mussorgsky's music had enriched Debussy's vocabulary and encouraged its technical freedom and expressive immediacy.[32] In 1908 (while writing the first part of The Nightingale), Stravinsky noted in his diary, "Why should I be following Debussy so closely, when the real originator of the operatic style was Mussorgsky?"[33] He met Debussy after a performance of The Firebird in 1910, began Petrushka before a signed portrait of Debussy, and pored over his music (along with Scriabin's) while writing Zvezdoliki. While his admiration for Debussy was so intense in this period that he called Debussy "my father in music,"[34] at the time of the composition of The Rite of Spring, Stravinsky's attitude changed, turning unmistakably expressionist:

> I want to suggest neither situations nor emotions, but simply to manifest, to express them. I think there is in what are called "impressionist" methods a certain amount of hypocrisy, or at least a tendency towards vagueness and ambiguity. That I shun above all things, and that, perhaps, is the reason why my methods differ as much from those of the impressionists as they differ from academic conventional methods. Though I often find it extremely hard to do so, I always aim at straightforward expression in its simplest form. I have no use for "working-out" in dramatic or lyric music. The one essential thing is to feel and to convey one's feelings.[35]

Contrast this statement, quoted from a newspaper interview in 1911, with Stravinsky's much-discussed later view, as stated in his 1935 autobiography:

> I consider that music is, by its very nature, essentially powerless to *express* anything at all, whether a feeling, an attitude of mind, a psychological mood, a phenomenon of nature etc. *Expression* has never been an inherent property of music.[36]

The Stravinsky of 1911 was a man of totally different attitudes from the post-1917 expatriate.[37] One aspect, however, remained: in what he later acknowledged as "a rare form of kleptomania,"[38] Stravinsky took what he liked or needed for his own use from Debussy, Scriabin, Mussorgsky, and other sources, including folk and popular music.

While Rimsky-Korsakov's death in 1908 was a traumatic experience for Stravinsky,[39] his place was soon taken by Sergei Diaghilev.[40] In an article entitled "The Diaghilev I Knew," Stravinsky remembered that "everything he did was idealistic. Commercialism was entirely foreign to his nature. . . . Working for him meant working solely for the great cause of art . . . in an artistic atmosphere that was like an electric current."[41] Bronislava Nijinska remembered that "We Diaghilevtsky called ourselves the innovators who put art ahead of technique and career."[42] Diaghilev's training in musical composition, his experience exhibiting modern Russian painting, and his years as an official of the Imperial Theaters in St. Petersburg resulted in his unequivocal understanding that ballet must be created by the closest fusion of dance, painting, and music. This unified approach was responsible for Stravinsky's phenomenal public recognition and artistic growth between 1909 and 1913. Diaghilev described himself perhaps better than anyone:

> I am, firstly, a charlatan, though rather a brilliant one; secondly, a great charmer; thirdly, frightened of nobody; fourthly, a man with plenty of logic and very few scruples; fifthly, I seem to have no real talent. None the less, I believe that I have found my true vocation—to be a Maecenas; I have everything necessary except money—but that will come![43]

Diaghilev's own artistic convictions focused on a constant criterion: to what extent is the work of art based on the internal demands of the artist?[44] He wrote in *The World of Art,* "Man does not depend on exterior circumstances but on himself alone. One of the greatest merits of our times is to recognize individuality under every guise in every epoch."[45]

The World of Art provided a platform for conflicting ideas in the Russian fin-de-siècle, which in turn laid the foundation for the Russian avant-garde. The struggle was between extremes: Russian culture versus that of the West; art-for-art's-sake versus art of the individual; art of the past versus art of the future. Of the *World of Art* circle, Alexandre Benois and Nicolas Roerich, designers and scenarists respectively of *Petrushka* and *The Rite of Spring,* were the most important figures—other than Diaghilev—in the development of Stravinsky's genius. In themselves they represented opposites. Benois, an original founder of the dilettante group which became the *World of Art* circle, was the conservative, Europeanized, cautiously historical eclectic. He considered Diaghilev, who was introduced to the circle in 1895, too Russian, "barbaric," and "Scythian" in his interests and tendencies, and set himself the task of educating Diaghilev in the European visual arts. (Benois found Diaghilev a brilliant pupil and acknowledged that the tables were soon turned.[46]) Roerich came from the same St. Petersburg generation as Benois but played a minor role in *The World of Art;* he was spurned by Benois and other Europeanized members of the circle for his extensive interest and erudition in ancient Slavic culture. His work was of profound importance to the neonational revival of Russian peasant art, modeled on the English Arts and Crafts movement. The revival was begun by Moscow merchant Savva Mamontov and his wife at their estate, Abramtsevo, in the 1870s, and was continued by Princess Mariia Tenisheva at Talashkino in the 1890s and early 1900s. It gathered momentum after the revolution of 1905–1906[47] and lent urgency to Diaghilev's desire to produce the first truly Russian ballet. In 1906 the two parallel movements merged, as Roerich was drawn into the *World of Art* circle, exhibited by Diaghilev, and commissioned to design the sets depicting the vast reaches of the Russian steppes for the ballet on Borodin's Polovtsian dances from *Prince Igor.* It was also in the years following 1906 that Stravinsky began to move in *World of Art* circles.[48]

Stravinsky's *Firebird* (1909–10) was Diaghilev's first fully commissioned ballet and the first ballet to explore the realm of Russian folk tales. Like Kandinsky's early fairy-tale paintings, it relies strongly on thematic symbols. The effectively theatrical device of associating the human element in *The Firebird* with diatonic folk melody and the supernatural with exotic chromaticism was "borrowed" from Rimsky-Korsakov, but the notion of using the tritone to characterize evil points toward Stravinsky's more expressionist gestures in *Petrushka* and *The Rite of Spring.* The obsessive motoric rhythms in the Infernal Dance of Kastchei's subjects provide a foretaste of Stravinsky's preoccupation with the psychological properties of rhythm, which is a dominant factor in *The Rite.*

Stravinsky worked closely with the choreographer Michel Fokine during the composition of *Firebird,* as Fokine was himself a fine musician. His suggestions about the dramatic presentation of folk melody (fragmentation of the melody as a dramatic action is prepared, then full realization only when the complete action takes place)[49] proved useful to Stravinsky in his subsequent works. Diaghilev's ideals of synthesis demanded close collaboration, which often took the form of turbulent committee meetings over tea and shaped the ideas of all the artists involved. In the clash of egos a single purpose held: a Messianic zeal to claim for Russia, as Stravinsky put it to Romain Rolland in 1914, "the role of a fine, healthy barbaric state, full of germinating ideas that will inspire thought throughout the world."[50]

During this period Stravinsky developed a strong interest in ethnology. He later claimed that his early memories of peasant melodies and rhythm were remarkably concrete.[51] They furnished him with sounds and musical materials of such importance to his "Russian" period (1909–20) that his "powers of fabrication were able to tap some unconscious 'folk' memory," creating modal material which sounds genuinely aboriginal.[52] Stravinsky also dealt directly with folk material—a photograph taken in 1909 shows him transcribing a peasant song (Ill. 7-1). Richard Taruskin and Lawrence Mor-

Ill. 7-1. Photo of Igor Stravinsky transcribing peasant song in 1909 at Ustilug.
Courtesy Theodore Stravinsky estate.

ton have investigated Stravinsky's concealed use of Russian folk song in *The Rite of Spring,* for which there is no documentation. Taruskin finds that

> Rimsky-Korsakov sought in the songs of Russian folk ceremonial only thematic material, which he then subjected to a treatment in the style of the mainstream of European art music. . . . Stravinsky, by seeking in folk songs something far more basic to his musical vocabulary and technique, was to use them as part of his self-liberation from that artistic mainstream, and as things turned out, its downright subversion.[53]

Stravinsky had such respect for Roerich's knowledge of the roots of Russian culture that he suggested to Roerich that they collaborate on a primitive ballet. Benois, however, opined that the original idea of *The Rite* was Roerich's. He felt that Stravinsky was attracted by the idea of reconstructing the mysterious past because it gave him free rein in his search for unusual rhythms and sounds.[54] Stravinsky himself has connected the creation of *The Rite* with his rebellion against the traditional styles of his own *Firebird,* against the orchestral formulae and academic tonal constrictions of Rimsky-Korsakov's tutelage, against the "official" St. Petersburg musical establishment, and against his hated childhood.[55]

It is clear from Stravinsky's urgent and secretive correspondence with Roerich in the spring and summer months of 1910 (at the time when Stravinsky had the "fleeting vision" of the sacrifice of a maiden to propitiate Yarilo, the god of spring) that Roerich's ideas for the libretto were essential to Stravinsky's composing, and that Stravinsky had composed a preliminary musical sketch when conferring with Roerich in the spring of 1910. Why the idea for *Petrushka* intervened is less clear, but it was also a rebellious concept. At first, the central image of the work that became *Petrushka* was not a puppet, but "a man in evening dress, with long hair, the musician or the poet of romantic tradition. He placed several heteroclite objects on the keyboard and rolled them up and down. At this the orchestra exploded with the most vehement protestations—hammer blows, in fact."[56] Stravinsky's rebellion was expressed in "a sort of combat between the piano and the orchestra,"[57] which became the second tableau, the scene in Petrushka's cell. When Diaghilev heard this piece and the Russian Dance in September 1910, he urged theatricalizing the piano-orchestra idea, keeping the original spirit: "The real subject [became] the droll, ugly, shifting personage who was always in an explosion of revolt . . . a sort of guignol called Pierrot in France, Kasperle in Germany, and Petrushka in Russia."[58]

Benois, whose knowledge of the stage had been proven in several previous ballets, and who had a special feeling for the Petrushka character from his childhood memories, was brought in on the collaboration and began to set a libretto to the music Stravinsky had written. The scenario dramatized the "grief, and rage, and love as well as the hopeless despair" Benois heard when Stravinsky played the piano/orchestra combat for him in December 1910.[59] Benois described Petrushka as "the personification of the spiritual and suffering side of humanity."[60] Stravinsky thought of the puppet as having a double existence; the real Petrushka is the exuberant, immortally sassy "ghost" who, at the end of the ballet, thumbs his nose at the world, in general, and his enemy the Magician, in particular. The bitonal arpeggios characterizing this double-sided "key to the enigma of Petrushka"[61] opened up a new world of tonal expansion, the intent of which initially was to insult. Stravinsky "discovered" these arpeggios on the keyboard, one hand playing black keys, the other white, a tritone apart (Ex. 7-2).

Ex. 7-2. Stravinsky, *Petrushka*, Second Tableau, [49], mm. 1–6, Petrushka chord.

The multifaceted musical portrayal of Petrushka is achieved in the Second Tableau by abrupt and extreme shifts of mood, color, texture, and tempo as well as by rapidly changing meters, which caused trouble for the dancers throughout the ballet. Stravinsky plumbs the depths of Petrushka's humiliation, fears, amorous desires, longing for freedom, and impulsive sassiness in many-layered passages of psychological simultaneity. One instance of this writing occurs during the Magic Trick in the First Tableau (at [32] of the 1911 version). Debussy singled out this tonally ambiguous passage for praise: "There is in it a kind of sonorous magic, a mysterious transformation of mechanical souls which become human by a spell of which, until now, you seem to be the unique inventor."[62] This scene reveals the three puppets— Petrushka, the Ballerina, and the Moor—hanging in their little theater in the midst of the Shrovetide Fair; they are brought to life by the Magician. ("Their coming to life should be somehow accompanied by suffering," wrote Benois.[63]) Eerie chromatic sliding figures, shivering trills and tremolos, hesitant repeated-note figures, and downward fluttering arpeggiated gestures express the stirrings, not just of heartbeat and breath, but also of differing feelings and emotions in the three puppets before they begin the robustly pandiatonic Russian dance (Ex. 7-3). Much of the *Petrushka* score shows Stravinsky's developing emphasis on contrapuntal writing, but seldom with as much enigmatic, detailed concentration as in this "mysterious transformation" from the mechanical to the human psyche.

Another passage that explores Petrushka's deepest self occurs in the Second Tableau, when the clown attempts—and fails completely—to impress the Ballerina, who has entered his cheerless cell. Interrupted fragments of ostinati, off-beat chords, changing meters, twitching grace notes, constantly shifting string techniques—all in a jumble of notes representing different aspects of Petrushka's character in incoherent order—contribute to a bizarre, agitated expression of gawky, tormented desire (Ex. 7-4). These two subjective passages are the most contrapuntally complex and rhythmically fragmented in the work. Their intent in reaching into the realms of the inexpressible makes Petrushka a uniquely moving character rather than a merely colorful clown figure.

Further expressionistic distortions in *Petrushka* include bizarre orchestral effects and rhythmic irregularity (e.g., the Moor's grotesque dance with the Ballerina in the Third Tableau and the Bear's attempt at musical imitation of his keeper in the Fourth) and the contrapuntal simultaneity demanded in the outer tableaux by the theatrical overlappings of events. Stravinsky's practice of disguising and distorting folk materials to serve his expressive purpose is another expressionist trait in this work.[64] "It is the composer's mentality which selects and subjugates the material, and this mentality cannot, of course, be disassociated from the qualities of the intellectual environment that surrounds it," wrote Boris Asaf'yev in 1929; in *Petrushka* Stravinsky "pulled out by the roots the choking weeds of academic dogma that flourished in a culture of security and prosperity and self-satisfied Philistinism."[65]

Constant brainstorming sessions by Diaghilev, Fokine, Nijinsky, and Benois, along with close correspondence and further meetings with Stravinsky, produced a stimulating synthesis of contributions. The tremendously successful production was highlighted by the unforgettable, grotesque characterization by Nijinsky (who had hitherto danced roles of beauty and seduction) in

The curtain of the little theater opens and the crowd sees three
puppets: Petrushka, a Moor, and a Ballerina.

Ex. 7-3. Stravinsky, *Petrushka*, First Tableau, [32], mm. 1–4.

Ex. 7-4. Stravinsky, *Petrushka,* Second Tableau, [57], mm. 1–5.

Ill. 7-2. Portrait of Vaslav Nijinsky as Petrushka. Stravinsky-Diaghilev Foundation, New York.

the title role (Ill. 7-2)[66] *Petrushka's* great success in 1911, Stravinsky later remarked, "was good for me in that it gave me the absolute conviction of my ear just as I was about to begin *Le Sacre du Printemps.*"[67]

In early summer 1911, after the success of *Petrushka* and while making plans to meet Roerich at Talashkino to collaborate on the project both called "our offspring," Stravinsky explored nontonal vocabulary in settings of poetry by Russia's leading Symbolist poet of the day, Konstantin Balmont (1867–1943). The two Balmont songs for high voice and piano (1911), Stravinsky's first pieces written without a key signature, experiment with modality. The Symbolist/impressionist cantata for male chorus and large orchestra, *Zvezdoliki* (King of the Stars), is one of his most radical and most difficult compositions to perform. Stravinsky ventures far into atonal realms, setting the choral and orchestral forces on different tonal planes not just as an experiment in bitonality, but to symbolize the difference between the harvesting people of the earth and the mighty King of the Stars, whose word they obey.

The rhythmic aspect of *Zvezdoliki* stands in extreme contrast to that of *The Rite of Spring*. In *Zvezdoliki*, when the rhythm is not purely declamatory it is sublimely static. Harmonic experimentation takes precedence over other elements of music. The powerful unaccompanied chords of the opening choral "motto" (Ex. 7-5) provided Stravinsky with the tonally ambiguous major/minor harmony he later used frequently in *The Rite*. These chords contain further novel harmonic combinations, which create varying degrees of dissonant tension. *Zvezdoliki* was dedicated to Debussy, but the extraordinarily dissonant sound of the piece is only occasionally reminiscent of the French composer. In a postcard to Florent Schmitt written on 21 July 1911, during the composition of *Zvezdoliki*, Stravinsky indicates that he is "playing only Debussy and Scriabin."[68] It seems likely that the harmonic experiments in chords with tonal interferences (i.e., chords with built-in affirmation and negation of a tonal base, or simultaneous harmonic stress and resolution) were also influenced by Scriabin's harmonic innovations, as well as by the bitonal advances Stravinsky had made in *Petrushka*.

Ex. 7-5. Stravinsky, *Zvezdoliki*, opening motto. Reprinted by permission of C. F. Peters Corporation on behalf of the publisher Robert Forberg, Berlin.

Although Stravinsky later denied it, the use of Balmont's transcendental texts at this time in his development is important. Martin Cooper has written that in the last years of the Tsarist regime

> Russian society, influenced by artists and intellectuals, developed a prophetic, apocalyptic sense, dimly foreseeing the near end of the world it knew and the birth of some new era of which social reform and a universal heightening of spirituality were the only two clearly distinguished traits.[69]

Zvezdoliki serves as a stage—before beginning *The Rite*—in which Stravinsky explored musical expression of the mystical-transcendent aspect of the Russian spirit. It is a preparation for his purpose, in *The Rite*, "to express the sublime uprising of Nature renewing herself—the whole pantheistic uprising of the universal harvest."[70]

In July 1911 Stravinsky met with Nicholas Roerich to examine the important collection of Russian ethnic art at Talashkino. Although he had sketched one page of music and had worked with Roerich on the scenario of *The Rite* in the spring of 1910, not until September 1911, when every detail of the staging had been settled, was Stravinsky able to begin composing, "in a state of passion and excitement."[71] He wrote of Roerich, an essential catalyst for this work, "Who else could help me, who else knows the secret of our ancestors' close feeling for the earth?"[72]

Roerich (1874–1947) traced his lineage back to the Vikings and tenth-century Russian ancestry. In 1903–1904 he made several trips to ancient Russian cities, sketching early Russian architecture, and soon began a campaign for the preservation of ancient Russian art. In 1909 and 1910, during his involvement with the Diaghilev Ballet, he traveled to Italy, Germany, Holland, and England. His pantheistic paintings and theater designs reflect his interest in the "monumental, serene and noble" qualities that inspired him as he investigated the roots of Russian art from the Stone Age onward.[73] Because of this very serenity, his painting cannot in any way be called expressionist, but his essays of the period show a marked similarity in attitude and vocabulary to expressionist manifestos:

> We have become poor in beauty. . . . Dead is the great Pan! . . . Beauty is useless where exists the great depression of our age—all-powerful vulgarity . . . where the unusual is depressed by a thousand hands. . . . [Art] may arouse the consciousness to something pure and good. . . . In order to see, one has to bathe one's eyes with pure art, without methods, boundaries and conditions. Whoever sees thus will not return to the commonplace. . . . An inner necessity . . . developed the venture of the schools and museum in Talashkino . . . away from the marts, from profits and calculations.[74]

By pure art, Roerich meant art of antiquity, but he did not have a purely historical approach. His emphasis was on intuition and penetration of the spirit of the past.[75] (The ritual in *The Rite* is not an authentic one, but an amalgam with creative license.) Along with Diaghilev, his motto was "Away with academic forms!"[76] Because Roerich believed that "the most ancient and most modern thoughts are united,"[77] he emotionalized and dramatized primitive antiquity in his paintings. Like Stravinsky's other collaborators, Roerich had a keen understanding of music, for he taught composition at the Talashkino arts colony and was profoundly interested in combining musical and pictorial forms. His contact with Stravinsky dated back to 1905, when he began designing for the theater in St. Petersburg. He recalled that in 1909 Stravinsky, whose character in this period was dominated by "turbulent spontaneity," approached him with the idea that they jointly write a ballet. "After thinking it over, I suggested two ballets to him—one 'Rite of Spring,' and the other 'Game of Chess.' "[78] Roerich's approach to *The Rite* was based on the concept that in the "refined primitiveness of our ancestors . . . rhythm, the sacred symbol, and refinement of gesture were great and sacred concepts."[79] Stravinsky's correspondence with Roerich during the composition of *The Rite* (1910–12) expresses the "impatient expectation" with which the composer awaited Roerich's libretto version and his desire to "exchange constantly our ever new impressions—they are so necessary for refreshment in work."[80] What Stravinsky had seen at Talashkino provided him with vivid visual images, to which he excitedly referred in his feverish correspondence. He had also transcribed instrumental and vocal music from a folk musician there.[81]

Stravinsky hoped Diaghilev would produce the new ballet in the spring of 1912. Once begun, the composing of this piece—the only one in which Stravinsky allowed Dionysian forces to rule him—proceeded very swiftly and brought him "countless happy hours."[82] Between late September 1911 and early January 1912 he completed the first half of the work. He triumphantly reported to Roerich: "It seems to me that I have penetrated into the mystery of springtime, its lapidarian rhythms, and have experienced them together with the characters of our creation. Nevertheless, I am to blame."[83] Between

1 March and the middle of April 1912, the second half of the work was completed, "in a state of exaltation and exhaustion," with the exception of the final sacrificial dance, which Stravinsky could play, but did not yet know how to write.[84]

In May 1913, at the time of the first performance of *The Rite*, in Paris, Stravinsky described the new ballet as a "work of faith," in which he had striven "toward a somewhat vaster abstraction" than in *Firebird* and *Petrushka*. The "vaster abstraction" was the premise of portraying the primeval birth of spring. The sound of the Prelude "is the vague and profound uneasiness of a universal puberty." Its intent is to express

> the fear of nature before the arising of beauty, a sacred terror at the midday sun, a sort of pagan cry. . . . Each instrument is like a bud. . . . The whole orchestra . . . should have the significance of the birth of Spring. . . . The adolescents are Augurs of Spring, who mark in their steps the rhythm of spring, the pulse-beat of spring. . . . In their rhythms one feels the cataclysm of groups about to form. . . . The defining of forces [occurs] through struggle. . . . All are seized with terror [as] the Sage gives a benediction to the Earth . . . becoming one with the soil. His benediction is as a signal for an eruption of rhythm . . . like the new energies of nature. . . . When [the Chosen One] is on the point of falling exhausted, the Ancestors . . . glide toward her like rapacious monsters in order that she may not touch the ground; they pick her up and raise her toward heaven. The annual cycle of forces which are born again and which fall again into the bosom of nature, is accomplished in its essential rhythms.[85]

The "lapidary" concept of rhythm (sculpted in or engraved on stone) may have been inspired by Roerich, whose researches extended to the Stone Age. This concept was basic to Stravinsky's composition of *The Rite*[86] and to the meaning of spring in his own emotions of rebellion. It resulted in a new language of rhythm, which becomes the overwhelming force in the ballet, often reducing melodic and harmonic materials to objects, manipulated and hurled about by primitive rhythmic impulse. In the midst of work on the "Dance of the Earth," the final dance of the first scene, in which visual images of people drunk with spring were vividly in his mind, Stravinsky wrote a note on the sketch: "Music exists when there is rhythm, as life exists when there is a pulse."[87]

Béla Bartók's essays and books on folk music have provided evidence that the revolutionary aspect of Stravinsky's rhythm is largely derived from folk sources. Among the rhythmic features of *The Rite* and other works of his Russian period are strict $\frac{2}{4}$ dances with irregular, shifting accents and sections in quick tempi with asymmetrical meters. Bartók was convinced that Stravinsky was so steeped in these folk practices that he was able to create his own convincing derivations.[88]

The "Dance of the Earth" is a through-composed piling up of repetitive rhythmic elements in the mosaic fashion Bartók found so feverishly exciting in the primitive construction of folk dances.[89] The first element consists of eruptive, violently syncopated chords preceded by glissandi at the outset of the dance ([72]). The second is the short, interrupted irregular triplet motive in the horns (beginning at [74]). The third presents short bursts of sharply reiterated sixteenth notes in the trumpets (beginning 5 mm. before [76]), taken from the motoric sixteenths running throughout the dance in timpani, contrabasses, and violas. The fourth is an ascending whole-tone scale in quarter notes. This scale, at first only three notes in the background, gathers pitches and intensity to become the full six-note scale as the second and third elements are taken up by more instruments (from [76] on). At the height of this cumulative excitement of fours against threes, the eruptive first element recurs *fff* (at [78]), climaxing the rhythmic tension—and ending scene 1—with convulsive outbursts.

In the "Dance of the Earth," rhythmic disturbance and excitement tear at the fabric of a regular $\frac{3}{4}$ meter; in "Augurs of Spring," a regular $\frac{2}{4}$ meter is violated by syncopations and interruptions. In the more complex second half of the work, changing meters and asymmetrical rhythms are added to the explosive rhythmic devices. The most disturbing example is the martial dance glorifying the Chosen One (at [104]), a male dance of extreme violence ("I was thinking of Amazonians," quipped Stravinsky in his eighties[90]). It is introduced by a barbaric measure of eleven pulses *(marcato e pesante)* on a dissonant chord in the strings, combined with four timpani tuned at dissonant intervals, while the men appear from the wings, "as though for an ambuscade," and the women retire. The dance was imagined by Stravinsky as a ricochet of movement in rhythmic groups of twos and threes.[91] Although the basic rhythmic cell is simple (Ex. 7-6), rhythmic expectations are annihilated by constantly changing meters and strongly irregular bass accents in tuba and timpani. The enormous orchestral sound, stretched to its extreme ranges, is broken by unexpected rests or shifts in texture, adding to the constant sense of dislocation (Ex. 7-7). Although there is a recognizable ABA form in this dance, considerations of formal balance are outweighed by the rhythmic violence.

Ex. 7-6. Stravinsky, *The Rite of Spring,* "Glorification of the Chosen One," rhythmic cell.

The harmonic vocabulary makes use of the dissonant advances of *Zvezdoliki*. Basically tonal triads contain or are combined with tonal interferences, such as the major/minor ambivalence, unresolved appoggiaturas, and added ninths, elevenths, and thirteenths. The bitonal "Augurs" chord (at [13]) in the first dance offers a cell from which much harmonic material is derived. The practice of combining two tonalities in one chord is extended, so that a significant chord such as the one occurring at the mystical moment in Part I,

Ex. 7-7. Stravinsky, *The Rite of Spring,* "Glorification of the Chosen One, 2 mm. before–2 mm. after [106].

when the Sage blesses the earth with a kiss, could be seen as a polytonal aggregation of three triads (Ex. 7-8). This chord, which in 1913 represented to Ernest Ansermet "the maximum harmonic tension of which musical consciousness is capable,"[92] can also be thought of as an extension of Scriabin's harmonic language.

Ex. 7-8. Stravinsky, *The Rite of Spring,* "The Kiss of the Earth," 1 m. before [72].

Stravinsky may have been further encouraged to rely on his ear and his instinct by Schoenberg's Piano Pieces, Op. 11, which Michel Calvocoressi remembered Stravinsky reading with excitement in Paris, soon after their publication in 1911.[93] The stubborn atonality of the second Schoenberg piece may have influenced the entrance of the Sage's theme (from [64] to [72]), where tonal conflict between the chromatic ostinato figure and the surrounding texture is extreme and continuous. This conflict has its cause in the dramatic situation: the Sage must intrude his authority over the destructive youthful antagonisms of the "Ritual of the Rival Tribes." At climactic moments in these war games, chords occur that are built on tritones and tritone progressions, such as might be found in the harmonic vocabulary of Mussorgsky or Scriabin (Exx. 7-9a and b).

An expressionist attitude is also evident in the manner in which Stravinsky distorted folk songs both rhythmically and melodically in *The Rite.* The extended bassoon melody which opens the work is a Lithuanian folk song. By investigating the published collection acknowledged by Stravinsky as his source, Lawrence Morton found other Lithuanian melodies that appear to have been transformed in rhythm and mode (Exx. 7-10a–d). There is also much evidence in the *Sketches* that harmonies were often generated from these melodic materials (a practice common among all expressionist composers). Stravinsky created dissonant harmonies out of elements from modal folk melodies, or even accompanied a melody with a variant of itself.[94] The license to create a liberating language from expressive distortion and manipulation of pristine folk material was also Bartók's way of expressing his individual voice.

Stravinsky well remembered his iconoclastic rebellion against St. Petersburg academic tradition when he had forgotten all else about the origins of the work. As he remarked in 1959:

Ex. 7-9. Stravinsky, *The Rite of Spring,* "Games of the Rival Tribes." a. 4 mm. before [59]; b. 2 mm. before–3 mm. after [63].

> I was guided by no system whatever in *Le Sacre du Printemps*. When I think of the music of the other composers of that time who interest me—Berg's music which is synthetic (in the best sense), and Webern's, which is analytic—how much more *theoretical* it seems than *Le Sacre*. And these composers belonged to and were supported by a great tradition. Very little immediate tradition lies behind *Le Sacre du Printemps*, however, and no theory. I had only my ear to help me: I heard and I wrote what I heard. I am the vessel through which *Le Sacre* passed.[95]

Twenty years after the catastrophic reception the work received at its first performance, Stravinsky found it "impossible . . . to recall what were the

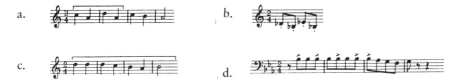

Ex. 7-10. a. Lithuanian fragment; b. Stravinsky, *The Rite of Spring,* "Augurs of Spring" ostinato [14]; c. Lithuanian fragment; d. Stravinsky, *The Rite of Spring,* "Augurs of Spring" melody [19].

feelings which animated me in composing *[The Rite]*."[96] His expressionist phase ended abruptly with its scandalous Paris premiere in May 1913. (Minor reverberations of Petrushka's anguish reappeared in Three Pieces for String Quartet, 1914.) Like Schoenberg, he claimed, "I was made a revolutionary in spite of myself."[97] In 1914 his interest turned to writing music that was (by 1921) "homogeneous, perfectly impersonal, and perfectly mechanical."[98] In subsequent years he erased from his mind the exaltation he had felt in composing *The Rite*, calling it "decadent music."[99]

At the work's first European, British, and American performances, many saw the antiromantic conception of a prehistoric birth of spring as purely savage. In his preoccupation with rhythm, Stravinsky had made no attempt to please the ear, had conveyed nothing more than something primitive and unformed.[100] The clash of tonal combinations had never been heard before.[101] Edward Dent complained that,

> Listening to Stravinsky is like wrestling with a new foreign language that is not based upon Latin or Greek . . . [and] entirely ignores the principles of syntax which we have been brought up to regard as logical and inevitable. . . . He does not pretend to argue; he just makes noises at us. . . . One has to go back and learn to take pleasure in the first physical impact of sound.[102]

On the other hand, a letter to the *New York Times*, headlined "Stravinsky and Psychoanalysis," argued, "Stravinsky did not so much say, 'Come, we are savages!' as he says, 'Come, we were once savages; let us see how it was, we intellectual people!' . . . *The Rite of Spring* is [only] a further proof that dancing is sex."[103] The music critic Jacques Rivière also recognized this vision of primal truth at the 1913 Paris premiere. Here at last, he wrote, was a frank, raw masterpiece which renounced the usual trickeries and softenings of Impressionism. The music was magnificently limited. Stravinsky's preoccupation was to utter everything expressly, specifically. The character of his music sprang from the will toward direct expression. Debussy indicates, but Stravinsky announces fully. For Rivière the work was a revelation of a new world: It is a biological ballet; a dance before man was; nothing but the bitterness of the struggle, the panic which accompanies the rising of the sap; nothing but the horrible work of cells. Spring is seen from the inside, in its effort, its spasm, its turning masses of protoplasm. We are plunged into lower realms, we assist the turbulence of birth. It is a prodigious spectacle of anguish.[104]

The artistic impulse to reach back to primitivism in order to find fresh means to fearless self-expression was basic to the *Brücke* painters. It is echoed in the animal paintings of Franz Marc, in the pre-Christian symbolism of Wassily Kandinsky, and in the sexual violence of Kokoschka's play and drawings for *Mörder, Hoffnung der Frauen*. In their time, expressionist works in many fields of art could have received the comment made by the musicologist and critic Louis Laloy, at whose home Stravinsky and Debussy first aired a four-hand version of *The Rite* in June 1912: "When they had finished

I. Erich Heckel, *Crystal Day*, 1913. Oil on canvas, 120 x 96 cm. Bayerische Staatsgemäldesammlungen, Munich. Legacy of Markus and Martha Kruss. Copyright 1992 ARS, New York.

II. Franz Marc, *Tiger*, 1912. Oil on canvas, 110 x 101 cm. Städtische Galerie im Lenbachhaus, Munich.

III. Wassily Kandinsky, *Sketch 1 for Composition VII*, 1913. Oil on canvas, 78 x 100 cm. Collection Aljoscha Klee, Bern. Copyright 1992 ARS, New York.

IV. Edvard Munch, *The Scream,* 1893. Tempera and casein on cardboard. 91 x 73.5 cm. National Gallery, Oslo. [Photo: Jacques Lathion]

there was no question of embracing, nor even of compliments. We were dumbfounded, overwhelmed by this hurricane which had come from the depths of the ages, and which had taken life by the roots."[105]

Select Bibliography

Asaf'yev, Boris. *A Book About Stravinsky*. Trans. R. F. French. Ann Arbor: UMI Research Press, 1982.

Benois, Alexandre. *Reminiscences of the Russian Ballet*. Trans. Mary Britnieva. New York: Da Capo, 1977.

Bowlt, John E. *The Silver Age: Russian Art of the Early Twentieth Century and the "World of Art" Group*. Newtonville, MA: Oriental Research Partners, 1979.

Buckle, Richard. *Diaghilev*. New York: Atheneum, 1979.

Calvocoressi, M. D. *Mussorgsky: His Life and Works*. Fair Lawn, NJ: Essential Books, 1956.

Druskin, Mikhail. *Igor Stravinsky: His Personality, Works and Views*. Trans. Martin Cooper. Cambridge: Cambridge University Press, 1983.

Lesure, François. *Press Book: Le Sacre du Printemps*. Geneva: Editions Minkoff, 1980.

Morton, Lawrence. *"Le Sacre du Printemps:* Literary and Musical Origins." *Tempo* 128 (March 1979): 9–16.

Pasler, Jann, ed. *Confronting Stravinsky: Man, Musician, and Modernist*. Berkeley: University of California Press, 1986.

Roerich, Nicholas. *The Realm of Light*. New York: Roerich Museum Press, 1931.

Solivanova, Nina. *The World of Roerich*. New York: International Art Center, 1922.

Stravinsky, Igor. *An Autobiography*. New York: Simon and Schuster, 1936.

———. "The Diaghilev I Knew." *Atlantic Monthly* 192 (November 1953): 33–36.

———. *Poetics of Music*. Trans. Arthur Knodel and Ingolf Dahl. New York: Random House, 1960.

———. *The Rite of Spring Sketches (1911–13)*. London: Boosey & Hawkes, 1969.

———. *Selected Correspondence*, vol. 1. Ed. Robert Craft. New York: Knopf, 1982.

Stravinsky, Igor, and Craft, Robert. *Expositions and Developments*. New York: Doubleday, 1962.

———. *Conversations with Igor Stravinsky*. Berkeley: University of California Press, 1980.

———. *Memories and Commentaries*. Berkeley: University of California Press, 1981.

Stravinsky, Theodore. *Catherine and Igor Stravinsky: A Family Album*. London: Boosey & Hawkes, 1973.

Stravinsky, Vera, and Craft, Robert. *Stravinsky in Pictures and Documents*. New York: Simon and Schuster, 1978.

Taruskin, Richard. "Russian Folk Melodies in *The Rite of Spring*." *Journal of the American Musicological Society* 33/3 (Fall 1980): 501–43.

Van den Toorn, Pieter C. *Stravinsky and The Rite of Spring: The Beginnings of a Musical Language*. Berkeley: University of California Press, 1987.

Van Vechten, Carl. *Music After the Great War and Other Studies*. New York: Schirmer, 1915.

Vlad, Roman. *Stravinsky*. 3d ed. Trans. F. Fuller. London: Oxford, 1978.

White, Eric Walter. *Stravinsky: The Composer and His Works*. Berkeley: University of California Press, 1966.

———. "Stravinsky in Interview." *Tempo* 97 (1971): 6–9.

CHAPTER EIGHT

Béla Bartók

> Those who paint a landscape for the sake of painting a landscape, those who write a symphony just for the sake of writing a symphony are in the best of cases good craftsmen. I cannot conceive of works of art other than as manifestations of their makers' limitless enthusiasm, despair, sorrow, anger, revenge, scorn, and sarcasm.
>
> Béla Bartók (1909)

Bartók's period of most intense expressionism, like Schoenberg's, dates from 1908 (with his abandonment of youthful romanticism) to 1923 (when his compositional attitudes were altered by wide public recognition and the neoclassical climate in music). During this period not all his works were expressionist. Like Beethoven, his ideal until his turn in the 1920s to Baroque models,[1] Bartók concentrated his main spiritual development in certain key works, which originated from particular psychological need. Bartók's expressionist works, like Schoenberg's and Webern's, were provoked by periods of agonizing personal crisis. His "spiritual loneliness"—which is also an intellectual loneliness—and his inability to find the "ideal companion," mentioned in his 1905 letter to his mother (quoted on p. 7), caused Bartók recurrent episodes of psychological and sexual turmoil, despair verging upon suicide, and subsequent salvation through work and composition.[2] String Quartets Nos. 1 and 2 and two stage works, *Duke Bluebeard's Castle* and *The Miraculous Mandarin,* were important feats of culmination and resolution in this expressionist period.

Not surprisingly, Bartók's spiritual progress through crises was paralleled by his development of a unique expressive musical language. But, as in similar situations with Webern's oeuvre, because of the late acceptance of Bartók's two important expressionist stage works and their publication only in the 1920s, these works are now available to the public in considerably *less* expressionist, revised versions. Examinations of these revisions by György Kroó[3] and John Vinton[4] reveal Bartók's effort to tighten, balance, and make more publicly acceptable both the form and the content of his treasured stage works. According to Zoltán Kodály, Bartók's closest musical friend and collaborator, "In the works of his youth [Bartók] sought an outlet for the ups and downs of life in the verbose, animated, though somewhat loose forms. Later his ever increasing concentration thrust out every superfluity, everything inessential."[5] Kodály also insisted, as have others who knew him, that although in Bartók the scientist (collector and codifier) and the artist were inseparably merged,[6] "Any attempt to find some special or contrived scale in his works proved to be fruitless. . . . Most of [his] condemned dissonances spring from the melodies. . . . He has no 'system'; . . . the expression is dictated by the message."[7]

László Somfai, director of the Bartók Archive in Budapest, echoes this view:

> Beyond the formal surface of several movements or full compositions of Bartók a sophisticated plan, often a genuine "secret program," can be discovered, in many cases only from the manuscript sources. He did not make plans and precompositional determinations in elementary question[s] of musical grammar (such as key-structure, chords, motivic variation, etc.). "I never created new theories in advance," Bartók stated in the Harvard Lectures (1943). "This attitude does not mean that I composed without set plans and without sufficient control. The plans were concerned with the spirit of the new work and with technical problems (for instance, formal structure involved by the spirit of the work), all more or less instinctively felt." He was aware of the fact that intuition played a central role in his composition. There is ample evidence of this in the manuscripts.[8]

These statements are particularly true of the pre-1921 expressionist works and corroborate Bartók's own insistence, to his early biographer, Denijs Dille, that "All my music is in the first place a matter of feeling and instinct. Do not ask me why I have written thus and not otherwise. I can give only one answer to all this: I wrote the way I felt."[9]

Bartók's life, from earliest childhood, was punctuated by periods of the most acute psychological suffering. At one of his deepest points of crisis, he wrote in a letter, "I have a sad misgiving that I shall never find any consolation in life save in music," and followed this thought with a line of music, rather than try to describe his feelings in words.[10] Composing was self-revelation for Bartók, who was otherwise "just never really capable of conveying his emotions."[11] Kodály remembered that Bartók raised a "barbed-wire fence" around himself in self-defense, a consequence of being spoiled as a child and therefore oversensitive. He longed for affection, but introversion was a basic trait of his character; he was afraid of people and did not warm easily. He wished to experience unknown things, and he had gigantic willpower.[12] His profound inner tension may have resulted partly from a polarity inherited from his parents: his father was talented, restless, and "emotionally strenuous"; his mother was orderly, systematic, and also possessed of an iron will.[13] Antal Molnár, violist in the Waldbauer-Kerpely String Quartet, which introduced much of Bartók's music from 1910 on, recalled the unbridgeable contrast between his outer and inner life. This was particularly apparent when

Bartók performed as a pianist, "as if, under the effect of some demonic power, his whole being were discharging electricity," then, at the end of the performance, "standing . . . with his emotionless exterior, without any sign of his calling, the 'clerk'; bowing his head in reluctant thanks for the ovation."[14]

Bartók was born in 1881 in a small town in what is now Rumania. Both his parents were musical. His father, headmaster of the local agricultural school, founded a musical league and an orchestra in the town and composed dance pieces. Bartók's mother began his musical training on the piano. Traumatized in infancy (after a smallpox vaccination) by a painful and disfiguring rash which plagued him until he was five, Bartók was a serious, lonely child, who hid from strangers in embarrassment and had no playmates. Pneumonia, other illnesses, and the misdiagnosis of a curvature of the spine further hampered his early development in walking, talking, and even sitting to play the piano, which was his greatest early interest. He had barely begun a normal school life, at the age of seven, when his father died. Forced to support herself and her two children, his mother moved frequently, to locations then in Hungary but which later became part of the Ukraine, Czechoslovakia, and Rumania. She became a schoolteacher in places where her children—especially Béla, who showed great precocity—would receive the best education and further musical training. His extreme dependence on his mother may have been a factor in his inclination toward very young girls, whom he felt he could dominate. Both his wives were his young piano students when he married them.[15] His second wife, Ditta Pásztory, felt that his strong relationship with his mother, until her death when Bartók was 58, kept him from being aware of his own age. (The pursuit of fourteen-year-old Klára Gombossy when he was 34, and of violinist Jelly d'Arányi when she was still in her twenties and he 40, resulted in important expressionist works.) His colleagues and many who met him attest both to his childlike reactions and to his extreme reticence. Márta Ziegler, his first wife, said he claimed to be unable to speak any language.[16] Yet his music shows the fiery, passionate world beyond his reticence. His painfully withdrawn personality concealed a deadly serious inner compulsion.

Bartók's first years at the Academy of Music in Budapest (1899–1901) were interrupted by life-threatening illness and the advice of doctors to give up music as a career. His willpower and tremendous capacity for work overcame these obstacles, but under the orthodox academic influence of his German-trained composition teacher, János Koessler, Bartók gave up composing, investing his surprising energies instead in brilliant performances as a pianist. He was independently investigating the music of Wagner and Liszt, but a Budapest performance of Richard Strauss's *Thus Spake Zarathustra*, in 1902, inspired him to study many of Strauss's scores, where he found the "seeds of a new life."[17] He transcribed *Ein Heldenleben* for the piano, performed it to great acclaim, took up the reading of Nietzsche, and began composing again.

The idea of the hero central to *Ein Heldenleben* led to Bartók's first major work, the symphonic poem *Kossuth* (1903). Its composition coincided

Ill. 8-1. Róbert Berény, *Portrait of Béla Bartók* (1913). Oil on canvas, 67 x 46 cm. Private collection.

with rising nationalist resentment in Hungary against Habsburg oppression. For his symphonic history of Hungarian valor Bartók found in grotesque caricature of the Austrian national anthem an expressive use of irony, which soon became one of his central compositional characteristics. At the performance of *Kossuth* in January 1904, his dissonances were excused in the tide of nationalistic fervor, and he was suddenly—at age 23—the celebrated composer of the nation. But this success was short-lived, for Hungarian audiences preferred to "drown in their Merry Widows and other operettas."[18]

In 1904 Bartók had his first—accidental—encounter with true Hungarian folk song. Then, after bruising failure in the Anton Rubinstein piano and composition competitions in Paris in 1905, and with the encouragement of his new acquaintance Zoltán Kodály, Bartók turned to collecting folk song from the peasantry, whose way of life had remained much as it had been since the Middle Ages. He found salvation in his discovery of the abundant resources of pure folk song, which he regarded as a natural phenomenon, with its "instinctive transforming power of a communication entirely devoid of erudition."[19] He collected songs from the Hungarian, Rumanian, and Slovakian peasantry, as far removed from "the iron horse" as possible, in order to find examples untainted by urban culture. When he discovered, in 1913, that songs collected from the Arabs of the Sahara shared strikingly similar elements with those of the Ukraine, Persia, and parts of Rumania, he called this phenomenon an expression of "the brotherhood of peoples."[20]

Bartók's collecting years before World War I—from 1905 to 1914—coincide with the period in which the painters of *Die Brücke* were finding their expressionist sources in nature and primitivism, and when Kandinsky and Marc of *Der Blaue Reiter* were searching for a new purity and simplicity in the glass paintings of Bavarian peasants. Like these painters, Bartók was searching for creative renewal in age-old instinctual art. Unlike Stravinsky, Bartók never abandoned this source but derived from its material a personal language which grew and evolved organically over the entire span of his creative life. In his expressionist phase he subjectivized folk music through the prism of his creative need. For example, he told Denijs Dille (in 1937), "The extreme variety that characterizes our folk music is, at the same time, a manifestation of my own nature."[21] While Bartók used utmost scientific objectivity in cataloguing and studying the folk materials he collected, in many of his compositions he manipulated and distorted them in such a way as to exemplify a statement made by the German music historian Karl Wörner: "Expressionism can be subjective or objective, in that it represents something which stands outside the ego, but is reflected by the ego in a fully subjective way."[22]

At the same time as Bartók set out with Kodály to find the true roots of Hungarian musical culture among the peasants, his slightly older contemporary Endre Ady (1877–1919) was emerging as the first Hungarian poet to write about the miseries of the cruelly neglected Hungarian, Rumanian, and Slav minorities. Ady uncovered painfully disturbing social, sexual, and spiritual issues as well.[23] His social criticism was decisive in the formation of Bartók's world outlook, and its impact on Hungarian public opinion is comparable to Karl Kraus's on the Viennese. Ady rejected nationalism and proclaimed the equality of nations and minorities. While Kodály's interest in folk song never extended beyond Hungarian materials, Bartók, the idealist and humanist, collected from widely differing regions and nations. As he pursued this goal, living in primitive conditions in remote villages, gaining the confidence of singers of the oldest songs, he became as ardent a supranationalist as he had earlier been a nationalist. This philosophical development inevitably increased his personal and artistic alienation in nationalist Hungary.

His search was always for truth. Many observed that for Bartók only the entire truth was the real truth, and every detail must reflect the truth of the whole. "The crushing consequence of his integrity would never allow him to merge with anything he did not fully believe in."[24] While this characteristic isolated him in many ways, he was nevertheless "an artist and fighter powerfully moved by all the contradictions and revolt of his age."[25] Bartók was in close touch with swiftly moving political and artistic currents of his time. He and Kodály were the musical leaders in the Ady-influenced radical circle of intellectuals in Budapest, which included the (not-yet Marxist) philosopher Georg Lukács and the poet, novelist, and playwright Béla Balázs. The Lukács family was intimately acquainted with Bartók and gave him shelter in their home from May 1920 to March 1922. Balázs had accompanied Bartók and Kodály on their earliest folk collecting tours, and he provided libretti for *Duke Bluebeard's Castle* (1911) and *The Wooden Prince* (1913–

16). This intellectual circle was deeply concerned with the same issues that troubled Bartók—the Strindbergian theme of the conflict between the sexes, the sense of crisis in Western culture, and the consequent fight for modern art and ideas in opposition to entrenched ignorance and prejudice. Bartók and Kodály were present at Lukács's founding of the avant-garde theater Thália, which brought plays by Strindberg, Wedekind, and Ibsen to Budapest in the years 1904–1908.[26] Bartók subscribed, from its founding in 1908, to *Nyugat* [West], the Ady-influenced literary journal, in which the thought of Nietzsche, Rilke, and Strindberg was published, and which showed considerable interest after 1910 in Bergson, William James, Freud, and the psychoanalytical movement.[27] In those years it was the only periodical that published positive and penetrating reviews of Bartók's compositions.[28] The activities of this intellectual circle led to the founding, in 1911, of the New Hungarian Music Society by Bartók and Kodály and to exhibitions of Hungary's postimpressionist painters, who called themselves "The Eight."[29] In 1917–18 this circle sponsored an influential lecture series entitled "Free School for Humanistic Studies," in which Bartók took part. By then, both his creative work and his efforts on behalf of peasant music had established him as a hero of the younger generation of radicals, one of whom declared, "Bartók is the first artist who, liberated from sentimental romanticism and melancholy Impressionism, manages, in this most impressionistic age, to be monumental."[30]

In the years 1905–1907, while collecting folk songs, Bartók ceased composing, but in the summer of 1907, he fell passionately in love with the prodigiously talented and beautiful nineteen-year-old violinist Stefi Geyer, a pupil of Jenö Hubay, and he began to compose again. His first Violin Concerto is dedicated to her; it is his last work in a romantic style and was written "in a narcotic dream."[31] He confessed to her that it was "the most direct music" he had ever written; that it came "straight from my heart." The first movement, which begins with the solo violin singing Stefi's leitmotif (Ex. 8-1), is a monothematic portrait of the "idealized Stefi Geyer, transcendent and intimate." The second movement is "the lively Stefi Geyer, gay, witty and entertaining." It begins as shown in Ex. 8-2 and continues in a rambling, rhapsodic manner with playful musical references to shared experiences, the dates and places of which are noted in the manuscript. The third movement, intended to be the "cool, indifferent, silent Stefi Geyer," was never written, because it "would be hateful music." By mid-February 1908, when Bartók sent her the manuscript of the Violin Concerto, along with a poem by Béla Balázs ("No two stars are so far apart as two human souls"), Geyer had broken their relationship. Reading Nietzsche had changed Bartók from a born Catholic to a convinced atheist;[32] he maintained that "It isn't God who created man in his own image, after his likeness: *It is man who created God after his own likeness.*"[33] The overbearing manner in which he demanded that Geyer try to understand his atheism and berated her for her intellectual weakness gives some idea of the difficulties Bartók imposed upon his "ideal companion."[34] The end of this tortured relationship brought Bartók to the point of suicide.[35] After this crisis, Bartók's alternating bouts of spiritual intoxication and despair through his awareness that "mine is the domain of dissonances"[36] are reflected in the increasing expressionism of his compositions from 1908 to the early 1920s.

Ex. 8-1. Bartók, Violin Concerto No. 1/I, mm. 1–2. © Copyright 1946 by Hawkes & Son (London) Ltd; copyright renewed.

Ex. 8-2. Bartók, Violin Concerto No. 1/II, mm. 1–4.

By 1908 the magic of Richard Strauss had evaporated for Bartók.[37] In the summer of 1907 he had visited Max Reger, whose influence showed itself in the spiraling chromaticism of the Violin Concerto and the first movement of String Quartet No. 1 (1908), but the excesses of Romanticism soon seemed to him unbearable. In his thorough study of Liszt, Bartók stripped Liszt's later, less-known works of their external brilliance "to find the true essence of composing."[38] He felt no real Hungarian tradition for composing until he found the expressive strength and lack of sentimental superfluity in ancient Magyar folk song. Bartók's introduction in 1907 to the music of Debussy (through Kodály) reinforced his belief in the wealth of Eastern folk music as a source of new language for Western music.

In his first expressionist work, Fourteen Bagatelles, Op. 6 (completed in May 1908), Bartók began the process of developing a personal musical vocabulary, experimenting with language far in advance of its time. Stated in stark simplicity (an unconscious parallel to Adolf Loos's desire to rid art of ornament), the innovative Bagatelles result not only from Bartók's search for liberation from the major/minor tyranny of nineteenth-century musical language, but also from his extreme psychological state.

The creative fruits of Bartók's folk song researches are apparent in the capricious tempo changes of the dancelike seventh and eleventh bagatelles and the lamenting twelfth. In the fateful summer of 1907, after visiting Stefi Geyer and her family, Bartók had set out on an extended collecting trip in Transylvania, where he discovered the fundamental importance of the "hitherto unnoticed" pentatonic scale to Magyar music.[39] The fourth and fifth bagatelles are settings of ancient pentatonic melodies; all the harmonies are built on pentatony, which avoids the tonic-dominant function, provides what Bartók calls a "consonant" seventh (that is, its affect in pentatony is not dissonant), and supplies a basis for fourth chords and their inversions.[40] The first bagatelle shows Bartók's effort to avoid and expand major/minor tonality by means of bimodality (he sometimes calls this "polymodality"). He uses two key signatures—four sharps for the right hand, four flats for the left— and thereafter abandons key signatures entirely. The sixth bagatelle is another instance of modal ambiguity, in which the flowing melody in B consistently maintains an ambivalent third degree. In the third bagatelle, an expressive melody pivots on the tritone C–F-sharp with an ostinato figure centered on G. (The C–F-sharp tritone gains further meaning in 1911, when it becomes the basis of *Duke Bluebeard's Castle* and the *Allegro Barbaro*.)

The last eight bagatelles use the four-note Stefi Geyer leitmotif in varying ways.[41] In a letter written in September 1907 to Stefi Geyer (see above, p. 177, and note 10), Bartók had altered the leitmotif's major triad (see Ex. 8-1) to a minor one, expressing his disappointment and sorrow caused by her "human frailty" and his thoughts of suicide.[42] Perhaps guided by his studies of Liszt's thematic transformations, Bartók continued throughout his expressionist period to distort this leitmotif (which we shall call the Geyer motive) according to his expressive need. In the Bagatelles and subsequent works it no longer represents the outer reality of Stefi Geyer, but portrays an *inner* reality of feeling and becomes an important motive in Bartók's expressionist language.

In the capricious seventh bagatelle this motive descends and extends to a ninth. It is harmonized by mocking downward-arpeggiated chord clusters. The eighth bagatelle has weeping descending chromatic phrases in appoggiatura-clouded thirds, seconds, sixths, and finally tritones, often cadencing on a chord built on the motive. The ninth bagatelle is a series of three variations beginning on the inverted, rhythmically altered motive and ending with a tritone cadence. Chords built on the motive, at times in an augmented version, punctuate the tenth bagatelle, which makes use of a freely invented Magyar-like dance melody over an ostinato. Fourth chords derived from the melody make a strong statement toward the end, only to be swept aside by the downward motion of the motive in thirds at the cadence. Concentration on the interval of a fourth—both melodically (in the central *parlando* section) and harmonically (in the outer sections)—is the basis of the eleventh bagatelle, which is framed by chords based on the Geyer motive (mm. 2 and 4 and the final cadence). The twelfth is a moving lament, in B minor, on the alteration of the motive's major seventh to a minor seventh (Ex. 8-3).

In the thirteenth bagatelle—a funeral march of ambiguous tonality on two triads a tritone apart—the Geyer motive appears for once in its original version at the point in the score marked *meghalt* (she dies), five measures before the end. The final, bitter waltz—the fourteenth bagatelle, "My lover dances"—begins with a demented distortion of the sublime opening of the first movement of the Violin Concerto, accompanied with a distorted or "mistuned" dominant in which the notes of the dominant-seventh chord are replaced by adjacent semitones (Ex. 8-4).[43] Asymmetrical phrases, obsessive

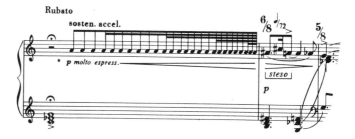

Ex. 8-3. Bartók, Fourteen Bagatelles, Op. 6/XII, mm. 1–2. New version © copyright 1950 by Boosey & Hawkes, Inc.; copyright renewed.

repetitions, rhythmic contortions and the fleeting, constantly changing, madly trilling Geyer motive whirl by in a savage nightmare akin to Berlioz's transformation of the *idée fixe* in the *Symphonie Fantastique*.[44] Bartók later orchestrated this bagatelle and combined it with the first movement of the Violin Concerto to form *Two Portraits*, Op. 5 (1906–16), with movements entitled "Ideal" and "Grotesque."

Ex. 8-4. Bartók, Fourteen Bagatelles, Op. 6/XIV, mm. 9–18.

The terse language of the Bagatelles, "devoid of all unessential decorative elements, deliberately using only the most restricted technical means,"[45] and filled with private meanings, inspired Busoni's exclamation "Finally, something really new!" when he heard them in June 1908.[46] Although Bartók later assigned tonalities to most of the Bagatelles,[47] the contradiction of tonal practices is very strong in them. In a letter written in 1910 to Frederick Delius, he referred to the Bagatelles as a

contradiction of the commonplace written . . . as a consequence of the peculiar mood I was in at the time, one which will probably never recur. . . . Since writing them I have regained some inner "harmony," so that, today, I am not in need of the contradictory accumulation of dissonances which express that particular mood. This may be the consequence of allowing myself to become more and more influenced by folk music.[48]

The First String Quartet, begun in February or March 1908 and completed in January 1909, clearly shows Bartók's "peculiar mood" and his way of regaining inner harmony. The first movement takes the first theme of the second movement of the Violin Concerto (*allegro giocoso*, see Ex. 8-2) and breaks it into a deeply grieving fugal opening (*lento, molto espressivo*, see Ex. 8-5), reminiscent of Beethoven's C-sharp minor String Quartet, Op. 131. (In transforming this idea and dividing it between the two violins, Bartók unconsciously approaches a dodecaphonic statement.) When Bartók pointed out to Stefi Geyer the relationship of this passage to her Violin Concerto, he wrote that it was his "funeral dirge."[49] The subsequent two movements of the First String Quartet (a work described by Kodály as "a return to life"[50]) are related to each other in their use of a twisting four-note semitone motive, and they grow steadily in rhythmic vigor. The expressive climax points in the final *allegro vivace* culminate in a sweeping pentatonic *adagio* folk melody (at [11] and 5 mm. before [35]), evidence of the tranquility Bartók found in peasant villages, collecting folklore.

Ex. 8-5. Bartók, String Quartet No. 1/I, Op. 7, mm. 1–3. Reprinted by permission of Boosey & Hawkes, Inc., sole agents for Kultura in the U.S.A.

The collecting of folk melodies provided Bartók the happiest days of his life,[51] and he passionately dedicated himself to this task:

This influence is most effective for the musician if he acquaints himself with folk music in the form in which it lives, in unbridled strength, amidst the lower people, and not by means of inanimate collections of folk music which anyway lack adequate diatonic symbols capable of restoring their minute nuances and thriving life. If he surrenders himself to the impact of this living folk music and to all the circumstances which are the conditions of this life, and if he reflects in his works the effects of these impressions, then we might say of him that he has portrayed therein a part of life.[52]

Bartók used the peasant materials he found in many ways. Most important to the development of his own personal language was his intent to "grasp in his works the spirit of this hitherto unknown music and to make this spirit (difficult to describe in words) the basis."[53] The change in the peasants' features when they sang, the traditions of their lives and festivities, the dusty environment in the villages, the grotesque quality of some of their instrumental tunes, and the bawdy nature of many texts were all absorbed by Bartók into the atmosphere of his works.

He chose particular attributes of peasants' homophonic musical language that freed him from the shackles of past musical practices. While orientally induced pentatony offered freedom from the tonic-dominant cadence and major/minor tyranny, old Church modes provided further fresh melodic and harmonic possibilities. Slovakian tunes characteristically made frequent use of the tritone in the Lydian mode. Rumanian peasants of Bihor also sang the augmented fourth in the majority of their melodies. The improvisational nature of much peasant song was an impetus to Bartók's interest in constant variation.[54]

The two basic types of folk rhythm—fixed tempo (for dances and work songs) and *parlando rubato* (for declamatory spontaneity)—offered incredible rhythmic variety. Hungarian declamation demanded the tonic accent and distinctive dotted rhythmic patterns. Slovakian rhythm often made use of syncopation, as well as dotted patterns from Hungary. Asymmetrical rhythms (particularly $\frac{5}{8}$ and $\frac{7}{8}$) were abundant, especially in Rumanian music, and attracted Bartók. By 1911, when he wrote *Duke Bluebeard's Castle*, he had assimilated elements from Hungarian, Slovakian, and Rumanian folk music into his language, much in the way Stravinsky had assimilated Russian folk elements by the time he wrote *The Rite of Spring* (also in 1911).

Western influences were also strong in Bartók's music of this period. In an essay for Liszt's centenary in 1911 (the same year that *Bluebeard* and the *Allegro Barbaro* were written), Bartók noted, "[Liszt's] works show a marvelous audacity of either form or invention . . . an almost fanatical striving for what is new and rare."[55] Since 1908, Bartók's music—particularly the Bagatelles—had faced mounting public hostility. Perhaps in contemplation of his own musical predicament, Bartók commented on the rejection of Liszt's compositions by the public: "Not all the stress should be laid upon forms, while great beauty—set ineffectively behind forms that may be imperfect— remains unnoticed."[56]

Debussy's melodic and harmonic vocabulary stimulated Bartók's tendency to project onto the vertical (harmonic) plane what came from the horizontal (melodic). This practice was the basis not only of fourth chords with the consonant seventh (seen in the fourth and fifth bagatelles) but also of chords built on tritones (from modal melodies)[57] and frequent chords built on transformations of the Geyer motive.

In 1909 Kodály and Bartók became acquainted with Arnold Schoenberg's First String Quartet,[58] and in 1910 Bartók had in his possession a manuscript of Schoenberg's Op. 11 piano pieces, before their publication.[59] However, this influence on Bartók's music grew only gradually, reaching its height in the works of the early 1920s.

In 1909, Bartók suddenly and secretly married his sixteen-year-old piano student, Márta Ziegler. Béla, Jr., was born in 1910. In spite of his new domestic situation, Bartók wrote to Delius in 1910, "I am very much alone here apart from my one friend, Kodály; I have nobody to talk to."[60] A concert of his music in Budapest, on 12 February 1911, was sabotaged by members of the orchestra, who thought Bartók a crazy genius and openly mocked him.[61] From March to September 1911, he wrote his one-act opera, *Duke Bluebeard's Castle,* which deals with the tragedy of solitude.

The text of the opera was not intended as a libretto; it was published in 1910 as a "mystery play" by Béla Balász. It is a Symbolist drama, owing much to the influence of Maeterlinck. It was written for Bartók, "only in the sense that one of two parched and exhausted wanderers might strike up a song to encourage the other, more weary than himself, to sing too," wrote Balász. "I wanted to depict a modern soul in the primary colors of folk song. . . . I wanted the same thing as Bartók. We had the same will and the same youth."[62] Balász had been close to Bartók since 1905. Balász's sympathy and interest in the new Hungarian music rooted in folk melody, combined with his modern psychological approach, attracted Bartók to the theater.

The opera is a psychological drama of the spiritual conflict between Duke Bluebeard, who is rumored to have murdered his previous wives, and his bride Judith, whose loving warmth, curiosity, and jealousy eventually destroy their relationship and her life. Balász's prologue sets the stage within the soul; the seven vaulted doors of Bluebeard's fortress (a cave hewn from solid rock) are the secrets of his inner life, which he cannot share, and which Judith passionately wants opened and revealed to her. Neither the contest of wills, nor the brilliant characterization of Bluebeard and Judith, nor the rooms behind the doors provide any real dramatic action. Yet the themes of the play— eternal spiritual loneliness, the irreconcilable differences between man and woman, and the tensions growing out of the nature of this polarity—are so close to Bartók's expressive need that the work achieves an intensely personal, extraordinarily powerful psychological impact.

Bartók's desire to write a truly Hungarian opera (earlier operas presented in Hungary were Italian or Wagnerian in style) was inspired by the fluid declamation of Debussy's *Pelléas et Mélisande;* Bartók was determined to serve Hungarian declamation through the use of the *parlando rubato* he found in folk music. The vocal parts are allowed an intimate simplicity, while the orchestra colors and characterizes each scene. As each door is opened, the orchestra provides a "view" of the room beyond, then delves further into a "reflection" on the effect the new revelation has on the relationship between Bluebeard and Judith.

There are themes for each experience—the Armory, the Treasure room, the Garden, the Kingdom, the Lake of Tears, and the final room, in which the wives are found—but none is more important than the blood motive, a symbolic semitone first heard harmonically in high woodwinds and horns (Ex. 8-6), as in the darkness, Judith feels the damp walls of the castle. On the discovery of the first room, the Torture chamber, the semitone motive grows shrill and dominates the scene. It appears again when Judith sees blood on the weapons of the Armory, the second room. At times the harmonic dissonance of the blood symbol is mitigated by its melodic version. In the Armory, as Bluebeard reassures Judith that what she sees is cool, soothing blood from fresh wounds, lower winds and strings make use of melodic semitones (2 mm. before [51]). Judith sees blood on the precious jewels of the Treasure room ([58]–[59]); and she discovers that some of the flowers of the Garden are blood-red ([68], melodic), but others are blood-soaked ([71]). In the central scene of the opera, the vast Kingdom behind the fifth door is filled with light, and the blood motive is virtually absent until Judith presses on to open the sixth door. As the tension between Bluebeard's restraint and Judith's will increases, melodic chromatic figures dominate the orchestral texture (beginning at [85]). In the sixth room, the Lake of Tears, the minor second becomes a descending, dotted weeping motive (4 mm. after [91]). As the tension rises before the opening of the final door, the blood motive, melodic and harmonic, saturates the texture ([112]). Judith has guessed the final secret, that the rumors of Bluebeard's murders are true. But when she demands the seventh key and opens the seventh door, she finds Bluebeard's wives—alive. The blood motive is heard one last time in Judith's horrified, broken, vocal line, "Living, breathing, they live here!" (2 mm. before [123]). Because Judith revealed this secret, she must join the three previous wives (who represent morning, midday, and evening) as the wife of midnight, locked away in a living death, while Bluebeard must remain forever alone in the dark fortress of his inviolable soul.

JUDITH. The walls are sweating! Tell me, Bluebeard, Why this moisture on my finger?

Ex. 8-6. Bartók, *Duke Bluebeard's Castle*, Op. 11, [11]. © Copyright 1921 by Universal Edition; copyright renewed. Used by permission of Boosey & Hawkes, Inc., and European American Music Distribution Corporation.

While the underlying theme is horrifying, the opera is filled with love. Bluebeard is ever gentle and wise, longing for Judith's unquestioning devotion. The Geyer motive, which continued to obsess Bartók, is significantly used in the opera. It is most often sung in descending forms by Judith, as she lovingly calls Bluebeard's name and offers to bring light to the darkness of his castle. As she grows more curious after seeing the first room, asks for more keys, and later snatches the third key from Bluebeard, an ascending, dotted, or ornamented version of the motive characterizes her feminine will. The motive is also associated with Bluebeard's love for Judith and his suffering as she questions his love. This motive, hidden in Bartók's scores of this period, is an important kernel of his personal language, a musical idea which changes as it reflects his experience with love—or with loneliness in the absence of his ideal of love.

Tritone motives are used in expressions of desire ([7], 2 mm. before [82]), of conflict ("Why so stubborn?" starting 7 mm. after [86]), and of jealousy ([105], 2 mm. before [109]), all emotions of polarity. Bluebeard sings the tritone F-sharp–C at two important moments: when Judith suspects that the murdered wives are behind the seventh door (2 mm. after [115]), and when he utters his final words, "forever, forever," as he is left alone (5 mm. before [140]). This particular tritone relationship is the symbolic tonal basis for the entire arch structure of the opera. The total darkness of Bluebeard's life and his castle is represented by F-sharp minor. As Judith enters his life, increasing light is cast from the open doors, and there is progression away from this key until, at the opening of the fifth door, revealing Bluebeard's vast Kingdom, C major, the key of light, is sounded in spacious orchestral phrases augmented by an organ. However, as Judith insists on opening more doors, shadows pass, doors swing shut, the light dims, and the tonal progression moves again to the darkness of F-sharp minor.

According to György Kroó,[63] Bartók made many important alterations to his opera between 20 September 1911 (when he completed it for a competition) and December 1921 (when the piano score was published). While there were no major stylistic changes, he changed dynamics, interpretation, and vocal parts; as had Webern, Bartók added metronome markings, dynamics, and tempo indications; in particular, he shortened the whole work and substituted a different ending. The original had an open conclusion and was 25–30 measures longer than it is in print. The final F-sharp–C tritone was missing. Bartók apparently recognized the potential symmetry of the form in his third version, which was used as preparation for publication. In its published version the opera ends, as Kroó puts it, with a "quasi-rhyme" of its prelude, and a much greater concentration in form is achieved.

In the well-known *Allegro Barbaro* for piano, written in 1911, soon after the opera, Bartók was preoccupied with the F-sharp–C tritone relationship in a modal framework. This fiery, rebellious piece, with its rhythmic propulsion and asymmetrical phrase lengths, also has biting sforzando appearances of the Geyer motive (extended to a ninth chord) in the middle section, followed by a crucial moment when the chord built on the motive appears, *dolce,* in two measures of arrested motion before the dynamic rhythm begins again. The *Allegro Barbaro* originated as an answer to a critic's remark, when he played a piano concert in Paris in 1910, that Bartók the Hungarian represented barbarism.[64] The anger and demoniacal expression released in this piece became important characteristics of Bartók's scherzo movements.

Around 1911, many elements basic to Bartók's unique expressive language reached maturity. In justifying his particular development of tritone harmonies, Bartók claimed that where other composers might have arrived at similar results at about the same time—intuitively or by using speculative methods—he (in making use of the Lydian fourth of Slovakian peasants' music) had imitated Nature; "for the peasants' art is a phenomenon of Nature."[65] Significantly, he also confessed to Delius in 1910, "I may say that my own motive for collecting folk songs is really not 'the thirst for scientific knowledge.' "[66] Rather, what he sought from his collecting was spiritual and creative nourishment. Because of his passionate interest in the phenomena of nature, the organic, natural development of his musical language was unimpeded by theories or sharp shifts in style, even when the circumstances of his life caused interruptions in his serious composing.

Bartók suffered an extended period of profound artistic isolation in the years 1911–17. As he was composing *Bluebeard*, he began to give up hope of hearing his music performed.[67] His opera was rejected as unperformable in a Hungarian national competition. The New Hungarian Music Society, which he and Kodály had founded in an attempt to organize independent concerts of modern works, foundered for lack of support. His Hungarian publishers were no longer interested in his new works, piano concert engagements abroad did not materialize, and Bartók withdrew from all public musical life in 1912. He felt that reactionary official musical circles had put him to death. Anything he supported would be pre-judged as suspect, and the only solution was "to write for my writing desk only"[68] and to pursue his research in the field of folk music more actively.

Bartók traveled widely, in 1913 finding among the nomadic Arabian peasants of Biskra, bordering the Sahara desert, narrowly confined melodies similar to the very melismatic, highly ornamented and orientally colored melodies he had discovered among primitive Rumanians in 1912. The catastrophe of war in 1914 threw him into a state of paralysis and depression which alternated with a "devil-may-care" attitude. Prevented from traveling to Rumania by the war, he was deeply anxious about the devastation of his beloved Transylvania, the part of Rumania in which his experiences had been the richest.[69]

In the summer of 1915, while collecting Slovakian materials, Bartók met the fourteen-year-old daughter of a forester who was helping him contact the peasants. The girl, Klára Gombossy, apparently accompanied Bartók on his tours in the area and formed a year-long relationship with him. This idyll provoked a compulsive series of compositions, culminating in Bartók's most aggressively expressionist theater work, *The Miraculous Mandarin*. Gombossy and her friend Wanda Gleiman had been inspired to write poetry by a young poet who had recently been killed in the war. Three of the highly erotic texts of Bartók's first song cycle, Op. 15, are said to have been written by Gombossy; a fourth—the most sensual—is said to be by Gleiman, and the origin of the fifth is uncertain. The mystery of the texts is further complicated by accusations of plagiarism and the fact that Bartók did not allow publication of these songs during his lifetime. Although of inferior literary quality, the poems deal with love, loneliness, and death, subjects close to Bartók's expressive need at the time. He set three poems (Gombossy's) in February 1916 (I, Spring: "My Love"; II, Summer: "Lying and Longing"; and V, Autumn: "In the Valley"). The autumnal preoccupation with bleak solitude and death in the last one seems to have urged Bartók on to set five poems by Endre Ady, his admired compatriot, which also dealt with autumn, loss, and death. Ady's love poems ignored the taboos of sexuality; they recorded all the nuances of mood in the man-woman relationship frankly and outspokenly, with unparalleled intensity of feeling and audacity of expression.[70] Bartók chose five poems, out of the nine Ady volumes he owned, for a second song cycle, Op. 16, composed between February and April 1916. During the following summer he wrote the remaining two songs of Op. 15: III, "Night of Desire," to a text by Wanda Gleiman; and IV, Winter: "In Vivid Dreams." In September 1916 his relationship with Klára Gombossy was broken.[71]

The two song cycles, Opp. 15 and 16, are unique in Bartók's oeuvre. The texts all suggest slow music. Their intimate, direct expression makes telling use of the personal musical vocabulary Bartók had evolved since 1907, particularly the harmonic. The songs weigh again the questions of love and death which arose in *Duke Bluebeard's Castle*. Bartók wrote his wife Márta in 1909: "Earlier I didn't feel this way, until I came to the conclusion that the real work of a human being is to communicate the most meaningful experiences and the most decisive passions of his life as precisely as in a biography."[72]

The longest of the Op. 15 songs (III, "Night of Desire") is dramatic and forms the emotional high point of the cycle. The phrase "This is the night of wild desire" is set to the Geyer motive, now descending over five notes of a ninth chord, as it does in the seventh bagatelle. The opening and closing piano harmonies (Ex. 8-7) are based on the Geyer chord, F-sharp–A–C–E, clouded by neighboring tones E-sharp and C-sharp. The same harmony occurs at the words "Let me not burn on love's pyre" (m. 64). The final vocal statement of the title phrase changes to a pure, pentatonic melody over gradually rising harmonies based on the Geyer motive. A slow, erotic waltz theme occurs at the words "Painful torture, blissful torture" (mm. 28–31) and again, varied, at "A night alive with burning passion" (mm. 45–48). This slow waltz idea forms the basis of the first and the last of the Op. 16 Ady songs ("Autumn Tears" and "I Cannot Come to You") and reappears importantly in *The Miraculous Mandarin*, when the Girl dances to seduce the Mandarin.

The text of the first song, "My Love," compares love to the blazing heat of midday. The Geyer motive appears twice, in reference to glowing, flaming passion. Hollow perfect fourths, fifths, and parallel tritones express summer heat in the accompaniment of the second song, "Lying and Longing." At the

Ex. 8-7. Bartók, Op.15/III, m. 1. © Copyrights 1958, 1961 by Universal Edition (London); copyrights renewed; used by permission of European American Distributors Corporation.

words "Under leafy branches summer holds back," this stark effect is relieved by seventh and ninth chords "clouded" by semitone contradictions.

The text (by an unspecified author) of the fourth song, "In Vivid Dreams" echoes Bartók's continuing desire for the "perfect companion whom my soul has waited for." The final song, "In the Valley," makes use of tone clusters (which are in complete contrast to the tonal orientation in the rest of the cycle), a falling theme, and a postlude of octaves in contrary motion surrounding tone clusters, as the poet sees signs of death in the icy waters of a pond in autumn.

The Op. 15 songs show greater economy of means than do the Ady songs of Op. 16. The concise expressive directness of the folk idiom prevails. Pentatonic turns, *parlando rubato,* and much use of melodic fourths characterize the vocal lines, which are more irregular and use a generally wider vocal range than is found in *Bluebeard.* Reflecting the rapid changes of mood in the Ady poems, the Op. 16 songs are often dominated by the piano accompaniment, particularly in the fourth song, "Alone with the Sea" (a song of the emptiness after lovers have parted), the third, "Lost Content" (a suicidal mood in which the poet's bed, once made for dreams, becomes a symbolic coffin), and the second, "Autumn Echoes" (a dramatic scene in which a prematurely aged man, amidst the rot of autumn, awakens to gaze about himself in silence).

Of the Op. 16 songs, only the first and fifth have the bold simplicity of Op. 15. The motivic cell of the fifth song is a falling melodic fourth (introduced by an upper semitone, thus outlining a tritone) on the words "I die, alas." It is reflected in piano interludes of parallel and mirrored fourth chords, or parallel fourths and tritones with their resultant combinations of sevenths. Again the subject of this song is loneliness and longing: "I cannot come to you." In both cycles, Bartók's style (for his writing desk only) grows more extreme in its dissonance, and his tonal orientation becomes so clouded by contradictions, that his own phrase, "polymodal chromaticism" (which Bartók preferred to "atonality," as atonality offered no fundamental tone), seems the best description.[73]

In these years Bartók was finding greater possibilities of expression in the extended freedom of a disintegrating tonal system,[74] as he examined the few works of Arnold Schoenberg in his possession. Much as Webern often did in his first measures before he understood the twelve-tone method, Bartók, in the opening measures of the first and the third movements of his Second String Quartet (Exx. 8-8a and b), with their expressive distillation of his emotional agonies of 1915–17, shows a tendency toward the dodecaphonic. Although the overall tonal scheme of the three movements of the Second Quartet can be construed as centered on A–D–A, the materials of the first and third movements create in themselves a tonal ambiguity, which János Kárpáti calls "free tonality."[75]

Ex. 8-8. Bartók, String Quartet No. 2, Op. 17. a. I, mm. 1–3; b. III, mm. 1–4.
© Copyright 1920 by Universal Edition; copyright renewed. Used by permission of Boosey & Hawkes, Inc.,and European American Music Distributors Corporation.

In 1926, after his expressionist period, Bartók said, enigmatically, "In my art I am guided by Rembrandt-like ideas."[76] His first two string quartets, when seen as culminations of previous works and in the light of his suicidal moods at the times of their composition, do seem to present self-portrait-like moments of reflection. The first and third movements of the Second Quartet are slow; the second is a scherzo. The three movements are closely integrated by motivic relationships. Although the first movement is a sonata form and the second a rondo, development or variation of the motives is constant and dramatic. The main materials of the quartet are surprisingly interrupted by unprepared intrusions of seemingly unrelated motives or themes, a practice undoubtedly inspired by Beethoven's late quartets. These interruptions seem to be autobiographical allusions. For example, the climactic point of the development section of the first movement is interrupted (at [15]) by the re-peated notes typical of a Hungarian peasant lament. A unison pentatonic phrase (2 mm. after [19]) is suddenly interjected into the agitated complexi-ties of the recapitulation; it is followed by three gestures, separated by pauses, that have the effect of sighs. A simple unison scalewise minor third, suddenly and significantly announced at the end of the recapitulation (5 mm. before [21]), gains in importance in the subsequent movements.

The Scherzo also contains surprising interjections which unbalance an otherwise predictable formal scheme, this time with much more pronounced expressive contrast. The movement is in a rondo form, using a *barbaro* type of main theme of Arabian folk character—built on a repeated minor third chromatically elaborated to expand to a major third—accompanied by drum-ming patterns (4 mm. before [1]). This theme is preceded by a hard tritone figure. The effect of the movement is dancelike, wild, and vividly uninhibited. The rhythm moves from duple meter to a triple meter, and then to a whirling, rushing combination of $\frac{3}{4}$, $\frac{6}{8}$, and $\frac{4}{4}$ for the final *prestissimo*, in an intensifica-tion derived from old dance forms. However, this physical propulsion is ca-priciously interrupted by (feminine) *dolce tranquillo* melodic fragments, in direct conflict with the impatient (masculine) minor-third motive of the Ara-bian dance figure (Ex. 8-9).[77] The *dolce* melody prevails and dominates an extremely contrasting, transparently lyrical section until the hard tritone fig-ure takes the stage again. The moment of greatest dissonance in the move-ment occurs at [38], when fourth and tritone chords dominate, *con gran passione*, followed by a last, lonely, sad statement of the *dolce* melody before the *prestissimo* sweeps it aside. Perhaps Dille's account of the rupture in Bar-tók's relationship with Klára Gombossy, twenty years his junior, in Septem-ber 1916, may illuminate the conflict in this scherzo-rondo movement: "Since in the matter of friendship Bartók was exigent, and he did not succeed in dominating this young girl of decided and independent character, quarrels were not long in coming."[78]

The final movement of the quartet is slow, introverted, extremely con-centrated, and contemplative. It makes use of themes from the Opp. 15 and 16 songs (much as meaningful phrases from Mahler's songs had generated ideas for his symphonies). The theme on fourths, which rises quietly out of the total dissonance of the opening, closely resembles a melody to the words "Since joy he never knew now awakens his longing" in the second Ady song. A second theme *(dolce)* seems derived from the setting of the words "Let me not burn on love's pyre," in Op. 15/III. A strange atmosphere of mirrored fourth chords *(con sordino* at [4]) recalls a passage preceding the final "I die, alas," of the last Ady song. Bartók himself found this movement "difficult to define."[79] The intensity of its extremely terse expression is devastating (fol-lowing the hyperemotionalism of the first movement and the electrifying vi-tality of the second), with its atmosphere of utter desolation and resignation.

Kodály—who was personally closer to Bartók than anyone else—wrote (in 1918 after the first performance of this work) that while the First String

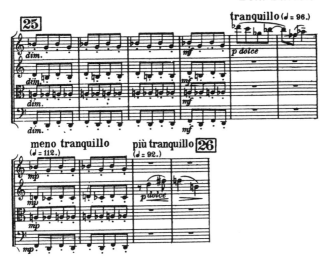

Ex. 8-9. Bartók, String Quartet No. 2, Op. 17/II, [25]–[26].

Quartet was a gradual return to life, the Second was an "Episode," in which sorrow has the last word but not the decisive one:

> The whole work, although musically perfect in form, gives the impression of direct experience. . . . This is not "program music," it does not require a written explanation, it speaks for itself. Whatever it has to say, it says clearly, with music. But it says something. . . .[80]

Bartók's musical vocabulary, built on the expressive power of concentrated intervallic cells and isolated gestures saturated with private meaning, tends toward abstraction in the final movement of the Second Quartet. Schoenberg's music may have influenced this work and the radical works of the following period, 1917–22, but in all ways, particularly the creative, Bartók was adamantly individual. Moreover, the origins of his personal musical vocabulary can be found in the Bagatelles of 1908—before he knew any of Schoenberg's music. He wrote about this influence, in a letter of 1920, "His music is a little strange to me, but it has shown some new music possibilities which were not suspected before him . . . I feel my works, even the most recent, to be so essentially different from Schoenberg!"[81]

In this period acquaintance with the Russian works of Stravinsky became important to Bartók, particularly *The Rite of Spring*, his favorite of Stravinsky's works. He played *The Rite* in its four-hand piano version with both his wife and his colleague Ernst von Dohnányi at the time that he was composing *The Miraculous Mandarin*, which shows its influence. (It is important to realize that although the *Allegro Barbaro* was completed before *The Rite of Spring*, it represents a point of *unconscious* relationship with

Stravinsky.) In Stravinsky's work, Bartók was critical of "mannerisms too often repeated" and the disturbing broken mosaiclike construction resulting from Stravinsky's "lack of a large conception";[82] but he called *The Rite* the apotheosis of Russian folk music.[83] While attempting in these years a synthesis between his Eastern culture and the developments of modern Western music, Bartók maintained that "the greatest influence was exercised on me by the peasants of our country."[84] Nevertheless, in his radical works of this period—the Songs, Opp. 15 and 16; Second String Quartet, Op. 17; Piano Études, Op. 18; *Miraculous Mandarin*, Op. 19; Improvisations for Piano, Op. 20; and the two Sonatas for Violin and Piano, 1921 and 1922—Bartók reached deeply into nonserial atonality, as had Schoenberg, and exploited primitive oriental dynamism, as had Stravinsky, while ever more profoundly and succinctly expressing his inner world.

In 1913 Béla Balász commissioned Bartók to compose music for his fairy tale, *The Wooden Prince*.[85] The neglect of *Duke Bluebeard's Castle*, of which Bartók was especially fond, impelled him to compose this ballet, which would compensate for the static nature of the one-act opera with colorful action, making a double bill practicable. *The Wooden Prince* (Op. 13), a fairy-tale pantomime (1914–16), was an unparalleled success at the Budapest Opera in May 1917, but after seeing several performances of the work, Bartók stated (in 1925) that he did not like it.[86] Although it reflects "the situation in which a woman prefers the poem to the poet, the picture to the painter,"[87] this work is not expressionist but is important in that its success in 1917—in the face of wartime destruction and high tensions in the Royal Opera House—led to a production of *Bluebeard* a year later. These performances and the premiere of the Second String Quartet, in turn, led to the beginning, also in 1918, of a long-term agreement with Universal Edition, the Viennese publishing firm. From 1918 on Bartók's compositions became known in the musical capitals of Europe and America, and his isolation from the public was broken.

The devastating political changes in these years provoked his desire to emigrate. "There never has been a darker period in the history of our country," Bartók wrote in 1920. "Red Terror and White Terror alternately following upon four years of war and starvation have left Hungary a mere shadow of its former self." Since the revolutions in 1919, all foreign performers had shunned Hungary. The idealist, pacificistic socialist government, which replaced the Habsburg rule, and the subsequent dictatorship of the proletariat under Béla Kún favored Hungarian talent and set up a musical directorate on which Bartók, Kodály, and Dohnányi served. But retribution for these efforts was severe in the reactionary period following the collapse of the dictatorship at the end of July 1919. All reforms were annulled, important musicians—such as Egisto Tango (who had conducted Bartók's two stage works), Kodály, and Dohnányi—were dismissed, and an anti-Semitic, anti-liberal attitude produced total demoralization.[88] Because Rumania had gone to war against Hungary, it was no longer possible for Bartók to pursue folk song researches in his beloved Transylvania. He felt "hopelessly cut off from the one thing which is as necessary to me as fresh air is to other people—the possibility of going on with my studies of folk music in the countryside." [89] After a trip to collect folk songs from Slovakian and Rumanian peasants in the summer of 1918, further searches in what to him were the most beautiful regions of all, Eastern Europe and the Balkans, were prevented by the painful political turmoil.

In an issue of *Nyugat* (1 January 1917), Bartók found the text of *The Miraculous Mandarin* by Menyhért Lengyel, a plot he called "marvelously beautiful," [90] perhaps because its shockingly raw, violent subject exposed the predatory greed and ruthlessness sweeping Europe in this period. In the tonal language of Bartók's pantomime setting, Eastern pentatony and primitive folk melody meet and conflict with the full range of Western chromatic vocabulary. Bence Szabolcsi, an early colleague of Bartók's and author of his first scholarly biography, wrote that Bartók's hatred of inhumanity was "incandescent, elementary, and more frantic at this stage than ever before or after"; Bartók "dared to stage primeval nature itself as a protest, in Asian disguise, against the free-for-all Europe of 1919 which brought dishonor to the continent." [91]

Bartók altered Lengyel's libretto considerably [92] and composed his most expressionist score not as a ballet but as a "grotesque" pantomime, in which music is used gesturally—often so explicitly that he later found it necessary to revise the more erotic sections in hopes of gaining its performance. The plot concerns three city Thugs who lure men into their attic hideout, by means of a Girl posing as a prostitute, and then rob them. There are three seductions: of an impoverished old Rake, a penniless Young Man, and a strange Oriental Mandarin, who represented Natural Man to Bartók. He used the story as a vehicle to express his hatred for war and the destructive violation of nature by mankind, and he was inspired to extremely rapid composition in the same way Stravinsky was by the scenario of *The Rite of Spring*. Aside from the outward manifestations of expressionist intent—in setting, plot, and vivid orchestral extremes—the musical vocabulary of the work is built on Bartók's private expressionist language.

The framework of the pantomime is the modern Western city, filled with greed, noise, machines, and human violence. The city and the Thugs are characterized by "hellish music, full of an awful noise of crowds, clatter, clanging, and tooting of horns." [93] Whenever the Thugs break into the action to victimize a "customer," this music (in $\frac{6}{8}$) violates the texture. When the third Thug rises from his position on the bed to bully the Girl into carrying out her seductions, aggressive melodic fourths rising through the orchestra serve as a phallic symbol. They reappear at the final erotic climax of the work (at [108]), as the Mandarin's desire is fulfilled by her embrace. [94]

The Girl is musically characterized by a malleable three-note chromatic cell (circled in Ex. 8-10), which at first is hesitant. The Geyer motive appears in her theme (bracketed in Ex. 8-10), in the seduction of the Young Man (4 mm. after [23], also [25]), and in its original ascending form as part of the erotic waltz the Girl dances for the Mandarin (see Ex. 8-11). The music of her forced seductions becomes more expansive as her technique improves with growing confidence. She is still shy when the Young Man enters, and her dance for him is in ⁵⁄₄, ornamented with exotic chromatic turns and trills to describe her desire for him.

Ex. 8-10. Bartók, *The Miraculous Mandarin*, The Girl's theme, [11]–2 mm. after [12]. © Copyright 1925 by Universal Edition; copyright renewed. Used by permission of Boosey & Hawkes, Inc., and European American Music Distribution Corporation.

The entrance of the Mandarin, who represents all that is alien to the city environment, is preceded by "mistuned" pentatonic chords, built on perfect fourths and tritones. The gigantic, unconquerable force of his desire for the Girl is represented by obsessive minor thirds. (This use of musical symbol may shed light on the mysterious function of minor thirds in the Second Quartet.) Grotesque orchestral effects describe the effect of the Mandarin's weird presence, leading to a dramatic clash of primitive forces. The Girl, terrified, begins a slow waltz of seduction (derived from the Opp. 15 and 16 songs), the melody of which shows the Mandarin's power over her. It is ingeniously formed of the Mandarin's minor third (x), the two outer notes of the Girl's three-note chromatic cell (y), and the Geyer motive (z) in Ex. 8-11. The dance becomes increasingly erotic. At the climax [59], the Girl sinks into the Mandarin's lap, but his embrace frightens her. She tears herself away, and the Mandarin chases her to a feverishly ornamented, Arabian-style theme built on a minor third (often notated as the oriental augmented second; see Ex. 8-12), accompanied by drummming patterns (as in the Scherzo of the Second String Quartet).

Ex. 8-11. Bartók, *The Miraculous Mandarin*, waltz melody, 6 mm. before [45]–2 mm. after [45].

Ex. 8-12. Bartók, *The Miraculous Mandarin,* [62], mm. 3–7.

When Bartók wrote about Stravinsky's "strange repetition 'à la ostinato' " of short recurring primitive motives, which "create an air of strange feverish excitement," he was comparing Stravinsky's Russian sources with similar occurrences in Rumanian music for wind instruments and in Arab peasant dances.[95] He also uses "rapidly chasing sets of motives" in this central scene of *The Miraculous Mandarin.* Glissando appearances of the Girl's chromatic cell are interjected into the chase, but pentatonic melody and tritone chords predominate, until insistent chordal minor thirds in the trombones penetrate the texture as the Mandarin catches the Girl. The Thugs leap out of hiding, seize the Mandarin, and attempt three times to murder him—by suffocation, stabbing, and hanging him from the light fixture—as the music becomes bizarrely descriptive. The Mandarin, a force of nature, is incapable of dying, and each time he is murdered his minor thirds revive, ascending with his desire or descending in his loneliness. As he is hanging, staring at the Girl, a textless chorus of voices is heard, sighing, weeping, and wailing his minor thirds. The Girl, who symbolizes humanity caught between barbarous forces, orders the Thugs to cut the Mandarin down; she no longer resists his embrace. With the consummation of his desire ([108]), his wounds begin to bleed and he dies, in a twentieth-century "love-death" framed in horror.

The score of this work, to which Bartók was very attached,[96] gave him considerable trouble after its completion. John Vinton has chronicled Bartók's revisions, which significantly lessened the raw shock of the fully expressionist original version.[97] In 1924 Bartók cut 70 percent of the erotic scene between the Girl and the Young Man. He weakened orgiastic aspects of the long embrace of the Girl and the Mandarin (musical climaxes in which the Mandarin's lust is fulfilled and his wounds begin to bleed). As with the revisions of *Bluebeard,* Bartók added clarity and cohesion to the form by echoing in the final scene formulas from earlier scenes. The work was first published in its more symmetrical form. It remained unperformed because of its subject matter until 1926, when it had a single scandal-ridden performance in Cologne and was withdrawn by order of Konrad Adenauer, then mayor of the city. After this performance Bartók arranged the concert suite (lacking the entire choral portion) and wrote to his editor, "This music definitely does express emotional happenings—as opposed to the current objective, reasoned, etc. tendencies."[98] In the late 1920s or early 30s he revised the finale further, again weakening sexual connotations in the final embrace, and changing the musical emphasis to a more transcendental, quiet ending, with a greater feeling of repose. The work was republished in 1936 (the version now available), but performances of the pantomime have been few and far between. In John Vinton's words, "Had the work been first performed in Berlin as Bartók wanted, or in Paris, and had Universal Edition been more adept at publicity, *The Miraculous Mandarin* might have gained a following comparable to that of *Le Sacre du printemps*."[99]

This "grotesque" pantomime, written during the months of revolution and counterrevolution (October 1918–May 1919) was Bartók's last work for the stage. In the turmoil and political repression of this period, Bartók was isolated from contact with peasants, but he began systematic analysis and arrangement of his folk materials. Kodály observed that Bartók, in revising his notations of folk songs with the help of his earlier recordings, took extremely seriously his responsibility to the original and notated every detail, even the tiniest ornamental notes.[100] László Somfai comments that this self-taught, highly developed technique of transcription was acquired by Bartók after 1919, in a desire to convey the individual idiosyncrasies and personal expression of each particular folk musician.[101]

Ill. 8-2. Rumanian vocal melody No. 79e, Bartók's *Rumanian Folk Music* (The Hague: Martinus Nijhoff, 1967). Courtesy Peter Bartók. Reprinted by permission of Kluwer Academic Publishers.

It was in this period that Bartók underwent a change in compositional attitudes, as he became more disillusioned about intellectual and artistic development in his own country and more aware of radical movements elsewhere. In articles published in 1920–21, he dealt with problems of synthesizing Eastern with modern musical language. "The music of our time," he wrote in 1920, "strives decidedly toward atonality. Yet it does not seem right to interpret the principle of tonality as the absolute opposite to atonality."[102] This conflict, along with the greater desire for formal organization (which affected his 1921 revision of *Duke Bluebeard's Castle*), can be seen in his last two expressionist works, the Sonatas for Violin and Piano, written in 1921– 22. They are dedicated to the violinist Jelly d'Arányi and were intended for performances with her in England and Western Europe.[103]

During the years of the conservative regime in Hungary, Bartók was viciously accused of high treason for his work with folk material other than Hungarian; the First and Second Violin Sonatas seem to be his poignant fare-well to peasant life. Slovakian and Rumanian characteristics appear promi-nently and poignantly in the experimental yet beautiful Second Sonata. It is a two-movement work of the slow-fast type, in which polymodal scales, whole-tone scales, chord clusters, fourth chords, tritone chords, drumming chords of major or minor seconds, and "mistuned" chords—an extended vocabulary of Bartók's atonal expressionist practices derived from folk materials—con-tradict tonal principles. A wide variety of rhythmic expression is exploited, from the spontaneous Rumanian *parlando rubato,* which dominates the slow first movement, to the unexpected accents in the otherwise strict meter of the dancelike first theme of the second movement.

The hauntingly beautiful melody which opens the first movement (Ex. 8-13a) is repeated subsequently in different forms. It returns in new variations before the recapitulation of the second movement and again at its poignant close, framing the robust dance rhythms of the second movement with nos-talgia. The scale of the first dance melody in the second movement (Ex. 8-13b) is derived from the opening notes of this nostalgic melody. In passages of climactic tension, Bartók makes use of extremes of range, dissonance, and wide intervals, a dramatic contrast in a piece which otherwise uses songlike melodic materials of the more primitive, narrow-ranged, but highly orna-mented type. Violin glissandi play a burlesque role in the Trio of the second movement. Violin harmonics, *sul ponticello,* and tremolo effects—soon to preoccupy Bartók—are used for variation and dramatic color, but in no way take precedence over the musical materials of the Sonata.

Both Violin Sonatas come close to Schoenbergian ideas of atonality. The Second synthesizes modern Western musical language with the spirit of East-ern folk sources. Somfai has pointed out that it is based on folk-dancelike forms, bagpipe imitations, and the drawn-out, improvisatory type of folk la-ment, which lent itself both to Bartók's desire for constant variation and to his interest in the individual idiosyncrasies of folk musicians. In this period Bartók "felt more confident in his compositional innovations when they seemed to him to have some justification in the various kinds of folk music he studied scientifically."[104]

In 1923 Bartók received his first public commission, for the Dance Suite. Here he retreated from his recent radical style in hopes of more popular success. While in subsequent years he preoccupied himself increasingly with

Ex. 8-13. Bartók, Second Sonata for Violin and Piano, violin melody. a. I, mm. 4–6; b. II, mm. 5–12. © Copyright 1923 by Universal Edition; copyright renewed. Used by permission of Boosey & Hawkes, Inc.

classically balanced forms and attitudes in his compositions, he never completely abandoned the highly personal immediacy which had dominated the expressionist compositions from 1908 to 1923. He continued to believe that "the music of all the peoples of the world can be traced back to some common basis of primeval forms, primeval types and primeval styles"[105] and that this source for new musical language was, above all others, "clean, fresh, and healthy."[106]

Select Bibliography

Antokoletz, Elliott. *Béla Bartók: A Guide to Research.* New York: Garland, 1988.
Bartók, Béla. *Letters.* Ed. János Demény. Trans. P. Balabán and I. Farkas. Trans. rev. by E. West and C. Mason. Budapest: Corvina, 1971.
———. *Essays.* Selected and ed. Benjamin Suchoff. New York: St. Martin's Press, 1976.
———. *Black Pocket-Book: Sketches 1907–22.* Budapest: Editio Musica, 1987.
Béla Bartók: A Memorial Review. New York: Boosey & Hawkes, 1950.
Bónis, Ferenc. *Béla Bartók: His Life in Pictures and Documents.* Budapest: Corvina, 1980.
Breuer, János. "Bartók and the Arts." *New Hungarian Quarterly* 60 (Winter 1975): 117–24.
Crow, Todd. *Bartók Studies.* Reprints of articles from *The New Hungarian Quarterly.* Detroit: Information Coordinators, 1987.
Dille, Denijs, ed. *Documenta Bartókiana,* I–IV. Budapest: Akadémiai Kiadó, 1964–1970.
Gillies, Malcolm. *Bartók Remembered.* New York: Norton, 1990.
Gluck, Mary. *Georg Lukács and His Generation: 1900–1918.* Cambridge: Harvard University Press, 1985.
Kárpáti, János. *Bartók's String Quartets.* Trans. F. Macnicol. Budapest: Corvina, 1975.
Kodály, Zoltán. *The Selected Writings of Zoltán Kodály.* Trans. L. Halápy and F. Macnicol. Budapest: Corvina, 1974.

Kroó, György. *A Guide to Bartók*. Trans. R. Pataki and M. Steiner. Trans. rev. E. West. Budapest: Corvina, 1974.

———. "Data on the Genesis of Duke Bluebeard's Castle." *Studia Musicologica* 23 (1981): 79–123.

Pethö, Bertalan. "Béla Bartók's Personality." *Studia Musicologica* 23 (1981): 443–58.

Ránki, György, ed. *Bartók and Kodály Revisited*. Budapest: Akadémiai Kiadó, 1987.

Somfai, László. *Bartók's Workshop: Sketches, Manuscripts, Versions: The Compositional Process*. Budapest: Hungarian Academy of Sciences, 1987.

———, ed. *Documenta Bartókiana* V. Budapest: Akadémiai Kiadó, 1977.

Ujfalussy, József. *Béla Bartók*. Trans. R. Pataki. Trans. rev. E. West. Boston: Crescendo, 1972.

———. "1907–1908 in Bartóks Entwicklung." *Studia Musicologica* 24/3–4 (1982): 519–25.

Ujfalussy, József, and Breuer, János, eds. *International Musicological Conference in Commemoration of Béla Bartók*. Melville, NY: Belwin Mills, 1972.

Vinton, John. "The Case of the Miraculous Mandarin." *Musical Quarterly* 50/1 (1964): 1–17.

Weissmann, John S. "Notes Concerning Bartók's Solo Vocal Music (I)." *Tempo* 36 (1955–56): 16–25.

CHAPTER NINE

Charles Ives

> Maybe music was not intended to satisfy the curious definite-ness of man. Maybe it is better to hope that music may always be a transcendental language in the most extravagant sense.
>
> Charles Ives (1919)

Charles Ives (1874–1954) in many ways sums up musical expressionism. He had many attitudinal similarities to other composers we have discussed: like Mahler, Ives weaves all of experience, the sublime and the ordinary, into the fabric of his music. Like Webern, Ives felt that his music contained ethical value, which was the most important thing about it. Rebelling, as did Stravinsky and Bartók, against academic limitations, Ives went to the same source they did—common folk—for the materials of his unique musical language. Reverence for his native soil and his country's earlier rural ways shaped his musical outlook, as it did Bartók's. Never uprooted and transplanted, Ives nevertheless felt—as Stravinsky had about his homeland—a treasured past slipping away in the increasing mechanization of America. His entire creative life was spent memorializing earlier heroes, Puritan forebears, carefree boyhood, and New England village life.

Deeper than these similarities is the fact that the metaphysical basis of music was all-important to Charles Ives. He called it "something that may be seen in the cosmic landscape of Art = Philosophy."[1] It is the force he gleaned from the Concord Transcendentalists and recognized in Beethoven, whose spirit he felt he was continuing in his composing.[2] Art was intended by nature to be a part of life, "a reflection, subconscious-expression, or something of that sort, in relation to some fundamental share in the common work of the world."[3] Like Schoenberg, Ives seems to have understood the psychological implications of his profound belief in artistic intuition. He knew that when he was composing or writing about his composing, he was getting something out of his system that had been there for some time.[4]

In the recent emphasis on experimentalism in Ives, comparatively little attention has been paid to the idealistic and subjective aspects of his music which place him among the expressionist composers. Yet Elliott Carter, studying Ives's *Essays Before a Sonata,* found "how close Ives's thinking was to that of the expressionists, for whom the inner world was of prime importance, and for whom art was not an object but a means of embodying his own spiritual vision."[5] Charles Wilson Ward has written that Ives's recognition of the intensely subjective nature of art and his belief that music expresses the inner world of a composer's personality are similar to the views of the European expressionists.[6] Christopher Ballantine and Stuart Feder[7] have further explored the subjective realm in Ives's music.

Ives's musical experiments, continued from ideas initiated in his boyhood by his father, were steps in the development of his expressive language. But so important to Ives were the values expressed in his music, and so crucial the problem of translating artistic intuition into musical sounds, that he wrote to Henry Cowell, "Music may resent going down on paper!"[8] It was the spirit that mattered. To Nicholas Slonimsky, about to conduct *Three Places in New England* in Paris in 1931 (the first orchestral performance of Ives's work in Europe), Ives wrote, "Just kick into the music as you did in the Town Hall. Never mind the exact notes or the right notes, they're always a nuisance. Jes let the spirit underneath the stuff sail up to the Eiffel Tower and on to Heaven."[9] Pure novelty or purely abstract musical endeavor not arrived at naturally or spontaneously usually ended up in the category Ives labeled "n.g.": No good. When he caught his music tilting toward abstract system, he gave himself a lashing:

> Occasionally something made in this calculated, diagram, design way may have a place in music, if it is primarily to carry out an idea, or a part of a program . . . but generally or too much or alone as such it is a weak substitute for inspiration or music. It's too easy, any high-school student (unmusical) with a pad, pencil, compass and logarithm table and a mild knowledge of sound, and instruments (blown or hit) could do it. It's an artificial process without strength though it may sound busy and noisy.[10]

It was Ives's opinion that "abstract things in art [are] one of two things: a covering up, or ignorance of (or but a vague feeling of) the human something at its source—or just an emasculated piece of nice embroidery!"[11] "What I had in mind . . . by 'new' was something that gives one a sense, whether remote or vivid, of that constant organic flow going on in all life, the outward form of which may appear quite different to different men."[12]

In *The Unanswered Question,* for chamber orchestra (1906), elements of experimentation are put to the service of an inner vision, articulated by Ives himself in a specific philosophical program:

> The strings play *ppp* throughout with no change of tempo. They are to represent "The silences of the Druids—Who Know, See and Hear Nothing." The trumpet intones "The Perennial Question of Existence," and states it in the same tone of

voice each time. But the hunt for "The Invisible Answer" undertaken by the flutes and other human beings, becomes gradually more active, faster and louder through an *animando* to a *con fuoco*.[13]

The irreconcilability of these elements and the inability to find the answer provide a layered musical process Ives frequently used to express his view of life's experiences. The strings *(largo molto sempre)* produce serene triadic and pandiatonic harmonies like those in Beethoven's "Heiliger Dankgesang"; the trumpet's enigmatic questioning phrase avoids both the tonality and the $\frac{4}{4}$ metrical feeling of the strings; and the increasing agitation of the flutes' atonal response disturbs neither of the other elements. Polytonality, simultaneous polymeters and/or tempi, and the combination of widely disparate elements—all important facets of Ives's musical expressionism—are already apparent in this early work.

Ives shared with other expressionists deep-rooted rebellions, most of which lasted his lifetime. The earliest was his rebellion against the academicism of Yale's Horatio Parker, who felt that Ives wrote in too many keys at once. As Ives grew out of his own youthful musical tastes he further rebelled against turn-of-the-century musical attitudes: "Magnifying the dull into the colossal produces a kind of 'comfort'—the comfort of a woman who takes more pleasure in the fit of fashionable clothes than in a healthy body."[14] Smugness about material "comfort" was an irritant common to expressionists. Arnold Schoenberg wrote in the Foreword to the 1911 edition of *Harmonielehre*, "Our time seeks much. But above all our time has found comfort. . . . Comfort as world-view! The least possible agitation, no shock. Those who so love comfort will never seek where it is not certain that it will be found."[15]

Ives often fulminated against the common attitude that "Beauty in music is too often confused with something that lets the ears lie back in an easy chair."[16] When enraged by this aspect of the music of his time, he would wax colorful: "Why should music be so even, so grooved in?—so smooth [that] our ears must become like unto feather beds, our muscles all drop out, and we have to have false-teeth ears to hear it with!"[17] Ives often castigated gentility in music as "emasculated art." As punching bag for his anger he chose Rollo, the unimaginative, literal-minded little boy of Jacob Abbott's multivolume series of lessons for conventional upbringing.[18] Little Rollo is subjected to so many trials and duties by his Victorian elders that by the time he enters school he is a miniature conformist prig, or what Ives, the robust athlete, liked to call an "old lady."

In the highly dissonant String Quartet No. 2 (1907–13), Ives makes his revolt against the prevailing genteel tradition in music crystal clear. The second movement *(Allegro con spirito)* was written in 1907 in reaction to concerts of the "nice" (a pejorative) Kneisel Quartet. At m. 31 the second violin, frequently characterized by marginal comments in the sketch as Rollo, emerges from a highly complex polymetric texture to play a diatonic F major solo followed by a burlesque cadenza *(andante emasculata—alla rubato),* marked "Elman!" in the sketch.[19] The three other instruments remonstrate with dissonance, violent rhythms *(Allegro con fisto),* and the words "Cut it out, Rollo!" The mocking character of the tempo indications (subsequently *presto, largo sweetota, largo soblato,* and again *allegro con fisto)* makes clear that Ives had no use for the sugary sentimentalism of much of the concert music of his day (Ex. 9-1). Rollo's conformity symbolized for Ives the roots of America's cultural inferiority complex. (Rollo is sent off to Europe for educational polish.) Ives spoke out against adopting European artistic standards merely because they were European. Like the mature Bartók, he did not believe in shallow nationalism: "If . . . [the composer] is true to none but the highest of American ideals (that is, the ideals only that coincide with his spiritual consciousness) his music will be true to itself and incidentally American."[20]

Ex. 9-1. Ives, Second String Quartet, II, mm. 31–38. © Copyright 1954 by Peer International Corporation.

Ives had many of the same fears that spurred the generation of expressionists. He feared the mechanistic aspect of American commercialism, a standardization which reduces the human being. Machinery of many sorts seemed an intrusion on his world. Automobiles, the telephone, the radio, recording machinery, elevators, the camera which might take his soul away— all bothered him profoundly. "The New River" (1911), a song for two-part chorus and chamber orchestra,[21] expresses Ives's direct, highly emotional criticism of the growing industrialization of America and the destruction of nature which accompanied it. A note added by the composer to the sketch of the 1913 solo song arrangement expresses his remembered outrage: "back from Zoar's Bridge, June 9th, 1911—Gas machine kills Housatonic!"[22] Like many of his songs, "The New River" is a "reflex, subconscious expression." As he often did when particularly aroused, Ives provided his own text. After a wild ragtime opening (marked "Fast and Rough"), which portrays the cheapening of his beloved Housatonic, the two-part chorus enters with the words

> Down the river comes a noise!
> It is not the voice of rolling waters.
> It's only the sounds of man,
> dancing halls and tambourine,
> phonographs and gasoline,
> human beings gone machine.

In the excerpt in Ex. 9-2, Ives vividly expresses the idea of inane, mechanical repetition ("human beings gone machine") with a phrase for the lower chorus part repeated six times in succession "as a kind of half drawl." Since the phrase is five eighth notes long and the upper part adheres to phrases of four quarter notes, the two parts never coincide, but continue mindlessly. A purposely vulgar quotation from the song "Tammany, Tammany" follows, with "Ta-ra-ra-boom-de-ay" as its text.

Ex. 9-2. Ives, "The New River," mm. 9–13, voice parts only. © Copyright 1970, 1971 by Peer International Corporation.

The song "The Cage" (1906) is based on Ives's experience observing a small boy watch a leopard pace ceaselessly back and forth in its cage at the zoo in Central Park.[23] Alienation, possibly caused by repetitiousness in the world of business, may have been represented by the words of his text: "Is life anything like that?" The song is marked to be played "evenly and mechanically, no ritard., decresc., accel. etc." The introduction consists of chords which grow ever shorter in duration (♩ ♩. ♩ ♪. ♪ ♪). Another version, called "In the Cage," for chamber orchestra, includes a two-note tympani ostinato in triplets, representing the leopard's steps. The effect of purposeful monotony is furthered both by the voice part, which is in syllabic eighth notes almost throughout, and by the harmony, which consists almost entirely of fourth chords.

Like Webern, Schoenberg, Berg, and Bartók, Ives sustained in early manhood a shattering personal loss—that of his remarkable father. "If I have done anything that is good in music, I owe it almost entirely to him and his influence," he wrote in a rare autobiographical letter.[24] George Ives, the youngest son of the prominent founder of the first savings bank in Danbury, Connecticut, was a strong individualist who taught his son and other children of the town that "You've got to know what you're doing [musically], and why you're doing it."[25] He involved Charles in empirical discoveries of the materials of music, insisting that listening comes first, technical explanations and terminology last. The result was a perennially open mind toward musical possibilities:

> Father used to say, "If one can use chords of 3rds and make them mean something, why not chords of 4ths? If you can have a chord of three notes and [one of] four, alternating and following, why not measures of $\frac{3}{4}$ then $\frac{4}{4}$, alternating and following? If the whole tones can be divided equally, why not half tones? . . . Why can't the ear learn a hundred other intervals if it wants to try?—and why shouldn't it want to try?"[26]

Yet no amount of eccentric experimentation interfered with the gift for meaning when George Ives was performing and conducting. He seems to have embodied the belief in human nature that is transcendental doctrine. When a music student complained that the town stonemason sang off-key in the Camp Meetings, George Ives—although he had perfect pitch and had been rigorously trained in all aspects of music—responded with an admonition to "Watch him closely and reverently, look into his face and hear the music of the ages. Don't pay too much attention to the sounds—for if you do, you may miss the music."[27] This attitude is echoed in his son's Epilogue to the *Essays Before a Sonata*: "My God! What has sound got to do with music! . . . Why can't a musical thought be presented as it is born. . . . That music must be heard is not essential—what it *sounds* like may not be what it *is*."[28]

It was the expressive qualities of George's music making that Charles particularly remembered: "He'd take a familiar piece and play it to make it mean more than something just usual. . . . He had the gift of putting something in the music which meant more sometimes than when some people sang the words."[29] George would play Schubert songs or familiar hymns on his cornet, insisting that the words should be known and thought of while he played. The memory of this instrumental expressivity led to Charles's practice of conceiving an instrumental work on a text and later writing a vocal version ("The Cage," "The Ruined River," and "The Housatonic at Stockbridge" are some examples of this method). Ives remembered especially the outdoor Camp Meeting services in Redding,

> where all the farmers, their families and field hands, for miles around, would come afoot or in their farm wagons. . . . Father, who led the singing, sometimes with his cornet or his voice, sometimes with both voice and arms, and sometimes in the quieter hymns with a French horn or violin, would always encourage the people to sing their own way. . . . There was power and exaltation in these great conclaves of sound from humanity.[30]

Children's Day at the Camp Meeting was memorialized in the Sonata No. 4 for Violin and Piano (1906–16). In the first movement Ives remembers that when it came their turn for a service, the children,

> especially the boys, liked to get up and join in the marching kind of hymns. . . . One day Lowell Mason's "Work, for the Night is Coming" got the boys going and keeping on between services, when the boy [Charles himself] who played the melodeon was practicing his "organicks of canonicks, fugaticks, harmonicks and melodicks."[31]

In his Sonata, Ives uses the children's hymn "Tell Me the Old, Old Story" (the chorus of which begins similarly to "Work, for the Night Is Coming) along with material from a Fugue in B-flat written by George Ives.[32] In a "foreshadowing" technique resembling that used by preluding organists, Ives first introduces isolated phrases from "Tell Me," arriving at a full statement of its refrain only at the climactic conclusion of the movement (beginning at m. 70). He achieves this climax by means of a frenetic piling up of motives representing the boys marching faster and faster, "reaching almost a 'Main Street Quickstep.'"[33]

Bandmaster George Ives's love of "accidental" counterpoint (such as that produced when two bands, playing different marches, converge from opposite directions—an idea notably similar to Mahler's concept of polyphony) is reflected in his son's love of all sorts of thematic and textural combinations. In Violin Sonata No. 4 this kind of simultaneity occurs in the frequent joining of George Ives's fugue with parts of the hymn tune (Ex. 9-3). In his development of material composed by his father, Ives could be said to be literally "writing his father's music" in the sonata, and the statement is at least metaphorically applicable to much of Ives's music.[34]

The second movement is deeply emotional, with a range broad enough to include both a profoundly felt meditation on the chorus of another children's hymn, "Jesus Loves Me," and its interruption by the almost brutal cross-rhythms of the movement's central section. This passage, marked *Alle-*

Ex. 9-3. Ives, Sonata for Violin and Piano, No. 4/I, mm. 16–19. Copyright © 1942 (renewed) by Associated Music Publishers, Inc.

gro (conslugarocko), was inspired by Ives's memory of the boys at the Camp Meeting throwing rocks into a nearby brook. Like Mahler, Ives frequently juxtaposed emotional and musical extremes without any transition. The freely rhapsodic opening *Largo* of the movement is written with very few bar lines. After several foreshadowings of the pentatonic opening phrase of "Jesus Loves Me," there is a complete statement of the chorus in the violin. A comparison with the original hymn shows how Ives, by means of octave displacement and interval distortion, bends the borrowed material to his own expressive needs (Ex. 9-4).

Ex. 9-4. a. William Batchelder Bradbury, "Jesus Loves Me," chorus; b. Ives, Sonata for Violin and Piano, No. 4/II, mm. 2–3, violin part only.

Although Ives put into music his memories of his father's "remarkable understanding of the ways of a boy's heart and mind",[35] he was equally proud of his strenuous New England upbringing and musical training. His father had not let him stop when the going got hard. At age twelve he was composing. At age fourteen he was the youngest professional organist in the state, practicing on a piano his father had rigged with foot pedals. He played drums in his father's band and practiced the drumming rhythms on the keyboard, using tone clusters—which later appeared in his compositions. His keyboard facility was so great that his father hoped he would become a concert pianist, but he was much too shy; "he couldn't face that being-alone on the stage in front of an audience."[36] In 1893 Ives was sent off to a preparatory school in New Haven in hopes of qualifying for admission to Yale. In New Haven he continued to serve as a professional church organist. In order to spare money for organ lessons in New York, he insisted that he could get along without a new overcoat and suggested sharing a single suit with his brother, Moss, who was still living at home in Danbury.[37]

In 1894, the year Ives entered Yale College, he began setting Psalms, under his father's guidance but with a strongly independent spirit. "Father let me do it, if I knew what I was doing and could play and sing them."[38] A saying of his father's must have spurred the new language he was using in his composing: "You won't get a wild, heroic ride to heaven on pretty little sounds."[39] In these early works, begun at the age of twenty, Ives set out on the path that culminates in his Fourth Symphony. His setting of Psalm 24 for unaccompanied chorus (1894) puts radically experimental means at the service of a strongly felt expressive purpose. Each verse of the psalm setting stresses a different, progressively larger interval (half tone, whole tone, minor third, major third, and so on). This procedure generates many new harmonies and leads to the kind of jagged melodic outline found in the European expressionists. More important, it enables Ives to express the meaning of the text with extraordinary dynamism (Ex. 9-5).

Ex. 9-5. Ives, Psalm 24, mm. 42–44. © 1955 Mercury Music Corporation.

Psalm 90, written for mixed chorus, organ, and bells, is a much longer and more ambitious work than Psalm 24. Originally conceived as early as 1894, the work was lost, and Ives recomposed it in 1923–24. It combines the experimental boldness of his early years with the transcendence of his mature compositional period, and, according to his wife, Harmony, it was the only one of his works with which he was satisfied.[40] Ives found the psalm's text deeply moving. To achieve a maximum of communicative intensity in his setting, he makes abundant use of musical symbolism, which, like Schoenberg's, is both traditional and newly invented. To portray sadness or sin, Ives uses the traditional ascending-descending chromatic half steps or descending chromatic half steps. He also invents a more personal musical symbolism at the opening of the psalm by providing single chords and two-chord progressions with specific meanings (Ex. 9-6). At the words "Thou turnest man to *destruction,*" the chord symbolizing "God's wrath against sin" returns, topped by an added major third, and then it appears in two upward transpositions (Ex. 9-7). Ives's text setting here is extremely vehement. The same chord reappears at the words "Thou carriest them away with a *flood*" and, later, at the words "anger" and "wrath."

Throughout the psalm, Ives's response to the text is varied and original, even leading to a *Sprechgesang*-like ascending phrase on the words "we fly

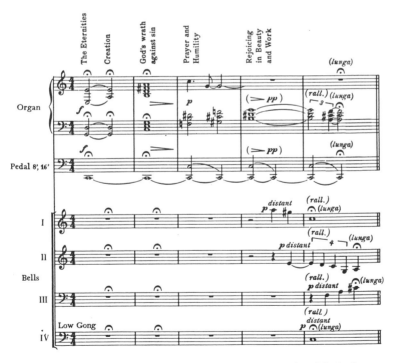

Ex. 9-6. Ives, Psalm 90, mm. 1–5. © 1966, 1970 Merion Music, Inc.

Ex. 9-7. Ives, Psalm 90, mm. 21–23.

away" (m. 74). The concluding section of the work is comparable to the ending of Mahler's *Das Lied von der Erde* in its Nirvana-like calm. As the chorus sings sustainedly in C major, accompanied by the organ in the open fifths and fourths of "The Eternities" and "The Creation," the bells, marked to be played "as church bells, in distance," set up three overlapping ostinati, also largely in C major, but colored by the notes G-sharp and C-sharp (Ex. 9-8). Since the ostinati do not coincide with the chorus or with one another, they suggest not only church bells but a music of planets moving eternally in their separate spheres.

Compulsion characterized Ives's approach to composing. His works seemed to conductors and critics of his time a "hodge-podge" of musical ideas,[41] yet his response to a suggested change in spelling in the song "Maple Leaves" was "I'd rather DIE than change a note of that!"[42] Even when asking himself, "Are my ears on wrong?"[43] Ives followed his convictions. His two greatest necessities seem to have been to carry on his father's musical and philosophical attitudes, and to live and create (since for him composing must come from living) in the most transcendental spirit possible. He drove himself to physical breakdown in order to obey his convictions. Vivian Perlis speculates that Ives's determination to write his life's work in half a lifetime (chiefly in the years 1894–1921) comes from the fact of his father's death at the age of 49, as well as knowledge of his own heart trouble, which was diagnosed in 1906.[44] Ives chose to be a businessman because "Father felt that a man could keep his music-interest stronger, cleaner, bigger, and freer, if he didn't try to make a living out of it."[45]

While he made a success out of his career in life insurance and became

Ex. 9-8. Ives, Psalm 90, mm. 111–15.

wealthy, Ives was far from a typical businessman. His personal secretary re-membered that he would be dictating a letter, "and all of a sudden something in the music line would come up in his head, and he'd cut off the letter and go into the music. I think that music was on his mind all the time."[46] He expressed deep gratitude to the fairness with which he was treated in his career, but at times, in his private diary, he admitted his discomfort in the business world:

> Too much shine and make-believe about these large offices—like a man digging potatoes in a dress suit. . . . A bad day underfoot/misunderstood as usual—if I could arrange my thoughts through my mouth as well as those that don't reach

the mouth it would be much more comfortable for me. . . . Most . . . businessmen don't practice what they preach.

The following week a big snow storm "relieves the routine lines in the business mind and makes them almost human."[47]

Ill. 9-1. Charles Ives in Battery Park, Manhattan, 1913. Ives Collection, Music Library, Yale University.

From 1898, when he began his business life in New York City, Ives composed evenings, weekends, and especially on holidays. He held prominent positions as a church organist until 1902, when, with added time on Sundays and a determination to write what he wanted to (rather than what was expected by a conservative congregation), he increased the pace of his experimental composing. He was engaged in 1905 to Harmony Twichell, who encouraged him as no one had since the death of his father. New self-confidence resulted in an outburst of advanced pieces: *Over the Pavements* (a study on the rhythms of passing foot traffic), *In the Cage, The Unanswered Question,* and its companion piece, *Central Park in the Dark,* among others. Around 1911 he was working on many pieces at once: *The New River, Three Places in New England,* "The Fourth of July" (the most radical movement of his *Holidays* Symphony), the Fourth Symphony, the Second *(Concord)* Piano Sonata, the Second String Quartet, and ideas for the *Universe* Symphony. He drove himself, taking Yankee pride in "stern but outdoors strength," both in his music and in his daily life.[48] This aspect of his character is an important determinant of his "dialect" of expressionism: "Dissonances . . . had a good excuse for being, and in the final analysis a religious excuse, because in the stern outward life of the old settlers, pioneers and Puritans, there was a life generally of inward beauty, but with a rather harsh exterior."[49] In contrast to some of the European expressionists (Berg, particularly), Ives felt that sensuality was a weak trait. He was further confirmed in this attitude by Harmony, who was a minister's daughter and objected, for example, to Whitman's poetry.[50]

The adjective "impressionist" finds its way into many discussions of Ives's music, perhaps because Ives often describes his works as pictures in sounds.[51] Further, in the Preface to his *Essays Before a Sonata,* he says the music

> is an attempt to present (one person's) impression of the spirit of transcendentalism that is associated within minds of many with Concord, Mass., of over a half century ago. This is undertaken in impressionistic pictures of Emerson and Thoreau, a sketch of the Alcotts, and a Scherzo supposed to reflect a lighter quality which is often found in the fantastic side of Hawthorne.[52]

Further reading shows that the word "impression" is used in a subjective sense. The essays tell more about Ives—and the impact of Emerson, Thoreau, Alcott, and Hawthorne on him—than they do about the Transcendentalists themselves. Reading Thoreau seems to have been Ives's greatest comfort when his father died.[53] Emerson was Ives's hero, and before that his father's and his grandmother's. Hawthorne provides an opportunity for Ives to recapture boyhood fantasies and prankish fun. (In his Hawthorne essay, Ives goes to careful lengths to say that his own point of view has nothing to do with the sin-obsessed puritanism more often associated with Hawthorne.) The Alcott movement and essay provide gentle reflection on the quiet village beauty of New England, which Ives so treasured that his later visits to his home in rapidly growing and changing Danbury were excruciatingly painful to him.[54] There are moments reminiscent of Impressionism in Ives's music, but the underlying intent is intensely subjective. There is often a programmatic subtext drawn deeply from the well of Charles Ives's life experience, particularly from events of great personal meaning to his extremely sensitive, emotional nature.

In "Emerson," the first movement of the Piano Sonata No. 2 (subtitled "Concord, Mass., 1840–1860," and written in 1911–15), Ives aimed to catch the spirit of the New England philosopher and poet in music; yet, since Ives identified closely with Emerson, much of the composer's own character is inevitably present in the score. In his introduction to the sonata, Ives stresses that Emerson

> wrote by sentences or phrases, rather than by logical sequence. His underlying plan of work seems based on the large unity of a series of particular aspects of a subject, rather than on the continuity of its expression. As thoughts surge to his mind, he fills the heavens with them, crowds them in, if necessary, but seldom arranges them along the ground first.[55]

Ives's "Emerson" proceeds by the same kind of free association of not necessarily linear, but related, ideas. The similarity of this concept to some of

Schoenberg's ideas around the same time is notable. (See Schoenberg's correspondence in 1909 with Busoni, quoted in chapters 4 and 5.)

In the original edition of the *Concord* Sonata (privately printed by Ives in 1921) the "Emerson" movement is divided into sections marked "prose" and "verse." These designations are used not only because Emerson wrote both prose and poetry but also to point out the different types of music in the movement: the more lyrical and somewhat more symmetrical verse sections, and the much freer prose sections. In the prose sections, which dominate the movement, Ives's realization that Emerson's thought did not consist of "little miniature ideas in frames"[56] leads to a constantly free juxtaposition and simultaneity of musical thoughts. The dense textures and dissonant harmony thus created correspond to Emerson's epic struggle to reconcile "the old Puritan canon . . . with his individual growth."[57] Wishing the performance of the movement to "have some of Emerson's freedom in action and thought,"[58] Ives uses few bar lines and stresses that the tempo should be variable, rather than constant.[59] Just as he got "a new angle of thought and feeling and experience" every time he read Emerson, Ives did not play the "Emerson" movement the same way each time, but "enjoyed playing this music and seeing it grow and feeling that it is not finished."[60] It is apparent from these remarks that Ives was more interested in the process of composition (including an element of spontaneous improvisation) than in the finished product; perhaps that is the reason many of his works exist in multiple versions.

Ives believed that musical form should be evolutionary rather than cut and dried:

> In this [*Concord*] Sonata they're spitting about, there is design—somewhat more than there should be, it seemed to me—and the form is obvious, but it isn't drabbed on every milestone on the way *up* or *to* or *on*. . . . A natural procedure in a piece of music . . . may have something in common [with] . . . a walk up a mountain. There's the mountain, its foot, its summit—there's the valley—the climber looks, turns, and looks down or up. He sees the valley, but not exactly the same angle he saw it at the last look—and the summit is changing with every step—and the sky.[61]

Nevertheless, the grand outlines of the three-part form of "Emerson" are clear (page numbers from the second edition): A (Exposition, p. 1 to the bottom of p. 7); B (Variations, in place of Development, p. 8 to p. 13, end of third brace); A' (quasi-Recapitulation, beginning with fugato, p. 13, fourth brace, to end of movement). The complexity of the movement is increased by the large number of themes; two are used cyclically in the Sonata as a whole, and four others are peculiar to the Emerson movement. The more important of the two cyclical themes, identified by Ives as "the Oracle," in fact begins with the opening motive from Beethoven's Fifth Symphony. As with most of Ives's quotations, its intent is to increase communication with the listener by evoking particular symbolic or psychological associations. In his *Essays Before a Sonata,* Ives makes clear that he attaches a wider and more transcendental meaning to the motto than that usually given it:

> There is an "oracle" at the beginning of the Fifth Symphony; in those four notes lies one of Beethoven's greatest messages. We would place its translation above the relentlessness of fate knocking at the door, above the greater human message of destiny, and strive to bring it towards the spiritual message of Emerson's revelations, even to the "common heart" of Concord—the soul of humanity knocking at the door of the divine mysteries, radiant in the faith that it *will* be opened—and the human will become the divine![62]

Ives further enriches his referential fabric by extending the "Oracle" with a free quotation from Zeuner's "Missionary Chant"—"Ye Christian heralds, go, proclaim/Salvation in Emmanuel's name"—a hymn which begins with the same pattern as the opening motive of Beethoven's Fifth Symphony.[63] Ex. 9-9 shows the complex texture that results when the "Oracle," continued as the "Missionary Chant," is stated in the bass, while the main theme of "Emerson" is developed in the top voice.

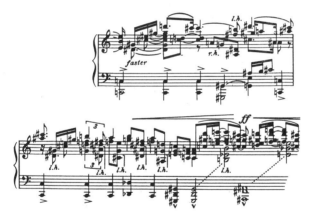

Ex. 9-9. Ives, Piano Sonata No. 2 (Concord Sonata), "Emerson," mm. 5–6. Copyright © 1947 (renewed) by Associated Music Publishers, Inc.

The intense, striving quality of the prose sections is balanced by the ecstatic lyricism of the variations (marked "verse"), which form the central part of the movement. Ives states his theme in extremely wide intervals in the first variation (p. 8, third and fourth braces). The second variation, according to a note added by the composer to the second edition, is meant to suggest "outdoor sounds over the Concord hills." In spite of the numerous accidentals, a sense of C major prevails in the variations, contrasting with the basically atonal music of the prose sections (Ex. 9-10).

Ex. 9-10. Ives, Piano Sonata No. 2 (Concord Sonata), "Emerson," p. 9.

In the second edition, Ives identifies the two sudden changes of tempo and texture in the recapitulation with "Emerson's sudden calls for a Transcendental Journey." The coda (p. 17, bottom brace) begins with a triumphal restatement of "Emerson's" main theme over an ostinato in the bass, which is almost always present from that point to the end of the movement. After the poignant, gradual fading of the main theme, the movement ends with a final statement of the "Oracle" and "Missionary Chant" in the middle voice (Ex. 9-11). The ostinato bass below it is reduced to a three-note pattern, while above, the repeated minor third C-sharp–E, whose dynamic fades from *pp* to *pppp*, is to "reflect the overtones of the soul of humanity and as they rise away almost inaudibly to the Ultimate Destiny." This passage is an example of the expressionist non-endings frequently found in Ives. Moreover, its alternating bass notes, with intimations of overtones in the treble, recall the musical symbol for night, sleep, or death used by Mahler and Schoenberg, and correspond closely to the motive of Marie's "waiting, which ends in her death" in Berg's *Wozzeck*.

*) To be heard as a kind of an overtone

Ex. 9-11. Ives, Piano Sonata No. 2 (Concord Sonata), "Emerson," last four mm. of p. 19.

The bursting energy of this movement conveys what Ives called Emerson's "thrust and dagger."[64] The "struggles of his soul" predominate over the "peace of mind which he commands even in his struggles."[65] These struggles of the soul were the composer's as well, as Ives found his way toward his own philosophy. World War I had the same crushing effect on his composing as it had on the European expressionist composers. A terrible tension built within him, for he felt that war was an expression of greed, started by "rich degenerates."

> The cause of all wars is cowardice. . . . When a man says he hates/doesn't believe in war, but believes it's got to come, he is a coward. He's afraid—he's the kind that makes war possible. He says you must be practical. . . . As soon as you are practical you are a coward."[66]

Much of his creative energy in 1915–16 was consumed by letters to newspapers on his theory that war is caused by a small number of men of large property in order to conserve or increase their property, and by his consequent development of a political theory limiting the amount of property one man can acquire.[67] With his profound optimism, Ives clung to President Wilson's ideals, and when the United States entered World War I on 6 April 1917, he plunged into patriotic efforts. Rejected on physical grounds in 1918, when he tried to enlist as an ambulance driver, Ives began a strenuous campaign to build his physical strength. At the same time he threw himself into the sale of Liberty Bonds, arguing that small bonds (Baby Bonds) would be an effective means of gathering support from the people at large—the people he had always believed in. On 1 October 1918, a severe heart attack brought on by these efforts effectively stopped his momentum. Thereafter he could not seem to keep his compositional ideas "up and sailing" the way he had been accustomed to.[68]

In the winter of 1919, while convalescing, Ives readied the *Concord* Sonata for private publication and wrote the *Essays* to explain what he intended in the music. Nowhere does he make clearer his subjective approach to composition than in his long disquisition on substance and manner in the *Essays*. In the Prologue he grapples with questions of the relationship of the subconscious to art: "Where is the line to be drawn between the expression of subjective and objective emotion?" Where does artistic intuition come from, the voice of God? or the voice of the devil? It is Ives's hope that the translation of artistic intuition into musical sounds will reflect "moral goodness," or "high vitality"; that music will become "a language so transcendent that its heights and depths will be common to all mankind."[69]

At the opening of the Epilogue, while recognizing that it is impossible for a prejudiced mind to contemplate the human qualities or attributes which lie at the source or primal impulse of an art inspiration, Ives forges on into the subjective realm; though it may be "tiresome," even "inartistic," he feels it is truer than the objective. Tracing the development of his own musical tastes from youth to maturity, Ives realizes that Wagner, instead of choosing spirit itself, chose the "representative" (as Emerson would say)—the lower set of values. The higher value—substance—is reality, quality, or spirit. The lower value—manner—is form and quantity. "Substance in a human-art-quality suggests the body of a conviction which has its birth in the spiritual consciousness. . . .[It] is somehow translated into expression by 'manner'—a process always less important than it seems." Ives recognizes that the two are inextricable, but "manner for manner's sake" as a basis of music is merely a way to reach fame; a "group-disease germ." Manner is always discovering partisans because it is the easy path of any particular idiom and can be catalogued, whereas

> substance is too indefinite to analyze in more specific terms. It is practically indescribable. Intuitions . . . will sense it—process, unknown. Perhaps it is an unexplained consciousness of being nearer God or being nearer the devil—of approaching truth or approaching unreality. It is a silent something felt in the truth of nature in Turner against the truth of art in Botticelli.

Among other examples, Ives sees Emerson as almost wholly substance, Poe as manner. Substance leans toward optimism, manner pessimism. "Beauty, in its common conception, has nothing to do with [substance]," Ives muses, and, for that matter, "Nobody knows what actual beauty is." But "substance can be expressed in music, and . . . is the only valuable thing in it. . . . Substance has something to do with character. Manner has nothing to do with it."[70]

One needs only to read Wassily Kandinsky's small book on his expressionist philosophy of art, *Über das geistige in der Kunst* (Concerning the Spiritual in Art), written in 1911, to see that passages correspond closely to Ives's thought and experience:

> Primitives . . . like ourselves . . . sought to express in their work only internal truths, renouncing in consequence all consideration of external form. . . . Neglect of inner meanings; . . . this vain squandering of artistic power is called "art for art's sake." . . . In periods of retrogression in the spiritual world . . . art ministers to lower needs, and is used for material ends. . . . The question "what?" disappears from art; only the question "how?" remains. . . . Art has lost her soul.[71]

Kandinsky represented the life of the spirit as an upward-moving triangle, at the top of which are those with the greatest vision. Similarly, Ives believed that "music (and all art, like all life) must be a part of the great organic flow, onwards and always upwards, or become soft in muscles and spirit, and die!"[72]

Ives's Fourth Symphony (1909–16), perhaps his finest work, caps the period of his most intense creative activity. The composer himself felt that its last movement "seems to me the best, compared with the other movements, or for that matter with any other thing I've done."[73] He told Henry Bellamann, "the aesthetic program of the work is . . . the searching questions of What? and Why? which the spirit of man asks of life."[74] The second, third, and fourth movements present differing answers to the question posed in the first one (Prelude).

Death and its transcendence seem to be at the center of the meaning of this symphony. In *Memos,* Ives hints at the incidents which inspired the final movement ("the apotheosis of the preceding content"): how "Nearer My God To Thee" ("Bethany") had sounded in the old Camp Meeting services led by his father; an incident showing one of the finest sides of his father's character; and the spontaneous singing of this hymn at a New York café after McKinley's assassination in 1901.[75] A similar moving communal response occurred after the sinking of the *Lusitania* in 1915, when a crowd of all classes joined in the dignified singing of "In the Sweet By-and-By" at a New York elevated station, "as a natural outlet for what their feelings had been going through all day long."[76] In 1910, during the composition of this symphony, the recurrence of Halley's comet may have inspired both musical and verbal symbols of transcendence over death in the first and last movements.

The Prelude of the Symphony begins with a tortured, chromatic *ff* question (Ex. 9-12), which becomes a motto and reappears in varied form at the beginning of the second and the fourth movements. In the first movement the question is followed by extreme contrast, as an ensemble of harp and two muted violins enters, playing a phrase from "Bethany," but "scarcely to be heard, as faint sounds in the distance." This starlike ensemble and its quotation are unobtrusively, almost subliminally, present throughout the rest of the Prelude, but their full significance is apparent only in the final movement.

Ex. 9-12. Ives, Fourth Symphony, I, mm. 1–2, strings only. Copyright © 1965 by Associated Music Publishers, Inc.

After a quotation of the opening phrase of "In the Sweet By-and-By," which probably recalls the communal experience following the sinking of the *Lusitania,* the rest of this short movement is dominated by Ives's version of the hymn "Watchman" ("Watchman, tell us of the night,/What its signs of promise are"). Ives uses this hymn because of the mood of expectancy it creates, and he treats both words and music with great freedom. He does this partly to avoid the hymn's over-rigid symmetry, but more importantly to increase its emotional intensity, filtering the borrowed material through his own psyche in order to make it serve his most urgent expressive purposes.

In order to enrich his communication with the listener, Ives presents the hymn in a *quodlibet* (or mosaic), mingling it with quotations of tunes whose texts and connotations are related to "Watchman." (This comparatively modest *quodlibet* foreshadows the grandiose montage at the end of the final movement.) To build suspense toward the climactic phrase of the hymn ("Traveller, yes; it brings the day"), Ives completely omits the phrase which precedes it, interpolating instead a one-measure general pause followed by two subjective utterances of "Traveller, yes!" Instead of the final phrase of Mason's hymn tune, he inserts his own text and music—"Dost thou see its beauteous ray?" After the chorus sings these words [8], chorus and orchestra drop out, leaving only the *ppp* "Bethany" ensemble. Thus Ives makes explicit that the "Bethany" group is meant to evoke the hymn's "glory-beaming star," with its connotations of belief and hope. As the movement draws to an evanescent subdominant closing, fragments of his added text phrase are repeated first urgently, then ever more quietly. With this indeterminate ending and textual question ("Dost thou see its beauteous ray?"), Ives creates a state of uncertainty and expectation which will be resolved in the last movement.

The second movement is a fantasy which resembles a series of fevered, expressionistic dream images. It reminds one of Strindberg's description of his *Dream Play* (quoted above, p. 16): "anything can happen; everything is possible and probable . . . imagination spins and weaves new patterns made up of memories, experiences, unfettered fancies, absurdities and improvisations." The movement consists largely of short sections contrasted by tempo, texture, and the widely differing nature of the materials Ives quotes. The unpredictable mixture of hymns, ragtime, popular songs, marches, and even a takeoff on polite salon music results in the chaos and distortion of a fevered dream. There are few transitions; more often, Ives "cuts" from one texture to another with cinematic rapidity or superimposes one type of material on another. He breaks the bounds of formal coherence and stretches the perceptive powers of the human ear to their utmost in order to record a human consciousness as it experiences the multiple vicissitudes of life. In his belief that "the fabric of existence weaves itself into a whole," Ives includes an almost overwhelming variety and complexity of textures and types of music in the movement.

This fantasy was composed at the same time as the "Hawthorne" movement of the *Concord* Sonata and is an expansion and elaboration of it. Ives (in Bellamann's program note) suggests that Hawthorne's short story "The Celestial Railroad," in which "an exciting, easy, worldly progress through life is contrasted with the trials of the pilgrims," may be considered an "incidental program" for the symphony movement.[77] The often distorted hymn quotations refer to the pilgrims' struggles and provide a foil to the wealth of livelier popular materials which dominate the movement. The sounds and rhythms of the steam engine (entering at [4], becoming "gradually faster and louder," and sounding its whistle three measures after [6]) relate to Hawthorne's story, but also to the important role of the railroad in the composer's life. Not only was Ives a commuter, but a childhood railroad fantasy shared with his father was a precious memory to him. As a boy in Danbury one of his favorite amusements was to create, with his younger brother, Moss, the "Ives Bros. RR" under the backyard clothesline (two barrels on the wash bench, an old stove pipe, the dinnerbell, part of a chicken coop as the cab, a brass spittoon as sandbox, a medicine indicator clock for a steam gauge, and a lot of saliva—renewed by soda-pop—going "sissle" as steam). George Ives would ride in the passenger car playing staccato passages and arpeggios on his violin, sounding "like the clicking of the car wheels especially when they were going over the switches. . . . How thankful we feel now, that father dreamed with us; how circumspect our lives would be now if he hadn't." Significantly, this passage from Ives's "Commuter's Diary" is followed by a philosophical reflection on his father's death:

> It is always "the minute after" life that everyone lives. Immortality is the complement of our present hope. If there is no present hope how can there be any immortality. . . . Faith is built on intuition and intuition on a series of experiences more or less subconscious.[78]

The entire movement leads up to the entrance of Ives's own *Country Band March* (1903). It is the breaking in of reality upon a dream; the subjective impression of a noisy, chaotic Fourth of July celebration. Ives concentrates not on "something that happens, but [on] the way something happens."[79] Starting with the introduction to the *Country Band March* [39], the movement's heaviest, most complex textures and loudest dynamics occur. Although the *March* predominates, many other tunes are quoted ("Yankee Doodle," "Turkey in the Straw," "Marching through Georgia," and "Long, Long Ago," to name only some of the best known) in a collage which accelerates to a final climax at [47] and then melts away quickly in the last three measures of the movement.

The third movement, a fugue based on two hymns, is a revision of the opening movement of Ives's First String Quartet (1896?). It is a retreat into formalism and ritualism which provides repose. Yet the movement is neither a dry exercise nor a parody. Its warmth and comparative simplicity make it an excellent foil for the complex movements which surround it and provide relief from their intense subjectivity.

The fourth and final movement of the Symphony answers the question posed in the first, and the answer is religious, communal, and transcendental. Ives called the movement "an apotheosis of the preceding content, in terms that have something to do with the reality of existence and its religious experience."[80] He wrote in *Memos*, "Not until I got to work on the *Fourth Symphony* did I feel justified in writing quite as I wanted to, when the subject matter was religious."[81] If the first movement asks a question whose answer is only hinted at by the scarcely audible "Bethany," in the last movement "Bethany" moves to center stage, showing that the answer to the question of existence is to be found in transcending the distractions of life and dreams (second movement) and moving nearer to God.

The finale begins with the "Battery Unit" (three drums, cymbal, and gong) playing slow march rhythms, which continue throughout and (in the manuscript) are notated to go on indefinitely after the rest of the orchestra is finished.[82] These slow march rhythms recall McKinley's funeral, for which Ives was moved to write his own *Memorial Slow March*, a part of which is quoted in the finale (mm. 40–63). The slow march rhythms suggest that Ives was preoccupied with death in this movement, but they also symbolize mankind's progress toward the ultimate transcendence with which the movement closes.

The whole finale is a constant, gradual crescendo of both dynamics and texture, leading through many quotations (largely of hymns) to the clearly tonal D-major *quodlibet*, which begins at m. 65. In this lofty *quodlibet* "Bethany" predominates, stated complete in the first violins and complemented by phrases from (among others) "Martyn," "Dorrnance," "Missionary Chant," and even a quotation from "As Freshmen First We Came to Yale."[83] In the coda (m. 72), the chorus enters wordlessly, repeating "Bethany" as part of an attenuating texture. A Nirvana-like atmosphere is created, similar to the ending of Ives's Psalm 90. The movement's culminating *quodlibet* is a communal apotheosis broad enough to embrace all humanity. Its multiple, layered quotations symbolize the different strata of human endeavor. The movement as a whole expresses mankind's advance toward perfectibility (in which Ives fervently believed) and an ultimate victory over death.

Elliott Carter, in "Expressionism and American Music," points out that "the same sort of thinking which formed the background of the Central European Expressionist movement also informed the thinking of artists . . . in the United States," and focuses on the independently arrived-at similarities in Ives's outlook and techniques. Carter recognizes as expressionist characteristics Ives's stress on truthfulness of expression and his inner necessity to express transcendental experiences.[84]

According to his partner, Jules Myrick, Ives was possessed of incredible idealism and felt that people "should communicate directly with each other on a personal basis, one to one. In his music, one finds this sense of immediacy of communicating almost tangible experiences."[85] As we have found in the work of other expressionist composers, Ives's expressive desires did not produce literal program music, but music in which the subjective dominates, even to the point of inchoateness. His playing of his own music shows—as Ives always counseled his performers—that gestures and spirit are more important than the right notes.[86] He told Bernard Herrmann that he was inspired by "something bigger than nice designs on paper,"[87] and Henry Bellamann that he "heard something else."[88]

The "something else" included an expressionist simultaneity in contrapuntal conception (much like Mahler's), which conveys diversity of experience by way of polytonal layers, polymeters, and superimposed conflicting tempi. Ives's profound antipathy to music that was boxed in, "nice and neat"[89] in its linear progression and formal cohesion, and his need to express his idea of organic flow result in an avoidance of literal repetition common to all expressionist composers. Like other expressionists, Ives felt music was the art of speaking extravagantly.[90] Yet, in order to intensify his meaning, he also embraced the expressionist opposite, an extreme of brevity and conciseness, in many of his songs (among them "Maple Leaves," "Ann Street," "Remembrance," "Duty," and "The Cage"). This reductive tendency was shared—independently—with Schoenberg and Webern. (Like Schoenberg, Ives was paradoxical. Paradox was necessary to the inclusive nature of Ives's art.)

As it was to expressionists (particularly to Webern and Bartók), the ethical aspect of his music was important to Ives. John Kirkpatrick remembers that Ives wanted to make music that would be good for the players' souls,[91] and Carter notes the influence on expressionism of mysticism, as a basis for the artist's sense of inner vision and disdain for the "material" world.[92] Ives was on this spiritual wavelength and shared it in the 1920s and 30s with the pianist Katherine Heyman, the composer and Whitman scholar Clifton Furness, and the younger Elliott Carter and John Kirkpatrick. Again, a paradox operates. The antagonism between the transcendental and old-time revivalist religion did not bother Ives. His quotations of hymns and vernacular tunes were "colloquial spots which the older generation of New Englanders (including mine) will get," he wrote to Nicholas Slonimsky in 1929.[93] His point was to enhance communication. Although his musical quotations are rarely literal—because they are subjectively altered—Ives felt anyone recognizing "Nearer My God, to Thee" and other such communally shared, deeply rooted American traditions, would understand his personal twists on meaning. However much Ives feared progress and change, he could not have seen how altered these traditions and values would become, for the context of much of his music is lost to the average listener—even the American—and must be resurrected by scholars. Yet the underlying spirit still conveys much of his meaning. Perhaps that spirit is best conveyed by a paragraph he wrote in 1924, a year after completing his last compositional work:

> Music is one of the many ways God has of beating in on man—his lives, his deaths, his hope, his everything—an inner something, a spiritual storm, a something else that stirs man in all of his parts and consciousness, and "all at once." . . . What this inner something is which begets all this, is something no one knows. . . . Music . . . no one knows what it is—and the less he knows he knows what it is the nearer it is to music—probably.[94]

Select Bibliography

Ballantine, Christopher. "Charles Ives and the Meaning of Quotation in Music." *Musical Quarterly* 65/2 (April 1979): 167–84.

Bellamann, Henry H. "Charles Ives: The Man and His Music." *The Musical Quarterly* 19/1 (January 1933): 45–58.

Block, Geoffrey. *Charles Ives: A Bio-Bibliography.* New York: Greenwood, 1988.

Carter, Elliott. "Expressionism and American Music." *Perspectives of New Music* 4/2 (Fall–Winter 1965): 1–13. Reprinted in *The Writings of Elliott Carter,* ed. Else Stone and Kurt Stone. Bloomington: Indiana University Press, 1977.

Cowell, Henry, ed. *American Composers on American Music.* Stanford, CA: Stanford University Press, 1933.

———, and Cowell, Sidney. *Charles Ives and His Music.* New York: Oxford University Press, 1955.

Feder, Stuart. "Decoration Day: A Boyhood Memory of Charles Ives." *The Musical Quarterly* 66/2 (April 1980): 234–61.

Henderson, Clayton W. *The Charles Ives Tunebook.* Warren, MI: Harmonie Park Press, 1990.

Hitchcock, H. Wiley. *Ives.* London: Oxford University Press, 1977.

———, and Perlis, Vivian, eds. *An Ives Celebration: Papers and Panels of the Ives Centennial Festival-Conference.* Urbana: University of Illinois Press, 1977.

Ives, Charles E. *Essays Before a Sonata, The Majority, and Other Writings.* Ed. Howard Boatwright. New York: Norton, 1961.

———. *Memos.* Ed. John Kirkpatrick. New York: Norton, 1972.

Kirkpatrick, John. *A Temporary Mimeographed Catalogue of the Music Manuscripts and Related Materials of Charles Edward Ives.* New Haven: Yale University Press, 1960.

———. "Ives as Revealed in His Marginalia." *Cornell University Musical Review* 4 (1961): 14–19.

Mellers, Wilfred H. *Music in a New Found Land.* New York: Knopf, 1965.

Perlis, Vivian. *Charles Ives Remembered.* New Haven: Yale University Press, 1974.

Perry, Rosalie Sandra. *Charles Ives and the American Mind.* Kent, OH: Kent State University Press, 1974.

Rossiter, Frank R. *Charles Ives and His America.* New York: Liveright, 1975.

Ward, Charles Wilson. "Charles Ives: The Relationship Between Aesthetic Theories and Compositional Processes." Ph.D. diss., University of Texas, Austin, 1974.

CHAPTER TEN

Synthesis of the Arts

> The artist must have something to say, for mastery over form is not his goal but rather the adapting of form to its inner meaning.
>
> Wassily Kandinsky (1911)

One of the most fascinating aspects of expressionism is the eradication of boundaries between the arts. Following Wagner, and in the spirit of Nietzsche's criticism of Wagner, no single art seemed adequate to express inner vision. Separation and specialization of the arts, a consequence of nineteenth-century materialism, was the antithesis of the organic, spiritual betterment expressionists strove for. Wagner had constructed "forms of effect on an entirely external basis."[1] The expressionist artist approached synthesis from an *internal* point of view, with the intention of affecting the subconscious, rather than merely the reason, of the spectator. Between 1907 and the outbreak of World War I, there was among expressionists a widespread yet single-minded desire to interrelate not only the various arts but also arts with ideas and philosophies. New techniques and achievements in expressionist synthesis must therefore be considered in light of the ideas which generated them.

Most of the works previously discussed in this book illustrate the urge toward synthesis of the arts. This attraction toward fusion originated in a desire for unity of vision. It was enhanced in theater and opera by modern techniques which focused on psychological depth of expression, while bold combinations of arts and ideas probing society's preconceptions dominated literary periodicals and artistic cabarets. Composers were freed for endeavors in secondary fields by the emphasis on meaning over form. The arts were no longer ends in themselves, but means to truthful perception. Mahler, Ives, Schoenberg, Webern, and Berg wrote texts or libretti for their vocal works, or they attempted plays. Schoenberg, Stravinsky, and Ruggles painted, and they often composed musical works with a strong visual attitude. There was constant reinforcement for these endeavors because of the uniquely high esteem in which music was held by painters, sculptors, poets, dramatists, and philosophers. For, as Schoenberg put it, music, more easily than the other arts, could express "the illogicality which our senses demonstrate . . . an expression of feeling, as our feelings, which bring us in contact with our subconscious, really are."[2]

Wassily Kandinsky, himself a trained musician, conceived most of his expressionist paintings as "compositions" or "improvisations" and was concerned with their "reverberations" [Klänge] in observers. He observed the current attitudes toward synthesis in his book, Concerning the Spiritual in Art (1911):

> The various arts are drawing together. They are finding in Music the best teacher. With few exceptions music has been for some centuries the art which has devoted itself not to the reproduction of natural phenomena, but rather to the expression of the artist's soul, in musical sound. A painter . . . naturally seeks to apply the methods of music to his own art . . . and so the arts are encroaching one upon another, and from a proper use of this encroachment will rise the art that is truly monumental.[3]

This striving toward musical expression had its roots in artists' endeavors to endow art and life with greater spiritual values. Kandinsky's purpose in art was "the expression of mystery in terms of mystery";[4] and Gustav Klimt spoke of the "spiritualization of form" (Vergeisterung der Form), a concept espoused by Adolf Loos, Schoenberg, and Schoenberg's pupils.[5] A line by the poet Else Lasker-Schuler, "A storm blows the holy ghost through the world," gave Herwarth Walden's periodical, Der Sturm, its symbol for the expressionist movement.

A fascination with mysticism, the occult, and numerology was often embodied in the antimaterialist desire of artists for transcendence. These preoccupations on the part of Scriabin, Ives, Webern, Berg, and Schoenberg contributed to the strong tendency toward the abstract in their expressionist experiments in synthesis. Expressionist composers' ideals of synthesis sometimes involved combinations of art and philosophy so visionary they were never completed. Expressionist utopianism, centered on the theme of the artist as a prophet in direct struggle with God and belief, evolved from Nietzsche's call for transcendence through extreme individualism.

Scriabin's immense ritual Mysterium, conceived in 1903 and intended to be performed by thousands in Tibet, was the most grandiose and apocalyptic of these visions. All the arts were to be employed, for Scriabin felt that the world's desire to be freed from the bonds of matter could only be fulfilled by a synthesis of the arts in the hands of a messiah—himself.[6] The listener was to be brought to an ecstatic state, and there was to be a final "dematerialization of the world."[7]

In 1911 (and independently of Scriabin, with whose music and ideas Ives later became acquainted), Ives conceived the idea of attempting to convey a subjective view of the earth and the heavens as he contemplated nature.[8] His *Universe Symphony* was an idea he continued to sketch, never completing it but leaving notes in the sketches in (the Transcendentalist's) hope that someone else might take up the work.[9] Although his was not Scriabin's messianic view, Ives had a mystic's attitude toward this work, which he intended to be "a presentation and contemplation in tones, rather than in music (as such), of the mysterious creation of the earth and firmament, the evolution of all life in nature, in humanity, to the Divine."[10]

In his text for the visionary oratorio *Die Jakobsleiter*, Schoenberg expressed the new spiritual insights he gained, after his marital difficulties, through his reading of Strindberg and of Balzac's *Séraphîta,* a popularization of the mystic theories of Swedenborg. Various philosophical points of view such as materialism and aestheticism are personified in the text, only to be rejected. The Chosen One (Schoenberg himself) will lead mankind to higher levels of spirituality by means of a new doctrine combining Judeo-Christian precepts with the Theosophical belief in reincarnation. Originally conceived as a theater work lasting three evenings, the oratorio remained a fragment, although Schoenberg was urgently attempting to complete it during the last year of his life.

Earlier works of synthesis reflected personal struggles with the radical changes in sexual and moral attitudes. The new psychological viewpoint demanded that the artist understand himself more clearly than before. As Kandinsky wrote to Schoenberg in 1911, "self-perception [should be] the root of the 'new' art, of art in general, which is never new, but which must enter into a new phase—today!"[11] This self-perception lies behind the autobiographical works of Strindberg, Wedekind, Kokoschka, Schoenberg, Webern, and Berg, who were preoccupied, before World War I, with dramatizing their own inner occurrences as representative of universal human conflicts. During their expressionist phase these artists were at their most self-revealing in works for the theater: Strindberg in chamber plays for his Intimate Theater (1907–10); Wedekind in his Lulu plays (1894–1903); Kokoschka in his early plays written for cabaret and Vienna's Kunstschau (1908–1909); Schoenberg in his one-act operas, *Erwartung* (1909) and *Die glückliche Hand* (1910–13); Webern in his play, *Tot* (1913); and Berg in his operas, *Wozzeck* (1914–21) and (to a lesser extent) *Lulu* (1928–35).

By 1907 the theater had been enhanced for expressionists as an ideal meeting place of the arts by advances in stagecraft modeled on music and based on a common obsession with spirit. The chief architects of these modern theories were Adolphe Appia and Gordon Craig. Working independently along very similar lines, they each found Wagner's music dramas mired in realism. They were determined to express the inner life of drama through stage settings that created mood by suggestion rather than by realistic detail. They used lighting that molded space and shapes, and they dramatized emotion through the psychological use of color. Music was at the root of their theories.

Appia had studied with Franz Liszt and had met Wagner at Bayreuth, where the productions disappointed him. He felt that music, not pure drama, should determine the form and substance of an operatic production. He devised a system of hieroglyphics to be used in the musical score for stage and lighting cues—a technique Schoenberg later appropriated for *Die glückliche Hand*. Above all, Appia wrote in his *Musik und die Inszenierung* (1899), light should not be used merely to illuminate painted flats but to bring out "the inner being of the outward seeming." [12] For his productions between 1910 and 1914 at Hellerau, near Dresden (in partnership with Emile Jaques-Dalcroze), Appia achieved a reduction to essentials in all media of the stage and a fusion of these media which became widely influential in theater arts.

As a young man, Gordon Craig composed music. He began his directing and designing career in London with productions of Purcell and Handel operas. His work centered on his belief that both theater and music originally sprang from movement. [13] As a director, he demanded entire and absolute control of the stage and all that happens on it, in order to achieve an art of "revelation" portraying states of mind distilled from the essence of the drama through lighting, settings, and movement. Craig tended further toward abstraction than did Appia, for he hoped to replace actors' faces with masks and the actor with the *Übermarionette*—a Nietzschean superpuppet. His autocratic approach limited his work as a director, but he was invited to Germany, Russia, and Italy to revitalize theater, and he exhibited widely in Europe. His book, *On the Art of the Theatre* (published in 1905 in English, French, and German), established him in Europe as an innovator of vision. Among others, Strindberg was strongly influenced by the powerfully spiritual quality of Craig's designs and ideas; and Max Reinhardt's revolutionary early productions of Gorky, Maeterlinck, Wedekind, Strindberg, and Wilde reflected Craig's expressionistic intensity. [14]

In 1903 Gustav Mahler, as director of the Vienna Opera, was also open to the new ideas of more meaningful synthesis of the arts. Appia's theories were discussed in the Vienna Secession; [15] and Reinhardt's productions, indebted to Craig's ideas, were widely known in Germany and presented in Vienna. (Hermann Bahr noted in his theater criticism of that year that Reinhardt was realizing the spiritual in something new and unique: a release from naturalism. [16]) In order to introduce the modern ideas of stagecraft into the tradition-encrusted Vienna Opera, Mahler appointed Alfred Roller, president of the Vienna Secession, as his scenic designer, and soon put him in charge of stage lighting and costumes as well. While Roller had no background in the theater, he shared with Mahler a selfless dedication to the spirit and integrity of each work of art. Like Mahler, Roller believed that "everything is in the score. . . . The production is only an art of framing, never the goal in itself." [17] Like Appia and Craig, Roller replaced stage scenery with stage spaces; and he reduced the expressive means of stage decoration to basic components, in what Hermann Bahr called "spiritualization of the scenic element." [18] Lighting played such an important part in the Mahler-Roller productions that a critic coined the term *Lichtmusik* for them. [19]

Roller's scene designs for the 1903 production of *Tristan und Isolde*, their first collaboration, exploit a plastic use of light and a psychological properties of color to enhance the drama. This production, given its first performance on the twentieth anniversary of Wagner's death, 21 February 1903, "marks the beginning of a new epoque in the lyric theater, and expresses a new aesthetic," wrote Hermann Bahr. [20] The critic Max Graf pointed out the psychological importance of complementary color choices: Act I was a symphony in reds, relieved by the light blue of sea and sky; Act II was a symphony in violet, with yellow contrast in the torch and foreboding dawn; Act III was grey. [21] Webern (whose secondary doctoral subject had been the history of art) noted in his diary the marvelous color contrasts in the first two acts, the irresistible sensuality of the second, and the unlimited sadness of the last act. [22]

There was fierce resistance among the entrenched officialdom of the Vienna Opera to the Mahler-Roller innovations, but Mahler insisted that, "What matters is the collaboration of all the arts. There is no future in the old standard cliches; modern art must extend to costumes, props, everything that can revitalize a work of art." [23] Mahler admonished the singers—whose sloppy, routine performances he uncompromisingly reformed—"What is most important in music is not to be found in the notes." [24] He demanded that they live—and therefore act—their parts with unprecedented psychological depth. Before drinking the love potion Tristan was a baritone, after it a tenor, he remarked. In the epoch-making Mahler-Roller production of Beethoven's *Fidelio* (1904), the traditionally robust Prisoners' Chorus became a mere octet of wormlike, emaciated figures, struggling toward the light. [25] A striking innovation in Mozart's *Don Giovanni* (1905) was the use of movable stage towers, which could close in upon intimate scenes or be pulled back for scenes requiring the full breadth of the stage. Merely turning these prismlike towers could transform an exterior scene into an interior one in thirty seconds, thereby maintaining a swift flow of action in this long opera, with its almost cinematic scene changes. Taking over as stage director (as well as conductor), Mahler often built his staging out of the singers' acting improvisations, while in musical rehearsals he demanded utmost precision, intensity, intelligence, and unremitting work. He conducted from memory, reflecting every nuance of expression in his face and requiring an astounding range of color and dynamic shading from the orchestra. Bruno Walter remembered that Mahler, with his intensely dramatic personality, "was able to penetrate the heart of the music and realize, within himself, the composer's dramatic vision." [26] This golden but brief period (1903–1907) of Vienna Opera productions under Mahler's and Roller's intense and uncompromising demand for psychological truth inspired and reverberated in the expressionist stage works of the younger Viennese—Schoenberg, Kokoschka, Webern, and Berg. At the same time, the efforts of Craig and Appia to reduce dramatic expression to essentials created a milieu in the theater for expressionism and its tendency toward the abstract.

Ideas of synthesis involving music were not confined to the elite world of opera and theater. Since the Secession movements in the 1890s, art journals had established a practice of including music, poetry, literature, and the fine arts in a kind of published *Gesamtkunstwerk*. An example is *Ver Sacrum* (Sacred Spring) 1898–1901, the magazine of the Vienna Secession, which published facsimiles of songs by Hugo Wolf and others. In the expressionist period, new journals took up this idea to fight cultural battles: *Erdgeist* (Earth Spirit, named after a Wedekind play), 1908, was a Viennese periodical "interested in all the arts"; *Der Merker* (The Observer), 1909–19, also Viennese, devoted an issue to Schoenberg, which reproduced his music, some of his paintings, his libretto for *Die glückliche Hand,* and his theoretical writings;[27] *Der Ruf* (The Call), Vienna, 1912–13, and *Der Zeit-Echo* (Echo of the Times), Munich, 1914, were also devoted to the "community of the arts." *Der Anbruch* (The Dawn), Vienna, 1918, and *Der Weg*, Munich, 1919, carried on a strong interest in the arts, but they turned increasingly political in tone as war devastated the artistic community. Herwarth Walden's Expressionist journal, *Der Sturm* (The Storm), centered for the most part in Berlin, 1910–32, seriously examined the question of synthesis of the arts and maintained a strong awareness of the important relationship of music to the other arts. In 1916–17 Lothar Schreyer wrote articles for *Der Sturm* on the need for unity of the arts; and, with Rudolf Blümner, an actor with musical interests, he opened a school for the development of Expressionist performance art which would provide trained performers and technicians for the *Sturm-Bühne* (theater of the Sturm circle). In this intense Expressionist movement, highly idealistic attitudes toward artistic unity (in contrast to Wagner's "juxtaposition" of the various art forms) prevailed, along with an attempt to create a "community of men" among both spectators and actors. Blümner (who worked with Reinhardt) invented for this theater the speaking style of Expressionist drama, with a musical approach. The first production of the *Sturm-Bühne,* on 16 October 1918, was August Stramm's *Sancta Susanna.* The theater disbanded when Schreyer went to the Bauhaus in 1921.[28]

A strong influence on the *Sturm-Bühne* activity came from Munich's *Blaue Reiter* group. From its inception in 1911, synthesis of the arts was basic to the philosophical concept of its leaders, Kandinsky and Marc. Their symbol, the Blue Rider, was St. George slaying the dragon of materialism, and their efforts involved the spiritual evolution of man through art. It was Kandinsky's idea to publish a "synthesized" book, which was intended to eliminate old narrow ideas and tear down the walls between the arts, "to demonstrate eventually that the question of art is not a question of form but one of artistic content."[29] The *Blaue Reiter Almanac* was published in 1912 in order to unite new international trends and stimulate the synthesis of the arts. There were to be two volumes, the second of which would have further developed ideas about theater with the collaboration of Hugo Ball, a theatrical producer. Ball and Kandinsky envisioned a "New Theater," to open in October 1914, and a new festival house, "The International Society for Modern Art," which would include theater, painting, music, and dance. The objective, aborted by the outbreak of war, was to have been no less than "the renaissance of society out of a union of all artistic means and powers."[30] Western theater of illusion was to have been supplanted by Eastern techniques of Japanese theater—stilts, masks, megaphones, and nonrealistic sets. The purpose was to affect the subconscious—rather than merely the reason—of the spectator. Although the second volume of the *Blaue Reiter Almanac* was also a war casualty, the first volume contained several articles on music (one by Schoenberg[31]) and reproduced facsimiles of three songs: Schoenberg's "Herzgewächse" (composed for the Almanac to a text by Maeterlinck), Berg's "Aus dem Glühenden" (Mombert), and Webern's "Ihr tratet zu dem Herde" (Stefan George).

The German cabaret movement was another fertile ground for the development of ideas of synthesis, particularly because of its satirical antiestablishment attitude. The popular music hall (in Germany, the *Tingeltangel*) was already a success to build upon. The Chat Noir of Montmartre was the model for Berlin's Überbrettl, founded in 1901 by Ernst Wolzogen, a German aristocrat who, like Hermann Bahr in Vienna, championed the avant-garde. The name "Überbrettl" was purposely Nietzschean ("super" stage, recalling the *Übermensch*, or superman), for beneath the humor was a serious purpose: to ennoble light theater and to mend the rift between concert music and the common people. Opposition to humorless naturalism was basic to the appeal of artistic cabaret. Among the innovations were performance improvisations and shadow plays incorporating music, the acting of puppets, and narration. Sung lyric poetry and ballads, either contributed by young, unknown literati or drawn from folk sources, were another immensely popular aspect of cabaret entertainment. These were often published in small illustrated books. Wolzogen sought out, for the Überbrettl, artists and performers who found opera and theater too narrow and wanted to link their talents to ideals, while he called himself "a dancing prophet in Nietzsche's sense" and played Master of Ceremonies.[32] Oskar Straus, a well-known operetta composer, provided most of the music; and Wolzogen also hired Schoenberg, in 1901, to contribute to the musical numbers. Schoenberg found inspiration for much of his early vocal music in the poetry of the Überbrettl circle; certainly the satirical tone of *Pierrot lunaire* harks back to the spirit of cabaret.

With the success of the Überbrettl, other literary cabarets sprang up in Berlin, Munich, and Vienna. Max Reinhardt's Schall und Rauch (Sound and Smoke), which opened in Berlin in 1901, evolved into the Kleines Theater (Little Theater), in which Reinhardt championed the disturbing and influential plays of Strindberg, Wedekind, Maeterlinck, and Gorky. Munich's first cabaret was also formed in 1901, by a group of painters, actors, and writers connected with the anti-royalist satirical weekly *Simplicissimus*. They called themselves Die elf Scharfrichter (The Eleven Executioners) and were determined to "execute" social hypocrisy. Here Frank Wedekind, recently released from a sensational trial and six months' imprisonment for ridiculing the Kaiser in verse, sang his own satirical poems, many of which dealt with erotic themes and street life, "in a brittle voice, slightly monotonous and quite untrained." Bertolt Brecht, strongly influenced by Wedekind, wrote, "It was the man's intense aliveness, the energy which allowed him to defy sniggering ridicule and proclaim his brazen hymn to humanity, that also gave him this personal magic."[33]

The first of Wedekind's semi-autobiographical Lulu plays, *Erdgeist* (Earth-Spirit), was first performed in the Elf Scharfrichter cabaret. Reinhardt produced series of Wedekind's plays in many European cities, often starring Wedekind himself, for his highly stylized acting, combining outrageously antinaturalist movements and grotesquely exaggerated speech, was essential to convey the meaning of these plays.[34] Hermann Bahr, watching the discomfiture of a Viennese audience at Reinhardt's production of *Erdgeist* in 1903, wrote: "The concern of art is not to soothe or lull people, but to startle and, as Schiller said, 'to discommode, spoil their comfort, put them into unrest and astonishment.' "[35] It was from the success of cabaret, as well as the idea that drama could emulate chamber music, that Reinhardt and Strindberg conceived their "chamber" theaters: Reinhardt's Kammerspielhaus (Chamber Playhouse) opened in Berlin in 1906, and Strindberg's Intimate Theater in Stockholm in 1908.[36]

It is a paradox typical of Vienna that Oskar Kokoschka's first experiments in radical expressionist theater came to life not in a cabaret characterized by the Nietzschean spirit, antiroyalist executioners, or smoke and noise, but in the coolly decorative *Jugendstil* surroundings of the Cabaret Fledermaus. The designer of this tiny but elegant theater was Josef Hofmann, a leader in the Wiener Werkstätte (Viennese Arts and Crafts) movement to commercialize and make of the material possessions of life an all-encompassing—but, in the expressionist sense, superficial—*Gesamtkunstwerk*. Hofmann's Palais Stoclet (1906) in Brussels, for which every piece of furniture, each practical object and casual ornament, even the clothing worn by the owners, was designed to correspond in form and style with the architecture, was the ultimate achievement of the Wiener Werkstätte. The Cabaret Fledermaus was also completely designed—down to the "hygienic elements"—in this manner. Yet the demands of Hofmann's and Kolo Moser's Wiener Werkstätte produced such versatile artists as Roller and Kokoschka, with their strong desire to invest synthesis with deeper meaning.[37]

Like Wedekind and Strindberg, Kokoschka was obsessed with the problem of honesty about sex, and no single art sufficed for what he called "the enticing abyss of Eros. . . . It took a world war with all its carnage to enable me to overcome this fatal confrontation."[38] The theme of his second production for the Cabaret Fledermaus, presented on 29 March 1909, was his struggle concerning woman *(Ich ringe um die Frau)*. It was a matinee of readings from his early literary work, along with a satirical play entitled *Eine Groteske.* Kokoschka was influenced by Strindberg's plays, which were produced frequently in Vienna in these years; he could not afford a ticket to the theater, so he read them all.[39] He was undoubtedly also influenced at this time, like so many others, by Otto Weininger's misogynist *Geschlecht und Charakter* (Sex and Character), published in 1903. A Wedekind-like discontinuity of scenes and an absurdist approach characterize the plot of *Eine Groteske;* the main character is a giant scarecrow cuckolded by his wife, who turns his head so that he cannot see her. He tells a parrot, "She eats men's souls," then sprouts antlers and commits suicide with an air pistol. Felix Salten wrote after this single performance:

> One saw, as it were, into a hot oven, into the fiery inner being of a stormy, aspiring, boiling youth. . . . The whole is a unique combustion. Not every artist's youth commences with such chaotic abundance, with such heat, with such spite, with so much vehemence and with such incredible tempo. . . . I will note the name O. Kokoschka . . . and will not be surprised if in a few years he is honored and laughed at, wondered at and mocked, as a great artist should be.[40]

Schoenberg may have seen this production. Toward the end of the play, a chorus of actors' heads appears briefly to speak lines of relative wisdom through holes cut in a backdrop—an effect Schoenberg subsequently used in *Die glückliche Hand,* the libretto of which was written only a little over a year later.

In July 1909 Kokoschka produced a second version of his satirical play, now called *Sphinx und Strohmann* (Sphinx and Scarecrow), along with his *Mörder, Hoffnung der Frauen* (Murderer, Hope of Women), in the Garden Theater of the International Kunstschau. This large exhibition included Viennese artists who, following Gustav Klimt's lead, had left the Vienna Secession in 1905. In *Mörder,* the battle of the sexes is more serious and complex than in Kokoschka's earlier work. As in many of Strindberg's nonrealistic plays, characters are typed only as Man or Woman. Fear and longing between the sexes are violent and poignant, as Men and Women confront and attempt to conquer each other through imprisonment, an orgy of lovemaking, and death. Kokoschka's compression of meaning, minimal indication of time and place, sketchy costumes made from rags, body painting, and demand for dynamic lighting forecast the style of later expressionist drama. Kokoschka directed, demonstrating for the actors the content of their roles in "gestures, various pitches, rhythms and choices of expression."[41] Semi-improvised music was loudly played by a small orchestra of drums, cymbals, clarinet, and bagpipe.[42] Later he wrote,

> In my first play I transgressed against the frivolity of our patriarchical civilization with my fundamental idea that man is mortal and woman immortal, that the

murderer wants to reverse these basic facts in the modern world. On this account I became the terror of the bourgeoisie *[Bürgerschreck]*.[43]

An idea of Kokoschka's expressive attitude in *Mörder* can be gathered from his violent drawings on the same subject published in *Der Sturm* in 1910 (Ill. 10–1).

In September 1909, Marie Pappenheim, Schoenberg's librettist for *Erwartung,* heard a rumor that Schoenberg was collaborating on an opera with Kokoschka.[44] Schoenberg was attempting to arrange a meeting with Kokoschka through the artist Max Oppenheimer.[45] Having just finished the swift composition and orchestration of *Erwartung,* Schoenberg seems to have been interested in consulting or even collaborating with Kokoschka on *Die glückliche Hand,* which like Kokoschka's theater works, was autobiographically engendered. Kokoschka wrote to Schoenberg:

> Aren't you also starting the theater piece on Monday[?] The man must be half-way between softness and brutality. Do you know by heart the inner, incessant, unstoppable screams, and shattering, and mysterious ascents, and slight physical structural changes. . . .[46]

Schoenberg is said (by Kokoschka) to have remarked,

> Kokoschka is one of those strong natures who can afford to express *themselves,* aware that they are thereby making their contribution to the expression of everyone and everything: the universe itself. This is without doubt the task of the great artist. Even if the lesser ones, and the public, call it Expressionism.[47]

Schoenberg and Kokoschka were affected by many similar influences. One was the life and work of Strindberg, whose writings began to appear in German translation in 1902. (From as early as 1887 Strindberg had written for the Vienna newspaper *Die Neue Freie Presse*.[48]) Max Reinhardt's startling productions of Strindberg's plays went on tour to Vienna and were reviewed by Hermann Bahr between 1903 and 1906.[49] So marked was the similarity of Schoenberg's and Strindberg's themes around 1912, the year of Strindberg's death, that both Webern and Berg remarked upon it in letters.[50] In Schoenberg's three expressionist dramatic works, these Strindbergian themes appear: the struggle between men and women; self-portrayal as an outcast champion of truth; the exploitation of the artist's subconscious for material; and a search for belief in the face of mockery and insult. In his theater works, Schoenberg makes use of Strindbergian innovations, such as dreamlike, disjunct scenes to convey psychological drama, universal character types (rather than named characters), and the concept of intimate, "chamber" theater, where each nuance of facial expression can be seen.

Like Strindberg, Schoenberg painted pictures remarkable for their use of color and the subjectivity of their content. His painting, begun in 1906,[51] gave him the same sort of satisfaction he derived from "making music."[52] Paintings in a naturalist style (Ill. 10-2) seem to have been his means of self-

Umfang acht Seiten

Einzelbezug: 10 Pfennig

DER STURM

WOCHENSCHRIFT FÜR KULTUR UND DIE KÜNSTE

Redaktion und Verlag: Berlin-Halensee, Katharinenstrasse 5 / Fernsprecher Amt Wilmersdorf 3524 / Anzeigen-Annahme und Geschäftsstelle: Berlin W 35, Potsdamerstr. 111 / Amt VI 3444

Herausgeber und Schriftleiter: **HERWARTH WALDEN**

Vierteljahresbezug 1,25 Mark / Halbjahresbezug 2,50 Mark / Jahresbezug 5,00 Mark / bei freier Zustellung / Insertionspreis für die fünfgespaltene Nonpareillezeile 60 Pfennig

JAHRGANG 1910 | BERLIN / DONNERSTAG DEN 14. JULI 1910 / WIEN | NUMMER 20

Zeichnung von Oskar Kokoschka zu dem Drama
Mörder, Hoffnung der Frauen

INHALT: OSKAR KOKOSCHKA: Mörder, Hoffnung der Frauen / PAUL LEPPIN: Daniel Jesus / Roman / ALFRED DÖBLIN: Gespräche mit Kalypso über die Musik / SIEGFRIED PFANKUCH: Liegt der Friede in der Luft / PAUL SCHEERBART: Gegenerklärung / KARL VOGT: Nissen als Theaterdirektor / MINIMAX: Kriegsbericht / Karikaturen

Mörder, Hoffnung der Frauen
Von Oskar Kokoschka

Personen:
Mann
Frau
Chor: Männer und Weiber.

Nachthimmel, Turm mit großer roter eiserner Käfigtür; Fackeln das einzige Licht, schwarzer Boden, so zum Turm aufsteigend, daß alle Figuren reliefartig zu sehen sind.

Der Mann
Weißes Gesicht, blaugepanzert, Stirntuch, das eine Wunde bedeckt, mit der Schar der Männer (wilde Köpfe, graue und rote Kopftücher, weiße, schwarze und braune Kleider, Zeichen auf den Kleidern, nackte Beine, hohe Fackelstangen, Schellen, Getöse), kriechen herauf mit vorgestreckten Stangen und Lichtern, versuchen müde und unwillig den Abenteurer zurückzuhalten, reißen sein Pferd nieder, er geht vor, sie lösen den Kreis um ihn, während sie mit langsamer Steigerung aufschreien.

Männer
Wir waren das flammende Rad um ihn,
Wir waren das flammende Rad um dich, Bestürmer verschlossener Festungen!

gehen zögernd wieder als Kette nach, er mit dem Fackelträger vor sich, geht voran.

Männer
Führ' uns Blasser!

Während sie das Pferd niederreißen wollen, steigen Weiber mit der Führerin die linke Stiege herauf.

Frau rote Kleider, offene gelbe Haare, groß,

Frau laut
Mit meinem Atem erflackert die blonde Scheibe der Sonne, mein Auge sammelt der Männer Frohlocken, ihre stammelnde Lust kriecht wie eine Bestie um mich.

Weiber
lösen sich von ihr los, sehen jetzt erst den Fremden.

Erstes Weib lüstern
Sein Atem saugt sich grüßend der Jungfrau an!

Ill. 10-1. Oskar Kokoschka, *Murderer, Hope of Women*, printed in *Der Sturm* 20 (July 14, 1910). Los Angeles County Museum of Art. The Robert Gore Rifkind Center for German Expressionist Studies.

training (he referred to them as "finger-exercises"):[53] he then subordinated technique to expression in caricatures of critics, art patrons, "Conqueror and Conquered." There are paintings of profound observation, tending toward the abstract, entitled "Thinking," "Hands" (Ill. 10-3), "Flesh," "Tears," and many "Visions" (see Ill. 4-2), which Schoenberg differentiated from portraits by professional painters: "I never saw faces but, because I looked into people's eyes, only their 'gazes.' . . . A painter, however, grasps with one look the whole person—I, only his soul."[54] Kandinsky exhibited two of these, along with two of the more naturalistic paintings, in the first *Blaue Reiter* exhibition, in December 1911.[55]

With Schoenberg, the development of his visual sense—along with the examples of synthesis in the theater from Mahler, Kokoschka, Reinhardt, and Strindberg—doubtless encouraged the desire, in his two expressionist operas, for total control over all the elements of theater production—what he called "making music with the media of the stage."[56] After showing his own libretto for *Die glückliche Hand* to Alma Mahler, he described his intentions to her in a letter of 7 October 1910:

> Colors, noises, lights, sounds, movements, looks, gestures—in short, the media which make up the ingredients of the stage—are to be linked to one another in a varied way. . . . It is all direct intuition. How I mean that you will understand best if I tell you I would most prefer to write for a magic theater. If tones, when they occur in any sort of order can arouse feelings, then colors, gestures, and movements must also be able to do this.[57]

In both *Erwartung* and *Die glückliche Hand*, Schoenberg specified color and lighting to heighten psychological impact; the climax of the latter opera is the crescendo of light, color, and storm that conveys the increasing pain of the Man's jealousy. Stage actions, moods, and gestures were specified in detail by the composer. Cues for all these directions are marked with hieroglyphics in the musical score of *Die glückliche Hand*, as Appia had recommended. When composing, Schoenberg visualized everything scenic;[58] he also sketched or painted his ideas for stage settings (Ills. 10-4 and 10-5). In an attempt to solve impracticalities and staging problems, Schoenberg constructed paper models of the latest stage machinery, such as turntables and moveable platforms that would swiftly change the scenery for *Erwartung* in the manner of the Roller-Mahler *Don Giovanni*. His stage directions indicate the performer's attitudes: in *Erwartung* the Woman must fear the wood; in *Die glückliche Hand* the acting ability of the Man was so much more important than his singing ability that his vocal type is not specified (a reference, perhaps, to Mahler's baritone/tenor Tristan).[59]

In 1911 Schoenberg met Reinhardt in hopes of a collaboration.[60] By 1913 he seems to have realized that much of what he was asking for was too demanding for the "limited resources" of the theater, and he suggested that *Die glückliche Hand* be realized in a film version with, as his choice for scenic

Ill. 10-2. Arnold Schoenberg, *Blue Self-portrait*, 1910. Oil on wood, 31 x 22 cm. Arnold Schoenberg Institute. Collection Lawrence and Ronald Schoenberg and Nuria Schoenberg Nono.

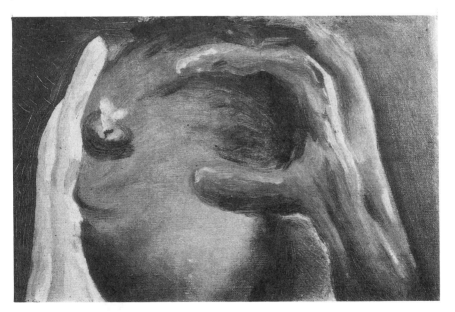

Ill. 10-3. Arnold Schoenberg, *Hands*, 1910. Oil on cardboard, 22 x 33 cm. Städtische Galerie im Lenbachhaus, Munich. Collection Lawrence and Ronald Schoenberg and Nuria Schoenberg Nono.

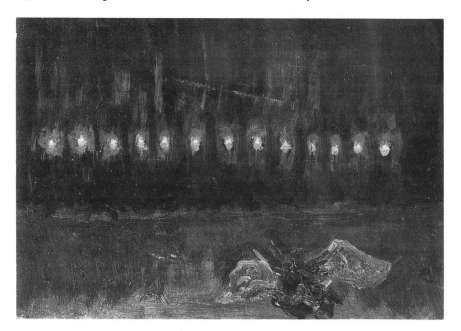

Ill. 10-4. Schoenberg, sketch for *Die glückliche Hand*, scene 1. Oil on cardboard, 22 x 30 cm. Arnold Schoenberg Institute. Collection Lawrence and Ronald Schoenberg and Nuria Schoenberg Nono.

Ill. 10-5. Schoenberg, sketch for *Die glückliche Hand*, The Man. Watercolor on paper, 27 x 13 cm. Arnold Schoenberg Institute. Collection Lawrence and Ronald Schoenberg and Nuria Schoenberg Nono.

designer, (1) Kokoschka, (2) Kandinsky, or (3) Roller.[61] While *Die Jakob-sleiter* was originally conceived as a vast stage work, employing massive choirs and orchestras and extending over three evenings,[62] it would not be "dramatic" in the traditional sense, Schoenberg wrote to Kandinsky in 1912. Rather, it would be "oratorio that becomes visible and audible. Philosophy, religion that are perceived with the artistic senses."[63] In 1917 Schoenberg still hoped to present his oratorio scenically, with Adolf Loos as designer.[64] By 1921 he admitted in an essay, "I am no man of the theater."[65]

Webern, caught up in the tremendous inner urgency of this project of Schoenberg's, wrote to Berg in 1917 that it was to be "a synthesis of an immense experience, of an unimaginable belief."[66] Toward the end of his intensive psychoanalysis with Dr. Alfred Adler, in October 1913, Webern also wrote an expressionist drama, *Tot: Sechs Bilder für die Bühne* (Dead: Six Scenes for the Stage). It is more modest but is an equally intense synthesis of experience and belief. While resisting his psychoanalysis, Webern had avidly read Strindberg and Swedenborg, seeking answers to his spiritual struggle. He sketched his ideas at first as the emotional skeleton of two musical movements.[67] Perhaps feeling that his ideas required a more dramatic form than pure music could offer, Webern wrote his play quickly, in a burst of creativity. He copied it in black ink for the dialogue and red for the stage directions—which well outnumber the lines of dialogue and cover all aspects of stage production. He sent it to Schoenberg, remarking that he felt it was dictated to him from beginning to end.[68] The play pleased Schoenberg, but he apparently rebuked Webern for quoting a large section from Swedenborg's *Vera Religio* in the final scene. Webern found Swedenborg's concept of "correspondences"—that in everything earthly there is a correspondence with the reality of God—so close to his own ideas that he was compelled to quote from the earlier work.[69]

Webern's play is static in action, like the dramas of Maeterlinck (in 1908 and 1910 Webern had begun operas on Maeterlinck texts). The characters are unnamed. The scenes are disjunct in the manner used by Strindberg in *To Damascus,* and they depict stages of psychological change in the principal characters—the Man and the Woman, whose son has died. The manuscript specifies dramatic lighting effects, according to season, time of day, and psychological mood. Webern describes details of each scene, even down to the particular alpine flowers along the mountain path where the Man and Woman seek the spirit of their son and are comforted by God's wonders in nature. He specifies detailed gestures for the actors. He prescribes graduated dynamics, expression, and the speed of delivery for the actors' spoken lines. As might be expected in Webern's work of this period, silences—framed by the sounds of bird song, a gurgling spring, or cowbells—signify the mystery of God's presence.

The play is full of psychological symbols. On a mountaintop, the Man remembers punishing his son for childish offenses; he agonizes over human will-to-power and hubris, and he prays for humility. In a village cemetery, the Woman realizes her grief is almost like egotism; she is comforted by the appearance of the Angel, who tells her the child is safe. In an alpine hut, the Man comes to an understanding of the Woman's more pragmatic, earthbound motherhood and accepts their mutual pain as their path to awareness of God. Webern attached so much personal significance to his play that, although he suppressed it (it would have been scorned in the New Objectivity following World War I), he kept it, carefully bound, and carried it in his rucksack on his desperate flight from Vienna to Mittersill when Russian troops occupied his home in 1945.[70]

After 1918, such Central European preoccupations with the dramatization of inner occurrences succumbed to more pressing issues of economic survival and social revolution; spiritual search turned to cynicism. Yet the expressionist composer's desire to be "the ideal stage director"[71] continued and is exemplified in the effective expressionist synthesis of the many arts of cabaret, opera, spoken drama, and film in Alban Berg's *Lulu*. In this work, Berg's strong sympathy for social outcasts is combined with his need to place himself at the emotional center of his opera. The legacy of expressionist synthesis is seen in Bertolt Brecht's collaborations with Weill, Hindemith, and Hanns Eisler, leading to the development of Brecht's (distinctly antiexpressionist) Epic Theater. The unquestioning faith in spontaneity upon which Dada was conceived, the surrender to the unconscious that was the basis of Surrealism, and the emphasis on instinctive human desires in Antonin Artaud's Theater of Cruelty are other aspects of this heritage. A strong and enduring expressionist legacy—but usually without expressionist music—can be traced in dance since Nijinsky. Perhaps the legacy of expressionist synthesis which brought the widest audience to expressionism is that of such silent films as *Metropolis* (1926). The original score—to be played live by a full symphony orchestra—was composed in direct collaboration with director Fritz Lang during the shooting of the film. Ironically, the neo-Wagnerian score does not catch the expressionist tone of this film.

Multilayered fusion, surpassing *Gesamtkunstwerk* and probing the depths of the unconscious, is unique to the expressionist concept of synthesis. Total control of the media of the stage was combined with psychological, spiritual, or social attitudes, which went well beyond doctrines of psychoanalysis, religion, or politics. Concern with finding, in personal experience, the kind of meaning which expressed a longed-for unity of all things, urged artists and composers to extend their powers, to break out of specialization, and to justify their encroachments into other arts as necessary to psychological truth. It is easy to find practical "failures" in the catalogue of these works of synthesis, but their integrity of vision is undeniable. Their reaction against realism/naturalism compelled expressionist composers, working in synthesis of the arts, to break the bonds of syntax, form, and logic, to reduce to essences the means of expression, and, in doing so, to sow the seeds of abstract art.

Select Bibliography

GENERAL

Bettlelheim, Bruno. *Freud's Vienna and Other Essays*. New York: Knopf, 1990.

Cooper, Martin. *Ideas and Music*. London: Barrie and Rockliff, 1965.

Hahl-Koch, Jelena, ed. *Arnold Schoenberg/Wassily Kandinsky: Letters, Pictures and Documents*. Trans. John C. Crawford. London: Faber, 1984.

Kandinsky, Wassily. *Concerning the Spiritual in Art*. Trans. M. T. H. Sadler. New York: Dover, 1977.

Pott, Gertrude. *Die Spiegelung des Sezessionismus im Österreichischen Theater*. Vienna: Wilhelm Braumüller, 1975.

Powell, Nicholas. *The Sacred Spring: The Arts in Vienna, 1898–1911*. Greenwich, CT: New York Graphic Society, 1974.

Vergo, Peter. *Art in Vienna: 1898–1918*. London: Phaidon, 1975.

APPIA, CRAIG, REINHARDT, MAHLER-ROLLER

Appia, Adolphe. *Musik und die Inszenierung*. Trans. Ulric Moore. Ithaca: Cornell University Press, 1929.

Volbach, Walter R. *Adolphe Appia, Prophet of the Modern Theatre*. Middletown, CT: Wesleyan University Press, 1968.

Craig, E. Gordon. *On the Art of the Theatre* (1911). London: Heinemann, 1957.

———. *Index to the Story of My Days*. New York: Viking, 1957.

Craig, Edward. *Gordon Craig: The Story of His Life*. London: Gollancz, 1968.

Innes, Christopher. *Edward Gordon Craig*. Cambridge: Cambridge University Press, 1983.

Reinhardt, Gottfried. *The Genius: A Memoir of Max Reinhardt*. New York: Knopf, 1979.

Sayler, Oliver, ed. *Max Reinhardt and His Theater*. New York: Brentano's, 1924.

Bahr, Hermann. *Glossen zum Wiener Theater, 1903–06*. Berlin: Fischer, 1907.

Bahr-Mildenburg, Anna. *Erinnerungen*. Vienna, 1921.

Blaukopf, Kurt. *Gustav Mahler*. Trans. I. Goodwin. New York: Praeger, 1973.

———, ed. *Mahler: A Documentary Study*. Trans. P. Baker, S. Flatauer, P. R. J. Ford, D. Loman, and G. Watkins. London: Thames and Hudson, 1976.

Graf, Max. *Der Wiener Oper*. Vienna: Humbolt, 1955.

La Grange, Henry-Louis de. *Mahler*, vol. 1. New York: Doubleday, 1973.

———. *Gustav Mahler: Chronique d'une vie*, vol. 2. Paris: Fayard, 1983.

Roller, Alfred. "Mahler und die Inszenierung." *Moderne Welt* 2/7 (1922–23): 5.

Specht, Richard. *Gustav Mahler*. Berlin: Deutsche Verlags-Anstalt, 1925.

Stefan, Paul. *Gustav Mahler: A Study of His Personality and Work*. Trans. T. E. Clark. New York: G. Schirmer, 1913.

Walter, Bruno. *Gustav Mahler*. Trans. Lotte Walter Lindt. New York: Schocken, 1974.

Willnauer, Franz. *Gustav Mahler und die Wiener Oper*. Vienna: Jugend und Volk, 1979.

Witeschnik, Alexander. *300 Jahre Wiener Operntheater*. Vienna: Fortuna, 1953.

JOURNALS, CABARET

Allen, Roy F. *German Expressionism and the Berlin Circles*. Göppingen: Kümmerle, 1974.

Gittleman, Sol. *Frank Wedekind*. New York: Twayne, 1969.

Kandinsky, W., and Marc, F., eds. *The Blaue Reiter Almanac* (1912). New Documentary edition. Ed. Klaus Lankheit. Trans. H. Falkenstein, M. Terzian, and G. Hinderlie. Reprint, New York: Viking Press, 1974.

Schreyer, Lothar. *Erinnerungen an Sturm und Bauhaus*. Munich: Langen, Müller, 1956.

Wolzogen, Ernst von. *Ansichten und Aussichten*. Berlin: Fontane, 1908.

K O K O S C H K A , S T R I N D B E R G , S C H O E N B E R G

Kallir, Jane. *Viennese Design and the Wiener Werkstätte*. New York: Galerie St. Etienne/ George Braziller, 1986.

Kokoschka, Oskar. *Dramen und Bilder*. Leipzig: Wolff, 1913.

———. *Schriften: 1907–1955*. Ed. Hans-Maria Wingler. Munich: Langen, Müller, 1956.

———. *My Life*. Trans. David Britt. London: Thames & Hudson, 1974.

Ritchie, James. *German Expressionist Drama*. Boston: G. K. Hall, 1976.

Schweiger, Werner J. *Der junge Kokoschka: Leben und Werk: 1904–1914*. Vienna: Brandstätter, 1983.

Whitford, Frank. *Oskar Kokoschka: A Life*. New York: Atheneum, 1986.

Lagercrantz, Olof. *August Strindberg*. Trans. Anselm Hollo. London: Faber, 1984.

Meyer, Michael. *Strindberg*. New York: Random House, 1985.

Crawford, John C. "Die glückliche Hand: Further Notes." *Journal of the Arnold Schoenberg Institute* 4/1 (June 1980): 69.

Kallir, Jane. *Schoenberg's Vienna*. New York: Galerie St. Etienne/Rizzoli, 1984.

Rufer, Josef. *Das Werk Arnold Schönbergs*. Basel: Bärenreiter, 1959.

Schoenberg, Arnold. *Texte*. Vienna: Universal Edition, 1926.

———. "Painting Influences." Trans. G. Zeisl. *Journal of the Arnold Schoenberg Institute* 2/3 (June 1978): 233.

CHAPTER ELEVEN

The Legacy of Expressionism

All changed, changed utterly:
A terrible beauty is born.
W. B. Yeats

The period of ascendancy of expressionism in twentieth-century music was brief. Introduced by the innovations of Strauss, Mahler, and Scriabin, it played a predominant role only from about 1908 to 1923. In Germany, there was a short-lived flowering of expressionism during the turbulent, revolutionary years immediately following World War I, a period when expressionism achieved its greatest popular acceptance. According to one contemporary observer, the expressionists were misunderstood and scorned until the horrors of the war sensitized and aroused the public. This heightened consciousness made possible expressionism's brief years of postwar success, but the public soon "fell back into the old complacency."[1]

The three most important composers of post–World War I Germany—Paul Hindemith (1895–1963), Kurt Weill (1900–1950), and the Austrian-born Ernst Krenek (1900–1991)—all came of age musically around 1920. All three were highly prolific, perhaps writing rapidly in response to the greatly increased pace of life following the war. Hurried composition may account for the frequent lack of stylistic consistency in their work. All three went through a period of musical expressionism in the early 1920s, departing from it around the middle of the decade as they pursued other stylistic directions. We must attempt to answer the fundamental question of whether, for the members of this second generation of composers, expressionism remains an "inner necessity," or whether it becomes simply an available, even fashionable, style or manner.

Unlike the earliest expressionists, whose overriding concern was usually their own subjectivity, the rising generation was eager to play an active part in the new, revolutionary society which seemed to be forming. This concern was expressed in the founding of two associations of artists and architects in Berlin in late 1918: the Novembergruppe and the Arbeitsrat für Kunst (Working Council for Art).[2] Founded by expressionist artists such as Max Pechstein and César Klein, these organizations attempted to bring the workers and the general public closer to art and to effect reforms in art education. Their early publications are characterized by the so-called *O Mensch* (O, Man) literary style, a broadly expressionist appeal to the "new man," who was supposed to emerge in the coming socialist Utopia (Ill. 11-1). In 1922, when the Novembergruppe decided to accept as members composers and writers "with a radical view of art,"[3] Kurt Weill joined and took an active part in discussions, which included politics as well as the arts. Although Paul Hindemith was never a member, he also participated in the important concerts of avant-garde music which the Novembergruppe produced in Berlin. These concerts frequently included literary recitations as well and were attended by many artists in fields other than music.

Ill. 11-1. Max Pechstein, cover for the revolutionary pamphlet *An alle Künstler* (To All Artists), 1919. Los Angeles County Museum of Art, cover of 83.11. The Robert Gore Rifkind Center for German Expressionist Studies. Copyright Max K. Pechstein.

Beginning about 1923, expressionism began to be replaced by what came to be called *Neue Sachlichkeit* (the New Objectivity), an artistic tendency characterized by down-to-earthness, clarity, simplicity, and realism, but also by a degree of "resignation and cynicism,"[4] as hopes for a new society faded and an atmosphere of business as usual took over in Germany. Although the Bauhaus (literally, House of Building), founded in 1919, had originally been strongly influenced by faculty members from the expressionist *Sturm* circle in Berlin, its new slogan in 1923 reflects the changing direction in the arts: "Art and Technology—a New Unity."[5] In 1925, Gustav Hartlaub's *Neue Sachlichkeit* exhibit in Mannheim confirmed the new tendency, and in the same year, the important Berlin critic Alfred Kerr could write (in a review of a broadly naturalistic comedy by the ex-expressionist Carl Zuckmayer) "Sic transit gloria expressionismi" (thus passes the glory of expressionism).[6] In opera the premiere of *Wozzeck* the same year marked musical expressionism's final triumph. By that time, Hindemith, Weill, and Krenek should no longer be considered expressionist composers.

Paul Hindemith's childhood was marked by poverty and family conflict. With grim determination, his father, a house painter who was a frustrated musician, pushed his three children toward the early development of their musical talents.[7] In spite of the family's straitened circumstances, Hindemith received excellent training in performance (violin; later viola) and composition at the Frankfurt Conservatory. The extraordinary facility with which he composed later led some critics to misinterpret Hindemith and his work as thoughtless; and his self-assurance (during the 1920s) as a cocky, wise-cracking *Musikant* (roughly, minstrel) tended to support this view. However, recent scholars have come to see that his public image masked a sensitive personality, one marked by pronounced depressive and choleric aspects.[8] In this context, it is particularly significant that Hindemith was drawn to visual and literary expressionism at exactly the time when he was trying to escape academic forms in his music. In a letter of 14 October 1917, the 21-year-old composer wrote that he had discovered an interesting magazine, *Das Kunstblatt* (The Art Journal, edited by Paul Westheim). The October 1917 issue was devoted to the pictures and literary works of Oskar Kokoschka and a catalogue of his works, which includes *Mörder, Hoffnung der Frauen,* the play Hindemith was to set two years later. His letter continued, "I don't know whether this kind of art would please you; it shows a completely 'ultra-overexcited' *[ultra-überspannte]* tendency, whose path I can scarcely understand properly. (Perhaps I must tread it myself. . . .)"[9]

The second movement of the Sonata for Cello and Piano, Op. 11, No. 3 (1919), marks the sudden beginning of expressionism in Hindemith's published works. Awareness of this movement's advance in style over the rest of the sonata caused the composer to provide a new opening movement in 1922.[10] The slow movement opens with a brooding, low-register melody in the cello which stresses tritone leaps. An extended crescendo, marked by relentlessly pounding tritone sonorities, leads to a *fff* climax. Functional harmony is rarely present. This stern and brooding movement clearly manifests the "depressive and choleric" sides of Hindemith's personality—traits which may have played a key role in leading him toward the formation of a personal style. The composer had written in a letter two years earlier, "I don't give a damn whether people like [my music] or not—as long as it's genuine and true."[11]

In 1919, Hindemith wrote his first stage work, a one-act opera based on Kokoschka's *Mörder, Hoffnung der Frauen*. Although this is one of the earliest operas based on a major expressionist dramatic work, Hindemith's eclectic setting rarely rises to the intensity of Kokoschka's conception. In a letter written to Hindemith in April 1920, his publisher objected to the "arbitrary, artificial" direction of recent works the composer had submitted. Hindemith answered with a stout defense of his development toward a more individual style in his works of 1919. He felt these compositions represented a real advance for him, and were

> purest, most natural, and not in the least "willful" music. . . . But they [Whitman Hymns, Op. 14; *Mörder, Hoffnung der Frauen;* and others] are still too much attached to all sorts of old-fashioned things. . . . A series of piano pieces (Op. 15) turned out better and in my new quartet (Op. 16) and, most of all, in the new songs (Op. 18), I have succeeded for the first time in doing what I always wanted, but was not able to do.[12]

Of the eight songs of Op. 18 (1920), three are composed to texts by expressionist poets: two by Else Lasker-Schüler, an important member of the Berlin *Sturm* circle, and one by Georg Trakl. Like Kokoschka's *Mörder, Hoffnung der Frauen,* both Lasker-Schüler texts deal with sexual conflicts; the second, entitled "Du machst mich traurig—hör" (You make me sad—listen) is an emotional statement of great urgency:

> I am so tired.
> I carry all the nights on my back
> Your night as well,
> Which your dreams transform so heavily.
> Do you love me?
> I blew the sad clouds from your forehead
> And made it blue.
> What will you do for me in my dying hour?

The slow tempo (the song is marked *"Langsam, klagend"* [Slow, plaintive]) and thickly dissonant piano writing of Hindemith's setting catch the brooding spirit of the text. The song is climaxed by three statements of the phrase "Do you love me?" at successively higher pitches (two are in the voice, the final one in the piano). The portrayal of emotion is vehement, direct, and uncompromising (Ex. 11-1).

For the third of his early one-act operas *(Sancta Susanna,* Op. 21, 1921),[13] Hindemith chose a text by August Stramm (1874–1915), the innovative expressionist whose poems and dramas had first been published by *Der Sturm.* In spite of its sparse, often fragmentary dialogue, *Sancta Susanna* is not an example of Stramm's most extreme "telegram style." In its subject matter, however, the play is even more shocking than *Mörder.* A young nun, Susanna, is stimulated by the sounds and odors which penetrate her cloister on

Ex. 11-1. Hindemith, Op. 18/VI, mm. 16–18. © B. Schott's Söhne, Mainz, 1922; © renewed. Used by permission of European American Music.

a fine spring evening and by a tale about an earlier nun, told her by the older Sister Klementia. Susanna conceives a sensual passion for Christ, and, at the climax of the play, she tears the loincloth from a statue of the crucified Savior and imagines that He is climbing down from the cross to embrace her. She refuses to repent, and the other nuns decide to wall her up behind the altar, denouncing her as "Satana" as the play ends. Because of the sacrilegious nature of Stramm's play (which Hindemith set almost word for word), the conductor Fritz Busch refused to perform the opera at the premiere of the other two one-acters (Stuttgart, 1921); its first performance took place the following year at Frankfurt, where it aroused protest.[14]

Hindemith considered *Sancta Susanna* the best of his three early erotic operas.[15] The music is much less derivative than that of *Mörder,* and the score, with its long, skillful buildup of tension, shows a high degree of musical and dramatic unity. Atmospheric tone painting is frequent, such as the use of running passages on three flutes (later piccolos) to represent the wind and a sinuous triplet figure to portray the enormous spider (itself a symbol of the devil) which appears at climactic points of the opera. As the dramatic tension reaches its highest level, Hindemith makes bold use of extremely dissonant polytonal complexes.

The success of his three provocative one-act operas in 1922 made Hindemith a hero to German avant-garde intellectuals,[16] and it is not surprising that he went on to complete another expressionist stage work the same year. This was *Der Dämon* (The Demon, Op. 28), a dance-pantomime with scenario by the writer and editor Max Krell. Like the three one-acters and the Lasker-Schüler songs, its theme is sexual. (The persistence with which Hindemith chooses texts of this nature during these years suggests that he himself may have been trying to work out some sexual/psychological problem in artistic terms.) The scenario of *Der Dämon* has strong overtones of sadomasochism. The characters are two young sisters and the Demon (his face is to be "a hard, wild mask of exotic shape"), who seduces and ultimately destroys them. Color symbolism appears in the many costume changes required.

The scenario calls for dances interspersed with short sections of silent pantomime. Hindemith's series of spontaneous character pieces record his emotional and musical response to the highly contrasting moods of the story. His use of a chamber ensemble furthers the unconstrained nature of this work, which marks the climax of Hindemith's expressionist phase. The variety of musical expression is extraordinary, ranging from improvisatory lyricism in the "Dance of Sadness and Desire," scored for solo flute, to the "Dance of the Red Frenzy," whose motoric rhythms and polytonality are to "unroll without resistance at an insane tempo." This is followed by the "Dance of Brutality" (also called the "Dance of the Whip-swinger" in the scenario), whose crude melody punctuated by heavy chords in the bass recalls Bartók's *Allegro Barbaro*.

In the many works Hindemith composed in 1922, brutal rhythmic vehemence is frequent enough to be identified as a definite facet of his musical style as well as an expression of the choleric side of his nature. It is found in the fourth movement of the Sonata for Solo Viola, Op. 25, No. 1, which is marked "Frenzied Tempo. Wild. Beauty of tone is secondary"; in the second movement of the Third String Quartet, Op. 22; in the "Shimmy" and "Ragtime" of *1922*, Suite for Piano, Op. 26; and in the "Finale: 1921" from the *Kammermusik* (Chamber music), Op. 24, No. 1, for twelve solo instruments, whose triplet ritornello for snare drum, accordion, and piano suggests bursts of machine gun fire. In *1922* and the finale of Op. 24, No. 1, Hindemith uses jazz, whose popularity was then sweeping Germany, as a metaphor for the speed and brutality of modern life. His "Directions for Use!!" of the final "Ragtime" of the Suite tells the player how to perform its relentless, mechanistic rhythmic repetitions: "Play this piece very wildly, but always very rigidly in rhythm, like a machine. Consider the piano in this case as an interesting kind of percussion, and treat it that way."

Along with the premiere of *Kammermusik* No. 1 at the 1922 Donaueschingen Festival, another highly contrasting new work by Hindemith appeared. This was *Die junge Magd* (The Young Servant Girl, Op. 23, No. 2), a cycle of six songs for contralto, flute, clarinet, and string quartet, to texts by the expressionist poet Georg Trakl. In a remarkable series of poems, whose pastoral tone is punctuated by images of decay and violence, Trakl tells, more by inference than by direct statement, the story of a servant girl who, having been seduced and abandoned, aborts her unborn child and subsequently dies herself. In spite of the nature of the text, Hindemith's setting marks the beginning of his transition away from expressionism. While this important and introspective song cycle is still expressionist in its text and its musical portrayal of mood and textual detail, the work's new concern for formal clarity, symmetrical phrasing, and textural transparency indicates the beginning of a new stylistic direction.

This change is even more apparent in *Das Marienleben* (The Life of Mary, Op. 27, 1922–23), a large song cycle for voice and piano on a text by Rainer Maria Rilke. Although some of the songs are intensely expressive ("Pietà," above all), Baroque forms and contrapuntal techniques predominate, supplanting detailed text expression. The reasons for the change in Hindemith's style seem to be grounded in his new vision of "the ethical necessities of music and the moral duties of the musician. . . . I began to envision an ideal of noble, and, as far as possible, perfect music, that I would some day be able to realize. . . ."[17] In 1925, he wrote to his publishers:

> I also believe that the reproaches made against most modern music are only too well deserved. . . . I am of the opinion that in the next few years the utmost orderliness will be called for, and I myself shall do everything I can to achieve it . . . I hope you will have noticed that I have been striving in all my recent things for the highest degree of purity and orderliness.[18]

Hindemith's urge for orderliness in fact went through various stages, manifesting itself first in emotional restraint and neobaroque usages; a rationalization of harmonic and tonal practices followed in the late 1920s and 30s.

Kurt Weill was born in Dessau, a city some sixty miles from Berlin. His father was a cantor and a composer of liturgical music. Although the influence of this religious background is frequently apparent in Weill's compositions, it was equally important to his development that Dessau, as the seat of the Duchy of Anhalt, had a well-known Court Theater, where both operas and dramas were performed. The Duke of Anhalt recognized Weill's precocious talents (the boy wrote his first opera at age eleven) and granted him free entry to the theater.[19] By the age of fifteen, Weill was already employed there as an accompanist. In 1918, he went to Berlin to pursue his musical studies, working for a few months with Wagner disciple Engelbert Humperdinck at the Berlin Hochschule für Musik (College of Music). In this period he also showed his first interest in politics, serving as president of the Hochschule's revolutionary Students' Council.[20] Perhaps becoming dissatisfied with academic routine, he left Berlin early in 1919, but he returned in the fall of 1920 to attend the composition master class of Ferruccio Busoni (1866–1924).

Weill's First Symphony (1921), written soon after he had entered Busoni's class, is strongly influenced by the expressionism of the immediate post–World War I period in Germany. Weill modeled his symphony on the *Festspiel* (Festival Play) by the expressionist writer Johannes R. Becher, entitled *Arbeiter Bauern Soldaten: Der Aufbruch eines Volks zu Gott* (Workers Farmers Soldiers: The Awakening of a People to God).[21] Although Becher was soon to become a doctrinaire Communist, *Arbeiter Bauern Soldaten* is more reflective of pacifism and mystical, ecstatic Christianity than of any party line.[22] Like Schoenberg's text for *Die Jakobsleiter*, it is a *Verkündigungsdrama* (drama of annunciation) in which three central characters (the Man, the Woman, and the Holy One) exhort war-weary humanity to follow the path to the Promised Land. In its idiom, the play is an extreme (if not very distinguished) example of expressionism, with grammatical distortions, highly charged language, and (at times) telegraphic compression. As in many expressionist plays, lighting and sound effects (many of which are musical) play an important role.

Arbeiter Bauern Soldaten must have appealed strongly to Weill by virtue of its double emphasis on socialism and the religious theme of the Promised Land, which related to his own background. His symphony is more clearly programmatic than most expressionist instrumental works, and it follows its literary model quite closely. Nevertheless, this composition by the young Weill exhibits the emotional involvement which is the hallmark of expressionism. The Symphony is some twenty minutes in length. It is written in three movements to be played without pause; they are connected by means of thematic transformations and cyclic recurrences. In one of the most striking of these recurrences, the massively dissonant opening progressions of the introduction (representing the armed clashes of war and revolution in the second part of Becher's play[23]) reappear in consonant, triumphant form at the end of the Symphony, when all these conflicts have been resolved. The main body of the first movement continues the representation of modern war. It is marked *Wild, heftig* (Wild, vehement), and with its screeching piccolos and *schmetternd* (blaring) brasses, it resembles an updated Mahler march movement. The second movement, *Andante religioso* (mm. 227–88) represents the plea of the Man and the Woman for their vision of peace.[24] Their pleading is not accepted without resistance, however, for at the climax of the movement the woodwinds' repeated entries, marked "shrill" and "stubborn," cause polytonal clashes. The final movement is the most strongly programmatic—a descendant of the finales of Beethoven's Ninth and Mahler's Second symphonies. A groping neobaroque theme, which represents the inadequacy of man's laborious efforts to find salvation, alternates with repeated statements of a chorale portraying man's discovery of God.[25] As the movement progresses, many highly affective markings appear, such as *Sehr ruhig, mystisch* (Very calm, mystical), when two solo violins play a lofty, *espressivo* duet over the final (partial) statement of the chorale in the bass (mm. 378–93). This passage probably refers to the "Light-Song" in Becher's play, the final ecstatic dialogue of the "voices of the Man and Woman in the light."[26] Next, a fanfare in the brass leads to the final triumphal march (mm. 399–406), marked *Jubelnd* (Exulting), and representing humanity's steady progression toward the Promised Land. Although the final cadence, marked *Sehr zuversichtlich* (Very confidently), would seem to call for a C-major chord, Weill surprisingly ends with C minor instead. Perhaps he realized that Germany's state hardly justified the utopianism with which Becher's play ends. Considering that Weill wrote the Symphony at age 21, it is surprisingly successful in its integration of the program of an expressionist play with purely musical demands of considerable complexity.

Shortly after the First Symphony, Weill's music begins to reflect the ideas of his teacher Busoni, the composer-pianist who was the principal prophet of neoclassicism. As early as 1907, in his *Sketch of a New Esthetic of Music*,[27]

Busoni had attacked what he called the "pseudo-emotion" and "lachrymose hysteria"[28] of Wagner and the post-Wagnerians. Busoni also rejected program music and dramatic music which duplicates the stage action.[29] He called instead for a reaffirmation of absolute musical form and, by 1920, was ready to launch his doctrine of *Junge Klassizität* (neoclassicism): "By 'new classicism' I understand the mastery, selection and exploitation of all the achievements of past experiments, their incorporation in firm and lovely forms."[30] Kurt Weill has described how Busoni's ideas helped young German composers distance themselves from expressionism:

> After the revolution in Germany we young musicians also were filled with new ideals, swollen with new hopes. But we could not shape the new that we longed for; we could not find the form for our content. We burst the fetters, but we could not do anything with the acquired freedom. . . . Thus, through the years of seclusion from the outside we underwent a spasm of excess which lay on the breast like a nightmare and which we yet loved because it made us free. Then Busoni came to Berlin. Through the agility of his clear-sighted intellect and through the transcending vastness of his creative genius, he was able to display a synthesis of all stylistic types of recent decades, a new restrained, sediment-free art, a *"Junge Klassizität."*[31]

Written only a year after the First Symphony, Weill's ballet-pantomime *Die Zaubernacht* (The Magic Night, 1922), shows the adaptability of his creative nature. His rapid absorption of Busonian influence is manifest in *Die Zaubernacht*'s transparent textures and straightforward, songlike melodies. Weill later called it the first work in which his eventual "simple style" could be recognized.[32] Through the success of *Die Zaubernacht* Weill met Georg Kaiser (1878–1945), a prolific and talented expressionist playwright already well known for *Die Bürger von Calais* (The Burghers of Calais, 1914), *Von Morgens bis Mitternacht* (From Morning to Midnight, 1916) and *Gas I* and *II* (1918 and 1920). Their first effort at collaboration, in 1924, a full-length ballet, was never completed.[33] Kaiser then suggested his earlier one-act play *Der Protagonist* (1920; produced in 1922), which he had actually envisioned as an opera, and which included two important pantomimes. The plot concerns the leading actor of a traveling company in Elizabethan England. His overinvolvement with his roles leads him to Dionysian states from which he can scarcely return when his acting is over. The first comic pantomime leaves him maniacally gay, but at the climax of the second, which is a tragic drama of jealousy, he murders his own sister (with whom there is a suggestion of an incestuous relationship) when she happens to come onstage.

The score of *Der Protagonist,* finished in 1925, reflects both Weill's search for a new musical style and his continuing involvement with expressionism. The music is busily contrapuntal and quite dissonant, although clear tonal poles are stressed. Neoclassicism and expressionism are both present, the former particularly in the first pantomime, whose relationship to the *commedia dell'arte* must have reminded Weill of Busoni's *Arlecchino* (Harlequin, 1914–

16). The idea of casting the pantomime into the musical form of theme and variations is Busonian, but the influence of Stravinsky's early neoclassical works is even more apparent: The stage orchestra in the pantomime approximates the instrumentation of Stravinsky's Octet (1922–23), and the ostinato of Weill's theme is reminiscent of *L'Histoire du Soldat* (The Soldier's Tale, 1918), whose German-language premiere in 1923 (with Hindemith playing the solo violin part)[34] was an event of great significance for Germany's composers.

However, the second pantomime and the scene which precedes it are true expressionist music drama. Here the music (in accord with the advice the Protagonist gives the musicians) is continuous, and the libretto calls for the pantomime to be acted "dramatically, with lively expression and passionate movement" rather than the stylized performance of the first pantomime. The opening of the second pantomime is characterized by numerous tempo changes, which portray the changing emotions of its characters. As the jealousy of the Protagonist (who is playing a deceived husband) mounts, the music expresses the growing tension by means of an ostinato (alternating major second, from [18] on) accompanied by ever-increasing rhythmic motion. At the point when his acted jealousy has gotten beyond control, his sister bursts in to tell him that she has a lover. Unable to distinguish reality from his art, the Protagonist stabs her. This passage shows such typically expressionist musical characteristics as frequent changes of texture and tempo (at [32] and [37]), extreme dissonance, and vocal "shouting" and "hoarse whispering." The continued use of two-note ostinato (particularly in the timpani before [32] and celesta at [33]) provides a degree of thematic coherence (Ex. 11-2).

The juxtaposition of expressionism and neoclassicism in *Der Protagonist,* although handled with skill and effectiveness, shows that expressionism was no longer an inner necessity for Weill, as it probably was at the time of the First Symphony. By 1925, expressionism had become for him only one possible style in which to write effective dramatic music. Soon after completing *Der Protagonist,* he came to consider its degree of musical complexity too alienating to the audience, and he continued to simplify and clarify his style. This process antedates Weill's collaboration with Brecht by several years. By the time of their first joint effort (the *Mahagonny Songspiel,* 1927), Weill had developed what he and Brecht called the "gestic" style, which rejects psychological characterization in favor of the "clear and stylized expression of social behavior of human beings towards each other."[35] This was accomplished musically through the "rhythmic fixing of the text"[36] and the use of popular dance rhythms. It continued to be the essence of Weill's approach to musical theater until the mid-1930s.

During his sheltered upper middle class upbringing in Vienna, Ernst Krenek wrote novels as well as music. He later studied philosophy for a few semesters at the University of Vienna.[37] From 1916 on, he studied composition with Franz Schreker, following him to Berlin in 1920, when Schreker

Ex. 11-2. Weill, *Der Protagonist,* 5 mm. before [32]–[33], m. 3. Copyright 1926; copyright renewed; English translation (by Lionel Salter) copyright 1978 by Universal Edition A.G., Vienna.

was appointed director of the Hochschule für Musik. In the artistic turbulence of postwar Berlin, Krenek became acquainted with such important figures of the musical avant-garde as the pianist-composer Eduard Erdmann and the conductor Hermann Scherchen. Partly under their influence, his style, which had been moderate up to that time, became atonally radical.

Krenek himself dated the beginning of his expressionist period from his String Quartet No. 1, Op. 6 (1921),[38] a work which was important in establishing his reputation. Its seven brief movements, to be played without pause, are connected by cyclic reminiscences. The style is predominantly dissonant, and the music shows Krenek's great interest in the contrapuntal combination of themes. Bartók's influence can be seen particularly in the pounding rhythms of the fast movements and in "bimodal" passages where the melody avoids the notes of the ostinato accompaniment. Extreme expressionist melodic gestures abound, particularly in the transitions linking the movements. The seventh movement is a double fugue. As its climax approaches, the music becomes more and more rhetorical and sectional, and the *fff* climax recalls Beethoven's *Grosse Fuge,* another work which combines counterpoint with extreme rhythmic vehemence.

In a conscious wish to carry on the symphonic tradition of Gustav Mahler, Krenek, who was then married to Mahler's daughter Anna, wrote three major symphonies by the time he was 23.[39] In the final Adagio of the monumental Second Symphony (Op. 12, 1922), which Krenek considers his foremost work of the period, an extended solo for the combined first and second violins recalls similar passages in the Adagio finale of Mahler's Ninth and the Adagio of his Tenth. However, the expressionist melodic gestures at the culmination of Krenek's one-voiced passage are infinitely more expansive (Ex. 11-3). Krenek may well have had this passage in mind when he later wrote that "in the last movement there are passages expressing pain with an intensity that I wish I could produce again."[40] Of the climax of the concluding Adagio, he said,

> I remember vividly that [at its first hearing] . . . the impression prevailed that if this accumulation of sound would continue only a little further the hall would

Ex. 11-3. Krenek, Symphony No. 2/III, last 11 mm. of [94]. © Copyright 1924, 1952 by Universal Edition A.G., Vienna.

cave in, or some catastrophe of unforeseeable magnitude occur. . . . While listening to the recordings [of a later performance] I pass each time through a state of curious excitement when the end of the piece approaches. As I see it now, the rhythmic rigidity which was present in that period is in a peculiar way made the emotional subject matter of the piece. To me the Second Symphony seems to denote a terrific elemental force raging against stifling confinement, as if a blind giant would batter the walls of a cave in which he is imprisoned.[41]

The ending of the Symphony combines rhythmic implacability with massive orchestration and extreme dissonance, which remains unabated as the work ends with a *fff sforzando*.

Later in 1922, Krenek composed his first work for the operatic stage, *Der Zwingburg* (The Tyrant's Castle, Op. 14). As an adolescent, he had developed "strong sympathies for left and far left causes,"[42] and his turn to the theater was partly caused by the wish to propagate his political and social ideas.[43] The libretto for *Der Zwingburg* was provided by a friend of Krenek's, a young doctor who later died at Auschwitz, and it was revised, at Krenek's request, by Franz Werfel.[44] The libretto strongly reflects the influence of Ernst Toller, the expressionist and revolutionary whose plays were popular at the time. The symbolic plot, which has strong political overtones, concerns an unseen giant who lives in a castle (which should also look like a factory) and dominates the lives of his people by means of the pounding rhythms played by an Organ-grinder who is under his spell. As this "scenic cantata" begins, the tyrant has decided to let his people have freedom for a day. The Organ-grinder is tied up so that he cannot play, and the manifestations of freedom blossom, including the love of the unnamed Man and Woman. The Man creates a "Barlach-like" statue, symbolizing artistic freedom, and marshals the workers against the tyrant's castle. However, the Organ-grinder is released by the throng, and, as he starts to play, the workers lose their freedom and revert to their mechanical tasks. In the more optimistic ending added by Werfel, the Organ-grinder hints of salvation at a far future time. Thus the libretto, like Schoenberg's *Die Jakobsleiter*, Webern's drama, *Tot*, and the Becher play used by Weill, relates to the expressionist *Verkündigungsdrama* (drama of annunciation).

The motoric ostinati, extreme dissonances and jagged melodies Krenek uses in *Der Zwingburg* are typical of musical expressionism, but it is less easy to understand why he often introduces consonant, tonal passages in this and other works of his expressionist period.[45] Krenek relates these juxtapositions of different styles to the influence of surrealism,[46] but it seems more reasonable to assume that they reflect his wish (conscious or unconscious) to reach a larger public. He himself has written of his inner conflict between "pure, uncompromising creation" and "the achievement of practical results in terms of 'this world,' whose current problems were a permanent challenge to me."[47]

In 1923, Krenek completed a work which he considered (along with the

Second Symphony) the most mature of his early output—an operatic setting of Oskar Kokoschka's play *Orpheus und Eurydike,* composed at Kokoschka's request.[48] The play was begun in 1915, shortly after Kokoschka received a severe head wound in battle. Originally "spoken, whispered in ecstacy, in delirium, wept, implored, howled in the anxiety and fever of the nearness of death,"[49] it was later reworked by Kokoschka, and in its completed form (1918) is his longest and most fully realized drama. In a visionary, dreamlike succession of scenes, he reinterprets the ancient myth to express the irreconcilable love-hate relationship between Man and Woman. The drama is a psychological working-out of the turbulent love affair he had earlier experienced with Alma Mahler. The autobiographical nature of the work is made specific by the appearance of the Greek words *allos makar* (roughly, "happiness is otherwise," but also an anagram of Alma-Oskar) on the ring which Orpheus has given Eurydike.[50] *Allos makar* is also the title of a group of three poems by Kokoschka concerning the hopeless nature of his relationship with Alma, which he had written and illustrated in 1913[51] (Ill. 11-2).

Ill. 11-2. Oskar Kokoschka, *The Man, Lying in the Lap of the Woman,* 1914. From *Allos Makar,* in *Zeit Echo* 1, No. 20 (1915). Lithograph, 6 x 5 ¹³⁄₁₆″. Los Angeles County Museum of Art, 83.1.1205b. The Robert Gore Rifkind Center for German Expressionist Studies.

Krenek took a highly intuitive, expressionist approach to setting Kokoschka's play:

> I was not in the least deterred by the fact that the book, on first reading, did not seem to make much sense to me. Again I wrote the music in feverish haste, as in a dream, once in a while grasping the implications of the text in a flash, then again groping in the dark, following my creative instinct rather than intellectual perception. Only much later did it become clear to me that Kokoschka's play

too, in a very subtle way, centered around the idea of human freedom. Ostensibly preoccupied with the purely technical problems of creating music for its own sake and according to its own laws, as I thought I understood them at the time, I acted in regard to the essential expressive contents of my music like a sleepwalker. I do not think that this condition interfered with the quality of my music—rather the opposite. But if I had more clearly realized what I was doing, I might have more consciously developed what was hinted at in those early works.[52]

The music is less Bartókian than *Der Zwingburg,* and more unified in style, in spite of occasional triadic passages. The score abounds in the "wild gestures, violent contrasts, cutting dissonances and improbable melodic leaps" which Krenek feels are characteristic of musical expressionism.[53] As the opera opens, a progression of massive, dissonant chords is followed by a web of contrapuntal voices as intricate and contorted as any web of lines to be found in a Kokoschka drawing (Ex. 11-4).

Ex.11-4. Krenek, *Orpheus und Eurydike,* Prelude, mm. 1–4. Copyright 1925 by Universal Edition; copyright renewed.

Orpheus und Eurydike is the last major expressionist work by Krenek. About this time he became tired of what he saw as the "overheated emotionalism" of this style, and he began to dream of a "cool, detached, objective music that would rely on perfect construction."[54] The decisive stimulus for this change was provided by visits to Paris while he was living in Switzerland in 1924–25. He was deeply impressed by the "happy equilibrium, perfect poise, grace, elegance and clarity" of the French music of the period, and by the "relations of the French musicians with their public."[55] His neoclassically oriented Concerto Grosso No. 2, Op. 25, and Concertino, Op. 27 (both 1924), were the immediate results of this experience, but in a 1925 speech, Krenek further affirmed the idea that music must abandon chromaticism and other means toward psychological individualization and return to tonic and dominant. Moreover, he maintained that "art does not represent anything nearly as important as we would like to think. . . . To live is necessary, but not to create art."[56] This is the theoretical background of Krenek's highly successful opera *Jonny spielt auf* (Jonny Strikes Up, 1925–26), in which jazz is combined with a tonal, Puccini-like idiom.

"These atonalists!" wrote Schoenberg to Kandinsky in 1922, in an irritable reference to the younger generation of German composers: "all these people aren't peddling their own skins but yours and mine."[57] Schoenberg was right in the sense that his pioneering expressionist works, along with those of Bartók and Stravinsky, were an important liberating influence on Hindemith, Weill, and Krenek. Although all three composers were labeled "atonalists" in the press because of their predominantly nontriadic idiom, examination of some of their expressionist works has shown that their atonality is in fact much less rigorous than Schoenberg's, as it is often mitigated by tonal references. All three wrote significant works in an expressionist idiom, and all of them were inspired by expressionist drama or poetry. However, in no case did expressionism become their definitive style, though Krenek admitted returning to it "perhaps relatively, off and on."[58]

There is no easy answer to the question of whether expressionism remained a real compulsion for this second generation of expressionist composers, or whether it was only a convenient style in which to write. Hindemith's expressionist music would seem to present the clearest case for inner necessity, as it frequently reflects his character traits (his tendency toward irritability and anger, in particular). Weill, on the other hand, varies his style at will, according to circumstances. Only his First Symphony is a truly expressionist work. Krenek himself maintained that musical expressionism was "rather a 'style' " to him, not an inner necessity,[59] but this statement must be accepted with caution in light of what he has written of his emotional involvement in the finale of the Second Symphony and his feverish, intuitive approach to *Orpheus und Eurydike*.

Even during the 1908–23 period, when expressionism predominated, new, divergent musical directions were increasingly apparent. As early as 1907, Busoni's *Sketch of a New Esthetic of Music* prophesied neoclassicism, and his opera *Arlecchino* provided a practical realization of his theories. Strauss retreated from the expressionism of *Elektra* in *Der Rosenkavalier* (1910) and continued this retreat even more decisively in *Ariadne auf Naxos* (1912; final version 1916). It was the works of Stravinsky, however, which provided the major impetus toward neoclassicism. Among the most important of these were *L'Histoire du Soldat* (1918), with its rejection of the Wagnerian *Gesamtkunstwerk* esthetic; *Pulcinella* (1919–20), a ballet based on the music of Pergolesi; and the Octet (1922–23).

During the period 1923–50, neoclassicism predominated in music. Most of the works written during these years show a partial return to classical or

Baroque form and style, and expressive content is often subordinate to formal considerations. Several tendencies related to neoclassicism were also important during the same years: *Neue Sachlichkeit,* as exemplified in the Brecht-Weill collaborations of the late 1920s and early 1930s (*The Threepenny Opera,* 1928; *Mahagonny,* 1927–29, and others); the work of *Les Six* (Honegger, Milhaud, Auric, Poulenc, Tailleferre, and Durey), founded on Erik Satie's ideas, which rejected both Wagner and Debussy and turned instead to a "music of everyday,"[60] reflecting music hall and other popular influences; and Socialist Realism, a simplified, conservative, folk-influenced style that was dictated to the composers of Soviet Russia by their government in the 1930s (certain works of Aaron Copland, such as *Billy the Kid,* 1938, and *A Lincoln Portrait,* 1942, reflect these tendencies toward simplification and accessibility).

Constructivism was also an important force during the 1923–50 period. In 1921, Schoenberg had remarked to his pupil Josef Rufer that he had "made a discovery which will ensure the supremacy of German music for the next hundred years."[61] This was twelve-tone technique, which appeared in a movement of the Five Piano Pieces, Op. 23 (1920–23); in two movements of Serenade, Op. 24 (1920–23); and throughout the Suite for Piano, Op. 25 (1921–23).[62] From the advent of these works, twelve-tone technique remained a dominant organizational principle in the music of Schoenberg. The same is true of Webern, beginning with *Drei Volkstexte,* Op. 17 (1924–25) and *Drei Lieder,* Op. 18 (1925). Bartók also developed and perfected his own very individual type of constructivism in his works of the 1920s and 30s.

Although neoclassicism and constructivism predominated during the second quarter of the twentieth century, in certain works expressionism was still a determining force. After his initial twelve-tone works (particularly the Suite for Piano and the Wind Quintet, Op. 26, 1923–24), Schoenberg gradually found a balance between construction and expressivity, and some works of his late years are recognizably expressionist in character. Two such compositions are the String Trio, Op. 45 (August 20–September 23, 1946), and *A Survivor from Warsaw,* Op. 46 (August 11–23, 1947).[63] It is significant that both were written at the direct impulse of very strong emotions: the String Trio was composed immediately following a major cardiac crisis in August 1946 and (according to the composer) describes in detail his illness and medical treatment;[64] *A Survivor from Warsaw,* for which Schoenberg wrote his own text, was composed after he learned that his niece had been shot in a Nazi camp.[65]

A Survivor from Warsaw, written for *Sprechgesang* narrator, male chorus, and orchestra, shows that Schoenberg had lost nothing of his expressionist intensity when the subject was sufficiently compelling: in his text a survivor of the Warsaw ghetto tells how a group of Jewish prisoners, abused and threatened with death by a brutal Nazi sergeant, defiantly sing the traditional Hebrew prayer "Shema Yisroel." From the very start of the piece, where a distorted bugle call and a military drum roll instantly set the scene, extreme orchestral colors and constantly changing textures and rhythms create a nightmare atmosphere of great vividness. As the Jews, ordered by the sergeant, begin to "count off," an extraordinary crescendo and an accelerando of irregular rhythms occur. The narrator's words are, "they began again, first slowly: one, two, three, four, became faster and faster, so fast that it finally sounded like a stampede of wild horses. . . ." The crescendo builds to an orchestral tutti and the outbreak of the male chorus in "Shema Yisroel." Earlier, the narrator's words "It was painful to hear them moaning and groaning," motivate the appearance of three statements of the traditional descending half-tone sighing figure often used by Schoenberg.[66] As in the String Trio, high, shrill sounds (in this case four oboes and four clarinets, two muted trumpets *f,* and violins I and II *ff*) serve as additional representations of pain (Ex. 11-5). The work as a whole is expressionist in its use of open form.

Ex. 11-5. Schoenberg, *A Survivor from Warsaw,* mm. 44–46. Used by permission of Belmont Music Publishers, Pacific Palisades CA 90272.

In spite of the leading role of neoclassicism between 1923 and 1950, the continuing influence of expressionism was widespread, even in America and the Soviet Union. Carl Ruggles and Dmitri Shostakovich were both strongly affected by this legacy. Ruggles (1876–1971), along with Charles Ives, deserves to be ranked as one of the most important American expressionists. This was recognized in 1932, when Nikolai Lopatnikoff, in a review of Ruggles's *Portals* (1925), identified Ruggles as "a composer who stands closest to the highly individualized expressionistic method."[67] Ruggles belonged to the same generation as Ives and Schoenberg, but he reached artistic maturity much later, writing most of his music between 1920 and 1950. By 1920, he was aware of much of the legacy of expressionism, and this knowledge helped him form his own individual style.

Ruggles was strongly drawn toward the sublime and the transcendental. He favored the spontaneous over the cerebral and sought mystical identification between man and the mightiest forces of nature. The sources of his musical and philosophical ideas were mainly German. In a 1906 lecture delivered at a music club in Lawrence, Massachusetts, he stated that "modern music really begins with Wagner. . . . I feel [in Wagner] the escape from the confines of tradition . . . the surge, the blood beats of humanity. . . . The supreme cry of his soul . . . is the Prelude to *Tristan and Isolde.*" He praised Strauss and Franck, and he admired Debussy's music, although he found it lacking in spirituality: "If he would only go up into the mountains where the wind blows large and free, and watch the sun rise."[68]

By 1919 Ruggles had worked through these early influences and said that he now "swears by Schoenberg,"[69] whose short expressionist pieces showed the way to the "varied and quick-shifting moods" of the opera Ruggles was writing. This was *The Sunken Bell,* based on Gerhart Hauptmann's Symbolist play,[70] a project which absorbed his creative energy from 1912 until 1923, when Ruggles abandoned it and destroyed the fair copy. By the end of his work on *The Sunken Bell,* his ideas of rebellion had crystallized. In a 1922 lecture, he uses picturesque language to attack the genteel tradition, which was very strong in music, and acclaims Whitman as the artist who first challenged it successfully. According to Ruggles, the music of Grieg, Franck, and McDowell shows "drivelling, cheap sentimentalism . . . [it is] a reflection of the black-walnut marble-top period . . . Venus de Milo with a clock in her belly. . . . Now think of Walt Whitman coming clean out of that mess." Like Ives, Ruggles extols "substance" as opposed to "manner." Among American composers, he praises the ferocity of Leo Ornstein (b. 1892) and the early radicalism of Henry Cowell (1897–1965).[71]

It is significant that Ruggles chose a line from William Blake for the epigraph to his 1924 orchestral work, *Men and Mountains:* "Great things are done when men and mountains meet."[72] Like Blake, Ruggles was a man "visited with a fire from heaven,"[73] a mystic who struggled to communicate his personal vision directly. The mysticism he found in Walt Whitman was his inspiration in *Portals* (1925), for thirteen strings. Concerning this work, Ruggles told Dorothy Canfield Fisher,

[the work of art] takes form gradually in one's unconscious mind until something, perhaps something quite unrelated, comes along and happens to crystallize it and bring it to consciousness. In this case the re-agent was Walt Whitman's lines

What are they of the known
But to ascend and enter the Unknown?

Ruggles compares the recurrences of the work's main theme to "a series of portals opening to new vistas. . . . A mystical concept—as indeed Whitman *was* mystical."[74]

Sun-Treader (1926–31) is Ruggles's longest work (seventeen minutes); it is written for large orchestra, including six horns and five trumpets. The composer himself seems to have recognized that the work defined his full maturity and creative vigor. While working on *Sun-Treader* he wrote to Henry Cowell: "More and more I'm gaining that complete command of line which, to me, is the basis of all music. There is absolutely no comparison between that which I've done with that which I'm doing now."[75]

Ruggles found his title and epigraph for *Sun-Treader* in a Robert Browning poem expressing admiration for Shelley in the lines "Sun-Treader,/Light and Life be thine forever!"[76] Throughout the work, arching, aspiring melodic lines and constantly dissonant textures combine to create an atmosphere of unrelieved, white-hot emotional tension. The first thirteen measures of the work present the main theme, a single, continuous melodic gesture covering an enormous range (Ex. 11-6). The melody's structure reflects a concept which had crystallized in the composer's mind around 1925. In a letter to his wife from that year, Ruggles reported that *Portals* was "in a new scheme of composition," which "eminates [sic] from not repeating any note until the tenth."[77] Nonrepetition of pitches, until ten different ones had been sounded, remained a compositional rule-of-thumb for Ruggles from 1925 on, but it never attained the status of a system.

Sun-Treader is a one-movement work characterized by drives toward ecstatic climaxes, which are extremely loud and full (such as those around

Ex. 11-6. Ruggles, *Sun-Treader*, mm. 1–13, melody only. © 1954 by Theodore Presser Company.

mm. 111 and 160). Although the high emotional tension is somewhat re-lieved by quieter, introspective passages, it always reappears, and the work ends, in a manner typical of Ruggles, with a long-held, highly dissonant tutti chord with dynamic markings *ff p < fff*. The work's emotional subtext is surely the striving of the artist toward the mystical, transcendental realms symbol-ized by the sun. The work is formally clear but strongly expressionist in its emotional thrust and its melodic, harmonic, and rhythmic idiom. As Charles Seeger has written, Ruggles's technique "shows a curious ratio between or-ganization and fantasy," with a "vast preponderance of fantasy."[78]

From the early 1930s, his musical creativity seems to have declined, and Ruggles devoted more and more of his time to painting. He considered his music and his painting equal expressions of the same basic creative spirit,[79] and some of his more abstract art works, such as "Tree of the Inner Eye," can be seen as the visual equivalent of his musical phrases (Ill. 11-3).

Ill. 11-3. Carl Ruggles, *Tree of the Inner Eye* (1947?). India ink on white paper and blue body color on re-verse of glass, 59.5 x 47 cm. Carl Ruggles Archive, Music Library, Yale University.

In 1931, in a Guggenheim Foundation application that was rejected, Ruggles expressed his wish to go to Europe and meet Schoenberg, Berg, and Webern, "these men who are experimenting as I am."[80] Indeed, Ruggles's mature music reflects an intuitive approach to composition comparable to that in Schoenberg's free atonal works. Unlike Schoenberg, Ruggles remained faithful to this largely free approach, and he never subscribed to more sys-tematic constructivism, as Schoenberg did in his twelve-tone works. Ruggles's melodic style bears a superficial resemblance to that of Schoenberg's atonal works, but his melodies, while equally strong in expressivity, are more vo-cally conceived, in a somewhat Wagnerian manner. Ruggles's approach to form is basically much more straightforward than that of Schoenberg in his atonal works, with a frequent use of almost literal recapitulation. In content, Schoenberg's music of the period 1908–20 is the more varied, reflecting both inward psychological probing and transcendental urges; Ruggles is almost always preoccupied in his music with striving toward lofty grandeur.

Ives and Ruggles met around 1927[81] and gradually became close friends, drawn together by the independence of mind which they shared and by their mutual respect for each other's musical integrity. Ives's openness to his musical environment—its popular elements in particular—contrasts with Ruggles's much more exclusive approach. As Ruggles once jotted down:

> I'm a Lone Eagle
> A Talisman
> Proclaiming the
> Destiny of Shapes
> The Shapes of Great
> Communications.[82]

Although both Ruggles and Ives frequently revised their compositions, their methods of doing so were diametrically opposed: Ruggles "would be chiseling off a bit here, off something there, and then balance it way over somewhere else,"[83] all in the stubborn search for perfection. On the other hand, Ives's constant tinkering with and adding to his compositions reflects an all-inclusive, quasi-improvisational attitude toward his materials. Both are united in their hatred of the genteel tradition and their urge to express the transcendental. However, while Ives draws on the American collective unconscious to reach this goal, Ruggles is always the "Lone Eagle," the isolated artist wrapped in a lonely struggle to reach and express the Sublime.

Dmitri Shostakovich (1906–75) is not usually considered a composer much affected by expressionism. Indeed, many of his works lean toward neoclassicism, Socialist Realism, or the more popular style of his many film scores. But some of his most significant compositions arise from a strong inner necessity. To convey his meaning in these works, Shostakovich employs extremes of orchestration, texture, dynamics, and tempo, along with dissonant atonality, savage accents, obsessive rhythms and ostinati, and unexpected contrasts. To clarify and enhance communication with his audience, he also makes masterful use of tone painting, musical symbolism, and quotations from popular and folk music and from his own previous work. All these characteristics reflect his affinity to expressionism and, in particular, to Mahler, Berg, and the proto-expressionist, Mussorgsky.

It was Shostakovich's misfortune to live his entire life under a totalitarian regime. His need for self-expression was great: "so many unsaid things collect in the soul, so much exhaustion and irritation lie as a heavy burden on the psyche. And you *must* unburden your spiritual world or risk a collapse. Sometimes you feel like screaming."[84] Forced throughout his life to wear a "mask of loyalty" to the Soviet regime, to sign or deliver statements and speeches written for him,[85] Shostakovich could express himself freely only through his music, and even this was subject to periodic restraint by the state. His life under totalitarianism is vividly portrayed in *Testimony,* his memoirs as told to Solomon Volkov. This book is one of the most revealing biographies by a composer and is crucial to the understanding of Shostakovich's creative psychology.[86]

Throughout his creative career, his expressionist music exhibits a dichotomy that has its roots in his character. Shostakovich recognized his affinity with the nineteenth-century Russian satirist Nikolai Gogol,[87] which is reflected in his music's frequent, bitter irony; but his kinship with Dostoevsky's compassion for human suffering is at least equally important to his compositions.

Although Shostakovich always wanted to communicate with his audience, at the times of his greatest persecution he resorted to a kind of cryptic or disguised communication. Much later, he admitted that he had actually been afraid that his music would be understood and that he would be betrayed by informers in the audience.[88] As persecution lessened, his communication became more specific and overt, in accord with his conviction that his music should be an "active force."[89] His most explicit works are the texted Thirteenth and Fourteenth symphonies. The Fourteenth shows his expressionism at its strongest. It is saturated throughout with the fear of death, which Shostakovich believed was "the strongest emotion of all."[90]

Shostakovich's so-called Storm and Stress period (1926–36), the years of his youthful expressionism,[91] corresponds roughly to the post-revolutionary era, when free artistic expression was still permitted in the USSR. In the earlier works of this period, Shostakovich's Gogol-like characteristics predominate. Like Bartók's Bagatelles (which Shostakovich may well have known), his 1927 *Aphorisms* for piano already show many of his important artistic traits: biting sarcasm, alienation, nose-thumbing dissonance, obsessiveness, and a preoccupation with the macabre. This penchant for the macabre is evident in the seventh piece, "Dance of Death," as the *Dies irae* melody is transformed into a fast waltz—a procedure resembling Bartók's treatment of the Stefi Geyer motive in the fourteenth Bagatelle.

As the basis of his first surviving opera, *The Nose* (1927–28), Shostakovich chose a short story by Gogol. The outrageous plot (concerning a nose which is accidentally separated from its owner and assumes an independent existence) serves as the vehicle for a caustic satire on Russian officialdom and the snobbery of the upper classes. This work dates from the period when Shostakovich was associated with the great avant-garde theater director Meyerhold and played stage piano in his production of Gogol's *The Inspector General.* The music of the opera is expressionist in its constant, manic exaggeration and shows Shostakovich's gift for musical satire and orchestral parody. In order to project the text clearly, *parlando* declamation is used almost throughout, and there are very few arias.

Shostakovich's next opera, *Lady Macbeth of Mzensk* (1930–32), is a much more serious and mature creation than *The Nose*. Shostakovich felt empathy with the murderous, lustful heroine, Katerina Ismailova, justifying her crimes as the revolt of a superior being against the stultifying dullness and repression of society in provincial Russia. In the fourth and final act, in which Katerina and her lover are deported to Siberia, the composer reveals the deeply compassionate side of his nature. Like Dostoevsky, Shostakovich felt a profound sympathy for the oppressed and for deported convicts in particular. This is apparent both in the libretto of the closing act and in the lyrical and consonant music—reminiscent of Mussorgsky—given to the convicts' chorus and to their spokesman.[92]

The first three acts, effectively combining tonality and free atonality, make expressionistic use of lurid colors and extreme contrasts. The score is characterized by an intense, at times animalistic, eroticism; for instance, in the bedroom scene (Act I, scene 3), the sexual intercourse of Katerina and her lover is explicitly depicted by thrusting trombone slides ([186] to [187]).[93] The eroticism of *Lady Macbeth* owes much to Berg's *Wozzeck*, which Shostakovich had seen eight or nine times in Leningrad in 1927.[94] (A crescendo on one note, similar to that in *Wozzeck*, appears in *Lady Macbeth*.[95]) In addition, Shostakovich seems to have taken from Berg the idea of the highly dramatic interludes ("entr'actes") which connect the scenes. After a minor character (the Seedy Lout) discovers the corpse of the husband Katerina has murdered, the orchestra launches into a *galop* in the style of Offenbach (Entr'acte between Act III, scenes 6 and 7)—an ironic allusion which is as effective as the fast polka for out-of-tune tavern piano suddenly heard in *Wozzeck*.[96]

Lady Macbeth, Shostakovich's powerful, highly original expressionist work, shows his rapid development into one of the great operatic composers of the twentieth century. It is therefore particularly tragic that in the midst of its great initial success, the opera was brutally attacked in *Pravda* in 1936. In "Chaos Instead of Music," an article Shostakovich believed was written by Stalin himself,[97] it is described as

> a deliberately dissonant, confused stream of sound. Fragments of melody, embryonic phrases appear—only to disappear again in the din, the grinding, the screaming. . . . This music is built on the basis of rejecting opera. . . . [It] carries into the theater and the music the most negative features of "Meyerholdism" infinitely multiplied.[98]

This attack and the subsequent rejection of Shostakovich and his music in Soviet Russia had a devastating effect on the composer. He considered the day the article was published the most "memorable" of his life,[99] and in the period which followed, he lived with constant fear, deep depression, and thoughts of suicide.[100] He never wrote another serious opera or ballet.

Although Soviet composers were allowed more freedom of expression during the years of World War II, Shostakovich was again traumatized by the cultural crackdown begun by Stalin's minister of culture, Zhdanov, in 1946. It was not until after the death of Stalin in 1953 that the composer felt he could once again put before the public music which expressed his deepest emotions. He initially denied that his powerful Tenth Symphony (1953) had a specific program.[101] Years later, he disclosed in *Testimony* that the symphony is about Stalin and the Stalin years, and that its second movement (Scherzo) is a musical portrait of the dictator.[102]

In this Scherzo, all musical factors combine to present a truly terrifying vision of Stalin's brutality and the fear and hysteria it aroused. The tempo is extremely fast (♩=176), the accents in the strings savage, the snare drum rhythms like machine guns. In the middle section of the movement little imagination is required to hear the scurrying of frightened rats (or victims) in the frenzied sixteenth-note runs of the woodwinds ([82]) and screams in the high string accents which follow (after [83]). This wild, sometimes raucous movement, with its *sffff* ending, is all the more powerful because of its brevity. The third movement is a darkly playful *Ländler* à la Mahler. In this movement, the musical motto formed from the German spelling of Shostakovich's name (D Es C H = D E-flat C B) makes its first appearance in this symphony.[103] Heard first in disguised form (mm. 1–3), the motto plays an increasingly dominant role as the movement progresses. In the Finale, material from the Stalin movement returns ([180]), becoming increasingly loud and threatening, but at its climax the D Es C H motto enters triumphantly, *fff* ([184]), symbolizing Shostakovich's survival and moral victory over Stalin.

The Eighth String Quartet (1960), an intense autobiographical distillation of the Tenth Symphony, is a key expressionist work. The D Es C H motive dominates obsessively. The Quartet was written after a visit to survivors of the Dresden firebombing and is dedicated to the "memory of the victims of fascism and war." However, many quotations from his earlier works—which make the quartet's meaning "clear as a primer" according to Shostakovich—show that he is once again reliving the Stalin years.[104] Like Joseph K. (in Kafka's *The Trial*), Shostakovich had experienced the trauma of nameless terror during those years, and in the Eighth Quartet he seeks to exorcise that terror by constant repetition of his personal motto. By using personal musical quotations, he increases direct communication with his audience. His concern with unmistakable meaning then leads him to use texts in some of his most important late works.

The bare and brooding first movement of the Eighth Quartet is largely a contrapuntal meditation on D Es C H, interspersed with self-quotations from earlier works including the First and Fifth symphonies. The frantic pace and extreme accents of the following Scherzo recall the "Stalin" movement of the Tenth Symphony. At the movement's climax, Shostakovich introduces a Jewish theme (from his Second Piano Trio, Op. 67, 1944, a work which was itself a tribute to the Jews slaughtered by Hitler's SS in the Ukraine).[105] Here he makes clear, as he does in many other works, his pity for the Jews in the face of their oppression in anti-Semitic Russia. In the fourth movement (Largo), however, the most important quotation occurs (Ex. 11-7). Introduced by the heavy tread of marching feet and a reference to the *Dies irae* (mm. 21–25), there is an extensive, moving statement of the revolutionary prisoners' song "Tormented by the Weight of Bondage." By quoting this song, known to every Russian, Shostakovich evokes sympathy for all victims of oppression. Like Ives, he uses quotation in order to awaken definite psychological associations in his hearers.

Ex. 11-7. Shostakovich, Eighth String Quartet/IV, mm. 19–35.

In his Thirteenth Symphony (1962), a setting of five poems by the much younger Yevgeni Yevtushenko, Shostakovich arrived at the point of fully overt, explicit communication. Like the expressionists during and after World War I, he turned in this work from introspection to an activist political stance. Setting the Yevtushenko poems, particularly the opening "Babi Yar," was an act of great courage, as the poem had already aroused much controversy in official Soviet circles. Although "Babi Yar" deals primarily with the slaughter of some 70,000 Jews by the Nazi SS and their Russian and Ukrainian helpers in 1941,[106] the poem is also a general indictment of the persecution of Jews and of Russian anti-Semitism in particular. This subject inspired Shostakovich to one of his most powerful creations. He set the text (for bass solo and unison male chorus) so that every word can be heard and understood.

The setting of "Babi Yar" is rich in highly emotional musical imagery. For the menacing opening, Shostakovich combined the lowest instruments of the orchestra in a relentless funeral march chorale (reminiscent of the "Bruder Martin" movement of Mahler's First Symphony). A countermelody in muted brass and intermittent entrances of a chime (a symbol of death) add to the atmosphere of bleak foreboding. Much later in the movement, anticipating the words "the wind whistles through the wild grass over Babi Yar," the opening material returns, *fff espressivo,* augmented by chilling 32d-note runs in the upper woodwinds.

After experiencing a serious heart attack in 1966, Shostakovich turned from the societal concerns of the Thirteenth Symphony to the deeply personal and introspective Fourteenth (1969), a work which deals with death. He conceived this symphony as a continuation of Mussorgsky's *Songs and Dances of Death,* which he had orchestrated in 1962.[107] The eleven texts, given to bass and soprano soloists in alternation, are mostly somber in tone. Ten are by Western European poets (Lorca, Apollinaire, and Rilke); the single text originally written in Russian (No. 9, by the Russian-German poet Küchelbeker) is the only one which is somewhat consoling and optimistic in content.

The Fourteenth Symphony is so different from Shostakovich's previous works as to suggest that at age 63 the composer had found a fresh musical style. The work combines a new economy of means (the orchestra is reduced to nineteen strings plus percussion) with a higher degree of dissonance and greater emotional concentration than he had previously achieved. Many orchestral gestures reflect the new musical language of Polish avant-garde, for Shostakovich was able to renew contacts with the music of foreign composers in the 1960s.

Although the symphony is tightly unified, Shostakovich achieves great variety as he evokes the many guises of death. His deft use of musical metaphor is evident throughout. The slow tempo and sparse textures of the first song ("De profundis" by Lorca) are violently contradicted by the second song's nightmarish, unrelenting exaggeration of Spanish popular style, as its text (Lorca's "Malagueña") describes death wandering in and out of a tavern. The six Apollinaire settings, which form the central part of the symphony, are marked by moments of great intensity. In "The Suicide" (No. 4) the words "The second [lily] grows out of my heart/ Which disintegrates in suffering, eaten by worms" motivate a piercing scream in the high violins, which then descends in sixteenth notes to a Mahlerian death motive in undulating thirds (Ex. 11-8). The tenth song ("The Poet's Death") recapitulates the symphony's opening, and the eleventh ("The Conclusion") is gripping in its complete lack of sentimentality. The opening words, "Death is all-powerful," set to a rising half-step motive in staccato eighth notes, determine the uncompromising tone of this finale. Soon, the voices rise to a *fff* climax on the concluding words, "When we think ourselves in the midst of life/ [Death] dares to cry in our midst." At this point, the *fff* reentrance of the percussion (wood-block and tom-tom) expresses irrefutable finality. Next, the dynamics return to *pp,* and the entire work concludes unyieldingly with a Bergian crescendo and a written-out accelerando on a highly dissonant chord in the strings.

Ex. 11-8. Shostakovich, Fourteenth Symphony/IV, mm. 1–3 of [60]. © Copyright 1970 by MCA Music Publishing.

The life experience of Shostakovich, which he described as "gray and miserable," led him to the conclusion that "fear is always with us."[108] A report of his 1959 visit to the United States noted that he was "highly nervous, a chain-smoker with darting eyes and fidgeting hands, ill at ease most of the time."[109] Yet Shostakovich was able to overcome his fear through the essential integrity of his finest music. In spite of the compromises he had to make in order to stay alive and the mask he felt forced to wear, he managed to express his deepest emotions in music and to make a reality of his profound conviction that music can attack evil.[110]

Although the music of Roger Sessions (1896–1985) and Elliott Carter (b. 1908) is for the most part too rationally constructed for either man to be regarded as primarily an expressionist, both of these important American composers of the generation following Ives and Ruggles partook of the legacy of expressionism. Sessions, who was one of the first to bring a knowledge of the work of Schoenberg, Berg, and Webern to younger American composers, and to make that knowledge an integral part of his own music, wrote in 1952 that undue emphasis was being given to the twelve-tone method rather than to the expressive crisis which Schoenberg's music embodies.[111] For Carter, although he was fully aware of Viennese expressionism, the primary influence was Ives, who had been his mentor when Carter was a teen-ager. The influence of Ives's Second String Quartet is unmistakable in Carter's conception of his own Second Quartet (1959):

My new quartet treats the four performers with even greater individualization than did [the First]—as I see it is all about the problems, the pleasures, of human cooperation. Who's to be leader, what happens when the leader goes too far etc. This kind of thinking interests me a great deal and I try to find some kind of system of oppositions and cooperations which give form to the entire work.[112]

The living American composer whose music most strongly continues the spirit of expressionism is Leon Kirchner. Born in Brooklyn in 1919, Kirchner moved with his family to Los Angeles at the age of nine, and came of age in the 1930s and 40s amidst the intellectual and artistic excitement created by the presence on the West Coast of many important European emigrés.

Not only the musical, but the intellectual surroundings were amazing. The density of the magnificent mentalities there . . . they were practically the generators of the city. Thomas Mann, Lion Feuchtwanger—I attended many of the readings at his house. He would invite young novelists and their friends to come to the house to read their first chapters. God that was wonderful.[113]

Aldous Huxley, Bertrand Russell, and Theodore Dreiser were other intellectuals with whom Kirchner came into contact.[114] His broad intellectual and humanistic interests continue to the present.

Although Kirchner also studied with Sessions and Ernest Bloch, he acknowledges that his musical life, as both composer and performer (conductor and pianist), has remained "deeply centered" in the work of his first important composition teacher, Arnold Schoenberg.[115] Kirchner has never adopted Schoenberg's twelve-tone technique, but he shares with his teacher the "sheer musical urge" characteristic of Schoenberg's freely atonal, expressionist works. Schoenberg's deep knowledge of three centuries of music also aided Kirchner in developing a keen sense of form and tradition. His studies with Schoenberg gave him the courage to stay outside the compositional fashions (serialism, total organization) which were pervasive in the 1950s and 60s.[116]

Kirchner's volatile, mercurial temperament is basic to his music. Aaron Copland, in an early review, fully recognized the force of Kirchner's personality as expressed in his music. After a Kirchner performance, Copland felt that he had made contact

not merely with a composer, but with a highly sentient human being; of a man who creates his music out of an awareness of the special climate of today's unsettled world. Kirchner's best pages prove that he reacts strongly to that world; they are charged with an emotional impact and explosive power that is almost frightening in its intensity. . . . We get the impression of a creative urge so vital as to burst all bonds of ordinary control. It is this "out of control" quality that gives any of his works enormous excitement.[117]

Kirchner himself has eloquently stated his compositional credo:

An artist must create a personal cosmos, a verdant world in continuity with tradition, further fulfilling man's "awareness," his "degree of consciousness," and bringing new subtilization, vision and beauty to the elements of experience. It is in this way that the Idea, powered by conviction and necessity, will create its own style, and the singular, momentous structure capable of realizing its intent.[118]

As with Schoenberg in his free atonal music, Kirchner's choice of notes and chords is not a technical one but an emotional decision involving the composer's entire being: "To me the quality of music goes beyond simply putting together notes. I look for a chord that will resonate somewhere deep in my soul. My whole heart is involved in the choice of notes."[119]

The Trio for Violin, Cello and Piano (1954), an important work of Kirchner's early maturity, gives a good idea of his expressionism.[120] The first movement is basically monothematic, but its succinct thematic material experiences far-reaching psychological metamorphoses. These emotional states are expressed in frequent, extreme changes of character and tempo. Passages marked "wild!" "appassionato," "lyrically, tenderly," "powerfully," and "coming from nowhere, almost out of control" follow each other in quick succession (mm. 19–31). Cadenzalike sections occur often, not only in the virtuoso piano part but in the violin and cello as well, and accelerandos and ritardandos are frequent. Although the movement falls into a free but clear three-part form reinforced by tonal references at important structural points, there is throughout a feeling of high drama and improvisatory spontaneity. As the composer has stated,

A great piece of music sets up a kind of anxiety as it unfolds: what will happen next? What follows then produces a kind of catharsis. In a way, music that has real quality stirs something in the human consciousness; if one listens intently, one cannot help but be a changed human being.[121]

Like earlier expressionists, Kirchner believes that the aim of art is to change humanity. He stands out as a highly individualistic, humanistically oriented composer who has had to live through a rationalistic, science-dominated period. It is to his credit that he has never become cynical or succumbed to what he calls the "fetish of complexity,"[122] which has often alienated audiences during the second half of the twentieth century.

It is by no means accidental that a significant revival of musical expressionism occurred in the 1960s—a decade of political turmoil and revolt in some ways comparable to the years immediately before and after World War I. During these years, Luigi Nono, Alberto Ginastera, and Peter Maxwell Davies all wrote works which reflect in different ways the heritage of musical expressionism.

Although the early compositions of Nono (1924–90) were strictly twelve-tone, he soon found that a freer idiom was necessary in order to express and communicate his political concerns. He nevertheless rejected the "chance" music of Cage and attacked, in typically expressionist terms, both Cage and Joseph Schillinger[123] for their "cessation of spiritual activity," prevalence of automatism and materialism, and segregation of spirit and matter.[124] An engaged Communist, Nono told his students they needed to have a political viewpoint as well as compositional technique.[125] In his own works, a strong political stance is balanced by a humanistic dedication to "love of life."

Nono's 1961 opera *Intolleranza* (dedicated to Schoenberg, whose daughter, Nuria, married Nono in 1955) embodies his ideas for a new music theater. Nono has written that these ideas have their origin in Schoenberg's *Die glückliche Hand,* a work he praises for the independence of its sung text and mimed action and for the dual role of the chorus as a musical and a static visual element. He also calls attention to the polemical, revolutionary character of Schoenberg's text, which Nono connects to the stylistic and technical radicalism of the work as a whole.[126]

The musical style of *Intolleranza* is apparent even in the look of the published score, which is reproduced directly from the broad, bold, and seemingly hurried strokes of the composer's manuscript. Masses of orchestral sound and a large body of percussion are used to produce mostly big, sometimes brutal, effects, though there are some quiet, chamberlike passages as well. In spite of the novelty of having sounds and projections emanate from changing locations in the theater, *Intolleranza* is so strongly influenced by *Die glückliche Hand,* by Ernst Toller's expressionist play *Masse Mensch* (1920), and by the work of Brecht and Meyerhold,[127] that it is primarily a summation of the previous achievements of expressionist musical theater.

Looking back over his career, the Argentinian composer Alberto Ginastera (1916–83) divided his creative work into three periods: "objective nationalism" (to 1948), "subjective nationalism" (to 1958), and "neo-expressionism" (from 1958).[128] As the increasing success of his music enabled Ginastera to spend longer periods in the United States and Europe, the elements of Argentine folk music, which initially marked his style, progressively receded. At the same time—since Ginastera believed that a good composer should be "disposed to capture all the stimuli which arrive from the outside world"[129]—his compositions increasingly reflected the influence of the avant-garde of the 1960s. But when he says that content should determine form, that he feels a "spiritual urgency" in the "necessity to create,"[130] and that "transcendence" is the most important quality in a work of art,[131] Ginastera speaks as a true musical expressionist.

The opera *Bomarzo* (1966–67) is an outstanding example of Ginastera's "neo-expressionist" third period. The libretto is filled with lurid, hallucinatory episodes. Duke Pier Francesco Orsini, an *angst*-laden, neurotic hunchback, has been poisoned; as he is dying, he recalls the emotional events of his life. Of the opera's fifteen scenes, the central thirteen are devoted to flashbacks, most of which are decidedly Freudian in tone. As was true of Ginastera's previous opera, *Don Rodrigo* (1963–64), the influence of Berg's *Woz-*

zeck is strongly present in *Bomarzo*. And like *Wozzeck*, *Bomarzo* is divided into fifteen scenes separated by musical interludes; and in both operas, the final interlude is intended to transcend the immediate dramatic circumstances and make a direct appeal to the audience's humanity. As Berg does in *Wozzeck*, Ginastera structures many scenes on forms from instrumental music.

The musical style and dramatic approach of *Bomarzo* also owe much to *Wozzeck*. In the vocal lines, there is considerable use of *Sprechgesang* and melodrama, as well as wide-intervaled atonal lyricism. However, the Bergian expressionist idiom is updated to include the pitch bends, tone clusters, and semi-aleatory textures characteristic of the avant-garde of the late 1950s and 1960s.

Up to 1965, the works of the British composer Peter Maxwell Davies (b. 1934) reflect an interest in combining serialism with late-medieval and early-Renaissance compositional techniques. Around 1965, however, Davies's music entered a radically new phase. *Revelation and Fall* (1965–66; based on a section of a prose poem by Georg Trakl) marks a "remarkable rebirth,"[132] ushering in a stylistic change marked by "expressionistic conflicts."[133] *Revelation and Fall* is the first of several works of dramatic or semidramatic expressionism by Davies, others in this vein include *Eight Songs for a Mad King* (1969) and the dance work *Vesalii Icones* (1969).

For the text of *Revelation and Fall*, Davies chose three paragraphs from Trakl's nine-paragraph prose poem "Offenbarung und Untergang."[134] These paragraphs portray the stations in the wanderings of the lonely poet (a ruined tavern, a forest at night) by means of a sometimes irrational flow of powerful images. Since Trakl, perhaps the most gifted of expressionist poets, was a member of the Vienna circle surrounding Kraus, Schoenberg, and Kokoschka—and was in fact present while Kokoschka painted the famous double portrait of Alma Mahler and himself (*The Bride of the Wind*, Ill. 1-5)—Davies's choice of a Trakl text brings his listeners back to one of the principal fountainheads of expressionism.

In view of Webern's important settings of Trakl in his Opp. 13 and 14, it would seem logical to look for points of Webern's influence in *Revelation and Fall*. However, Schoenberg's *Pierrot lunaire* is actually a stronger influence, just as it had been the main influence on Webern's Op. 14. Like *Pierrot*, *Revelation and Fall* is a semidramatic work. In its original performances, the soprano soloist wore a scarlet nun's habit, her lectern was in the form of a black cross, and the specially built percussion instruments were in the shape of large futuristic sculptures.[135]

At the climax of the piece, Davies returns to the primeval scream of expressionism. Following a very quiet passage, the words "Einbrach ein roter Schatten mit flammendem Schwert in das Haus" (A red specter with flaming sword broke into the house) are screamed and shouted by the singer through a megaphone. She is at first accompanied by a railway guard's whistle, a rachet on a clock mechanism, and a large bass drum, all *fff*. Later (m. 185), a note instructs that she is to shout the words "ein roter Schatten" over and over until the end of the measure, "becoming ever more hysterical."

In spite of some notable quiet passages, *Revelation and Fall* is in many ways an outrageous work, intended to shock. Like Mahler, Davies does not shrink from consciously "ugly" sounds. His purpose appears to have been threefold: to express and work out the conflicts—presumably religious—in his own nature; to shake the British audience out of its complacency, thereby breaking down the remainders of the genteel tradition in British music; and, as he states explicitly in his introduction to *Eight Songs for a Mad King*, "to explore certain extreme regions of experience" (Davies's italics).[136]

Although we have pointed to Ruggles, Kirchner, Shostakovich, Nono, Ginastera, and Davies as composers whose work most obviously embodies the continuing importance of the expressionism of the first quarter of the twentieth century, the influence of the pioneering expressionist works of this period is much more pervasive. It decisively affected the further development of twentieth-century music in ways which could not be negated by later, contradictory developments, be they neoclassicism, neoromanticism, constructivism, or minimalism. The revolutionary expressionist legacy, which includes freedom of musical form, directness and forcefulness of musical expression, extensions of instrumental and vocal techniques, and immensely widened possibilities in melody, harmony, texture, and coherence, became a part of twentieth-century musical language.

The expressionist eruption of 1908–23 was essentially an outburst of repressed feeling. The urgent need for expression and communication led to new musical techniques. The search for emotional truth resulted in the overturning of traditional concepts of beauty, and music was perceived as an expressive *language* rather than the "play of sounding forms."[137] As the deepest, most direct expression of intense emotions and transcendental yearnings, music was not a diversion to the expressionists, but a profound experience. Among the many "isms" of modernism, it was from expressionist compulsion that "a terrible beauty" was born.

Select Bibliography

Bailey, Walter B. *Programmatic Elements in the Works of Schoenberg.* Ann Arbor: UMI Research Press, 1984.

Becher, Johannes R. *Um Gott.* Leipzig: Insel, 1921.

Briner, Andres. *Paul Hindemith.* Zürich: Atlantis, 1971.

Busoni, Ferruccio. *Entwurf einer neuen Ästhetik der Tonkunst.* Trieste: Schmidt, 1907.

———. *Sketch of a New Esthetic of Music.* Trans. Th. Baker. New York: G. Schirmer, 1911.

25 Jahre neue Musik: Jahrbuch 1926 der Universal-Edition. Vienna: Universal, 1926.

Gay, Peter. *Weimar Culture.* New York: Harper and Row, 1968.

Gilbert, Steven E. "Carl Ruggles (1876–1971): An Appreciation." *Perspectives of New Music* 10/1 (Fall–Winter 1972): 274.

Harrison, Lou. *About Carl Ruggles.* Yonkers: Oscar Baradinsky at the Alicat Bookshop, 1946.

Hindemith, Paul. *A Composer's World.* Cambridge: Harvard University Press, 1952.

Hindemith Jahrbuch. 1970–   .

Jarman, Douglas. *Kurt Weill.* Bloomington: Indiana University Press, 1982.

Kemp, Ian. *Hindemith.* London: Oxford University Press, 1970.

Kirchner, Leon. "I sometimes think I dreamed all of this, and perhaps I have." *Harvard Magazine* 77/3 (November 1974): 47.

Kirkpatrick, John. "The Evolution of Carl Ruggles: A Chronicle Largely in His Own Words." *Perspectives of New Music* 6/2 (Spring–Summer 1968): 147.

Kleimann, Helga. *Die Novembergruppe.* Berlin: Gebr. Mann, 1969.

Kokoschka, Oskar. "*Allos makar.*" *Zeit-Echo: Ein Kriegs-Tagebuch für Künstler* 20/1 (1915): 300.

Kowalke, Kim W. *Kurt Weill in Europe.* Ann Arbor: UMI Research Press, 1979.

Krenek, Ernst. "Self-Analysis." *New Mexico Quarterly* 23/1 (Spring 1953): 5.

———. *Zur Sprache gebracht.* Munich: Langen-Müller, 1958.

———. *Horizons Circled: Reflections on My Music.* Berkeley: University of California Press, 1974.

Lopatnikoff, Nikolai. "An American in Berlin." *Modern Music* 9/2 (January–February 1932): 90.

MacDonald, Ian. *The New Shostakovich.* London: Fourth Estate, 1990.

Neumeyer, David. *The Music of Paul Hindemith.* New Haven and London: Yale University Press, 1986.

———, and Schubert, Giselher. "Arnold Schoenberg and Paul Hindemith." *Journal of the Arnold Schoenberg Institute* 13/1 (June 1990): 3.

Nono, Luigi. "The Historical Reality of Music Today." *Score* 27 (July 1960): 41.

———. *Texte: Studien zu seiner Musik.* Ed. Jürg Stenzl. Zürich: Atlantis, 1975.

Norris, Christopher, ed. *Shostakovich: The Man and His Music.* Boston and London: Boyars, 1982.

Paul Hindemith: Zeugnis in Bildern [Testimony in Pictures]. 2d ed. Trans. Everett Helm. Mainz: Schott, 1961.

Peterson, Elliot. "The Music of Carl Ruggles." Ph.D. diss., University of Washington, 1967.

Pruslin, Stephen, ed. *Peter Maxwell Davies: Studies from Two Decades.* Tempo Booklet No. 2. London: Boosey & Hawkes, 1979.

Rexroth, Dieter, ed. *Erprobungen und Erfahrungen: Zu Paul Hindemiths Schaffen in den Zwanziger Jahren.* Veröffentlichungen des Paul-Hindemith-Institutes Frankfurt, vol. 2. Mainz: Schott, 1978.

Rubsamen, Walter H. "Schoenberg in America." *Musical Quarterly* 37/4 (October 1951): 469.

Salzman, Eric. "Carl Ruggles: A Lifetime is Not Too Long to Search for the Sublime." *Hi-Fi/Stereo Review* (September 1966): 53.

Sanders, Ronald. *The Days Grow Short: The Life and Music of Kurt Weill.* New York: Holt, Rinehart and Winston, 1980.

Schubert, Giselher. *Hindemith.* Reinbek bei Hamburg: Rowohlt, 1981.

Schwarz, Boris. *Music and Musical Life in Soviet Russia.* 2d ed. Bloomington: Indiana University Press, 1983.

Seeger, Charles. "Carl Ruggles." *Musical Quarterly* 18/4 (October 1932): 578.

———. "In Memoriam: Carl Ruggles." *Perspectives of New Music* 10/2 (Spring–Summer 1972): 171.

Sessions, Roger. "Some Notes on Schoenberg, and the Method of Composing with Twelve Notes." *Score* 6 (May 1952): 7.

Skelton, Geoffrey. *Paul Hindemith: The Man behind the Music*. New York: Crescendo, 1975.

Smalley, Roger. "Some Recent Works of Peter Maxwell Davies." *Tempo* 84 (Spring 1968): 2.

Sollertinsky, Dmitri, and Sollertinsky, Ludmilla. *Pages from the Life of Dmitri Shostakovich*. Trans. Graham Hobbs and Charles Midgley. New York and London: Harcourt Brace Jovanovich, 1980.

Trakl, Georg. *Poems*. Trans. Lucia Getsi. Athens, OH: Mundus Artium, 1973.

Urtubey, Pola Suárez. *Alberto Ginastera*. Buenos Aires: Editiones Culturales Argentinos, 1967.

Volkov, Solomon, ed. *Testimony: The Memoirs of Dmitri Shostakovich*. Trans. Antonina Bouis. New York: Harper and Row, 1979.

Wörner, Karl H. *Neue Musik in der Entscheidung*. 2d ed. Mainz: Schott, 1956.

Notes

PREFACE

1. There is, to our knowledge, no book-length study of expressionism in music. Luigi Rognoni's *The Second Vienna School: Expressionism and Dodecaphony,* trans. Robert W. Mann (London: Calder, 1977), perhaps comes closest, but much of this work is devoted to the subsequent development of twelve-tone music. Indeed, so few musical scholars have dealt with expressionism in music that the field has been left largely to literary scholars and cultural historians.

2. The term began appearing in German music periodicals such as *Melos* as late as 1920. See Jost Hermand, "Expressionism and Music," in *Expressionism Reconsidered,* ed. Gertrud Pickar and Karl Webb (Munich: Fink, 1979), pp. 59ff.

3. John C. Crawford, "The Relationship of Text and Music in the Vocal Works of Schoenberg, 1908–1924," Ph.D. diss., Harvard University, 1963.

4. Principal descriptions of expressionism in music include Arnold Schering, "Die expressionistische Bewegung in der Musik," in *Zur Einführung in die Kunst der Gegenwart* (Leipzig: Seemann, 1919), pp. 139ff.; Ernst Bücken, *Führer und Probleme der neuen Musik* (Cologne: Tonger, 1924), pp. 149ff.; Nicolas Slonimsky, *Music Since 1900* (New York: Norton, 1937), p. xvii; Robert Wiedman, "Expressionism in Music," Ph.D. diss., New York University, 1955; Jan Maegaard, "Some Formal Devices in Expressionistic Works," *Dansk Aarbog for Musik Forsning* (1961): 69; H. H. Stuckenschmidt, "Was ist musikalischer Expressionismus," *Melos* 36/1 (January 1969): 1; Will Hofmann, Karl Wörner, and Walter Maunzen, "Expressionismus," *Die Musik in Geschichte und Gegenwart* III: 1658; Wörner, *Die Musik in der Geistesgeschichte* (Bonn: Bouvier, 1970), pp. 26ff. Hermand, p. 58, provides a useful summary of some of the previous writings on this topic.

5. Elliott Carter, "Expressionism and American Music," *Perspectives of New Music* 4/2 (Fall–Winter 1965): 1–13; reprinted in *The Writings of Elliott Carter,* ed. Else Stone and Kurt Stone (Bloomington: Indiana University Press, 1977), pp. 230–43.

6. See particularly *Expressionism as an International Literary Phenomenon,* ed. Ulrich Weisstein (Paris: Didier, and Budapest: Académiai Kiadó, 1973).

7. "Belief in technique as the only means of salvation would have to be suppressed, and the urge for truthfulness encouraged." Arnold Schoenberg, "Problems in Teaching Art" (1911), in *Style and Idea,* ed. Leonard Stein, trans. Leo Black (Berkeley and Los Angeles: University of California Press, 1984), p. 368.

8. Joseph Kerman, *Contemplating Music: Challenges to Musicology* (Cambridge: Harvard University Press, 1985), pp. 12, 18.

9. Hermand, p. 65.

10. For example, see the essays in the exhibition catalogue *The Spiritual in Art: Abstract Painting 1890–1945* (Los Angeles: Los Angeles County Museum of Art, and New York: Abbeville Press, 1986).

I. TWENTIETH-CENTURY EXPRESSIONISM

1. We use the lower case for terms which denote a tendency rather than a movement. We subscribe to the description of modernism as "not so much a movement as a sensibility or a mood that could give rise to movements of very different kinds" (Robert Wohl, Introduction, *The Lost Voices of World War I,* ed. Tim Cross [Lon-

don: Bloomsbury: 1988], p. 2). While Expressionism existed as a movement in German literary and visual arts, it never attained the self-awareness of a movement in music. We distinguish between the movement (Expressionism) and the more universal concept (expressionism), as does John Willett in *Expressionism* (New York: McGraw-Hill, 1970).

2. Arnold Schoenberg, letter to Wassily Kandinsky, 18 January 1911, in *Arnold Schoenberg/Wassily Kandinsky: Letters, Pictures and Documents,* ed. Jelena Hahl-Koch, trans. J. C. Crawford (London: Faber, 1984), p. 23. Emphasis Schoenberg's.

3. Bartók, letter to his early biographer, Denijs Dille, quoted in Israel Nestyev, "Prokofiev and Bartók: Some Parallels," in *International Music Conference in Commemoration of Béla Bartók 1971,* ed. J. Ujfalussy and J. Breuer (New York: Belwin Mills, 1972), p. 105.

4. Anton Webern, letter to Alban Berg, 12 July 1912, unpublished.

5. Charles Ives, letter to Henry Bellamann, in Bellamann, "Charles Ives: The Man and His Music," *Musical Quarterly* 19/1 (January 1933): 48.

6. Kasimir Edschmid, "Über den dichterisch Expressionismus," *Tribüne der Kunst und Zeit* I (1919): 39.

7. Herbert Read, *The Meaning of Art* (London: Faber, 1931, rev. 1972), p. 222.

8. Ibid., emphasis added.

9. Two publications which take an international view of expressionism are Richard Brinkmann, *Expressionismus: Internationale Forschung zu einem internationalen Phänomen* (Stuttgart: Metzler, 1980); and Ulrich Weisstein, ed., *Expressionism as an International Literary Phenomenon* (Paris: Didier, and Budapest: Académiai Kiadó, 1973).

10. Marit Werenskiold, *The Concept of Expressionism: Origin and Metamorphoses,* trans. Ronald Walford (Oslo: Universitetsforlaget, 1984), pp. 5–34. The Fauves (1904–1908) had an important influence on the early phase of German Expressionist art (see Jean Leymarie, *Fauves and Fauvism* [Geneva and New York: Skira/Rizzoli, 1987], pp. 85–100), and constitute the aspect of early French modernism with which Expressionist painters had the most in common.

11. Schoenberg, Breslau lecture on *Die glückliche Hand* (1928), in *Schoenberg/Kandinsky Letters,* p. 105.

12. Oswald Spengler, *The Decline of the West,* ed. Arthur Helps, trans. C. F. Atkinson (New York: Knopf, 1962), p. 59.

13. On the relationship between the ideas of Mahler and Adler, see William McGrath, *Dionysian Art and Populist Politics in Austria* (New Haven: Yale University Press, 1975).

14. H. H. Stuckenschmidt, *Arnold Schoenberg,* trans. Humphrey Searle (New York: Schirmer, 1978), pp. 29, 31, 34–35, 43.

15. Hans Moldenhauer and Rosaleen Moldenhauer, *Anton von Webern* (New York: Knopf, 1979), p. 137.

16. Ibid., p. 244.

17. Much of Ives's later life was spent promoting his idea that the majority should govern the country directly, without politicians standing between the people's vote and the instrument of government. For Ives's essays on these matters, see his *Essays Before a Sonata, The Majority, and Other Writings,* ed. Howard Boatwright (New York: Norton, 1961), pp. 137ff. Frank Rossiter, in *Charles Ives and His America* (New York: Liveright, 1946), discusses the social and economic factors which explain much of Ives's character and attitudes.

18. Wassily Kandinsky, *Concerning the Spiritual in Art,* trans. M. T. H Sadler (1911; reprint New York: Dover, 1977), pp. 12, 15.

19. *Schoenberg/Kandinsky Letters,* p. 25. Italics added.

20. Wassily Kandinsky used the term most frequently. See his "On the Question

of Form" in *The Blaue Reiter Almanac,* ed. W. Kandinsky and F. Marc, New Documentary edition, ed. Klaus Lankheit, trans. H. Falkenstein, M. Terzian, and G. Hinderlie (1912; reprint New York: Viking Press, 1974), p. 153.

21. See Lewis Wickes, "Schoenberg, *Erwartung,* and the Reception of Psychoanalysis in Musical Circles in Vienna until 1910/11," *Studies in Music* 23 (1989): 88–106.

22. Stefan Zweig, *The World of Yesterday* (New York: Viking Press, 1943), pp. 33–35, 69.

23. Robert Craft, *Present Perspectives* (New York: Knopf, 1982), p. 227.

24. See Carl E. Schorske, "Politics and Patricide in Freud's *Interpretation of Dreams,*" in *Fin-de-siècle Vienna: Politics and Culture* (New York: Knopf, 1980), p. 186; and Peter Gay, "How the Modern World Began," *Horizon* 15/2 (Spring 1973): 14.

25. Otto Weininger, *Sex and Character,* trans anon. (London: William Heineman, 1906), p. 85. Weininger, an anti-Semitic Jew who believed the Jewish race and culture was an embodiment of the "feminine-chaotic" principle, whereas the Aryan was the embodiment of the masculine-creative principle, committed suicide only a few months after the publication of his book. See Allan Janik and Stephen Toulmin, *Wittgenstein's Vienna* (New York: Simon & Schuster, 1973), pp. 71–74.

26. Bartók, letter to his mother, 10 September 1905, in Béla Bartók, *Letters,* ed. János Demény, trans. P. Balabán and I. Farkas, trans. revised by E. West and C. Mason (Budapest: Corvina, 1971), p. 53.

27. Willi Reich, *The Life and Work of Alban Berg,* trans. Cornelius Cardew (London: Thames & Hudson, 1965), p. 22. See also Donald Harris, "Berg and Frida Semler," *International Alban Berg Society Newsletter* 8 (Summer 1979): 11, and Mosco Carner, *Alban Berg: The Man and the Work* (London: Duckworth, 1975), pp. 6–7.

28. Stuckenschmidt, p. 94. Stuckenschmidt surmises that the marriage was perhaps under strain earlier, at the birth of Schoenberg's second child, Georg, in September 1906, because of "continual struggle with material circumstances and perpetual worries. Schoenberg kept [Mathilde] apart from his circle of friends; she did not accept invitations to Mahler's house and her name was not mentioned in Schoenberg's exchange of letters with Strauss. . . . Up to the time of his second marriage Schoenberg prevented third persons . . . even friends, from having a glimpse of his private life" (ibid., p. 88). Mathilde was the sister of Alexander Zemlinsky, Schoenberg's close friend and teacher.

29. Arnold Schoenberg, Berlin diary, 7 January 1912, cited in Joseph Rufer, *The Works of Arnold Schoenberg,* trans. Dika Newlin (London: Faber, 1962), p. 34. This attitude is remarkably similar to one expressed by Richard Wagner, who wrote, "What makes me love music so unutterably is that it keeps everything secret while it says the most unthinkable things; this makes it, literally, the only true art." Letter to Princess Karoline Wittgenstein, 12 April 1858, quoted in Friedrich Blume, *Classic and Romantic Music: A Comprehensive Survey,* trans. M. D. Herter Norton (New York: Norton, 1970), p. 117.

30. Theodor W. Adorno, *Philosophy of Modern Music,* trans. Anne Mitchell and Wesley Blomster (New York: Seabury, 1973), p. 46.

31. Bartók, letter to his mother, 10 September 1905, in *Letters,* p. 53.

32. Nietzsche carried Emerson's lectures with him when he traveled and annotated his copy. There are many reverberations of Emerson's thought in Nietzsche's, including reference to Zoroaster (Zarathustra is a variant spelling), the Gay Science (Nietzsche's *Die fröhliche Wissenschaft*), and the possible derivation of Nietzsche's *Übermensch* from Emerson's Oversoul. See Gay Wilson Allen, *Waldo Emerson* (New York: Viking, 1981), pp. 378, 469; also Walter Kaufmann's Introduction to his translation of Nietzsche's *The Gay Science* (New York: Random House, 1974), pp. 7–13.

The point is significant in relation to the similarity of many of Charles Ives's philosophical attitudes to those of expressionist composers of whom he had no knowledge when writing his music.

33. Bartók, letter to Irmy Jurkovics, 15 August 1905, in *Letters,* p. 50, emphasis Bartók's.

34. Nietzsche, *Thus Spake Zarathustra,* Collected Works, Vol. 11, ed. Oscar Levy (New York: Russell, 1964), p. 12.

35. *Schoenberg/Kandinsky Letters,* pp. 54–55.

36. Rudolf Steiner, *An Autobiography,* trans. Rita Stebbing (Blauvelt, NY: Rudolf Steiner Publications, 1977), pp. 294, 320. After deep study of Goethe's writings on natural science, then of Nietzsche's philosophy, and after several years' experience in the newly founded Theosophical Society in Vienna (1890) and in Berlin (1900–13), Steiner began around 1902 to develop Anthroposophy: "Knowledge produced by the higher self in man." From 1905 on, feeling an impending catastrophe, he traveled and lectured widely in Europe in an effort to heal the spiritual blindness of his generation. His contact with both Kandinsky and Kafka is documented. Schoenberg may have known Steiner in Berlin (1901–1902), as they frequented the same circle of intellectuals. See Hartmut Zelinsky, "Der 'Weg' der 'Blauen Reiter': zu Schönbergs Widmung an Kandinsky in die Harmonielehre," in *Arnold Schönberg/Wassily Kandinsky, Briefe, Bilder und Dokumente einer aussergewöhnlichen Begegnung,* ed. Jelena Hahl-Koch (Salzburg: Residenz, 1980), p. 234.

37. See Wilhelm Worringer, *Abstraction and Empathy: a Contribution to the Psychology of Style* (1908), trans. Michael Bullock (New York: International Universities Press, 1953). See also Worringer, *Form in Gothic* (1912), trans. Herbert Read (London: G. P. Putnam, 1927).

38. Some important members of this group were Ernst Ludwig Kirchner, Karl Schmidt-Rottluff, Erich Heckel, Max Pechstein, Otto Mueller, and (for a short period) Emil Nolde. The group was active in Dresden and Berlin between 1905 and 1913.

39. Members of *Der blaue Reiter* included Wassily Kandinsky, Franz Marc, Gabriele Münter, Alexei von Jawlensky, Marianne von Werefkin, and August Macke. These artists were not as tightly organized as those of *Die Brücke;* they emphasized the spiritual purposes of art and were active in Munich from 1911 until the outbreak of World War I.

40. Kokoschka moved to Berlin in 1910 and participated in expressionist activities around Herwarth Walden's journal *Der Sturm;* Schiele and Gerstl remained in Vienna and died tragically young. These Viennese artists worked as individuals.

41. Quoted in Peter Selz, *German Expressionist Painting* (Berkeley: University of California Press, 1957), p. 165.

42. Kandinsky, letter to Sir Michael Sadler, in Michael Sadler, *Modern Art and Revolution* (London: Hogarth, 1932), pp. 18–19.

43. Hermann Bahr, *Expressionismus* (Munich: Delphin, 1920), p. 84. This book was completed before World War I.

44. Bahr, quoted in Selz, p. 10.

45. Read, pp. 226–28.

46. Ibid.

47. A careful distinction must be made between expressionism and Abstract Expressionism, a term used only for painting. Abstract Expressionism combines the nonobjectivity of abstractionism (begun by Kandinsky) and the personal viewpoint of expressionism—both of these being fused by the post–World War II New York school of painters (Pollock, De Kooning, Tobey, and others), in order to arrive at a new vision.

48. *Schoenberg/Kandinsky Letters,* p. 23.

49. Arnold Schering, "Die expressionistiche Bewegung in der Musik," in *Zur Einführung in die Kunst der Gegenwart* (Leipzig: Seemann, 1919), pp. 139ff.

50. Arnold Schoenberg, "Franz Liszt's Work and Being," in *Style and Idea,* ed. Leonard Stein (Berkeley: University of California Press, 1984), p. 443.

51. Kandinsky, "On the Question of Form," *Blaue Reiter Almanac,* p. 149.

52. Arnold Schoenberg, Breslau lecture on *Die glückliche Hand, Schoenberg/ Kandinsky Letters,* p. 105. In his *Harmonielehre* (Vienna and Leipzig: Universal, 1911), p. 15, Schoenberg writes: "On the lowest level, art is simply imitation of nature. But soon it is nature imitation in the more extended meaning of the concept, not only imitation of outer, but also of inner nature. . . . On its highest level, art concerns itself exclusively with inner nature."

53. Ernst Stadler, "Form ist Wollust." Poem quoted in Weisstein, p. 32.

54. Schoenberg, Breslau lecture, in *Schoenberg/Kandinsky Letters,* p. 105.

55. Walter and Alexander Goehr, "Arnold Schoenberg's Development towards a Twelve-Note System," in *European Music in the Twentieth Century,* ed. Howard Hartog (London: Routledge and Kegan Paul, 1957), p. 87.

56. August Strindberg, Preface to *A Dream Play* in *Six Plays of Strindberg,* trans. Elizabeth Sprigge (New York: Doubleday, 1955), p. 193.

57. Hans Steffen, ed., *Der deutsche Expressionismus,* 2d ed. (Göttingen: Vanderhoeck and Ruprecht, 1970), p. 102. [All translations unless acknowledged, are by the present authors.]

58. For a discussion of musical prose, see Schoenberg's essay "Brahms the Progressive," in *Style and Idea,* pp. 411ff.

59. Anton Webern, *The Path to the New Music,* trans. Leo Black (London and Vienna: Universal, 1963), p. 55.

60. Theodor Däubler, *Der neue Standpunkt* (Leipzig: Insel, 1916), p. 179.

61. Henry-Louis de La Grange, *Mahler,* vol. 1 (New York: Doubleday, 1973), p. 55; and Natalie Bauer-Lechner, *Recollections of Gustav Mahler,* trans. Dika Newlin, ed. Peter Franklin (Cambridge: Cambridge University Press, 1980), pp. 155–56.

62. Adorno, p. 20. Unfortunately, a mistranslation at this point in the text obscures Adorno's original meaning.

63. Schoenberg, *Harmonielehre,* p. 484.

64. Charles Ives, *Memos,* ed. John Kirkpatrick (New York: Norton, 1972), p. 130.

65. Ibid., pp. 42, 44, 47, 49, 56, 120.

66. Luigi Rognoni, *The Second Vienna School: Expressionism and Dodecaphony,* trans. R. W. Mann (London: Calder, 1977), pp. 1, 4, and 43.

67. See Robert P. Morgan, "Secret Languages: The Roots of Musical Modernism," in *Modernism: Challenges and Perspectives,* ed. Monique Chefdor, Ricardo Quinones, and Albert Wachtel (Urbana: University of Illinois Press, 1986), p. 33.

68. Schering, p. 145.

69. Allen Edwards, *Flawed Words and Stubborn Sounds: A Conversation With Elliott Carter* (New York: Norton, 1971), p. 84.

70. Jan Maegaard, "Some Formal Devices in Expressionistic Works," *Dansk Aarbog for Musik Forsning* (1961): 75.

71. Schoenberg, "Problems in Teaching Art," in *Style and Idea,* pp. 367–69.

2 . FORERUNNERS I: WAGNER AND STRAUSS

1. H. H. Stuckenschmidt, *Schoenberg: His Life, World, and Work,* trans. Humphrey Searle (New York: Schirmer Books, 1978), p. 33.

2. Thomas Mann, "Suffering and Greatness of Richard Wagner," in *Essays of Three Decades,* trans. H. T. Lowe-Porter (New York: Knopf, 1947), p. 348.

3. Richard Wagner, "Opera and Drama" (1851), Pt. III, in *Richard Wagner's Prose Works,* trans. William Ashton Ellis (New York: Broude Brothers, [1966]), vol. 2, p. 350.

4. Ibid., p. 356. Wagner does not employ the term in this essay, however.

5. Wagner, "The Music of the Future" (1860), *Prose Works*, vol. 3, pp. 328–29.

6. Wagner, "Opera and Drama," Pt. II, pp. 205–206.

7. Ibid., pp. 224–27.

8. Wagner, "The Destiny of Opera" (1871), *Prose Works*, vol. 3, pp. 149–50.

9. "Opera and Drama," Pt. III, pp. 335–47.

10. Wagner, "Beethoven" (1870), *Prose Works*, vol. 5, p. 103.

11. Ibid., p. 95. Wagner paraphrases Schopenhauer here. Cf. Arthur Schopenhauer, *The World As Will and Representation*, vol. 1, trans. E. F. J. Payne (Indian Hills, CO: Falcon's Wing, 1958), p. 260.

12. Wagner, "Beethoven," p. 96.

13. Jack M. Stein, *Richard Wagner and the Synthesis of the Arts* (Detroit: Wayne State University Press, 1960), p. 170.

14. Particularly in "A Pilgrimage to Beethoven" (1840), *Prose Works*, vol. 7, p. 21; "Beethoven," vol. 5, p. 57; and "The Destiny of Opera," vol. 5, p. 127.

15. Wagner, "A Pilgrimage to Beethoven," p. 42.

16. Stein, pp. 131–32.

17. Theodor Adorno, *Versuch über Wagner* (Berlin: Suhrkamp, 1952), p. 198.

18. From a letter to Mathilde Wesendonck, in *Richard Wagner an Mathilde Wesendonck*, 2d ed., ed. Wolfgang Golter (Berlin: Duncker, 1904), p. 144.

19. *Parsifal*, piano-vocal score (Mainz: Schott, 1911), stage direction on p. 124.

20. "Beethoven," p. 69. Wagner here follows Schopenhauer in arguing that music, like dreams, is the direct expression of "inward-facing consciousness." See "Beethoven," p. 68.

21. Mann, p. 313.

22. Beethoven, Op. 130/I, beginning of development; Op. 131/III; and particularly the opening section of the last movement of the Ninth Symphony.

23. Theodor Adorno, "Zur Partitur des 'Parsifals,' " in *Moments musicaux* (Frankfurt: Suhrkamp, 1964), p. 55.

24. Rollo Myers, ed., *Romain Rolland/Richard Strauss Correspondence* (Berkeley and Los Angeles: University of California Press, 1968), p. 126.

25. Ibid., p. 190.

26. Richard Strauss, *Recollections and Reflections*, ed. Willi Schuh (London and New York: Boosey & Hawkes, 1973), p. 156.

27. See the chapter on Strauss in Barbara Tuchman, *The Proud Tower: A Portrait of the World before the War* (New York: Macmillan, 1966), p. 340.

28. *Rolland/Strauss Correspondence*, pp. 139, 112.

29. Mario Praz, *The Romantic Agony*, trans. Angus Davidson, 2d ed. (London and New York: Oxford University Press, 1951), p. 158.

30. Strauss, *Recollections*, p. 156.

31. Ibid.

32. Ibid. For an example of Strauss's dramatic use of bitonality, see *Salome*, piano-vocal score (Berlin and Paris: Fürstner, 1905), mm. 2–6 of [215].

33. Strauss, letter to his wife, 17 May 1906, in *Der Strom der Töne trug mich fort: Die Welt um Richard Strauss in Briefen*, ed. Franz Grasberger (Tutzing: Schneider, 1967), p. 169. Schoenberg and Zemlinsky also attended this first performance in Austria (Stuckenschmidt, p. 67).

34. Willi Reich, "Aus Alban Bergs Jugendzeit," *Melos* 22/2 (February 1955): 37.

35. Lewis Wickes, "Schoenberg, *Erwartung*, and the Reception of Psychoanalysis in Vienna until 1910/1911," *Studies in Music* 23 (1989): 95.

36. D. J. Bach, "*Elektra* von Richard Strauss," *Arbeiter-Zeitung* (Vienna) 21/85 (20 March 1909): 1–2, as quoted in Wickes, "Schoenberg, *Erwartung*," pp. 97–98 and nn. 72, 73, 74.

37. Norman Del Mar, *Richard Strauss* (New York: Free Press of Glencoe, 1962), vol. 1, p. 290.

38. Strauss, *Recollections,* p. 155.

39. Ibid.

40. Eric Salzman, *Twentieth-Century Music: An Introduction,* 2d ed. (Englewood Cliffs, NJ: Prentice-Hall, 1974), p. 11.

41. See, however, Salzman, ibid., pp. 10–11, 94–96; Donald Mitchell, *The Language of Modern music,* 2d ed. (London: Faber, 1966), pp. 29ff.; and Allen Edwards, *Flawed Words and Stubborn Sounds: A Conversation with Elliott Carter* (New York: Norton, 1971), p. 84.

42. After the first Milan performance of *Rosenkavalier* Italian Futurists demonstrated against Strauss's "debasement" of his previous progressive stance (see Strauss, *Recollections,* p. 159).

43. Stuckenschmidt, pp. 61–76.

44. Ibid., p. 73.

3 . FORERUNNERS II: MAHLER AND SCRIABIN

1. Henry-Louis de La Grange, *Mahler,* vol. 1 (New York: Doubleday, 1973), pp. 51, 72. The breadth of Mahler's education resembles Webern's.

2. Ibid., pp. 58, 64.

3. Gustav Mahler, *Selected Letters,* ed. Knut Martner, trans. Eithne Wilkins, Ernst Kaiser, and Bill Hopkins (London: Faber, 1979), p. 233.

4. Ibid., p. 329.

5. La Grange, pp. 741–42. Mahler had previously adapted a story by Ludwig Bechstein to serve as the text for his *Das klagende Lied* (ibid., p. 52).

6. Mahler, *Selected Letters,* p. 212.

7. Ibid.

8. La Grange, p. 791.

9. Gustav Mahler, Symphony No. 2/V, [39]. This music is anticipated instrumentally at [7] and [21].

10. Natalie Bauer-Lechner, *Recollections of Gustav Mahler,* trans. Dika Newlin, ed. Peter Franklin (Cambridge: Cambridge University Press, 1980), p. 32.

11. Ibid., p. 34.

12. Ibid., p. 174.

13. Mahler, *Selected Letters,* p. 233.

14. Bauer-Lechner, p. 130.

15. Mahler, *Selected Letters,* p. 179.

16. Ibid., p. 54; letter to Josef Steiner dated 17 June 1879.

17. La Grange, p. 169. Strauss perceived Mahler's conducting as deriving from Wagnerian tradition, since Wagner's conducting had been marked by similar traits.

18. Bauer-Lechner, p. 173.

19. La Grange, p. 749.

20. Ibid., p. 21.

21. Bauer-Lechner, p. 173.

22. Mahler, *Selected Letters,* pp. 193, 206.

23. Theodor Adorno, *Mahler: Eine musikalische Physiognomik* (Frankfurt: Suhrkamp, 1960), p. 14.

24. La Grange, pp. 784–85.

25. La Grange, program notes for Los Angeles Philharmonic performances of Mahler's Eighth Symphony, 29 and 30 April and 1 May 1976.

26. Josef Rufer, *The Works of Arnold Schoenberg,* trans. Dika Newlin (London: Faber, 1962), pp. 115–16.

27. Quoted by Karl Heinz Füssl in his Foreword to the Eighth Symphony (Mahler, *Sämtliche Werke*, vol. 8 [Vienna: Universal, 1977]).

28. Mahler, *Selected Letters*, p. 294.

29. Füssl, Foreword to the Eighth Symphony.

30. Paul Bekker, *Gustav Mahlers Symphonien* (Berlin: Schuster and Loeffler, 1921), p. 271.

31. La Grange, *Mahler*, p. 803.

32. Mahler, *Selected Letters*, p. 212.

33. Bauer-Lechner, pp. 155–56.

34. Kurt Blaukopf, *Gustav Mahler*, trans. Inge Goodwin (New York: Praeger, 1973), p. 181; and Dieter Schnebel, "Das Spätwerk als Neue Musik," in Arnold Schönberg et al., *Gustav Mahler* (Tübingen: Wunderlich, 1966), p. 164.

35. Mahler, letter to Bruno Walter, summer 1904 (*Selected Letters*, p. 279).

36. Ibid., p. 179.

37. Mahler, letter to Max Kalbeck, January 1902 (ibid., p. 262).

38. Alma Mahler, *Gustav Mahler: Memories and Letters*, ed. Donald Mitchell, trans. Basil Creighton (Seattle: University of Washington Press, 1975), pp. 70, 100.

39. Erwin Ratz, *Revisionsbericht* of Sixth Symphony, in Mahler, *Sämtliche Werke*, vol. 6 (Lindau: Kahnt, 1963).

40. Alma Mahler, p. 122.

41. Bauer-Lechner, p. 173.

42. Adorno, p. 96.

43. Erwin Ratz, "Zum Formproblem," in Schönberg et al., p. 112.

44. Arnold Schoenberg, "Gustav Mahler," in *Style and Idea*, ed. Leonard Stein, trans. Leo Black (Berkeley and Los Angeles: University of California Press, 1984), p. 463.

45. Webern's Symphony, Op. 21 (1928), belongs to a later period.

46. Hans Redlich, *Alban Berg* (Vienna: Universal, 1957), p. 94.

47. Alban Berg, *Letters to his Wife*, ed. and trans. Bernard Grun (New York: St. Martin's Press, 1971), pp. 147–48.

48. Dika Newlin, *Bruckner, Mahler, Schoenberg*, 2d rev. ed. (New York: Norton, 1978), pp. 198–99.

49. See John C. Crawford, "The Relationship of Text and Music in the Vocal Works of Arnold Schoenberg, 1908–1924," Ph.D. diss., Harvard University, 1963, pp. 104–105.

50. Ibid., pp. 34–36.

51. Blaukopf, p. 237; and Hans Mersmann, "Gustav Mahlers 'Lied von der Erde,' " *Melos* 2/7 (1 May 1921): 56.

52. Hermann Scherchen, "Das neue Führertum in der Musik," *Die Erhebung*, ed. Alfred Wolfenstein (Berlin: Fischer, 1920), vol. 2, pp. 265–67. Although Scherchen greatly admired Schoenberg and was later to conduct important performances of his music, he writes that Schoenberg's "visions and creations belong to the far future" (p. 269).

53. Bekker, p. 167.

54. Scriabin, quoted in William W. Austin, *Music in the 20th Century* (New York: Norton, 1966), p. 72.

55. Faubion Bowers, *The New Scriabin: Enigmas and Answers* (New York: St. Martin's Press, 1983), p. 51. On the basis of his contact with and inspiration from Scriabin, Pasternak decided himself to become a composer—and later changed his mind.

56. Martin Cooper, *Ideas and Music* (London: Barrie and Rockliff, 1965), p. 127.

57. Faubion Bowers, *Scriabin: A Biography of the Russian Composer*, (Tokyo and Palo Alto: Kodansha International, 1969), vol. 2, p. 240.

58. Bowers, *New Scriabin*, p. 52.

59. For a detailed account of the sources of Scriabin's doctrine, see Manfred Kelkel, *Alexandre Scriabine: Sa vie, l'ésoterisme et le langage musical dans son oeuvre* (Paris: Honoré Champion, 1978), bk. 2, pp. 1–72.

60. Bowers, *Scriabin*, vol. 2, pp. 54, 61, 63.

61. Arnold Schoenberg, *Harmonielehre* (Vienna and Leipzig: Universal, 1911), p. 364.

62. English translation in Bowers, *Scriabin*, vol. 2, pp. 131–35.

63. Ibid., p. 107.

64. Kelkel, bk. 2, pp. 22, 27.

65. Bowers, *Scriabin*, vol. 2, p. 205.

66. Ibid., pp. 206–208.

67. Sabaneiev program notes, ibid., p. 208.

68. Bowers, *New Scriabin*, p. 111. See mm. 3–4 of [3], piano part.

69. For examples, see Kelkel, bk. 3, p. 77.

70. George Perle, *Serial Composition and Atonality: An Introduction to the Music of Schoenberg, Berg, and Webern*, 6th ed., rev. (Berkeley, Los Angeles, and Oxford: University of California Press, 1991), p. 41.

71. Bowers, *New Scriabin*, pp. 206–208.

72. Ibid., p. 135.

73. Ibid., p. 107.

74. Rollo H. Myers, "Scriabin: A Reassessment," *The Musical Times* 1367 (January 1957): 17.

75. Vera Stravinsky and Robert Craft, *Stravinsky in Pictures and Documents* (New York: Simon and Schuster, 1978), p. 62.

76. Ibid., pp. 29, 605 nn. 49 and 51.

77. For Scriabin's influence on Berg, see James Marshall Baker, "Alexander Scriabin: The Transition from Tonality to Atonality," Ph.D. diss., Yale University, 1977, vol. 1, p. 53; vol. 2, p. 472.

78. H. H. Stuckenschmidt, *Schoenberg: His Life, World, and Work*, trans. Humphrey Searle (New York: Schirmer Books, 1978), p. 254.

79. Allen Edwards, *Flawed Words and Stubborn Sounds: A Conversation with Elliott Carter* (New York: Norton, 1971), p. 40.

4 . ARNOLD SCHOENBERG

1. Arnold Schoenberg, program note to a performance of his works in Vienna, 14 January 1910. Cited in Willi Reich, *Arnold Schoenberg: A Critical Biography*, trans. Leo Black (New York: Praeger, 1971), p. 49.

2. Ibid., pp. 56–57.

3. *Jakobsleiter* dates from Jan Maegaard, *Studien zur Entwicklung der dodekaphonen Satzes bei Arnold Schönberg*, vol. 1 (Copenhagen: Hansen, 1972), p. 91.

4. Arnold Schoenberg, "Problems in Teaching Art" (1911), in *Style and Idea*, ed. Leonard Stein, trans. Leo Black (Berkeley: University of California Press, 1984), p. 365.

5. Arnold Schoenberg, *Harmonielehre* (Leipzig and Vienna: Universal, 1911), p. 15.

6. Ibid., p. 466.

7. Schoenberg, letter to Busoni, 24 August 1909. In Antony Beaumont, trans. and ed., *Ferruccio Busoni: Selected Letters* (London and Boston: Faber, 1987), p. 396.

8. H. H. Stuckenschmidt, *Schoenberg: His Life, World and Work*, trans. Humphrey Searle (New York: Schirmer Books, 1978), pp. 16, 18.

9. Ibid., p. 22.

10. Information from Nuria Schoenberg Nono, July 1988.

11. Carl E. Schorske, *Fin-de-siècle Vienna: Politics and Culture* (New York: Knopf, 1980), pp. 119–20.

12. Henry de La Grange, *Mahler* (New York: Doubleday, 1973), p. 411.

13. Stuckenschmidt, p. 34.

14. Schorske, p. 299.

15. Ibid., p. xxix.

16. Gertrud Pott, *Die Spiegelung des Sezessionismus im Österreichischen Theater* (Vienna: Braumüller, 1975), p. 169.

17. Schoenberg, letter to Kokoschka, 3 July 1946, Library of Congress, unpublished.

18. Stuckenschmidt, p. 31; and Max Graf, "Das Wiener Café Grössenwahn," *Neues Öesterreich* (11 February 1951): 1.

19. By 1913 Schoenberg's library included Kant, Schopenhauer, Bergson, Nietzsche, and Plato as well as Balzac, Dehmel, Rilke, Kraus, Stefan George, Hauptmann, Maeterlinck, and 28 volumes of Strindberg (Stuckenschmidt, p. 183).

20. Allan Janik and Stephen Toulmin, *Wittgenstein's Vienna* (New York: Simon and Schuster, 1973), p. 102.

21. Schorske, p. 344.

22. Paul Stefan, *Das Grab in Wien: Eine Chronik 1903–1911* (Berlin: Reiss, 1913), p. 122.

23. Paul Stefan, "Wie es früher bei Schönberg-Abenden zuging," *Der Ruf* 4 (May 1913): 22.

24. Stuckenschmidt, p. 94.

25. Jan Meyerowitz, *Arnold Schönberg* (Berlin: Colloquium, 1967), p. 15.

26. Schoenberg, "Testamentsentwurf" (unpublished), Schoenberg Archive, Arnold Schoenberg Institute, Los Angeles. Short excerpt in English translation in Jane Kallir, *Arnold Schoenberg's Vienna* (New York: Galerie St. Etienne/Rizzoli, 1984), p. 28.

27. Will Grohmann, *Kandinsky* (New York: Abrams, [n.d.]), p. 52.

28. Stuckenschmidt, pp. 31, 33.

29. Interview with Schoenberg by Paul Wilhelm, *Neues Wiener Journal,* 10 January 1909. Reprinted in *Arnold Schönberg Gesammelte Schriften,* vol. 1, ed. Ivan Vojtech (Frankfurt: Fischer, 1976), p. 157.

30. Alma Mahler, *Gustav Mahler: Memories and Letters,* ed. Donald Mitchell, trans. Basil Creighton (Seattle: University of Washington Press, 1975), pp. 256–57. This passage shows Schoenberg's unconscious tendency to describe himself when writing about other composers he admires—a tendency which is particularly apparent in his 1912 Mahler lecture (Schoenberg, *Style and Idea,* p. 449).

31. The third movement ("Litanei") was finished on 11 July 1908, the second (Scherzo) on 27 July 1908. Josef Rufer, *The Works of Arnold Schoenberg* (London: Faber, 1962), pp. 29, 126.

32. The appearance of the tune "Ach, du lieber Augustin" in Schoenberg's sketches as early as the fall of 1907 suggests that his marriage had been failing for some time before his wife left in the summer of 1908. See Albrecht Dümling, *Die fremden Klänge der hängenden Gärten: Die öffentliche Einsamkeit am Beispiel von Arnold Schönberg und Stefan George* (Munich: Kindler, 1981), p. 161.

33. Stuckenschmidt, p. 116.

34. Stefan George, "Entrückung" (Rapture), trans. the authors.

35. George, "Entrückung," in his *Works,* 2d. rev. ed., trans. Olga Marx and Ernst Morwitz (Chapel Hill: University of North Carolina Press, 1974), p. 269.

36. Schoenberg, "Analysis of the Four Orchestral Songs, Op. 22," trans. Claudio Spies, in *Perspectives of Schoenberg and Stravinsky,* rev. ed., ed. Benjamin Boretz and Edward T. Cone (New York: Norton, 1972), p. 27.

37. Quoted in Anton Webern, "Schönbergs Musik," in Alban Berg et al., *Arnold Schönberg* (Munich: Piper, 1912), p. 40.

38. Dümling, pp. 83–96.

39. Maegaard, vol. 1, p. 64.

40. Rufer, pp. 34–35.

41. Schoenberg, "The Relationship to the Text" (1912), in *Style and Idea*, p. 144.

42. Webern, p. 43.

43. Schoenberg, *Harmonielehre*, p. 471.

44. This type of *Klangfarbenmelodie,* in which fragments of a pitched melody pass from one instrument to another, has become the more widely accepted application of the term.

45. Arnold Schoenberg, *Berliner Tagebuch,* ed. Josef Rufer (Frankfurt: Propyläen, 1974), p. 11.

46. Schoenberg, "My Evolution" (1948), in *Style and Idea*, p. 79.

47. Schoenberg, in an undated letter to Busoni (probably 27 or 28 August 1909), states: "The librettist (a lady), acting on my suggestions, has conceived and formulated everything just as I envisaged it." (Beaumont, p. 399.)

48. *Arnold Schönberg Gedenkausstellung 1974,* ed. Ernst Hilmar (Vienna: Universal, 1974), p. 203; and Lewis Wickes, "Schoenberg, *Erwartung,* and the Reception of Psychoanalysis in Musical Circles in Vienna until 1910/11," *Studies in Music* 23 (1989): 96 and nn. 65 and 66.

49. Egon Wellesz, *Arnold Schoenberg,* trans. W. H. Kerridge (London: Dent, 1925), p. 28.

50. See above, p. 18 and n. 60.

51. Webern, pp. 45–46.

52. Rufer, *Works of Schoenberg,* p. 34.

53. Schoenberg, letter to Busoni, undated, but probably 13 or 18 August 1909 (Beaumont, p. 389).

54. Schoenberg, letter to Kandinsky, 24 January 1911, in *Arnold Schoenberg/Wassily Kandinsky: Letters, Pictures and Documents,* ed. Jelena Hahl, trans. John C. Crawford (London: Faber, 1984), p. 23.

55. Schoenberg, "Composition with Twelve Tones (I)," in *Style and Idea*, pp. 217–18.

56. Recent scholars have achieved good analytical results by taking the text of *Erwartung* as their point of departure. See particularly Siegfried Mauser, *Das expressionistische Musiktheater der Wiener Schule* (Regensberg: Bosse, 1982), pp. 20–201.

57. Climaxes: (1) mm. 110–12; (2) mm. 153–57; (3) mm. 190–93; (4) mm. 347–48; (5) mm. 415–16; (6) m. 424.

58. At mm. 158, 193, and 348.

59. See mm. 110–12.

60. Lyric sections: (1) mm. 5–10; (2) mm. 19–22; (3) mm. 50–68; (4) mm. 97–100; (5) mm. 231–53, 257–73; (6) mm. 350–410.

61. The relationship is a serial one: motive c. is the retrograde inversion of motive b., and motive a. can be derived from motive c. by reversing the order of the first two notes.

62. These words were also important symbols to early expressionist poets and playwrights. In Kokoschka's play *Der brennende Dornbusch* (The Burning Thornbush, 1911) moonlight appears as a symbol of feminine sexuality, while blood takes on significance as a symbol of human vitality in this play and in *Mörder, Hoffnung der Frauen.*

63. Berg, *Wozzeck,* III, 4, mm. 302–305.

64. See above, p. 35 and Ex. 2–11.

65. M. 352; see also mm. 296–97.

66. Theodor W. Adorno, *Philosophy of Modern Music,* trans. Anne Mitchell and Wesley Blomster (New York: Seabury, 1973), p. 42.

67. *The Berg-Schoenberg Correspondence: Selected Letters,* ed. Juliane Brand, Christopher Hailey, and Donald Harris (New York and London: Norton, 1987), p. 11 n.; and Stuckenschmidt, pp. 139–44.

68. Alma Mahler-Werfel, *Mein Leben* (Frankfurt: Fischer, 1963), p. 66.

69. Rufer, *Works of Schoenberg,* p. 154.

70. The full score was completed on 18 November 1913 (ibid., p. 37).

71. Reinhard Johannes Sorge's *Der Bettler* (The Beggar), usually accepted as the earliest "Ich-Drama," did not appear until 1911.

72. Schoenberg, "New Music: My Music," in *Style and Idea,* p. 105.

73. Schoenberg, letter to Emil Hertzka (ca. 1913), in *Arnold Schoenberg Letters,* ed. Erwin Stein, trans. Eithne Wilkins and Ernst Kaiser (Berkeley and Los Angeles: University of California Press, 1987), pp. 43–45.

74. Stravinsky, who heard a rehearsal of *Pierrot* in 1912, criticized the aesthetics of the work as a "retrogression to the out-of-date Beardsley cult." (Igor Stravinsky, *Autobiography* (New York: Simon and Schuster, 1936), p. 67.

75. Schoenberg, *Berliner Tagebuch,* p. 34.

76. Religious themes were also important to expressionist visual aritists at this time. See, for example, Max Pechstein's twelve woodcuts *Das Vater Unser* (The Lord's Prayer), 1921.

77. Schoenberg, letter to Kandinsky, 20 July 1922 (*Schoenberg Letters,* pp. 70–71).

78. Schoenberg, *Die glückliche Hand,* full score (Vienna: Universal, 1917) pp. 3–4.

79. Hans Redlich, *Alban Berg: The Man and His Music* (New York: Abelard-Schumann, 1957), pp. 65–66; Hans Moldenhauer and Rosaleen Moldenhauer, *Anton von Webern* (New York: Knopf, 1979), p. 140.

80. Kandinsky had had conversations with Rudolf Steiner and had attended the latter's lectures in Munich. See Karl H. Wörner, *Die Musik in der Geistesgeschichte: Studien zur Situation der Jahre um 1910* (Bonn: Bouvier, 1970), p. 181.

81. Schoenberg, letter to Richard Dehmel, December 1912 (*Schoenberg Letters,* p. 36).

82. Webern, letter to Berg, 27 June 1912, unpublished.

83. Schoenberg, letter to Dehmel, 13 December 1912 (*Schoenberg Letters,* p. 35).

84. For Schoenberg's plan for this symphony, see Rufer, *Works of Schoenberg,* pp. 115–16.

85. Ibid., p. 153. The text of *Die Jakobsleiter* is given in Arnold Schoenberg, *Texte* (Vienna: Universal, 1926), pp. 39–65.

86. Jean M. Christensen, "Arnold Schoenberg's Oratorio 'Die Jakobsleiter'," Ph.D. diss., UCLA, 1979, vol. 1, p. 53.

87. Schoenberg, *Die Jakobsleiter,* in *Texte,* p. 45.

88. Ibid., p. 62. This is an idea taken from Emanuel Swedenborg, by way of Balzac's *Séraphîta,* which Schoenberg acknowledges as the source in his published text.

89. Wörner, p. 199.

90. Part I of the work is completed in *particell* (short score) form, with indications of instrumentation, but there are only scattered sketches for Part II. Part I has been published in an orchestral score and a piano reduction, both prepared by Schoenberg's pupil Winfried Zillig. Full score: Schoenberg, *Die Jakobsleiter: Oratorium für Soli, gemischten Chöre und Orchester* (Vienna: Universal, 1980); piano-vocal score: *Die Jakobsleiter* (Los Angeles: Belmont, 1974).

91. Reich, p. 112.

92. Schoenberg, "My Evolution," in *Style and Idea*, pp. 89–90.

93. Schoenberg, "Composing with Twelve Tones" (I), ibid., p. 223. See also Anthony Payne, "Schoenberg's *Jacob's Ladder*," *Tempo* 75 (Winter 1965–66): 21–22.

94. Karl Kraus, *Die letzten Tage der Menschheit* (Vienna: Verlag "Die Fackel," 1918–19).

95. *Die Jakobsleiter*, piano-vocal score, p. 136.

96. Christensen, vol. 1, p. xvi.

97. Schoenberg, *Style and Idea*, p. 464.

5 . ANTON WEBERN

1. Theodor W. Adorno, "Berg and Webern—Schoenberg's Heirs," *Modern Music* 8 (January–February 1931): 31. In an article on the occasion of the first performance of Webern's Five Pieces for Orchestra, Op. 10, in Zürich, Adorno further states: "Like almost no other, Webern's music corresponds to the demands of expressionism. Without permitting the question of its valid objectivity, it is satisfied with the pure presentation of the subjective which cannot be divorced from musical material." In *Anbruch* 6 (1926), quoted in Friedrich Wildgans, *Anton Webern*, trans. E. T. Roberts and H. Searle (London: Calder, 1966), pp. 166–67.

2. Webern, letter to Berg, 12 July 1912, unpublished. We are indebted to Maria Halbich-Webern for permission to quote from her father's unpublished letters to Berg and Schoenberg.

3. Ibid., and letters to Schoenberg, 10 and 30 August 1910, partly quoted in Hans Moldenhauer and Rosaleen Moldenhauer, *Anton von Webern: A Chronicle of His Life and Work* (New York: Knopf, 1979), pp. 132–33, 709.

4. Moldenhauer and Moldenhauer, p. 190.

5. See Walter Kolneder, *Anton Webern: An Introduction to His Works*, trans. Humphrey Searle (London: Faber, 1968), p. 83. See also Webern's correspondence with Schoenberg in Moldenhauer and Moldenhauer, chap. XII.

6. Webern, letter to Schoenberg, 23 June 1910, in Moldenhauer and Moldenhauer, p. 113.

7. Webern, letter to Schoenberg, 23 July 1912, Library of Congress. This remark parallels Ives's attitude, expressed in a letter to Elliott Carter, 12 June 1944, that "Art = Philosophy." Reproduced in Vivian Perlis, *Charles Ives Remembered* (New Haven: Yale University Press, 1974), pp. 140–41.

8. Moldenhauer and Moldenhauer, p. 31.

9. *Anton Webern Festschrift*, ed. Ernst Hilmar (Vienna: Universal, 1983), p. 60.

10. Webern, letter to Berg, 19 July 1912, quoted in Moldenhauer and Moldenhauer, p. 162.

11. Webern, "Der Lehrer," in Alban Berg et al., *Arnold Schönberg* (Munich: Piper, 1912), p. 86.

12. Webern, "Schönbergs Musik," ibid., p. 22.

13. Arnold Schoenberg, *Harmonielehre* (Vienna and Leipzig: Universal, 1911), p. 466.

14. Arnold Schoenberg, "How One Becomes Lonely" (1937), in *Style and Idea* ed. Leonard Stein, trans. Leo Black (Berkeley: University of California Press, 1984), p. 41.

15. Erwin Stein, "Anton Webern," *Musical Times* 87 (January 1946): 14–15. Arnold Elston, a student of Webern's, told composer Leon Kirchner that Webern's playing of his own music was so passionate—accompanied with anguished breathing, sighs, etc.—that it was embarrassing to be present. (Authors' conversation with Leon Kirchner, Cambridge, MA, March 1981.) Otto Klemperer confessed to Webern that he had difficulty approaching his music, whereupon Webern played some for him. "He played with enormous intensity and fanaticism. Passionately! When he had fin-

ished, I said, 'You know, I cannot conduct it that way. I'm simply not able to bring that enormous intensity to your music. I must do as well as I can.' " From *Conversations With Klemperer*, ed. Peter Heyworth (London: Faber, 1973), p. 94. But since 1945, Webern's art has been characterized by the avant-garde as "almost passionless." See Reginald Smith Brindle, *The New Music: The Avant-Garde since 1945*, 2d ed. (Oxford and New York: Oxford University Press, 1987), p. 6.

16. Eugene Lehner, interview with the authors, 4 August 1987, Tyringham MA,; see Dorothy L. Crawford, "An Interview With Eugene Lehner," *Journal of the Arnold Schoenberg Institute* 12/1 (June 1989): 49–50. Theodor Adorno remembered that he and Berg "once concocted a Webern parody, consisting of a single quarter-note rest under a quintuplet bracket and garnished with every conceivable symbol and performance notation, which to top it off, was then to fade away." Theodor W. Adorno, *Alban Berg: Master of the Smallest Link*, trans. J. Brand and C. Hailey (Cambridge: Cambridge University Press, 1991), p. 27.

17. Webern, letter to Berg, 29 March 1912, unpublished.

18. Hans Swarowsky, *Wahrung der Gestalt*, ed. Manfred Huss (Vienna: Universal, 1979), p. 231.

19. Felix Greissle lecture, 20 August 1959, Princeton University.

20. Swarowsky, p. 228.

21. Ibid., p. 236.

22. Webern, letter to Schoenberg, 24 May 1911, unpublished, Library of Congress.

23. Webern, letter to Schoenberg, 11 December 1913, quoted in Moldenhauer and Moldenhauer, p. 183.

24. *Anton Webern: Weg und Gestalt in Selbstzeugnissen und Worten der Freunde*, ed. Willi Reich (Zurich: Arche, 1961), pp. 15–17. While at the University of Vienna, Webern attended rehearsals of Mahler's Third, Fifth, and Sixth symphonies and played the Third on the piano with Egon Wellesz before its performance in 1904.

25. Heinrich Isaac, *Choralis Constantinus II*, ed. Webern, in *Denkmäler der Tonkunst in Österreich* 16/32 (Graz: Akademische Druck und Verlagsanstalt, 1959): vii–xii. Webern's introduction is partially reprinted, trans. Leo Black, in *Die Reihe 2: Anton Webern* (London: Universal, 1975), pp. 23–25.

26. Stefan George, *Der siebente Ring* (1907), translation the authors'. The outpouring of emotion in these poems was inspired by Maximin, George's ideal of spiritual grace,who died in 1904, one day after his sixteenth birthday. Many people were shocked when the poems were first published.

27. This speechlike vocal declamation is undoubtedly influenced by Debussy's *Pelléas et Mélisande*, which Webern had heard in Berlin in 1908. He returned for a second performance and wrote to Schoenberg, "O God, I cannot express how beautiful it was. I have surrendered unreservedly to this impression." Webern, letter to Schoenberg, 6 December 1908, in Moldenhauer and Moldenhauer, p. 104.

28. Webern's process of composing with tonal references in this period, then rejecting them when readying his songs for publication, is documented in several of the George songs by Reinhold Brinkmann, who found this "liquidation of the fundamental tones" in the manuscripts of Op. 3/I, III, and V. Brinkmann, "Die George-Lieder 1908/09 und 1919/23—ein Kapitel Webern-Philologie," in *Beiträge der Österreichischen Gesellschaft für Musik 1972/73*: 40–50.

29. See Moldenhauer and Moldenhauer, pp. 266, 269, 585. Edward Steuermann commented: "Present Webern performances are much too rigid. Webern himself was the freest interpreter of his own music that could be imagined." (Gunther Schuller, "Conversation with Steuermann," *Perspectives of New Music* 3 [Fall/Winter 1964]: 22–34.)

30. Webern wrote to Schoenberg of his need to express in his works his growing

grief for his mother's death on 17 July 1912, only a few days after his similar letter to Berg.

31. Arnold Schoenberg, "Anton Webern: *Klangfarbenmelodie,*" in *Style and Idea,* ed. Leonard Stein, trans. Leo Black (Berkeley: University of California Press, 1984), pp. 484–85; see also H. H. Stuckenschmidt, *Arnold Schoenberg: His Life, World and Work,* trans. Humphrey Searle (New York: Schirmer Books, 1977), p. 442, for Schoenberg's chronological notes about Webern's desire to surpass his teacher by exaggerating everything Schoenberg was doing.

32. Anton Webern, *The Path to the New Music,* ed. Willi Reich, trans. Leo Black (London: Universal, 1975), p. 54.

33. Schoenberg, letter to Busoni, undated, but probably 13 or 18 August 1909, in Antony Beaumont, trans. and ed., *Ferruccio Busoni: Selected Letters* (London and Boston: Faber, 1987), p. 389. In his *Harmonielehre,* written in 1911, Schoenberg commented on the "gasping" chords in mm. 5 and 6 of Webern's Op. 5/I: "Why this [harmony] is so and why it is right I cannot say in detail at present. In general it appears natural to anyone who accepts my view of the nature of dissonance. But I believe firmly that it is right, and a number of others believe this too. It seems that the chromatic scale could be made responsible for the sequence of chords. The chords are mostly in such a relation that the second one contains as many notes as possible which are chromatic heightenings of the first chord. But these rarely occur in the same part" (quoted in Kolneder, p. 58).

34. Berg, quoted, ibid., p. 45.

35. Webern, letter to Schoenberg, 31 May 1911, quoted in Moldenhauer and Moldenhauer, p. 126.

36. Erwin Stein, "Alban Berg and Anton von Webern," *The Chesterian* 26 (October 1922): 33–40.

37. Webern, letter to Schoenberg, 13 January 1913, quoted in Moldenhauer and Moldenhauer, p. 126.

38. Alma Mahler, *Gustav Mahler: Memories and Letters,* 3d ed., ed. Donald Mitchell, trans. Basil Creighton (Seattle: University of Washington Press, 1975), p. 70.

39. Webern, letter to Berg, 20 August 1928, quoted in Moldenhauer and Moldenhauer, p. 129.

40. Webern, letter to Berg, 12 July 1912, unpublished. See also Wolfgang Schreiber, *Gustav Mahler in Selbstzeugnissen und Bilddokumenten* (Hamburg: Rowohlt, 1971), p. 148.

41. Quotes from a review of the first performance, one of the great musical scandals of the early twentieth century, appear in Kolneder, p. 63; and Moldenhauer and Moldenhauer, p. 171.

42. Moldenhauer and Moldenhauer, p. 128.

43. Webern, letter to Schoenberg, 30 August 1909, quoted, ibid., p. 126.

44. Webern, letter to Berg, 12 July 1912, unpublished.

45. Richard Hoffman calls this "rhythmic dissonance" in "Webern's Six Pieces, Opus 6 (1909)," *Perspectives of New Music* 6/1 (1967): 75–77.

46. Webern, *Path,* p. 21.

47. Webern, letter to Berg, 16 July 1910, quoted in Moldenhauer and Moldenhauer, p. 132.

48. Webern often wrote in letters about Mahler's music that it was "dictated"; for example, see ibid., p. 321. Rilke apparently also felt that God dictated to him what he must say; see Rainer Maria Rilke, *The Book of Hours* (London: Hogarth Press, 1961), p. 28.

49. Webern, letter to Schoenberg, 17 January 1911, quoted in Moldenhauer and Moldenhauer, p. 140.

50. Ibid., p. 165. See also Wildgans, pp. 50–66.

51. Wittgenstein, letter to Ludwig von Ficker (n.d., between 1914 and 1919) quoted in Allen Janick and Stephen Toulmin, *Wittgenstein's Vienna* (New York: Simon and Schuster, 1973), p. 192. There are many other parallels between Wittgenstein and Webern; chief among them are their approach to mysticism, the ethical stance in their work, and their crystalline structures. See Ray Monk, *Ludwig Wittgenstein: The Duty of Genius* (New York: Penguin, 1991).

52. Webern, letter to Schoenberg, 4 December 1910, quoted in Moldenhauer and Moldenhauer, p. 113.

53. Webern, *Path,* p. 51.

54. Stuckenschmidt, p. 444.

55. Webern, letter to Schoenberg, 25 July 1911, unpublished, Library of Congress.

56. Webern, letter to Schoenberg, 23 August 1911, quoted in Moldenhauer and Moldenhauer, p. 149.

57. Webern, letter to Schoenberg, 18 September 1911, ibid.

58. Webern, letter to Berg, 30 October 1911, unpublished.

59. Webern, letter to Berg, 23 November 1911, unpublished.

60. Webern traveled to Vienna and Prague for performances of Mahler's Eighth Symphony, played the celesta in the Prague performance, and made a pilgrimage to Mahler's grave in Vienna. On 22 January 1912, Schoenberg wrote in his Berlin diary: "Webern will not be in Berlin on the fifth of March, when Rosé plays my First Quartet here. I am sorry, because he is the only friend who knows the work; the only one who relates to it warmly. He is going to Vienna, to hear Mahler's Eighth Symphony. I would gladly go also. This shows, however, that he doesn't depend on me so exclusively as he would like to make me believe. Discussion about it in the evening with Mathilde. The result: We are half and half angry. Naturally she goes too far; for on certain grounds (G) [erstl] she has a need to find fault with Webern. I reminded her that I myself actually behaved often no better toward Mahler; that parents to children, children to parents behave themselves badly. That good is really an abstraction and nothing is absolute. That there are no absolutely good and faultless people. And that I never will forget in how many other cases Webern behaves excellently to me. But she refuses to understand. She remains rigidly with her assertion and hardly listens." Arnold Schönberg, *Berliner Tagebuch,* ed. Josef Rufer (Frankfurt: Propyläen Verlag, 1974), p. 10.

61. Webern, letters to Schoenberg, 17 November and 4 December 1912, quoted in Moldenhauer and Moldenhauer, pp. 165, 167.

62. Webern, letter to Schoenberg, 17 March 1913, quoted, ibid., p. 191.

63. Webern, letter to Schoenberg, 3 June 1913, quoted, ibid., p. 191.

64. Webern, letter to Berg, 24 July 1913, unpublished.

65. Webern, letter to Schoenberg, 31 July 1913, Library of Congress.

66. Dr. Alfred Adler (1870–1937), a favored member of Freud's inner circle since 1902, had introduced Dr. David Joseph Bach, a close friend of Schoenberg's, to Freud's Wednesday meetings in 1906. Bach was a member until Adler's split with Freud. Another close associate of Schoenberg's, Max Graf, was also a member from 1902 until Adler's exit. See Lewis Wickes, "Schoenberg, *Erwartung,* and the Reception of Psychoanalysis in Musical Circles in Vienna Until 1910/11," *Studies in Music* 23 (1989): 89–90. A more immediate recommendation for treatment by Alfred Adler was made by Webern's physician and by Schoenberg's friend Dr. Oskar Adler, both of whom knew Dr. Alfred Adler.

67. Webern, letter to Berg, 24 June 1913, unpublished.

68. Webern, letters to Schoenberg, 5 and 6 August, 16 and 29 September 1913, Library of Congress. See Moldenhauer and Moldenhauer, pp. 178–81.

69. Karl Kraus, *Die Fackel* 47/378–383 (July–September 1913): 73.

70. "Psychoanalyse ist jene Geisteskrankheit für deren Therapie sie sich hält." Aphorism quoted in Karl Kraus, *Auswahl aus dem Werke,* ed. Heinrich Fischer (Munich: Kösel Verlag, 1957), p. 48.

71. Webern, letter to Schoenberg, 29 September 1913, Library of Congress. For the Freud-Kraus conflict, see Peter Gay, *Freud: A Life for Our Time* (New York: Norton, 1988), p. 215. Freud, for his part, railed at the "unbridled vanity and lack of discipline of this talented beast, Karl Kraus."

72. Webern, letter to Schoenberg, 7 October 1913, quoted in Moldenhauer and Moldenhauer, p. 192. Italics added.

73. Webern, letter to Schoenberg, 24 November 1913, quoted, ibid.

74. Webern, "Third String Quartet," Lehmann Collection, Pierpont Morgan Library, quoted by permission of Maria Halbich-Webern. Translation the authors'.

75. Webern, *Three Orchestral Songs* (1913/14) (New York: Carl Fischer, 1968). Translation the authors'.

76. Webern, letter to Schoenberg, 24 November 1913, in Moldenhauer and Moldenhauer, p. 192.

77. This symbol appears in the work of Jakob Böhme, the late sixteenth- early seventeenth-century mystic, whose thought had influenced Webern since his student days.

78. Webern, letter to Schoenberg, 12 September 1912, quoted in Moldenhauer and Moldenhauer, p. 204.

79. Ibid., p. 199.

80. *Tot* (1913), Stage-play in Six Scenes. Manuscript in Webern Collection, Paul Sacher Stiftung, Basel.

81. "Op. 3, No. 3," in Lehmann Collection, Pierpont Morgan Library, New York.

82. "Op. 6," in Lehmann Collection, Pierpont Morgan Library.

83. Lehmann Collection, Pierpont Morgan Library.

84. See Moldenhauer and Moldenhauer, pp. 196–98, 204.

85. Willi Reich, "Anton von Webern," *Die Musik* 22 (August 1930): 814, quoted in Moldenhauer and Moldenhauer, p. 198.

86. In a letter to Nicolas Slonimsky, dated 14 January 1937, Webern explained, "I wrote, in the years between 1911 and 1913, with long interruptions, about twenty pieces, as expressions of musical lyricism, and selected five of them to include in opus 10." He gave the dates: I, 28 June 1911; II, 13 September 1913; III, 8 September 1913; IV, 19 July 1911; V, 6 October 1913. (Slonimsky, *Music Since 1900* [New York: Scribners, 1971], p. 1316.)

87. Erwin Stein, "Fünf Stücke für Orchester von Anton Webern," *Pult und Taktstock* 5/6 (May–June 1926): 109–13.

88. When published with Op. 13 in 1926, "Die Einsame" was changed considerably from its 1914 "Op. 7" version: the mezzo-soprano line, at first characterized by the widest possible extremes of range and intervals, was smoothed out by octave transpositions and changed to soprano. Instruments were changed and dynamics were made less extreme. The "Op. 7" manuscript is in the Lehmann Collection, Pierpont Morgan Library.

89. See Rudolf Stephan, "Zu einigen Liedern Anton Weberns," in *Beiträge der Österreichischen Gesellshaft für Musik* (1972/73): 135–44.

90. Webern, letter to Schoenberg, 26 November 1914, Library of Congress.

91. Webern, letter to Schoenberg, 11 November 1914, Library of Congress.

92. Webern, letter to Schoenberg, 24 November 1914, Library of Congress.

93. Webern, letters to Schoenberg, 3 and 17 January 1915, Library of Congress.

94. Webern attempted completely different approaches to a single poem, using various kinds of declamation and varying instrumental combinations. His struggle with atonality is expressed in his focus on ostinato techniques and his occasional

regression to tonality. See Anne C. Shreffler, "Webern's Trakl Fragments," paper given at the meeting of the American Musicological Society, Baltimore MD, November 1988.

95. Webern, letter to Schoenberg, 24 June 1917, quoted in Moldenhauer and Moldenhauer, p. 266.

96. Walter Kolneder, *Anton Webern: Genesis und Metamorphose eines Stils* (Vienna: Lafite, 1974), p. 70.

97. Webern, letter to Berg, 18 August 1918, quoted in Moldenhauer and Moldenhauer, p. 267.

98. Theodor W. Adorno, *Philosophy of Modern Music,* trans. A. Mitchell and W. Blomster (New York: Seabury, 1973), p. 42.

99. Joan Allen Smith, *Schoenberg and His Circle: A Viennese Portrait* (New York: Schirmer Books, 1986), p. 198.

100. Schoenberg, "New Music," 29 September 1923, in *Style and Idea,* p. 138.

101. Ibid., pp. 483–84.

102. Hans Moldenhauer, "Notes on Webern's 'Im Sommerwind' and Six Pieces for Orchestra, Op. 6," *Beiträge der Österreichischen Gesellschaft für Musik* (1972/73): 95–96. See Anton Webern, *Sketches* (1926–45), facsimile reproduction (New York: Fischer, 1968).

103. Webern, letter to Schoenberg, 7 July 1912, quoted in Moldenhauer and Moldenhauer, p. 161.

6. ALBAN BERG

1. Rosemary Hilmar, *Alban Berg: Leben und Wirken in Wien bis zu seinen ersten Erfolgen als Komponist* (Vienna: Böhlhaus, 1978]), p. 27.

2. Mosco Carner, *Alban Berg: The Man and the Work* (London: Duckworth, 1975), p. 7.

3. From a 1904 letter from Berg to his friend and mentor Hermann Watznauer, quoted in Willi Reich, *The Life and Work of Alban Berg,* trans. Cornelius Cardew (London: Thames and Hudson, 1965), p. 17.

4. Erich Alban Berg, *Der unverbesserliche Romantiker: Alban Berg 1885–1935* (Vienna: Österreichischer Bundesverlag, 1985), p. 20.

5. E. A. Berg, ed., *Alban Berg: Leben und Werk in Daten und Bildern* (Frankfurt: Insel, 1976), p. 12.

6. E. A. Berg, *Alban Berg,* p. 18; and Berg, *Der unverbesserliche Romantiker,* p. 72.

7. Donald Harris, "Berg and Frida Semler," *International Alban Berg Society Newsletter* 8 (Summer 1979): 10; and Alban Berg, *Letters to His Wife,* ed. and trans. Bernard Grun (New York: St. Martin's Press, 1971), p. 27.

8. Harris, p. 11.

9. Berg, letter to Helene Nahowski, 23 August 1909, Berg, *Letters,* p. 90.

10. Berg, letter to Helene, undated (March 1910), ibid., p. 101.

11. R. Hilmar, pp. 25–26.

12. E. A. Berg, *Der unverbesserliche Romantiker,* p. 64.

13. Ibid., p. 144.

14. Reich, *Berg,* p. 17.

15. Harris, p. 10.

16. Carner, p. 4.

17. Theodor W. Adorno, *Berg: Der Meister des kleinsten Übergangs* (Frankfurt: Suhrkamp, 1977), p. 32.

18. Berg, letter to Franz Nahowski, July 1910, Berg, *Letters,* p. 109.

19. R. Hilmar, p. 9.

20. Hans F. Redlich, *Alban Berg: The Man and His Music* (New York: Abelard-Schumann, 1957), p. 245.

21. Reich, *Berg,* p. 28.

22. Fritz Usinger, "Das Lebenswerk Alfred Momberts," in *Alfred Mombert: Ausstellung zum 25. Todestag* (Karlsruhe: Badische Landesbibliothek, 1967), p. 13.

23. Quoted in Reich, *Berg*, p. 32.

24. Schoenberg, letters to Berg, 13 January 1912 and 14 February 1912, in *The Berg-Schoenberg Correspondence*, ed. Juliane Brand, Christopher Hailey, and Donald Harris (New York and London: Norton, 1987), pp. 65, 74.

25. E. A. Berg, *Alban Berg*, p. 21. Altenberg's two poems and prose sketch are in his *Neues Altes* (Berlin: Fischer, 1919; 1st ed., 1911), pp. 45, 205, 87.

26. Altenberg, pp. 60–64.

27. Berg clarified the last line to read "And over both a gloomy haze still lingers, until the clouds have dispersed."

28. Adorno, p. 88.

29. Mark DeVoto, "Alban Berg's Picture Postcard Songs," Ph.D. diss., Princeton University, 1966, pp. 12–17, gives a full explanation of the ingenious procedures applied to the various ostinati in reaching the climax.

30. See Ex. 3-6b.

31. Berg, letter to Helene, undated (autumn 1912?): "I have once more played through Mahler's Ninth. The first movement is the most glorious he ever wrote. It expresses an extraordinary love of this earth, for Nature; the longing to live on it in peace, to enjoy it completely, to the very heart of one's being, before death comes, as it irresistibly does. The whole movement is based on a premonition of death, which is constantly recurring" (Berg, *Letters*, p. 147).

32. Ibid.

33. Mm. 1–19 and 20–38; see DeVoto, p. 38.

34. Schoenberg, letter to Berg, 14 January 1913, *Berg-Schoenberg Correspondence*, p. 147.

35. Reich, *Berg*, p. 41; and Ernst Hilmar, *Wozzeck von Alban Berg* (Vienna: Universal, 1975), p. 9.

36. Adorno, p. 36.

37. Berg, *Letters*, p. 161.

38. George Perle, *The Operas of Alban Berg*, vol. 1: *Wozzeck* (Berkeley and Los Angeles: University of California, 1980), p. 18.

39. Adorno, p. 110.

40. Berg, letter to Schoenberg, 10 April 1914 (*Berg-Schoenberg Correspondence*, p. 208).

41. Such as mm. 29–33 and 40–46.

42. Schoenberg, letter to Berg, 3 October 1912, *Berg-Schoenberg Correspondence*, p. 117.

43. For the sake of simplicity, this spelling, used by Berg, will be employed throughout, although the more authentic spelling *Woyzeck* is preferred by modern scholars when referring to Büchner's play.

44. E. Hilmar, p. 10; and Willi Reich, "Aus unbekannten Briefen von Alban Berg an Anton von Webern," *Schweizerische Musikzeitung* 93 (1 February 1953): 50.

45. Paul Elbogen, quoted in Douglas Jarman, *Alban Berg: Wozzeck* (Cambridge and New York: Cambridge University Press, 1989), p. 1.

46. A. J. H. Knight, *Georg Büchner* (Oxford: Blackwell, 1951), pp. 113–14.

47. Insel edition, ed. Wilhelm Hausenstein, which preserves the order established in Büchner, *Gesammelten Schriften*, vol. 1, ed. Paul Landau (Berlin: Cassirer, 1909). See E. Hilmar, p. 12.

48. Jack M. Stein, "From *Woyzeck* to *Wozzeck*: Alban Berg's Adaptation of Büchner," *Germanic Review* 47 (May 1972): 168.

49. Thomas M. Messer, *Edvard Munch* (New York: Abrams, n.d.), p. 84.

50. Soma Morgenstern, graveside eulogy for Berg, in E. A. Berg, *Der unverbesserliche Romantiker*, p. 186.

51. Kurt Blaukopf, "Autobiographische Elemente in Alban Bergs *Wozzeck*," Österreichische *Musikzeitschrift* 9/2 (May 1954): 156–57.

52. Reich, "Aus unbekannten Briefen . . . ," p. 50.

53. Extended formal analyses of *Wozzeck* appear in Berg's 1929 lecture (in Jarman, *Alban Berg: Wozzeck*, p. 154; and in Perle, *Wozzeck*, p. 38).

54. Berg, "The 'Problem of Opera,' " reprinted in Reich, *Berg*, p. 66.

55. Berg, *Wozzeck* lecture (Jarman, *Alban Berg: Wozzeck*, p. 160).

56. Ibid., p. 161.

57. Ibid., p. 165.

58. See above, pp. 18, 48.

59. Berg, *Letters*, p. 278.

60. Theodor Däubler, *Der neue Standpunkt* (Leipzig: Insel, 1916), p. 179.

61. Strauss, *Salome*, [227]–[313] and [355]–[361]. Strauss, however, uses various different pitches for the long-held trills.

62. Berg, *Wozzeck* lecture (Jarman, *Alban Berg: Wozzeck*, p. 167).

63. See Ex. 4-9.

64. See Exx. 4-6 and 3-10.

65. See Ex. 3-7d. The rhythmic pattern is actually introduced inaudibly in the
individual orchestral entries of the first crescendo (mm. 109–14).

66. Carner, p. 189.

67. Berg, letter to Erich Kleiber, quoted in E. Hilmar, p. 48.

68. See p. 35.

69. Hans Keller, "The Eclecticism of *Wozzeck*" (conclusion), *Music Review* 13/
2 (May 1952): 133. See Ex. 4-8.

70. Berg, *Wozzeck* lecture (Jarman, *Alban Berg: Wozzeck*, p. 169).

71. See Ex. 3-11.

72. Berg, "The 'Problem of Opera,' " in Reich, *Berg*, p. 64.

73. Ibid., pp. 117–18. According to Reich, the quotation is based on Berg's own
ideas.

74. Although tone-rows occur in the fifth of the Altenberg Songs and in *Wozzeck*
(Act I, scene 4), and the Chamber Concerto makes melodic use of all four row forms
(prime, inversion, retrograde, and retrograde-inversion), Berg does not fully adopt
twelve-tone technique until the second of his settings of "Schliesse mir die Augen
beide" (1925).

75. Adorno, p. 44.

76. The private program has been elucidated in Barbara Dalen, " 'Freundschaft,
Liebe, und Welt': The Secret Programme of the Chamber Concerto," in *The Berg
Companion*, ed. Douglas Jarman (London: MacMillan, 1989), p. 141.

77. English translation in Reich, *Berg*, pp. 143–48.

78. Ibid., pp. 147–48.

79. A–H–D–E = A–B–D–E, since *H* in German is B-natural (Dalen, p. 153).

80. Dalen, p. 166.

81. Mm. 157–69 of *Wozzeck*, I, 1, are the retrograde of mm. 6–14.

82. H. F. Redlich, *Alban Berg: Versuch einer Würdigung* (Vienna: Universal,
1957), p. 157.

83. Douglas Jarman, *The Music of Alban Berg* (Berkeley and Los Angeles: University of California Press, 1979), p. 241.

84. Berg, letter to Webern, 12 October 1925, in Ursula von Rauchhaupt,
Schoenberg, Berg, Webern: The String Quartets. A Documentary Study, trans. Eugene
Hartzell (Hamburg: Deutsche Grammophon Gesellschaft, 1971), p. 89.

85. Adorno, p. 136.

86. Berg, analysis of the *Lyric Suite*, in Rauchhaupt, p. 102.

87. Douglass Green, "Berg's De Profundis: The Finale of the *Lyric Suite*," *Inter-*

national *Alban Berg Society Newsletter* 5 (June 1977): 13; and George Perle, "The Secret Program of the *Lyric Suite*," ibid.: 4.

88. Berg, *Letters*, pp. 337–41.

89. Perle, "Secret Program," p. 7.

90. Berg, analysis of the *Lyric Suite*, in Rauchhaupt, p. 111.

91. Alban Berg, *Briefe an seine Frau* (Munich and Vienna: Langen and Müller, 1965), pp. 184–85.

92. Translation from Green, p. 13.

93. Although the vocal part has a range of almost four octaves, this problem can be, and has been, adjusted in performance. The first performance of the vocal version of the *Largo desolato* took place in New York on 1 November 1979.

94. Douglas Jarman, "Alban Berg, Wilhelm Fliess and the Secret Programme of the Violin Concerto," *International Alban Berg Society Newsletter* 12 (Fall–Winter 1982): 5.

95. Dates from Günter Seehaus, *Frank Wedekind* (Reinbek bei Hamburg: Rowohlt, 1974), p. 61.

96. Frida Semler Seabury, "1903 and 1904," *International Alban Berg Society Newsletter* 1 (December 1968): 5.

97. E. A. Berg, ed., *Alban Berg*, pp. 17, 94–97; Karl Kraus's introduction is reprinted in his *Grimassen, Ausgewählte Werke*, vol. 1 (Berlin: Volk und Welt, 1971), p. 51 (excerpts translated in Reich, *Berg*, pp. 156–59).

98. Jack M. Stein, "*Lulu*: Alban Berg's Adaptation of Wedekind," *Comparative Literature* 26/3 (Summer 1974): 233.

99. Ibid., p. 225n.

100. Reich, *Berg*, p. 158.

101. These tonal passages include the love theme of Lulu and Dr. Schön, which first appears in Act I, mm. 615–24; the duet of Alwa and Lulu, Act II, mm. 315–36; and the first variation on a tune by Wedekind, Act III, mm. 693–707.

102. Ernst Krenek, "Marginal Remarks re *Lulu*," *International Alban Berg Society Newsletter* 9 (Fall 1980): 10.

103. *International Alban Berg Society Newsletter* 6 (June 1978): 3.

7. THE PROBLEM OF EXPRESSIONISM IN STRAVINSKY

1. "Stravinsky frankly admits both his *Autobiography* and *Poetics* 'were written through other people.'" Paul Henry Lang, Editorial, *Musical Quarterly* 48/3 (July 1962): 370.

2. Mikhail Druskin, *Igor Stravinsky: His Personality, Works and Views*, trans. M. Cooper (Cambridge: Cambridge University Press, 1983), p. 1.

3. "A man has one birth place, one fatherland, one country—he *can* have only one country—and the place of his birth is the most important place in his life." Stravinsky, quoted in John Warrack, "Stravinsky as a Russian," *Tempo* 81 (Summer 1967): 9.

4. Claude Debussy, letter to Stravinsky, 24 October 1914, in Igor Stravinsky and Robert Craft, *Conversations with Igor Stravinsky* (Berkeley: University of California Press, 1980), p. 54.

5. Igor Stravinsky, *Poetics of Music*, trans. A. Knodel and I. Dahl (New York: Random House, 1960), pp. 10–11.

6. Igor Stravinsky and Robert Craft, *Memories and Commentaries* (Berkeley: University of California Press, 1981), p. 26.

7. Stravinsky, letter to his parents, 27 July 1901, in Vera Stravinsky and Robert Craft, *Stravinsky in Pictures and Documents* [hereafter *Pictures and Documents*] (New York: Simon and Schuster, 1978), p. 21.

8. Igor Stravinsky and Robert Craft, *Expositions and Developments* (New York: Doubleday, 1962), p. 18.

9. Igor Stravinsky, *An Autobiography* (New York: Simon and Schuster, 1936), p. 8.

10. *Memories and Commentaries*, p. 24.

11. Ibid., p. 30.

12. *Pictures and Documents*, p. 63.

13. *Conversations*, p. 48.

14. Ibid., p. 38.

15. Vladimir Stassov, whom Stravinsky called "one of my dearest old friends" (*Expositions and Developments*, p. 20), had been Mussorgsky's closest musical advisor throughout the composition of *Boris Godunov*. M. D. Calvocoressi, *Mussorgsky: His Life and Works* (Fair Lawn, NJ: Essential Books, 1956), p. 14. "Genuinely intuitive" was Stravinsky's assessment (*Conversations*, p. 44).

16. Stravinsky, letter to Vladimir Napravnik, 15 November 1932, in *Pictures and Documents*, p. 32.

17. *Conversations*, pp. 43–44.

18. *Memories and Commentaries*, p. 55.

19. "It is impossible to live in such a boiling pot unless one is indifferent to the life around one, and unless one looks upon the great Russian Revolution with hatred. As you know, we are of the opposite conviction." Letter from Stravinsky, July 1906, recipient not cited, in *Pictures and Documents*, p. 21.

20. *Memories and Commentaries*, p. 28. Dostoevski had liked music and had gone to concerts with Stravinsky's father (*Conversations*, p. 84).

21. *Conversations*, p. 57.

22. Ibid., p. 64.

23. *Pictures and Documents*, pp. 29, 605 n. 49.

24. Eric Walter White, *Stravinsky: The Composer and His Works* (Berkeley: University of California Press, 1966), p. 81.

25. Stravinsky, postcard to Florent Schmidt, 11 July 1911, in *Pictures and Documents*, p. 62.

26. Stravinsky, letter to Andrey Rimsky-Korsakov, 7 October 1911, ibid., p. 56.

27. Pieter C. van den Toorn, in *The Music of Igor Stravinsky* (New Haven: Yale University Press, 1983), discusses the octatonic scale as a "referential factor" (never acknowledged by Stravinsky) in his Russian works.

28. Calvocoressi, *Mussorgsky*, p. 94.

29. Ibid., p. 244. Bartók commented that "It did not fall to [Mussorgsky] to achieve perfection—he should be regarded as a forerunner of the tendency [to base art music on peasant music]." "The Relation of Folk Song to the Development of the Art Music of Our Time" (1921), in Béla Bartók, *Essays*, ed. Benjamin Suchoff (London: Faber, 1976), p. 325.

30. Ibid., p. 126.

31. Stravinsky first appeared in the Evenings of Contemporary Music in 1904, accompanying a horn player in one of the palaces of Catherine the Great (notes on Stravinsky in Lawrence Morton Collection, University of California, Los Angeles). The first public performance of his own music at these concerts was of an early piano sonata, on 27 December 1907, in the modest hall of the Petersburg Conservatory. Stravinsky himself performed there also, as accompanist in his Gorodetsky Songs (Druskin, p. 28).

32. See *Expositions and Developments*, p. 138; and Edward Lockspeiser, *Debussy: His Life and Mind*, 2 vols. (reprint, London: Cambridge University Press, 1978), vol. 1, pp. 48–49.

33. *Memories and Commentaries*, p. 133.

34. *Pictures and Documents*, p. 62.

35. Stravinsky, in an interview with M. D. Calvocoressi, *London Musical Times,* 1 August 1911, quoted in Carl Van Vechten, *Music After the Great War and Other Studies* (New York: Schirmer, 1915), pp. 92–93.

36. Stravinsky, *An Autobiography,* p. 83. "With [this book], largely ghostwritten by . . . Walter Nouvel, Stravinsky's career as self-mythologizer reached an early peak." Richard Taruskin, "Folk Melodies in *The Rite of Spring,*" *Journal of the American Musicological Society* 33/3 (Fall 1980): 502.

37. There is considerable evidence of these differences in attitude in *Pictures and Documents.* Robert Craft discusses the effect of World War I and the 1917 Revolution on Stravinsky's character and fortune (pp. 28–29) and his response to suffering: "The effect of suffering and grief . . . on Stravinsky's artistic beliefs was that he determined to keep his art and his life as nearly separate as possible instead of seeking an outlet for his feelings in music" (p. 37).

38. *Memories and Commentaries,* p. 110. His collaborator in the World War I years, C. F. Ramuz, called him "a man of prey," in *Souvenirs sur Igor Stravinsky* (Paris: N.R.F.; Lausanne: Mermod, 1929), quoted in White, p. 55.

39. *Conversations,* p. 45.

40. Richard Buckle, *Diaghilev* (New York: Atheneum, 1979), p. 115.

41. *Atlantic Monthly* 192 (November 1953): 33–36.

42. Bronislava Nijinska, *Early Memoirs,* trans. and ed. Irina Nijinska and Jean Rawlinson (New York: Holt, Rinehart and Winston, 1981), p. 313.

43. Sergei Diaghilev, letter to his stepmother, 1895, quoted in *Diaghilev: Costumes and Designs of the Ballets Russes* (New York: Metropolitan Museum of Art, 1978), n.p.

44. John E. Bowlt, *The Silver Age: Russian Art of the Early Twentieth Century and the "World of Art" Group* (Newtonville, MA: Oriental Research Partners, 1979), pp. 72–73.

45. *Diaghilev: Costumes and Designs,* n.p.

46. Alexandre Benois, *Reminiscences of the Russian Ballet,* trans. M. Britnieva (reprint, New York: Da Capo, 1977), pp. 150, 121, 179.

47. The Scythian Movement, 1907–17, "was a time of a great wave of interest in native Russian art, stripped of the hybridization with Western themes and forms that had predominated in the nineteenth century." Simon Karlinsky, "Igor Stravinsky and Russian Preliterate Theater," in *Confronting Stravinsky: Man, Musician, and Modernist,* ed. Jann Pasler (Berkeley: University of California Press, 1986), p. 5.

48. Druskin, p. 33.

49. Michel Fokine, *Memoirs of a Ballet Master,* trans. V. Fokine (Boston: Little Brown, 1961), p. 161.

50. Romain Rolland, *Journal des années de guerre,* 24 September 1914, quoted in Lockspeiser, vol. 2, p. 183.

51. *Expositions and Developments,* p. 36.

52. *Memories and Commentaries,* p. 98.

53. Taruskin, p. 543.

54. Benois, pp. 347–48.

55. Stravinsky said that he wrote *The Rite* to send everyone in his Russian past who had failed to recognize his genius "to hell." Robert Craft, *Present Perspectives* (New York: Knopf, 1984), p. 227. The hostility expressed by the Rimsky-Korsakovs and the St. Petersburg establishment to his first two successes with Diaghilev was an extremely painful experience, which cast a shadow on the composition of *The Rite* (*Pictures and Documents,* pp. 24–25).

56. Stravinsky, interview in *Les Nouvelles Littéraires* (8 December 1928), quoted in *Pictures and Documents,* p. 66.

57. Ibid.

58. Stravinsky, for pianola version of *Petrushka* (1928), ibid., p. 67.

59. Benois, p. 327.

60. Ibid., p. 326.

61. Stravinsky, for pianola version of *Petrushka*, in *Pictures and Documents*, p. 67.

62. Claude Debussy, letter to Stravinsky, 10 April 1913, in *Conversations*, pp. 48–49.

63. Benois, p. 326.

64. See Frederick W. Sternfeld, "Some Russian Folk Songs in Stravinsky's Petrouchka," reprinted in the Norton Critical Score of *Petrushka*, ed. Charles Hamm (New York: Norton, 1967), pp. 203–15.

65. Boris Asaf'yev, *A Book About Stravinsky*, trans. R. F. French (Ann Arbor: UMI Research Press, 1982), pp. 10, 22, 23.

66. Nijinsky's sister Bronislava remembered his dancing "as if he is using only the heavy wooden parts of his body. Only the swinging, mechanical, soulless motions jerk the sawdust-filled arms or legs upwards in extravagant movements to indicate transports of joy or despair" (Nijinska, p. 373).

67. *Expositions and Developments*, p. 137.

68. *Pictures and Documents*, p. 61.

69. Martin Cooper, *Ideas and Music* (London: Barrie and Rockliff, 1965), p. 256.

70. Stravinsky, "What I Wished to Express in *The Consecration of Spring*," interview originally in French in *Montjoie!* (Paris), 29 May 1913; English trans. Edward Burlingame Hill, in *Boston Evening Transcript*, 12 February 1916; quoted in *Pictures and Documents*, pp. 524–26. The original is reprinted in *Press Book: Le Sacre du Printemps*, ed. François Lesure (Geneva: Editions Minkoff, 1980), pp. 13–15. The authenticity of this interview seems settled in Stravinsky's correspondence with V. V. Derzhanovsky, quoted in *Selected Correspondence*, ed. R. Craft (New York: Knopf, 1982), vol. 1, p. 54, where it is made evident that Stravinsky only disavowed minor details in the Russian translation of his French interview, published for the premiere of *Le Sacre du Printemps*.

71. Stravinsky, letters to Nicholas Roerich, 15 July and 26 September 1911, in I. Vershinin, "I. Stravinsky's Letters to N. Roerich," *Muzyka* (8 August 1966): 57–63, trans. anon., in the Lawrence Morton Collection, University of California, Los Angeles. This translation was sent on 20 September 1966 to Lawrence Morton (who was then working on a major critical study of Stravinsky) by Igor Blazhkov (who may have been the translator). It differs from Stravinsky's, in Igor Stravinsky, *The Rite of Spring Sketches (1911–13)* [hereafter *Sketches*] (London: Boosey & Hawkes, 1969), Appendix II, pp. 27–31. Stravinsky's translation omits some passages, including references to Roerich's ideas as being essential to the composing of *The Rite of Spring*.

72. Stravinsky, letter to N. F. Findeizen, 2 December 1912, *Sketches*, Appendix II, p. 32.

73. Nina Solivanova, *The World of Roerich* (New York: International Art Center, 1922), pp. 50–52.

74. Nicholas Roerich, "Talashkino" (1908), in *The Realm of Light* (New York: Roerich Museum Press, 1931), pp. 294–306.

75. *Nicholas Roerich* (New York: Nicholas Roerich Museum, 1964), p. 3.

76. Roerich, "A Wreath for Diaghileff" (1930), in *The Realm of Light*, p. 321.

77. Roerich, "Sacre" (1930), address to the League of Composers, ibid., p. 186.

78. P. Belikov and B. Knyazeva, *Roerich* (Moscow: Moloday Gvardiya, 1972); unpublished translation by Courtney Collier (available at the Roerich Museum), pp. 58–64.

79. Roerich, "Sacre," p. 186.

80. Stravinsky, letters to Roerich, 27 July 1910 and 13 September 1911, translation in Lawrence Morton Collection.

81. Taruskin, p. 510 n. 17.

82. Stravinsky, letter to Maximilian Steinberg, 29 July 1913, in *Pictures and Documents*, p. 25.

83. Stravinsky, letter to Roerich, 6 March 1912, translation in Lawrence Morton Collection.

84. Stravinsky, "À propos *Le Sacre du Printemps*," *Saturday Review*, 29 December 1959, p. 29.

85. Stravinsky, "What I Wished to Express . . . ," in *Pictures and Documents*, pp. 524–26. Many versions of the Russian title appear in accounts of the progress of this composition; Stravinsky liked best "The Coronation of Spring." Roerich's idea was "The Great Sacrifice." Others were "Sacred Spring," "Holy Spring," and "The Innocence of Spring."

86. "I want the whole of my work to give the feeling of the closeness between men and the earth, the closeness between the lives of men and the soil, and I sought to do this through a lapidary rhythm." Stravinsky, letter to N. F. Findeizen, 5 December 1912, in *Sketches*, Appendix II, p. 33.

87. Ibid., p. 35.

88. See Béla Bartók, "The Influence of Folk Music on the Art Music of Today" (1920), in *Essays*, p. 317.

89. Bartók, "The Influence of Peasant Music on Modern Music" (1931), ibid., p. 343.

90. Stravinsky, *Sketches*, Appendix II, p. 33n.

91. Robert Craft, *"The Rite of Spring*: Genesis of a Masterpiece," in *Sketches*, p. xxii.

92. Quoted in Allen Forte, *The Harmonic Organization of The Rite of Spring* (New Haven: Yale University Press, 1978), p. 66n.

93. M. D. Calvocoressi, *Music and Ballet* (London: Faber, 1933), p. 227.

94. Lawrence Morton, *"Le Sacre du Printemps*: Literary and Musical Origins," *Tempo* 128 (March 1979): 9–16. Taruskin explores this further in "Russian Folk Melodies in *The Rite of Spring*."

95. Stravinsky, "À propos *Le Sacre du Printemps*," p. 37. It is interesting to note Scriabin's similar thought, expressed in 1914: "Individuality is a precious vessel from which the One drinks the knowledge of suffering and joy. I am only the vessel." Quoted in Faubion Bowers, *The New Scriabin* (New York: St. Martin's Press, 1983), p. 100. As we have seen, the thought is similar to Mahler's and Webern's feelings that their work was dictated to them. In any case, it is an attitude at odds with Stravinsky's later craftsmanlike viewpoint.

96. Stravinsky, *An Autobiography*, pp. 75–76.

97. Stravinsky, *Poetics of Music*, p. 11.

98. *Expositions and Developments*, p. 118.

99. Carlos Chavez, in *Stravinsky in the Theatre*, ed. Minna Lederman (New York: Da Capo, 1975), p. 127.

100. H. Colles, "The Fusion of Music and Dancing," *Times* (London), 12 July 1913, in Lesure, pp. 63–64.

101. C. H., "Stravinsky at Queen's Hall," *The Spectator*, 18 June 1921, ibid., p. 69.

102. Dent, "Le Sacre du Printemps," *The Nation and The Atheneum*, 18 June 1921, ibid., pp. 70–71.

103. B. G., "Stravinsky and Psychoanalysis," *New York Times*, 21 April 1924, ibid., p. 98.

104. Jacques Rivière, "Le Sacre du Printemps," *Nouvelle Revue Française*, November 1913, ibid., pp. 38–48.

105. Quoted in *Pictures and Documents*, p. 87.

8. BÉLA BARTÓK

1. Bartók, letter to musicologist Edwin von der Nüll, quoted in Mátyás Seiber, "Béla Bartók's Chamber Music," *Béla Bartók: A Memorial Review* (New York: Boosey & Hawkes, 1950), p. 29. Bartók wrote to his mother on 18 June 1903 that his sister should look upon his music as "composed by the 'future Beethoven of Hungary.' " *Béla Bartók, Letters,* ed. János Demény, trans. P. Balabán and I. Farkas, trans. rev. E. West and C. Mason (Budapest: Corvina, 1971), p. 25.

2. Denijs Dille, an early Bartók scholar and the first director of the Budapest Bartók Archives (1961–71), stated, "I believe there were several periods of crisis in Bartók's life. In my opinion Bartók's psychological make-up must be taken into consideration to understand and interpret his works." Quoted in Imre Antal, "Denijs Dille on His Collaboration with Bartók," *New Hungarian Quarterly* 63 (Autumn 1970): 207–15.

3. György Kroó, "Data on the Genesis of Duke Bluebeard's Castle," *Studia Musicologica* 23 (1981): 79–123.

4. John Vinton, "The Case of *The Miraculous Mandarin*," *Musical Quarterly* 50/1 (January 1964): 1–17.

5. Zoltán Kodály, *The Selected Writings of Zoltán Kodály,* trans. L. Halápy and F. Macnicol (Budapest: Corvina, 1974), p. 106.

6. Ibid.

7. Ibid., p. 90.

8. László Somfai, *Bartók's Workshop: Sketches, Manuscripts, Versions: The Compositional Process* (Budapest: Hungarian Academy of Sciences, 1987), pp. 3–4. Somfai continues, "Calculations of the proportions of a composition—with Fibonacci or other numbers—have not yet been discovered in Bartók's workshop. In composition he followed a natural instinct for balance and proportion" (p. 12). The full text of Bartók's 1943 remarks appears in his *Essays,* selected and edited by Benjamin Suchoff (New York: St. Martin's Press, 1976), p. 376.

9. Quoted in Israel Nestyev, "Prokoviev and Bartók: Some Parallels," in *International Musicological Conference in Commemoration of Béla Bartók, 1971* [hereafter *Commemoration 1971*], ed. József Ujfalussy and János Breuer (Budapest: Edition Musica, 1972), p. 139. Also quoted in *Bartók breviárium,* collected by Ujfalussy, ed. Vera Lampert (Budapest: Zenemükiadó, 1974), pp. 478–79.

10. Bartók, letter to Stefi Geyer, September 1907, in Bartók, *Letters,* pp. 86–87. The line of music has resemblances to the Bagatelle, Op. 6/XIII (titled "Elle est mort") and includes Stefi Geyer's "Leitmotiv," which he points out. He continues: "One letter from you, a line, even a word—and I am in a transport of joy, the next brings me almost to tears, it hurts so. . . . It is as if I am in a state of spiritual intoxication all the time. Just what one needs for work (composing)!"

11. Denijs Dille, quoted in Antal, p. 209.

12. Kodály, "Bartók the Man" (1946), in *Selected Writings,* pp. 98–101.

13. Ferenc Bónis, *Béla Bartók: His Life in Pictures and Documents* (Budapest: Corvina, 1980), pp. 9–10.

14. Molnár, quoted in Bónis, p. 8.

15. See Bartalan Pethö, "Bartók's Personality," *Studia Musicologica* 23 (1981): 454–57. Márta Ziegler was sixteen in 1909, when Bartók asked his mother to set her a place for lunch after her lesson. After dinner had also passed and the evening wore on, his mother asked if Márta should be getting home. Bartók replied she would be staying, as they had gotten married that day (p. 451). Ditta Pásztory, whom he married in 1923 after a sudden divorce, was 22 years younger than Bartók.

16. Quoted in Malcolm Gillies, *Béla Bartók Remembered* (New York: Norton, 1990), p. 22. See also memoirs of Antal Molnár and Béla Balazs, ibid., pp. 32–33, 36–37, on Bartók's reticence.

17. Bartók, "Autobiography" (1921), *Essays,* p. 409.

18. Bartók, quoted in Otto Deri, "Béla Bartók: A Portrait of His Personality Drawn from His Letters," *Current Musicology* 13 (1971): 90–103.

19. Bartók, "The Relation of Folk Song to the Development of the Art Music of Our Time" (1921), *Essays*, p. 321.

20. Bartók, letter to Octavian Beu, 10 January 1931, *Letters*, p. 201.

21. Quoted in Bence Szabolcsi, "Bartók's Principles of Composition," *Bartók Studies*, ed. Todd Crow (Detroit: Reprints in Music, 1976), p. 19.

22. Karl H. Wörner, "Expressionismus und Expressivismus in der Musik," in Wörner, *Die Musik in der Geistesgeschichte: Studien zur Situation der Jahre um 1910* (Bonn: Bouvier, 1970), p. 26.

23. In a letter to his Rumanian friend János Buşiţia, in January 1912, Bartók wrote that Ady "touched every painful and disquieting sore in contemporary Hungarian life" (*Letters*, p. 113). See also György Lukács, "The Importance and Influence of Ady," *New Hungarian Quarterly* 10/35 (Autumn 1969): 46–58. Other articles of interest about Ady in *New Hungarian Quarterly* are: László Ferenczi, "The Timeliness of Ady" 18/66 (Summer 1977); Neville Masterman, "Ady as Political Thinker" 19/72 (Winter 1978); Erzsébet Vezér, "Ady: Poet and Social Critic" 20/73 (Spring 1979).

24. Agatha Fassett, *The Naked Face of Genius: Béla Bartók's Last Years* (London: Gollancz, 1970), p. 82.

25. Bence Szabolcsi, his contemporary and author of the first scholarly biography of Bartók in Hungarian, quoted in Gillies, p. 89.

26. Mary Gluck, *Georg Lukács and His Generation: 1900–1918* (Cambridge: Harvard University Press, 1985), p. 63. Georg Lukács, *Record of a Life: An Autobiographical Sketch,* trans. R. Livingstone (London: Verso, 1983), gives firsthand material on this circle and Bartók's importance in it.

27. Gluck, pp. 90–91. Also see Béla Bartók, Jr., interview with László Somfai, "Béla Bartók Jun. on His Father," *New Hungarian Quarterly* 64 (Winter 1976): 193–96; an excerpt is reprinted in Gillies, pp. 29–32.

28. Marianne D. Birnbaum, "Bartók, Kodály and the 'Nyugat,' " in *Bartók and Kodály Revisited,* ed. György Ránki (Budapest: Akadémiai Kiadó, 1987), p. 61. See also Mary Gluck, "The Intellectual and Cultural Background of Bartók's Work," in the same volume.

29. See János Breuer, "Bartók and the Arts," *New Hungarian Quarterly* 16/60 (Winter 1975): 117–24. Róbert Berény, who painted Bartók's portrait in 1913, was one of "The Eight." He also wrote an article on Bartók's music. After 1910 Bartók played the piano for the openings of this group's exhibits.

30. Milos Náray, "Bartók Béla," editorial in *Ma* 3/2 (1917): 20; quoted in Gluck, p. 214.

31. Bartók, quoted in György Kroó, *A Guide to Bartók,* trans. R. Pataki and Maria Steiner, trans. rev. E. West (Budapest: Corvina, 1974), p. 40. The subsequent quotes describing Violin Concerto No. 1 are from a 1908 letter to Stefi Geyer, not included in *Letters,* but quoted by Kroó.

32. As Bartók matured, his atheism became a pantheism, and Goethe became one of his favorite writers. See Bence Szabolcsi, "Bartók and World Literature," in *Commemoration 1971,* p. 105. In 1916 Bartók joined the Unitarian Church, the humanist religion which began in Transylvania. See George Jellinek, "Bartók the Humanist," in Ránki, pp. 211–12.

33. Bartók, letter to Stefi Geyer, 6 September 1907, in *Letters*, p. 76.

34. See Bartók's letters to Stefi Geyer, 6 September and [middle of September] 1907, *Letters,* pp. 75–87.

35. "The *First String Quartet* is an internal drama, a kind of *retour à la vie:* the return to life of a man who had reached the shores of nothingness." Kodály, "Béla Bartók" (1921), in *Selected Writings*, p. 91.

36. Bartók, letter to Stefi Geyer, 6 September 1907, in *Letters,* p. 81.

37. Bartók, "Autobiography" (1921), in *Essays,* p. 409.

38. Ibid.

39. Kodály, "Bartók the Folklorist" (1955), in *Selected Writings,* p. 104.

40. Bartók, "The Folk Songs of Hungary" (1928), in *Essays,* p. 409.

41. Bartók had recently played pieces from Reger's *Aus meinem Tagebuch,* Vol. II, Op. 82, and may have had the model of a musical diary in mind. See Todd Crow, "Bartók's Fourteen Bagatelles: Thoughts from a Performer's Perspective," paper read at International Bartók Festival and Congress, Detroit, 1–21 March 1981.

42. *Letters,* pp. 83, 86.

43. See a full discussion by János Kárpáti, "The Mistuning Phenomenon in Bartók's Compositional Technique," in *Commemoration 1971,* p. 42; and in Kárpáti, *Bartók's String Quartets,* trans. F. Macnicol (Budapest: Corvina, 1975), pp. 137–58.

44. This bagatelle inspired Amy Lowell's poem "After Hearing a Waltz by Bartók," in which a jealous lover murders his rival at a dance only to drown in the blood of the corpse. Amy Lowell, *Sword Blades and Poppy Seeds* (New York: Houghton Mifflin, 1914), p. 155.

45. Bartók, "Introduction to *Béla Bartók Masterpieces for the Piano*" (1945), in *Essays,* p. 432.

46. Bartók, letter to Etelka Freund, 28 June 1908, in *Letters,* p. 89.

47. All except VIII, XIII, and XIV in 1910 (*Letters,* p. 98); and all except XIV in 1945 (*Essays,* p. 433).

48. Bartók, letter to Frederick Delius, n.d. [1910], in *Letters,* p. 105.

49. Denis Dille, "Angaben zum Violinkonzert, 1907," in *Documenta Bartókiana* II, ed. D. Dille (Mainz: Schott, 1965), p. 92.

50. Kodály, "Béla Bartók" (1921), in *Selected Writings,* p. 91.

51. Bartók, "The Folk Songs of Hungary" (1928), in *Essays,* p. 332.

52. Bartók, "The Influence of Folk Music on the Art Music of Today" (1920), ibid., p. 318.

53. Bartók, "The Folk Songs of Hungary" (1928), ibid., p. 333.

54. "I do not like to repeat a musical thought unchanged, and I never repeat a detail unchanged. This practice of mine arises from my inclination for variation and for transforming themes. . . . The extreme variety that characterizes our folk music is, at the same time, a manifestation of my own nature." Bartók, to Dille in 1937, quoted by Bence Szabolcsi, "Bartók's Principles of Composition," in Crow, *Bartók Studies,* p. 19.

55. Bartók, "Liszt's Music and Our Contemporary Public" (1911), ibid., p. 122.

56. Ibid., p. 124. See also the very complete discussion of this influence on Bartók by Lajos Bardos, "Liszt the Innovator," *Studia Musicologica* 17 (1975): 3–38.

57. Bartók, "The Folk Songs of Hungary" (1928), in *Essays,* p. 338.

58. Bónis, p. 19.

59. Dille, "Die Beziehungen zwischen Bartók und Schoenberg," *Documenta Bartókiana* II, p. 54.

60. Bartók, letter to Frederick Delius, June 1910, in *Letters,* p. 105. Márta devoted herself to Bartók, copying much of his music for him. But Everett Helm writes, "Differences between husband and wife began at an early date" ("Bartók," *High Fidelity,* November 1964, p. 74).

61. Dille, "On the Concert of February 12, 1911," *Documenta Bartókiana* II, p. 99.

62. Balász, quoted in József Ujfalussy, *Béla Bartók,* trans. Ruth Pataki, trans. rev. E. West (Boston: Crescendo, 1971), pp. 105, 109. There is much relevant material on Balász, his background (which was akin to Bartók's), personality, and attitudes, including quotations about Bartók from Balász's diary, in Gluck, *Georg Lukács and His Generation: 1900–1918.*

63. Kroó, "Data," pp. 79–123.

64. Bónis, "Bartók and Wagner," in *Bartók Studies*, p. 88.

65. Bartók, "The Folk Songs of Hungary" (1920), in *Essays*, p. 338.

66. Bartók, letter to Delius, n.d. [1910] in *Letters*, p. 105.

67. Bartók, letter to Delius, 27 March 1911, ibid., p. 111.

68. Bartók, letter to Géza Vilmos Zágon, 22 August 1913, ibid., pp. 123–24.

69. Bartók, letter to Buşiţia, 20 May 1915, ibid., p. 131.

70. John S. Weissmann, "Notes Concerning Bartók's Solo Vocal Music (I)," *Tempo* 36 (1955–56): 16–25. See also László Ferenczi, "The Timeliness of Ady," *New Hungarian Quarterly* 18/66 (Summer 1977): 32–35.

71. Denis Dille, "Sur les écrivants du texte de l'Opus 15," appendix to record notes for Bartók, *Hungarian Folk Songs* (Hungaroton SLPX11603).

72. Márta Ziegler, "Über Béla Bartók," in *Documenta Bartókiana* IV, ed. D. Dille (Budapest: Akadémiai Kiadó, 1970), p. 173.

73. Harvard Lectures (1943), in *Essays*, p. 370.

74. See Bartók's discussion of atonality in "The Problem of the New Music" (1920), ibid., pp. 455–63.

75. Kárpáti, *Bartók's String Quartets*, p. 16.

76. A 1926 interview, quoted by János Breuer, "Bartók and the Arts," *New Hungarian Quarterly* 16/60 (Winter 1975): 117.

77. When Bartók described a (Rumanian) peasant courting dance to Agatha Fassett, he showed her the wild tempo and the way the man dances around the woman, who must disapprove. "Love was created, it seems, for the benefit of man alone. The best a woman can do is to tolerate it with disapproval" (Fassett, pp. 188–89).

78. Dille, "Sur les écrivants du texte de l'Opus 15."

79. Kárpáti, *Bartók's String Quartets*, p. 186.

80. Kodály, quoted in Kroó, *Guide to Bartók*, pp. 93–94. In 1921 Kodály compared Bartók's crisis to Beethoven's: "All these works [of 1915–17] reveal a new manner of composition. Isolation and incessant work had a similar effect on Bartók as the progress of deafness on Beethoven. Alienated from the external world, turning inward, he reached into the furthest depths of his soul. He came to know the suffering that inspires poets to immortal beauty while at the same time consuming their lives. . . . We cannot approach works of such cryptic meaning with technical analyses; they must be listened to and felt" (Kodály, "Béla Bartók," in *Selected Writings*, p. 93).

81. Bartók, letter to Philip Heseltine (Peter Warlock), 24 November 1920, in *Documenta Bartókiana* V, ed. L. Somfai (Budapest: Akadémiai Kiadó, 1977), p. 140.

82. Ibid.; also Bartók, "The Relation of Folk Song to the Development of the Art Music of Our Time" (1921), in *Essays*, p. 325.

83. Bartók, "The Influence of Folk Music on the Art Music of Today" (1920), in *Essays*, p. 317; also Harvard Lectures (1943), ibid., p. 360.

84. Bartók, letter to Heseltine, 24 November 1920, in *Documenta Bartókiana* V, p. 140.

85. Lajos Lesznai, *Bartók*, trans. P. M. Young (London: Dent, 1973), p. 98.

86. Somfai, *Bartók's Workshop*, p. 49.

87. Béla Balázs, quoted in Ujfalussy, *Béla Bartók*, p. 135.

88. Bartók, "Hungary in the Throes of Reaction," written for *Musical Courier* 80/18 (April 1920), trans. C. Saerchinger, quoted in László Somfai, "Vierzehn Bartók-Schriften aus den Jahren 1920/21," *Documenta Bartókiana* V, pp. 15–138.

89. Bartók, letter to Buşiţia, May 1921, in *Letters*, p. 153.

90. Bartók, quoted in Kroó, *A Guide to Bartók*, p. 100. The libretto was written for the Russian ballet in 1912 at the request of Diaghilev, but the war intervened.

91. Szabolcsi, "Bartók's *Miraculous Mandarin*," in *Bartók Studies*, pp. 25, 33.

92. See the original libretto in *Bartók Studies*, pp. 111–16.

93. Ziegler, p. 177.

94. This musical symbol first appeared in the seventh of the diary-like Bagatelles (m. 9), as an accentuated, striking contrast to the capricious, staccato descending form of the Geyer motive.

95. Bartók, "The Influence of Peasant Music on Modern Music" (1931), in *Essays*, p. 343.

96. Szabolcsi, "Bartók's *Miraculous Mandarin*," in *Bartók Studies*, p. 24.

97. Vinton, pp. 1–17. See also Béla Bartók, *Black Pocket-Book: Sketches 1907–1922*, facsimile edition (Budapest: Editio Musica, 1987), folios 15–24, for sketches of many of the musical gestures and the original ending.

98. Vinton, p. 3.

99. Ibid., p. 17.

100. Kodály, "Bartók the Folklorist" (1955), in *Selected Writings*, p. 106. There is an illustration showing Bartók's revisions in colored ink, in Bónis, p. 92.

101. Somfai, interview with the authors, 27 June 1989, Bartók Archive, Budapest.

102. Bartók, "The Problem of the New Music" (1920), in *Essays*, p. 458.

103. Bartók's relationship with Jelly d'Arányi, whose family he had known as early as 1902 (when she was a child of nine), is described in Malcolm Gillies, *Bartók in Britain: A Guided Tour* (New York: Oxford University Press, 1989), pp. 131–44.

104. László Somfai, "The Influence of Peasant Music on the Finale of Bartók's Piano Sonata: An Assignment for Musical Analysis," which also gives analytical comments on the Second Sonata for Violin and Piano, in *Studies in Musical Sources and Style: Essays in Honor of Jan LaRue*, ed. Eugene K. Wolf and Edward A. Roesner (Madison: A-R Editions, 1990), p. 537. Sketches for the original ideas for the Second Violin Sonata are to be found in Bartók, *Black Pocket-Book*, folios 27v–30r. Somfai comments on the folk derivation of these ideas in *Bartók's Workshop*, p. 10.

105. Bartók, quoted in Bónis, p. 21.

106. Bartók, letter to Octavian Beu, 10 January 1931, in *Letters*, p. 201.

9. CHARLES IVES

1. Charles Ives, letter to Elliott Carter, 12 June 1944, in Ives Collection, Yale University.

2. Vivian Perlis, *Charles Ives Remembered* (New Haven: Yale University Press, 1974), pp. 87–88.

3. Ives, Postface, *114 Songs*, in *Essays Before a Sonata* [hereafter *Essays*], ed. Howard Boatwright (New York: Norton, 1961) p. 124.

4. Ives, Conductor's Note for the Fourth Symphony, in Ives Collection.

5. Elliott Carter, "Expressionism and American Music," *Perspectives of New Music* 4/2 (Fall–Winter 1965): 1–13; reprinted in *The Writings of Elliott Carter*, ed. Else Stone and Kurt Stone (Bloomington: Indiana University Press, 1977), pp. 230–43.

6. Charles Wilson Ward, "Charles Ives: The Relationship Between Aesthetic Theories and Compositional Processes," Ph.D. diss., University of Texas, Austin, 1974, p. 58.

7. Christopher Ballantine advises listening to Ives's music "musico-philosophically," and he compares Ives's symbolic use of quotation fragments to Jung's theory of dreams and their symbols. See Ballantine, "Charles Ives and the Meaning of Quotation in Music," *Musical Quarterly* 65/2 (April 1979): 167–84. Stuart Feder, a psychiatrist and psychoanalyst who has also studied composition, delves into Ives's relationship with his father and the evidence that the father remained present in the son's life after his death (when Ives was twenty) in a posthumous "collaboration." See Feder, "Decoration Day: A Boyhood Memory of Charles Ives," *Musical Quarterly* 66/2 (April 1980): 234–61.

8. Ives, letter to Henry Cowell, 4 December 1927, in Ives Collection.

9. Ives, letter to Nicholas Slonimsky, 28 May 1931, in Ives Collection. On 30 December 1931 Ives wrote to Slonimsky: "You're the only conductor that ever asked me to do anything. This score [which Ives had arranged for Slonimsky's Chamber Orchestra of Boston] would never have gotten off the shelf, if it hadn't been for you."

10. Marginal note, manuscript of sketch of the song "Majority" (1921) at m. 50, where twelve-tone principles are used; in Ives Collection. See John Kirkpatrick, "Ives as Revealed in His Marginalia," *Cornell University Musical Review* 4 (1961): 18. The note begins, "The plan of this, in orches[tra] parts, is to have each . . . complete the 12 notes (each in a different system) . . . & hold [the] last of [the] 12 . . . as finding its star. Occasionally. . . ." (etc.) Ives had previously used a twelve-tone row as an ostinato in *Tone Roads*, No. 3 (1915). J. Peter Burkholder, *Charles Ives: The Ideas Behind the Music* (New Haven: Yale University Press, 1985), p. 49, discusses the importance of distinguishing between Ives's concert music and his experiments designed to explore new technical possibilities, which Ives later called "hardly more than memos in notes."

11. Ives, *Memos*, ed. John Kirkpatrick (New York: Norton, 1972), pp. 97–98.

12. Ibid., p. 239.

13. Ives, Foreword to *The Unanswered Question* (New York: Southern Music, 1953).

14. Ives, *Essays*, p. 83.

15. Arnold Schoenberg, *Harmonielehre* (Leipzig and Vienna: Universal, 1911), p. vi: "Unsere Zeit sucht vieles. Gefunden aber hat sie vor allem etwas: den Komfort. . . . Der Komfort als Weltanschauung! Möglichst wenig Bewegung, keine Erschütterung. Die den Komfort so lieben, werden nie dort suchen, wo nicht bestimmt etwas zu finden ist."

16. Ives, *Essays*, p. 97.

17. Ives, *Memos*, p. 101.

18. Van Wyck Brooks, *The Flowering of New England* (New York: Dutton, 1936), p. 408, says that leading manufacturers saw themselves in their early stages as Rollo. The Rollo books were written in the 1860s (revised in the 1870s) by Jacob Abbott (1803–79), a New England author whose works bore such titles as *Young Christian Series*, *Learning to Read*, *Learning to Think*, *The Little Philosopher*, and *A Primer of Ethics*.

19. Sketch of String Quartet No. 2, in Ives Collection. The famous violinist Mischa Elman (1891–1967) must have seemed too Rollo-like to Ives.

20. Ives, *Essays*, p. 80.

21. This song exists in two published versions: Ives's 1913 solo song arrangement, on *114 Songs* (Redding, CT, 1922), p. 13; and Henry Cowell's orchestral arrangement of the original two-part choral setting (New York: Peer International, 1970). The latter is the source of the lower part used in Ex. 9-2, which Ives omitted in his solo song arrangement.

22. Ives, *Memos*, p. 162.

23. Ibid., p. 55.

24. Ives, letter to John Tasker Howard, 30 June 1930, ibid., p. 237.

25. Ibid., p. 47.

26. Ibid., p. 141.

27. Ibid., p. 132.

28. Ives, *Essays*, p. 84.

29. Ives, *Memos*, pp. 45–46.

30. Ibid., pp. 132–33.

31. Ives, note in score, Sonata No. 4 for Violin and Piano (New York: Associated Music Publishers, 1942), p. 21.

32. Ives, *Memos*, p. 165.

33. Ives, note in score, Sonata No. 4 for violin and piano. Structures based on

the foreshadowing of thematic material are frequent with Ives. He states that in his Sonata No. 3 for Violin and Piano, "the working-out develops into the themes, rather than from them. The coda consists of the themes for the first time in their entirety" (*Memos*, p. 69, n. 1). This technique was also used by Stravinsky, first in *The Firebird* and then extensively in *Petrushka* and *The Rite of Spring*.

34. Henry Cowell and Sidney Cowell, *Charles Ives and His Music* (New York: Oxford University Press, 1955), p. 12.

35. Ives, *Memos*, pp. 114–15.

36. Ibid., p. 103 n.

37. Ives, letter to George E. Ives, 3 December 1893, in Ives family correspondence, Ives Collection.

38. Ives, *Memos*, p. 47.

39. Ibid., p. 132.

40. John Kirkpatrick and Gregg Smith, editor's notes for their edition of Psalm 90 (Bryn Mawr: Merion Music, 1970), pp. 3–4.

41. Olin Downes, review of a concert on 29 January 1927, quoted in Cowell and Cowell, p. 102.

42. John Kirkpatrick, reminiscence in Perlis, p. 221. See also Nicholas Slonimsky's similar experiences with *Three Places in New England*, ibid., p. 150.

43. Ives, *Memos*, p. 71.

44. Perlis, p. 123.

45. Ives, *Memos*, p. 131.

46. Kathryn Verplanck, Ives's personal secretary before 1912, in Perlis, p. 50.

47. Ives, "Commuter's Diary," 16 February–2 March 1914, in Ives Collection. For Henry Bellamann, who published an article on Ives in *The Musical Quarterly* in 1933, Ives wrote a long memo on his feelings about business versus music. His draft in the Ives Collection at Yale shows his bitterness (the bracketed portions, which he omitted from his final version) toward professional musicians: "It is my impression that there is [a greater freedom from personal animosity, group prejudice] more open-mindedness [tolerance] and willingness to examine [intelligently and] carefully [and accurately] the premises underlying a new or unfamiliar thing [before condemning it], in the world of business than in the world of music. [Perhaps too, in the former, there is less personal bias, egoism, and group prejudice, with their limiting influence.]" This memo, which includes the statement quoted above in chap. 1, "The fabric of existence weaves itself into a whole . . . ," is quoted in full, omitting, of course, Ives's own deletions, in Henry H. Bellamann, "Charles Ives, the Man and his Music," *The Musical Quarterly* 19 (1933): 47–48.

48. Ives, *Memos*, p. 39. A schedule, in the Ives Collection, which had obviously been tacked on a wall or a door, gives a sample of Ives's "vacation" ideal while in Redding:

6:45–7:30	Chores (fire, coal, pump, spring water etc.)
7:30–7:45	Bach
7:45–8:15	Breakfast
8:15–11:00	Hard work [evidently composing?]
11–12:30	Farm work
12:30–1	Loaf
1–1:30	Lunch
1:30–2	Read
2–6	Farm work & wood & water trees
6–6:30	Rest (hard work)
6:30–7:30	Dinner (big)
7:30–8	Smoke and talk
8–9	Read (Jim to barn)

9–   To bed % D.C. @ coda
Farm work = potatoes, bunch corn, dry beans, burn weed, dig around not up
apple trees. Currant bushes, rye & flour (soy)
(Oct. 15 screens off) cut weeds spring

49. Ives, *Memos*, p. 130.
50. Ives admired Walt Whitman's poetry and set one of his texts, "Who goes
there," both as a choral piece and as a solo song. Harmony's influence on his attitudes
can be seen in a letter (11 October 1921) to Clifton Furness, an authority on Whitman. While agreeing with Furness that "Whitman . . . tells us with wonderful power
of the great life values," Ives admits, "I have read Whitman little lately. Mrs. Ives
doesn't like the over-human leer in his face." In Ives Collection.
51. But in *Essays*, p. 82, Ives remarks: "[Debussy's] substance would have been
worthier if his adoration or contemplation of Nature . . . had been more the quality
of Thoreau's. . . . Thoreau leaned toward substance and Debussy toward manner."
52. Ives, *Essays*, p. xxv. See also the manuscript reproduced in Perlis, p. 110.
53. "My Thoreau, that reassuring and true friend, who stood by me one 'low'
day, when the sun had gone down, long, long before sunset" (*Essays*, p. 67). This
comment has been interpreted by Howard Boatwright (the editor) as referring to George
Ives's death at the age of 49 in 1894, when Ives was a freshman at Yale.
54. Perlis, p. 82.
55. Ives, *Essays*, p. 22.
56. Ives, *Memos*, p. 188.
57. Ibid., p. 199 n. 3. Ives's comment refers specifically to the fugato beginning
at the fourth brace of p. 13 of the second edition (Ives's revision) of the Piano Sonata
No. 2: "Concord, Mass., 1840–1860" (New York and London: Associated Music
Publishers, 1947), and also to the movement as a whole.
58. Ives, *Memos*, p. 201.
59. Ives, End Notes to Piano Sonata No. 2, second edition.
60. Ives, *Memos*, pp. 79–80.
61. Ibid., p. 196.
62. Ives, *Essays*, p. 36.
63. John Kirkpatrick, Introduction to his unpublished edition of the *Concord
Sonata*.
64. Ives, *Memos*, p. 191.
65. Ibid., p. 199 n. 3.
66. Ives, "Commuter's Diary," 11–15 June 1914, Ives Collection.
67. Scrap Book I, Ives Collection.
68. Ives, *Memos*, p. 112.
69. Ives, *Essays*, Prologue, pp. 4–8.
70. Ibid., Epilogue, pp. 70–92.
71. Wassily Kandinsky, *Concerning the Spiritual in Art,* trans. Michael Sadler
(reprint, New York: Dover, 1977), pp. 1–9.
72. Ives, *Memos*, p. 136. In correspondence with Clifton Furness, who began
writing to Ives upon receipt of a copy of the *Concord* Sonata in 1921, and who was
himself struggling to compose, Ives commented further about his philosophy of organic "flow." Furness complained of a lack of cohesion in his own music. Drafting a
reply, Ives jotted down, "cohesion—grabbing at a life-preserver—something definite
to hold on to. The ocean is more important than one life—give it a chance." Letter
to Clifton Furness, 11 September 1932, in Ives Collection.
73. Ives, *Memos*, p. 66.
74. Quoted in John Kirkpatrick's Preface to Ives's Fourth Symphony (New York:
Associated Music Publishers, 1965), p. viii. Note the development of this idea out of
the germ of *The Unanswered Question*.

75. Ives, *Memos*, p. 66.

76. Ibid., pp. 92–93.

77. Kirkpatrick, Preface to Fourth Symphony, p. viii.

78. Ives, "Commuter's Diary," 5 June 1914, Ives Collection. This entry, written on the train commuting between Redding and New York, begins, "I fear I may get further and further away from my boyhood dreams."

79. Ives, *Essays*, p. 42.

80. Kirkpatrick, Preface to Fourth Symphony, p. vii.

81. Ives, *Memos*, p. 129.

82. Kurt Stone, "Ives's Fourth Symphony: A Review," *The Musical Quarterly* 52/1 (January 1966): 11.

83. Kirkpatrick, Preface to the Fourth Symphony, p. ix.

84. Stone and Stone, *The Writings of Elliott Carter,* pp. 230–43. This perceptive article is a report following the conference on expressionism at the Maggio Musicale, Florence, 1964. Carter combines this with a discussion of the "ultramoderns," who influenced him strongly when, as a high school student in the mid-1920s, he met Ives and accompanied him to concerts. Like others in the 1960s, Carter mistakenly equates constructivism and experimentalism with expressionism; he also includes Varèse's technique of fragmentation in his discussion of expressionistic vision.

85. Perlis, p. 35.

86. See Ives's performances of his own works in *Music of Ives: 100th Anniversary Album* (Columbia Records M4-3254, 1974).

87. Ives, letter to Bernard Herrmann, n.d., in Ives Collection.

88. Bellamann, p. 49.

89. See Ives's mocking song "On the Counter," 1920.

90. Ives, *Essays*, p. 52.

91. Perlis, p. 218.

92. Stone and Stone, p. 236. Ives shunned the material world. Modern inventions, such as the camera and the telephone, terrified him; and he would have little to do with newspapers, which he felt advanced his country's crass commercialism (Perlis, pp. 42, 99, 136).

93. Ives, letter to Slonimsky, 14 July 1929, Ives Collection.

94. Ives, memo on note paper of the St. James Palace Hotel, London, where the Iveses stayed August 7–19, 1924; written at the time of the death (12 August) of David Twichell, his close friend, New York roommate, and brother-in-law. (In Ives Collection.)

10. SYNTHESIS OF THE ARTS

1. Wassily Kandinsky, "On Stage Composition," in Kandinsky and F. Marc, eds., *The Blaue Reiter Almanac* (1912), New Documentary Edition, ed. Klaus Lankheit, trans. H. Falkenstein, M. Terzian, and G. Hinderlie (reprint, New York: Viking, 1974), pp. 190ff.

2. Schoenberg, letter to Ferruccio Busoni, 13 or 18 August 1909, in Busoni, *Selected Letters*, trans. and ed. Antony Beaumont (London: Faber & Faber, 1987), p. 389.

3. Wassily Kandinsky, *Concerning the Spiritual in Art*, trans. M. T. H. Sadler (New York: Dover Publications, 1977), pp. 19–20.

4. Kandinsky, preface to catalogue of second Neue Künstlervereinigung exhibition, Munich, September 1910, quoted in Will Grohmann, *Kandinsky* (New York: Abrams, n.d.), p. 86.

5. *Vergeisterung der Form,* a concept begun by Gustav Klimt and spread by Schoenberg and Adolf Loos to other countries, is mentioned in Otto Zoff, "Adolf Loos über sein [Michaelerplatz] Haus," *Der Merker* 3 (February 1912): 115.

6. Martin Cooper, *Ideas and Music* (London: Barrie and Rockliff, 1965), pp. 131–32.

7. William Austin, *Music in the Twentieth Century* (New York: Norton, 1966), p. 69.

8. In Ives's correspondence with Katherine Heyman (1928–31), Ives Collection, Yale University, there is much discussion of Scriabin, whose works Heyman was performing and for whose philosophy she was an apostle. In his music collection, Ives owned many piano works of Scriabin, including Piano Sonatas Nos. 4, 5, 8, and 9.

9. Charles Ives, *Memos*, ed. John Kirkpatrick (New York: Norton, 1972), pp. 106–108.

10. Ibid., p. 163.

11. Jelena Hahl-Koch, ed., *Arnold Schoenberg/Wassily Kandinsky: Letters, Pictures and Documents*, trans. John C. Crawford (London: Faber, 1984), p. 25.

12. Adolphe Appia, *Musik und die Inszenierung*, trans. Ulric Moore (Ithaca: Cornell University Press, 1929), p. 6.

13. E. Gordon Craig, *On the Art of the Theatre*, 1911 version (reprint, London: Heinemann, 1957), pp. 46–47.

14. See Oliver Sayler, ed., *Max Reinhardt and His Theater* (New York: Brentano's, 1924), p. 22; and Gottfried Reinhardt, *The Genius: A Memoir of Max Reinhardt* (New York: Knopf, 1979), p. 16.

15. Franz Willnauer, *Gustav Mahler und die Wiener Oper* (Vienna: Jugend und Volk, 1979), p. 126.

16. Hermann Bahr, *Glossen zum Wiener Theater, 1903–06* (Berlin: Fischer, 1907), pp. 236ff.

17. Willnauer, pp. 102, 128.

18. Ibid., p. 87.

19. Oscar Bie, in a review of *Tristan und Isolde*, 1903, quoted in Kurt Blaukopf, *Gustav Mahler*, trans. Inge Goodwin (New York: Praeger, 1973), p. 168. Mahler saw to it that Roller had all the technical rehearsal time he needed, but the long hours spent experimenting with lighting in the opera house became a source of bureaucratic complaints against Mahler's directorship.

20. Quoted in Henry-Louis de La Grange, *Gustav Mahler: Chronique d'une vie* vol. 2 (Paris: Fayard, 1983), p. 312.

21. Max Graf, *Der Wiener Oper* (Vienna: Humbolt, 1955), pp. 163ff.

22. La Grange, vol. 2, p. 326.

23. Kurt Blaukopf, *Gustav Mahler*, trans. I. Goodwin (New York: Praeger, 1973), p. 174.

24. "Das Wichtigste in der Musik steht nicht in den Noten." Richard Specht, *Gustav Mahler* (Berlin: Deutsche Verlags-Anstalt, 1925), p. 94.

25. Kurt Blaukopf, ed., *Mahler: a Documentary Study* (London: Thames & Hudson, 1976), p. 237.

26. Bruno Walter, *Gustav Mahler*, trans. Lotte Walter Lindt (New York: Schocken, 1974), pp. 81–82.

27. *Der Merker* 2 (June 1911).

28. Roy F. Allen, *German Expressionism and the Berlin Circles* (Göppingen: Kümmerle, 1974), pp. 261–67. See also Lothar Schreyer, *Erinnerungen an Sturm und Bauhaus* (Munich: Langen, Müller, 1956).

29. *Blaue Reiter Almanac*, p. 37.

30. Ibid.

31. Arnold Schoenberg, "The Relationship to the Text." Also included were articles by composer Thomas von Hartmann on "Anarchy in Music," Mussorgsky disciple Leonid Sabaneiev on "Scriabin's *Prometheus*," and a visionary article on "Free Music" by N. Kulbin.

32. Ernst von Wolzogen, *Ansichten und Aussichten* (Berlin: Fontane, 1908), p.

x. Wolzogen, aristocrat son of the Intendant of the Court Theater in Schwerin, Germany, was a poet, novelist, and musical journalist. He composed and functioned in all areas of music as a dilettante, while growing up in the theater. His older stepbrother, Hans, lived most of his life in Bayreuth as editor of the *Bayreuther Blätter*, which published Ernst's review—the only one—of Adolphe Appia's first pamphlet criticizing Wagnerian production philosophy.

33. From Brecht's 1918 obituary for Wedekind, quoted in Sol Gittleman, *Frank Wedekind* (New York: Twayne, 1969), p. 5.

34. Ibid., p. 22.

35. Bahr, p. 255.

36. Strindberg's "Memorandum on Intimate Theater" (1908) was widely influential. It is quoted in Michael Meyer, *Strindberg* (New York: Random House, 1985), p. 438.

37. See Peter Vergo, *Art in Vienna: 1898–1918* (London: Phaidon, 1975), pp. 148–52.

38. Oskar Kokoschka, *My Life*, trans. David Britt (London: Thames & Hudson, 1974), p. 27.

39. Ibid., p. 30. See also James Ritchie, *German Expressionist Drama* (Boston: G. K. Hall, 1976), p. 128.

40. Werner J. Schweiger, *Der junge Kokoschka: Leben und Werk: 1904–1914* (Vienna: Brandstätter, 1983), p. 46.

41. Kokoschka, *My Life*, p. 29.

42. Orrel P. Reed Jr., *German Expressionist Art: The Robert Rifkind Collection* (Los Angeles: University of California, 1977), p. 132. See also Kokoschka, *My Life*, p. 28; and Gertrude Pott, *Die Spiegelung des Sezessionismus im Österreichischen Theater* (Vienna: Wilhelm Braumüller, 1975), p. 169. Paul Zinner created the music.

43. Oskar Kokoschka, *Schriften*, ed. H. M. Wingler (Munich: Langen, Müller, 1956), p. 50.

44. Pappenheim, letter to Schoenberg, n.d, established by Brian Simms as early September 1909; Schoenberg Collection, Library of Congress.

45. Jane Kallir, *Schoenberg's Vienna* (New York: Galerie St. Etienne/Rizzoli, 1984), p. 90 n. 34.

46. Ibid.

47. Quoted in Kokoschka, *My Life*, p. 217.

48. Olof Lagercrantz, *August Strindberg*, trans. Anselm Hollo (London: Faber, 1984), p. 171. Schoenberg did not often acknowledge the influence of his contemporaries, but at the end of his life he wrote, in a letter to Jake Johnson, 30 June 1951, that he had read all of Strindberg's translated works "numerous times. . . . That made me one of his greatest disciples." Letter in Schoenberg Collection, Library of Congress.

49. Bahr, *Glossen*. The influence of Strindberg was strong among the Viennese avant-garde preoccupied with sex and destruction. Bruno Bettelheim, *Freud's Vienna and Other Essays* (New York: Knopf, 1990), pp. 2–16.

50. Webern, letter to Berg, 21 December 1911, on "spiritual communion" between artists: "Strindberg and Schoenberg! Rays of God!" in Hans Moldenhauer and Rosaleen Moldenhauer, *Anton von Webern* (New York: Knopf, 1978), p. 152; Berg repeated Webern's comments to Schoenberg, 23 December 1911, in Juliane Brand, Christopher Hailey, and Donald Harris, eds., *The Berg-Schoenberg Correspondence* (New York: Norton, 1987).

51. Arnold Schoenberg, "Painting Influences," trans. Gertrude Zeisl, *Journal of the Arnold Schoenberg Institute* 2/3 (June 1978): 239.

52. Halsey Stevens, "A Conversation With Schoenberg About Painting," ibid., p. 179.

53. Kandinsky, "The Paintings of Schoenberg," trans. Barbara Zeisl, ibid., p. 181.

54. Schoenberg, "Painting Influences," p. 237.

55. Kandinsky, letter to Schoenberg, 20 December 1911, in *Schoenberg/Kandinsky Letters,* p. 41.

56. Schoenberg, Breslau lecture on *Die glückliche Hand,* ibid., p. 105.

57. Quoted in John C. Crawford, *"Die glückliche Hand,* Further Notes," *Journal of the Arnold Schoenberg Institute* 4/1 (June 1980): 73.

58. Schoenberg, letter to Ernst Legal, Intendant, Kroll Opera, Berlin, 14 April 1930, in Josef Rufer, *Das Werk Arnold Schönbergs* (Basel: Bärenreiter, 1959), p. 15.

59. Schoenberg, letter to Fritz Soot, 18 November 1913, in *Arnold Schoenberg Letters,* ed. Erwin Stein, trans. Eithne Wilkins and Ernst Kaiser (Berkeley: University of California Press, 1987), p. 41: "Concerning the role of the Man . . . acting ability is the most important. . . . The singer should sing it who is best cut out for it, whether he is a tenor, a baritone, or a bass."

60. Webern, letter to Berg, 5 September 1911, unpublished.

61. Schoenberg, letter to his publisher, Emil Hertzka, n.d., in *Arnold Schoenberg Letters,* p. 44; the editor, Erwin Stein, one of Schoenberg's early composition students, presumes 1913 to be the year.

62. Webern, letters to Berg, 27 July, 2 and 8 August 1912, unpublished.

63. Schoenberg, letter to Kandinsky, 19 August 1912, in *Schoenberg/Kandinsky Letters,* p. 54. In the same letter, he reported to Kandinsky the completion of *Pierrot lunaire,* which had for him "perhaps no heartfelt necessity as regards its theme, its content, but certainly as regards its form." This work was useful to him as a "preparatory study" for the oratorio.

64. Schoenberg, letter to Loos, 19 June 1917, in F. Glück, "Briefe von Arnold Schönberg an Adolf Loos," *Österreichisches Musikzeitung* 16 (January 1961): 10.

65. Arnold Schoenberg, "Zemlinsky," in *Style and Idea,* ed. Leonard Stein, trans. Leo Black (Berkeley: University of California Press, 1984), p. 486.

66. "Diese Synthese einer ungeheuerlichen Erfahrung, eines unfassbaren Glaubens." Webern, letter to Berg, 12 July 1917, unpublished.

67. Webern, sketch of ideas for *Tot,* Webern collection, Paul Sacher Stiftung, Basel.

68. Webern, letter to Schoenberg, 6 November 1913, in Schoenberg Collection, Library of Congress.

69. Webern, letter to Schoenberg, 10 November 1913, ibid. Balzac's *Séraphîta* had likewise been based on long quotations from Swedenborg. Schoenberg himself had quoted Swedenborg (through Balzac) very briefly in *Die Jakobsleiter.*

70. Hans Moldenhauer, lecture at the Arnold Schoenberg Institute, 4 April 1983. The manuscript of the play is in the Webern Collection, Paul Sacher Stiftung, Basel.

71. Alban Berg, "A Word About Wozzeck," *Modern Music* 5 (November–December 1927): 22.

11. THE LEGACY OF EXPRESSIONISM

1. Max Krell, *Das Alles gab es einmal* (Frankfurt: Scheffler, 1961), p. 208.

2. John Willett, *Expressionism* (New York: McGraw-Hill, 1970), pp. 125–26.

3. Helga Kleimann, *Die Novembergruppe* (Berlin: Gebr. Mann, 1969), p. 74 n. 54.

4. Gustav Hartlaub (who is credited with inventing the term *Neue Sachlichkeit*), cited in Peter Gay, *Weimar Culture* (New York: Harper and Row, 1968), p. 122.

5. Willett, p. 190.

6. Gay, pp. 122–23.

7. Geoffrey Skelton, *Paul Hindemith: The Man Behind the Music* (New York: Crescendo, 1975), p. 29.

8. Andres Briner, "Ich und Wir—Zur Entwicklung des jungen Paul Hindemith," in *Erprobungen und Erfahrungen: Zu Paul Hindemiths Schaffen in den Zwanziger Jahren,* ed. Dieter Rexroth, Veröffentlichungen des Paul-Hindemith-Institutes Frankfurt, vol. 2 (Mainz: Schott, 1978), p. 29.

9. Peter Cahn, "Hindemiths Lehrjahre in Frankfurt," *Hindemith-Jahrbuch* 2 (1972): 45.

10. Ibid., p. 44. It is the 1922 first movement which is included in the published version of Op. 11, No. 3.

11. Letter to Emmy Ronnefeldt (May 1917), in Skelton, p. 51.

12. Andres Briner, *Paul Hindemith* (Zürich: Atlantis, 1971), pp. 24–25. Hindemith's words provide an interesting echo of Schoenberg's 1910 program notes for *Das Buch der hängenden Gärten* (see above, p. 73).

13. Hindemith's second opera is *Das Nusch-Nuschi,* Op. 20 (1921), a comic work based on an erotic libretto by Franz Blei.

14. Briner, "Ich und Wir," p. 27.

15. Gerhard R. Koch, "Musiktheater," in *Paul Hindemith: Katalogue seiner Werke* (Frankfurt: Städtische Musikbibliothek, 1970), p. 10.

16. Skelton, p. 63.

17. Paul Hindemith, introduction to the revised version of *Das Marienleben* (Mainz: Schott, 1948), p. iii.

18. Skelton, p. 80.

19. Ronald Sanders, *The Days Grow Short: The Life and Music of Kurt Weill* (New York: Holt, Reinhart and Winston, 1980), p. 20.

20. Ibid., p. 28.

21. In Johannes R. Becher, *Um Gott* (Leipzig: Insel, 1921), p. 130.

22. In 1924, Becher completely revised the play along more strictly Communist lines, significantly changing the subtitle to *Entwurf zu einem revolutionären Kampfdrama* (Sketch for a Drama of Revolutionary Struggle). See Kim Kowalke, *Kurt Weill in Europe* (Ann Arbor: UMI Research Press, 1979), pp. 25, 319 n. 51.

23. Becher, pp. 162–85.

24. See David Drew's analysis of the First Symphony in relation to Becher's play in the album notes to the recording (Angel S-36506).

25. Ibid.

26. Becher, p. 213.

27. Ferruccio Busoni, *Entwurf einer neuen Ästhetik der Tonkunst* (Trieste: Schmidt, 1907); *Sketch of a New Esthetic of Music,* English trans. by Th. Baker (New York: G. Schirmer, 1911).

28. Baker (trans.), *Sketch,* p. 37.

29. Ibid., pp. 5, 14.

30. Busoni, quoted in William Austin, *Music in the 20th Century* (New York: Norton, 1966), p. 114.

31. Kurt Weill, "Busoni und die neue Musik" (Busoni and the New Music), in Kowalke, p. 462.

32. "Topical Dialogue about *Schuloper* between Kurt Weill and Dr. Hans Fischer" (1930), in Kowalke, p. 522.

33. Sanders, p. 57.

34. Kowalke, p. 31.

35. Martin Esslin, cited in ibid., p. 117.

36. Kurt Weill, "Concerning the Gestic Character of the Text," in ibid., p. 493.

37. Friedrich Saathen, Introduction to Ernst Krenek, *Zur Sprache gebracht* (Munich: Langen-Müller, 1958), pp. 8–9.

38. Krenek, in a letter to the authors dated 23 October 1981, names "about Op. 6 to Op. 24" as his expressionist works.

39. Ernst Krenek, *Horizons Circled: Reflections on My Music* (Berkeley: University of California Press, 1974), p. 22.

40. Ernst Krenek, "Self-Analysis," *New Mexico Quarterly* 23/1 (Spring 1953): 12.

41. Ibid.

42. Krenek, *Horizons Circled*, p. 39.

43. Saathen, p. 9.

44. Krenek, *Horizons Circled*, pp. 36–37.

45. In *Der Zwingburg*, two examples of these more consonant sections are the chorale which follows the unveiling of the statue (2 mm. before [95]) and the elegiac gestures of the Organ-grinder's final passage (mm. 1407ff.), which recall *Das Lied von der Erde.*

46. Krenek, *Horizons Circled*, p. 22.

47. Krenek, "Self-Analysis," pp. 6–7.

48. Krenek, *Horizons Circled*, p. 38.

49. Oskar Kokoschka, letter to H. M. Winkler, 9 November 1950, quoted in Kokoschka, *Schriften: 1907–1955*, ed. Winkler (Munich: Langen-Müller, 1956), p. 467.

50. See Act II, scene 4 of the play and opera.

51. Published in *Zeit-Echo: Ein Kriegs-Tagebuch für Künstler* 20/1 (1915): 300; text also in Kokoschka, *Schriften*, p. 130.

52. Krenek, "Self-Analysis," pp. 13–14.

53. Krenek, *Horizons Circled*, pp. 23–24.

54. Ibid., p. 24.

55. Krenek, "Self-Analysis," p. 14.

56. Ernst Krenek, "Musik der Gegenwart," speech given 19 October 1925 at the Congress for Musical Esthetics, Karlsruhe; in *25 Jahre neue Musik: Jahrbuch 1926 der Universal-Edition* (Vienna: Universal, 1926), pp. 57–59.

57. Schoenberg, letter to Kandinsky, 20 July 1922, in *Arnold Schoenberg Letters*, ed. Erwin Stein, trans. Eithne Wilkins and Ernst Kaiser (Berkeley: University of California Press, 1987), p. 71.

58. Krenek, letter to the authors, 23 October 1981.

59. Ibid.

60. "Enough of clouds, of waves, of aquariums, of Ondines, and odors of the night; we need a music on the ground, A MUSIC OF EVERYDAY." Jean Cocteau, *Le Coq et l'arlequin* (Paris, 1918); in Austin, p. 166.

61. H. H. Stuckenschmidt, *Schoenberg: His Life, World, and Work*, trans. Humphrey Searle (New York: Schirmer Books, 1978), p. 277.

62. Dates from Jan Maegaard, *Studien zur Entwicklung des dodekaphonen Satzes bei Arnold Schönberg*, vol. 1 (Copenhagen: Hansen, 1972), pp. 95–110.

63. Dates from Josef Rufer, *The Works of Arnold Schoenberg*, trans. Dika Newlin (London: Faber, 1962), p. 73; and Stuckenschmidt, p. 485.

64. Stuckenschmidt, p. 479.

65. Walter H. Rubsamen, "Schoenberg in America," *Musical Quarterly* 37/4 (October 1951): 482.

66. Karl H. Wörner, *Neue Musik in der Entscheidung*, 2d ed. (Mainz: Schott, 1956), pp. 61–63.

67. Nikolai Lopatnikoff, "An American in Berlin," *Modern Music* 9/2 (January–February 1932): 91.

68. Ruggles Collection, Yale University. Other portions of this lecture appear in John Kirkpatrick, "The Evolution of Carl Ruggles: A Chronicle Largely in His Own Words," *Perspectives of New Music* 6/2 (Spring–Summer 1968): 149–50.

69. Interview with Ruggles, *Christian Science Monitor,* 13 September 1919.

70. Gerhart Hauptmann, *Die Versunkene Glocke,* 1896; English translation by Charles Henry Meltzer, 1899.

71. Lecture at the Whitney Studio Club, New York, 31 March 1922 (Ruggles Collection, Yale University). Other portions of this lecture are quoted in Kirkpatrick, p. 154.

72. From *Gnomic Verses,* in *The Poetical Works of William Blake* (London: Oxford University Press, 1913 [reprinted 1960]), p. 193.

73. Lou Harrison, *About Carl Ruggles* (Yonkers: Oscar Baradinsky at the Alicat Bookshop, 1946), pp. 18–19.

74. From an unpublished 1929 article by Dorothy Canfield Fisher, Ruggles Collection.

75. Ruggles, letter to Henry Cowell, 27 January 1928, quoted in Kirkpatrick, pp. 156–57. Anton Webern expresses a similar new confidence in his melodic writing ("long themes . . . something entirely different from before the war") in the Trakl settings which he wrote beginning in 1917 (see above, p. 121).

76. Robert Browning, "Pauline" (1833). Like Ives, Ruggles had a strong knowledge of nineteenth-century poetry. He has even been described as more intellectually involved with English literature than with music while he was studying at Harvard (Eric Salzman, "Carl Ruggles: A Lifetime Is Not Too Long to Search for the Sublime," *High Fi/Stereo Review,* September 1966: 56).

77. Ruggles, letter to Charlotte Ruggles, undated (December 1925?), Ruggles Collection.

78. Charles Seeger, "Carl Ruggles," *Musical Quarterly* 18/4 (October 1932): 589–90.

79. Salzman, p. 56.

80. Ruggles Collection.

81. S. E. Gilbert, "Carl Ruggles (1876–1971): An Appreciation," *Perspectives of New Music* 10/1 (Fall–Winter 1971): 224.

82. Ruggles Collection.

83. Lou Harrison, quoted in Vivian Perlis, *Charles Ives Remembered* (New Haven: Yale University Press, 1974), p. 200.

84. Solomon Volkov, ed., *Testimony: The Memoirs of Dmitri Shostakovich,* trans. Antonina W. Bouis (New York: Harper and Row, 1979), p. 29.

85. Maxim Shostakovich, the composer's son, quoted in Boris Schwarz, *Music and Musical Life in Soviet Russia,* 2d ed. (Bloomington: Indiana University Press, 1983), p. 645.

86. The reliability of these memoirs, smuggled out of Russia and published after Shostakovich's death, has been controversial, but their consistency of tone (bitterness, irony and black humor), makes them extremely convincing. Boris Schwarz, the leading American scholar of Soviet music, finds "the overall impression [of *Testimony*] . . . persuasive" (Schwarz, p. 576).

87. According to Dmitri Sollertinsky and Ludmilla Sollertinsky, *Pages from the Life of Dmitri Shostakovich,* trans. Graham Hobbs and Charles Midgley (New York and London: Harcourt Brace Jovanovich, 1980), p. 46, Shostakovich was very close to Gogol in temperament.

88. Volkov, p. 135.

89. Ibid., p. 159.

90. Ibid., p. 180.

91. Schwarz, p. 80.

92. In Act IV of *Lady Macbeth,* Shostakovich uses actual convict songs, which his mother had played to him when he was a child. Ian MacDonald, *The New Shostakovich* (London: Fourth Estate, 1990), p. 92.

93. All references to *Lady Macbeth of Mzensk* are to the original piano-vocal score (Moscow: State Musical Publishing House, 1935).

94. Schwarz, p. 127; and Volkov, p. 43.

95. The crescendo on one note similar to the one in *Wozzeck* (Act III, m. 109) is heard in Act I, scene 2 of Shostakovich's opera ([110]). The "immer zu" motive from Berg's opera (Act II, m. 504) appears in the entr'acte following Act I, scene 1 of *Lady Macbeth,* after [66].

96. Beginning of Act III, scene 3 (m. 122).

97. Volkov, pp. 113–14.

98. Quoted in Schwarz, p. 123.

99. Volkov, p. 113.

100. Ibid., p. 118.

101. Schwarz, p. 279.

102. Volkov, p. 141.

103. The motto had appeared earlier in such works as the Violin Concerto No. 1 (1947–48; revised 1955) and the Fifth String Quartet (1952).

104. Volkov, pp. 155–56.

105. Robert Stradling, "Shostakovich and the Soviet System, 1925–75," in Christopher Norris, ed., *Shostakovich: The Man and His Music* (Boston and London: Boyars, 1982), p. 211.

106. For details, see Roy Blokker and Robert Dearling, *The Music of Dmitri Shostakovich: The Symphonies* (Cranbury, NJ: Associated University Presses, 1979), pp. 134–35 n.

107. Shostakovich, Preface to *14. Symphonie,* Op. 135 (Hamburg: Sikorski, 1970).

108. Volkov, pp. 14, 204.

109. *Musical America* (1 December 1959); quoted in Schwarz, p. 318.

110. Volkov, p. 234.

111. Roger Sessions, "Some Notes on Schoenberg, and the Method of Composing with Twelve Notes," *Score* 6 (May 1952): 10.

112. Elliott Carter, letter to Peter Yates, 8 June 1959 (unpublished). Peter Yates Collection, University of California, San Diego.

113. Dorothy L. Crawford, interview with Leon Kirchner, Cambridge, MA, 30 December 1987.

114. Ibid.; and "I sometimes think I dreamed all of this, and perhaps I have," interview with Kirchner in *Harvard Magazine* 77/3 (November 1974): 47.

115. Kirchner, letter to Gerald Turbow, 13 March 1990, unpublished.

116. Kirchner, quoted in Hans Heinsheimer, "Zeroing In," *Opera News* 41/23 (16 April 1977): 13.

117. Aaron Copland, review of Kirchner's Duo for Violin and Piano (1947), *Notes* 7/3 (June 1950): 434.

118. Kirchner, quoted in Gilbert Chase, *America's Music,* 2d. ed. (New York and Toronto: McGraw-Hill, 1966), p. 570.

119. Heinsheimer, p. 13.

120. Other works which repay study from this point of view are the *Sonata Concertante* for violin and piano (1952) and the Piano Concerto No. 1 (1953).

121. Kirchner, quoted in Joseph Machlis, *Introduction to Contemporary Music* (New York: Norton, 1961), p. 605.

122. Kirchner, quoted in Joseph Horowitz, "Notes on the Program," *Leon Kirchner,* CD Elektra Nonesuch 79188-2 (1989).

123. Joseph Schillinger (1895–1943) developed a method for musical composition based on mathematical principles.

124. Luigi Nono, "The Historical Reality of Music Today," *Score* 27 (July 1960): 43–45. English translation of a lecture given by Nono at Darmstadt on 1 September 1959.

125. Luigi Nono, *Texte: Studien zu seiner Musik,* ed. Jürg Stenzl (Zürich: Atlantis, 1975), pp. 12–13 of Introduction.

126. Nono, "Möglichkeit und Notwendigkeit eines neuen Musiktheaters" (based on a 1962 lecture), in *Texte,* p. 92.

127. Nono himself discusses these sources in "Einige genaure Hinweise zu 'Intolleranza 1960,' " ibid., p. 70; and "Möglichkeit und Notwendigkeit," ibid., pp. 92–94.

128. Pola Suárez Urtubey, *Alberto Ginastera* (Buenos Aires: Editiones Culturales Argentinos, 1967), pp. 68–69.

129. Ibid., p. 12.

130. Ibid., pp. 11–12.

131. Ibid., p. 72.

132. Roger Smalley, "Some Recent Works of Peter Maxwell Davies," *Tempo* 84 (Spring 1968): 2.

133. Stephen Pruslin, ed., "Introduction: Nel mezzo del cammin—In Mid-flight," in *Peter Maxwell Davies: Studies from Two Decades,* Tempo Booklet No. 2 (London: Boosey & Hawkes, 1979), p. 2.

134. The complete text is printed in German and English in Georg Trakl, *Poems,* trans. Lucia Getsi (Athens, OH: Mundus Artium, 1973), p. 186.

135. Smalley, p. 5.

136. Peter Maxwell Davies, "A Note on the Music," *8 Songs for a Mad King* (London: Boosey & Hawkes, 1971), unpaged. We may assume that these "extreme regions of experience" include insanity, since Davies continues: "in No. 5, 'The Phantom Queen,' . . . the flute part hurries ahead in a 7:6 rhythmic proportion, the clarinet's rhythms become dotted, and its part displaced by octaves, the effect being *schizophrenic*" (emphasis added).

137. *"tönend bewegte Formen";* Eduard Hanslick, *Vom Musikalisch-Schönen,* 17th ed. (Wiesbaden: Breitkopf & Härtel, 1971), p. 59.

Index